# THE "SUMMA THEOLOGICA"

Nihil Obstat.

FR. INNOCENTIUS APAP, O.P., S.T.M.,
CENSOR THEOL.

Imprimatur.

EDUS. CANONICUS SURMONT,
VICARIUS GENERALIS.

WESTMONASTERII.

---

## APPROBATIO ORDINIS.

Nihil Obstat.

FR. VINCENTIUS McNABB, O.P., S.T.M.,
FR. LUCAS WALKER, O.P., S.T.L.

Imprimatur.

FR. BEDA JARRETT, O.P., S.T.L.,
PRIOR PROVINCIALIS ANGLIÆ.

IN FESTO S. CRUCIS,
*die 14 Sept.*, 1926.

*First published,* 1914.
*Second edition,* 1927.

# THE
# "SUMMA THEOLOGICA"

OF

# ST. ⌊THOMAS AQUINAS

PART II

(*FIRST PART*)

LITERALLY TRANSLATED BY

## FATHERS OF THE ENGLISH DOMINICAN
## PROVINCE

FIRST   NUMBER

(QQ. I.—XLVIII.)

LONDON

## BURNS OATES & WASHBOURNE LTD.

PUBLISHERS TO THE HOLY SEE

*Made and Printed in Great Britain*

# CONTENTS

## TREATISE ON THE LAST END

## TREATISE ON HUMAN ACTS

### I. Of those Acts which are Proper to Man

#### (a) The Nature of Voluntary Acts in General

#### (b) The Nature of Elicited Voluntary Acts

#### (c) The Nature of Commanded Voluntary Acts

#### (d) The Division of Human Acts

v

# TREATISE ON THE LAST END

# THE "SUMMA THEOLOGICA"

## FIRST PART OF THE SECOND PART

### PROLOGUE.

SINCE, as Damascene states (*De Fide Orthod.* ii. 12), man is said to be made to God's image, in so far as the image implies *an intelligent being endowed with free-will and self-movement*: now that we have treated of the exemplar, *i.e.*, God, and of those things which came forth from the power of God in accordance with His will; it remains for us to treat of His image, *i.e.*, man, inasmuch as he too is the principle of his actions, as having free-will and control of his actions.

### QUESTION I.

#### OF MAN'S LAST END.

*(In Eight Articles.)*

IN this matter we shall consider first the last end of human life; and secondly, those things by means of which man may advance towards this end, or stray from the path: for the end is the rule of whatever is ordained to the end. And since the last end of human life is stated to be happiness, we must consider (1) the last end in general; (2) Happiness.

Under the first head there are eight points of inquiry: (1) Whether it belongs to man to act for an end? (2) Whether this is proper to the rational nature? (3) Whether a man's actions are specified by their end? (4) Whether there is any last end of human life? (5) Whether one man can have several last ends? (6) Whether man ordains all to the last end ? (7) Whether all men have the same last end ? (8) Whether all other creatures concur with man in that last end ?

## FIRST ARTICLE.

### WHETHER IT BELONGS TO MAN TO ACT FOR AN END ?

*We proceed thus to the First Article :—*

*Objection* 1. It would seem that it does not belong to man to act for an end. For a cause is naturally first. But an end, in its very name, implies something that is last. Therefore an end is not a cause. But that for which a man acts, is the cause of his action; since this preposition *for* indicates a relation of causality. Therefore it does not belong to man to act for an end.

*Obj.* 2. Further, that which is itself the last end is not for an end. But in some cases the last end is an action, as the Philosopher states (*Ethic.* i. 1). Therefore man does not do everything for an end.

*Obj.* 3. Further, then does a man seem to act for an end, when he acts deliberately. But man does many things without deliberation, sometimes not even thinking of what he is doing; for instance when one moves one's foot or hand, or scratches one's beard, while intent on something else. Therefore man does not do everything for an end.

*On the contrary*, All things contained in a genus are derived from the principle of that genus. Now the end is the principle in human operations, as the Philosopher states (*Phys.* ii. 9). Therefore it belongs to man to do everything for an end.

*I answer that*, Of actions done by man those alone are properly called *human*, which are proper to man as man. Now man differs from irrational animals in this, that he is master of his actions. Wherefore those actions alone are properly called human, of which man is master. Now man is master of his actions through his reason and will; whence, too, the free-will is defined as *the faculty and will of reason*. Therefore those actions are properly called human which proceed from a deliberate will. And if any other actions are found in man, they can be called actions *of a man*, but not properly *human* actions, since they are not proper to man as man.—Now it is clear that whatever actions proceed from a power, are caused by that power in accordance with the nature of its object. But the object of the will is the end and the good. Therefore all human actions must be for an end.

*Reply Obj.* 1. Although the end be last in the order of execution, yet it is first in the order of the agent's intention. And it is in this way that it is a cause.

*Reply Obj.* 2. If any human action be the last end, it must be voluntary, else it would not be human, as stated above. Now an action is voluntary in one of two ways: first, because it is commanded by the will, *e.g.*, to walk, or to speak; secondly, because it is elicited by the will, for instance the very act of willing. Now it is impossible for the very act elicited by the will to be the last end. For the object of the will is the end, just as the object of sight is colour: wherefore just as the first visible cannot be the act of seeing, because every act of seeing is directed to a visible object; so the first appetible, *i.e.*, the end, cannot be the very act of willing. Consequently it follows that if a human action be the last end, it must be an action commanded by the will: so that there, some action of man, at least the act of willing, is for the end. Therefore whatever a man does, it is true to say that man acts for an end, even when he does that action in which the last end consists.

*Reply Obj.* 3. Such like actions are not properly human actions; since they do not proceed from deliberation of the reason, which is the proper principle of human actions. Therefore they have indeed an imaginary end, but not one that is fixed by reason.

## SECOND ARTICLE.

### WHETHER IT IS PROPER TO THE RATIONAL NATURE TO ACT FOR AN END ?

*We proceed thus to the Second Article :—*

*Objection* 1. It would seem that it is proper to the rational nature to act for an end.   For man, to whom it belongs to act for an end, never acts for an unknown end.   On the other hand, there are many things that have no knowledge of an end; either because they are altogether without knowledge, as insensible creatures: or because they do not apprehend the idea of an end as such, as irrational animals.   Therefore it seems proper to the rational nature to act for an end.

*Obj.* 2. Further, to act for an end is to order one's action to an end.   But this is the work of reason.   Therefore it does not belong to things that lack reason.

*Obj.* 3. Further, the good and the end is the object of the will.   But *the will is in the reason* (*De Anima* iii. 9).   Therefore to act for an end belongs to none but a rational nature.

*On the contrary*, The Philosopher proves (*Phys.* ii. 5) that *not only mind but also nature acts for an end*.

*I answer that*, Every agent, of necessity, acts for an end. For if, in a number of causes ordained to one another, the first be removed, the others must, of necessity, be removed also.   Now the first of all causes is the final cause.   The reason of which is that matter does not receive form, save in so far as it is moved by an agent; for nothing reduces itself from potentiality to act.   But an agent does not move except out of intention for an end.   For if the agent were not determinate to some particular effect, it would not do one thing rather than another: consequently in order that it produce a determinate effect, it must, of necessity, be determined to some certain one, which has the nature of an end.   And just as this determination is effected, in the rational nature, by the *rational appetite*, which is called the will; so, in other things, it is caused by their natural inclination, which is called the *natural appetite*.

Nevertheless it must be observed that a thing tends to an end, by its action or movement, in two ways: first, as a thing, moving itself to the end,—as man; secondly, as a thing moved by another to the end, as an arrow tends to a determinate end through being moved by the archer, who directs his action to the end. Therefore those things that are possessed of reason, move themselves to an end; because they have dominion over their actions, through their free-will which is the *faculty of will and reason*. But those things that lack reason tend to an end, by natural inclination, as being moved by another and not by themselves; since they do not know the nature of an end as such, and consequently cannot ordain anything to an end, but can be ordained to an end only by another. For the entire irrational nature is in comparison to God as an instrument to the principal agent, as stated above (I. Q. XXII., A. 2 *ad* 4: Q. CIII., A. 1 *ad* 3). Consequently it is proper to the rational nature to tend to an end, as directing (*agens*) and leading itself to the end: whereas it is proper to the irrational nature to tend to an end, as directed or led by another, whether it apprehend the end, as do irrational animals, or do not apprehend it, as is the case of those things which are altogether void of knowledge.

*Reply Obj.* 1. When man of himself acts for an end, he knows the end: but when he is directed or led by another, for instance, when he acts at another's command, or when he is moved under another's compulsion, it is not necessary that he should know the end. And it is thus with irrational creatures.

*Reply Obj.* 2. To ordain towards an end belongs to that which directs itself to an end: whereas to be ordained to an end belongs to that which is directed by another to an end. And this can belong to an irrational nature, but owing to some one possessed of reason.

*Reply Obj.* 3. The object of the will is the end and the good in universal. Consequently there can be no will in those things that lack reason and intellect, since they cannot apprehend the universal; but they have a natural appetite or a sensitive appetite, determinate to some particular good. Now it is clear that particular causes are moved by a universal cause: thus the governor of a city, who intends the common good, moves, by his command, all the particular departments of the city. Consequently all things that lack reason are, of necessity, moved to their particular ends by some rational will which extends to the universal good, namely by the Divine will.

## Third Article.
### WHETHER HUMAN ACTS ARE SPECIFIED BY THEIR END ?

*We proceed thus to the Third Article :—*

*Objection* 1. It would seem that human acts are not specified by their end. For the end is an extrinsic cause. But everything is specified by an intrinsic principle. Therefore human acts are not specified by their end.

*Obj.* 2. Further, that which gives a thing its species should exist before it. But the end comes into existence afterwards. Therefore a human act does not derive its species from the end.

*Obj.* 3. Further, one thing cannot be in more than one species. But one and the same act may happen to be ordained to various ends. Therefore the end does not give the species to human acts.

*On the contrary*, Augustine says (*De Mor. Eccl. et Manich.* ii. 13): *According as their end is worthy of blame or praise, so are our deeds worthy of blame or praise.*

*I answer that*, Each thing receives its species in respect of an act and not in respect of potentiality; wherefore things composed of matter and form are established in their respective species by their own forms. And this is also to be observed in proper movements. For since movements are, in a way, divided into action and passion, each of these receives its species from an act; action indeed from the act which is the principle of acting, and passion from the act which is the terminus of the movement. Wherefore heating, as an action, is nothing else than a certain move-

ment proceeding from heat, while heating as a passion is
nothing else than a movement towards heat: and it is the
definition that shows the specific nature.   And either way,
human acts, whether they be considered as actions, or as
passions, receive their species from the end.   For human
acts can be considered in both ways, since man moves himself, and is moved by himself.   Now it has been stated above
(A. 1) that acts are called human, inasmuch as they proceed
from a deliberate will.   Now the object of the will is the
good and the end.   And hence it is clear that the principle
of human acts, in so far as they are human, is the end.   In
like manner it is their terminus: for the human act terminates
at that which the will intends as the end; thus in natural
agents the form of the thing generated is conformed to the
form of the generator.   And since, as Ambrose says (*Prolog.
super Luc.*) *morality is said properly of man,* moral acts
properly speaking receive their species from the end, for
moral acts are the same as human acts.

*Reply Obj.* 1. The end is not altogether extrinsic to the
act, because it is related to the act as principle or terminus;
and it is just this that is essential to an act, viz., to proceed
from something, considered as action, and to proceed
towards something, considered as passion.

*Reply Obj.* 2. The end, in so far as it pre-exists in the
intention, pertains to the will, as stated above (A. 1 *ad* 1).
And it is thus that it gives the species to the human or
moral act.

*Reply Obj.* 3. One and the same act, in so far as it proceeds
once from the agent, is ordained to but one proximate end,
from which it has its species: but it can be ordained to
several remote ends, of which one is the end of the other.
It is possible, however, that an act which is one in respect of
its natural species, be ordained to several ends of the will:
thus this act *to kill a man,* which is but one act in respect of
its natural species, can be ordained, as to an end, to the safe-
guarding of justice, and to the satisfying of anger: the result
being that there would be several acts in different species of
morality: since in one way there will be an act of virtue, in

another, an act of vice.   For a movement does not receive
its species from that which is its terminus accidentally, but
only from that which is its *per se* terminus.   Now moral ends
are accidental to a natural thing, and conversely the relation
to a natural end is accidental to morality.   Consequently
there is no reason why acts which are the same considered
in their natural species, should not be diverse, considered in
their moral species, and conversely.

### Fourth Article.

#### Whether There Is One Last End of Human Life ?

*We proceed thus to the Fourth Article :—*

*Objection* 1. It would seem that there is no last end of
human life, but that we proceed to infinity.   For good is
essentially diffusive, as Dionysius states (*Div. Nom.* iv.).
Consequently if that which proceeds from good is itself good,
the latter must needs diffuse some other good: so that the
diffusion of good goes on indefinitely.   But good has the
nature of an end.   Therefore there is an indefinite series of
ends.

*Obj.* 2. Further, things pertaining to the reason can be
multiplied to infinity: thus mathematical quantities have no
limit.   For the same reason the species of numbers are infinite, since, given any number, the reason can think of
one yet greater.   But desire of the end is consequent on the
apprehension of the reason.   Therefore it seems that there
is also an infinite series of ends.

*Obj.* 3. Further, the good and the end is the object of the
will.   But the will can react on itself an infinite number of
times: for I can will something, and will to will it, and so on
indefinitely.   Therefore there is an infinite series of ends
of the human will, and there is no last end of the human will.

*On the contrary,* The Philosopher says (*Metaph.* ii. 2) that
*to suppose a thing to be indefinite is to deny that it is good.*
But the good is that which has the nature of an end.   Therefore it is contrary to the nature of an end to proceed indefinitely.   Therefore it is necessary to fix one last end.

*I answer that,* Absolutely speaking, it is not possible to proceed indefinitely in the matter of ends, from any point of view. For in whatsoever things there is an essential order of one to another, if the first be removed, those that are ordained to the first, must of necessity be removed also. Wherefore the Philosopher proves (*Phys.* viii. 5) that we cannot proceed to infinitude in causes of movement, because then there would be no first mover, without which neither can the others move, since they move only through being moved by the first mover. Now there is to be observed a twofold order in ends,—the order of intention, and the order of execution: and in either of these orders there must be something first. For that which is first in the order of intention, is the principle, as it were, moving the appetite; consequently, if you remove this principle, there will be nothing to move the appetite. On the other hand, the principle in execution is that wherein operation has its beginning; and if this principle be taken away, no one will begin to work. Now the principle in the intention is the last end; while the principle in execution is the first of the things which are ordained to the end. Consequently, on neither side is it possible to go on to infinity; since if there were no last end, nothing would be desired, nor would any action have its term, nor would the intention of the agent be at rest; while if there is no first thing among those that are ordained to the end, none would begin to work at anything, and counsel would have no term, but would continue indefinitely.

On the other hand, nothing hinders infinity from being in things that are ordained to one another not essentially but accidentally; for accidental causes are indeterminate. And in this way it happens that there is an accidental infinity of ends, and of things ordained to the end.

*Reply Obj.* 1. The very nature of good is that something flows from it, but not that it flows from something else. Since, therefore, good has the nature of end, and the first good is the last end, this argument does not prove that there is no last end; but that from the end, already sup-

posed, we may proceed downwards indefinitely towards those
things that are ordained to the end.   And this would be
true if we considered but the power of the First Good, which
is infinite.   But, since the First Good diffuses itself according to the intellect, to which it is proper to flow forth into
its effects according to a certain fixed form; it follows that
there is a certain measure to the flow of good things from
the First Good from Which all other goods share the power
of diffusion.   Consequently the diffusion of good does not
proceed indefinitely, but, as it is written (Wisd. xi. 21),
God disposes all things *in number, weight and measure*.

*Reply Obj.* 2.   In things which are of themselves, reason
begins from principles that are known naturally, and
advances to some term.   Wherefore the Philosopher proves
(*Poster.* i. 3) that there is no infinite process in demonstrations,
because there we find a process of things having an essential,
not an accidental, connection with one another.   But in
those things which are accidentally connected, nothing
hinders the reason from proceeding indefinitely.   Now it is
accidental to a stated quantity or number, as such, that
quantity or unity be added to it.   Wherefore in suchlike
things nothing hinders the reason from an indefinite process.

*Reply Obj.* 3.   This multiplication of acts of the will
reacting on itself, is accidental to the order of ends.   This
is clear from the fact that in regard to one and the same
end, the will reacts on itself indifferently once or several
times.

## FIFTH ARTICLE.

### WHETHER ONE MAN CAN HAVE SEVERAL LAST ENDS ?

*We proceed thus to the Fifth Article :—*

*Objection* 1.   It would seem possible for one man's will to be
directed at the same time to several things, as last ends.
For Augustine says (*De Civ. Dei* xix. 1) that some held man's
last end to consist in four things, viz., *in pleasure, repose,
the gifts of nature, and virtue*.   But these are clearly more
than one thing.   Therefore one man can place the last end
of his will in many things.

*Obj.* 2. Further, things not in opposition to one another do not exclude one another. Now there are many things which are not in opposition to one another. Therefore the supposition that one thing is the last end of the will does not exclude others.

*Obj.* 3. Further, by the fact that it places its last end in one thing, the will does not lose its freedom. But before it placed its last end in that thing, *e.g.*, pleasure, it could place it in something else, *e.g.*, riches. Therefore even after having placed his last end in pleasure, a man can at the same time place his last end in riches. Therefore it is possible for one man's will to be directed at the same time to several things, as last ends.

*On the contrary*, That in which a man rests as in his last end, is master of his affections, since he takes therefrom his entire rule of life. Hence of gluttons it is written (Phil. iii. 19): *Whose god is their belly :* viz., because they place their last end in the pleasures of the belly. Now according to Matth. vi. 24, *No man can serve two masters*, such, namely, as are not ordained to one another. Therefore it is impossible for one man to have several last ends not ordained to one another.

*I answer that*, It is impossible for one man's will to be directed at the same time to diverse things, as last ends. Three reasons may be assigned for this. First, because, since everything desires its own perfection, a man desires for his ultimate end, that which he desires as his perfect and crowning good. Hence Augustine says (*De Civ. Dei* xix. 1): *In speaking of the end of good we mean now, not that it passes away so as to be no more, but that it is perfected so as to be complete*. It is therefore necessary for the last end so to fill man's appetite, that nothing is left beside it for man to desire. Which is not possible, if something else be required for his perfection. Consequently it is not possible for the appetite so to tend to two things, as though each were its perfect good.

The second reason is because, just as in the process of reasoning, the principle is that which is naturally known, so in the process of the rational appetite, *i.e.*, the will, the principle needs to be that which is naturally desired. Now this must needs be one: since nature tends to one thing only. But the principle in the process of the rational appetite is the last end. Therefore that to which the will tends, as to its last end, is one.

The third reason is because, since voluntary actions receive their species from the end, as stated above (A. 3), they must needs receive their genus from the last end, which is common to them all: just as natural things are placed in a genus according to a common form. Since, then, all things that can be desired by the will, belong, as such, to one genus, the last end must needs be one. And all the more because in every genus there is one first principle; and the last end has the nature of a first principle, as stated above. Now as the last end of man, simply as man, is to the whole human race, so is the last end of any individual man to that individual. Therefore, just as of all men there is naturally one last end, so the will of an individual man must be fixed on one last end.

*Reply Obj.* 1. All these several objects were considered as one perfect good resulting therefrom, by those who placed in them the last end.

*Reply Obj.* 2. Although it is possible to find several things which are not in opposition to one another, yet it is contrary to a thing's perfect good, that anything besides be required for that thing's perfection.

*Reply Obj.* 3. The power of the will does not extend to making opposites exist at the same time. Which would be the case were it to tend to several diverse objects as last ends, as has been shown above (*ad* 2).

### Sixth Article.

#### WHETHER MAN WILLS ALL, WHATSOEVER HE WILLS, FOR THE LAST END ?

*We proceed thus to the Sixth Article :—*

*Objection* 1. It would seem that man does not will all, whatsoever he wills, for the last end. For things ordained to the last end are said to be serious matter, as being useful. But jests are foreign to serious matter. Therefore what man does in jest, he ordains not to the last end.

*Obj.* 2. Further, the Philosopher says at the beginning of his *Metaphysics* (i. 2) that speculative science is sought for its own sake. Now it cannot be said that each speculative science is the last end. Therefore man does not desire all, whatsoever he desires, for the last end.

*Obj.* 3. Further, whoever ordains something to an end, thinks of that end. But man does not always think of the last end in all that he desires or does. Therefore man neither desires nor does all for the last end.

*On the contrary,* Augustine says (*De Civ. Dei* xix. 1): *That is the end of our good, for the sake of which we love other things, whereas we love it for its own sake.*

*I answer that,* Man must, of necessity, desire all, whatsoever he desires, for the last end. This is evident for two reasons. First, because whatever man desires, he desires it under the aspect of good. And if he desire it, not as his perfect good, which is the last end, he must, of necessity, desire it as tending to the perfect good, because the beginning of anything is always ordained to its completion; as is clearly the case in effects both of nature and of art. Wherefore every beginning of perfection is ordained to complete perfection which is achieved through the last end. Secondly, because the last end stands in the same relation in moving the appetite, as the first mover in other movements. Now it is clear that secondary moving causes do not move save inasmuch as they are moved by the first mover. Therefore secondary objects of the appetite do not move the appetite, except as ordained to the first object of the appetite, which is the last end.

*Reply Obj.* 1. Actions done jestingly are not directed to any external end; but merely to the good of the jester, in so far as they afford him pleasure or relaxation. But man's consummate good is his last end.

*Reply Obj.* 2. The same applies to speculative science;

which is desired as the scientist's good, included in complete and perfect good, which is the ultimate end.

*Reply Obj.* 3. One need not always be thinking of the last end, whenever one desires or does something: but the virtue of the first intention, which was in respect of the last end, remains in every desire directed to any object whatever, even though one's thoughts be not actually directed to the last end. Thus while walking along the road one needs not to be thinking of the end at every step.

## Seventh Article.

### WHETHER ALL MEN HAVE THE SAME LAST END ?

*We proceed thus to the Seventh Article :—*

*Objection* 1. It would seem that all men have not the same last end. For before all else the unchangeable good seems to be the last end of man. But some turn away from the unchangeable good, by sinning. Therefore all men have not the same last end.

*Obj.* 2. Further, man's entire life is ruled according to his last end. If, therefore, all men had the same last end, they would not have various pursuits in life. Which is evidently false.

*Obj.* 3. Further, the end is the term of action. But actions are of individuals. Now although men agree in their specific nature, yet they differ in things pertaining to individuals. Therefore all men have not the same last end.

*On the contrary,* Augustine says (*De Trin.* xiii. 3) that all men agree in desiring the last end, which is happiness.

*I answer that,* We can speak of the last end in two ways: first, considering only the aspect of last end; secondly, considering the thing in which the aspect of last end is realized. So, then, as to the aspect of last end, all agree in desiring the last end: since all desire the fulfilment of their perfection, and it is precisely this fulfilment in which the last end consists, as stated above (A. 5). But as to the thing in which this aspect is realized, all men are not agreed as to their last end: since some desire riches, as their consummate good; some, pleasure; others, something else. Thus to every taste the sweet is pleasant; but to some, the sweetness of wine is most pleasant, to others, the sweetness of honey, or of something similar. Yet that sweet is absolutely the best of all pleasant things, in which he who has the best taste takes most pleasure. In like manner that good is most complete which the man with well-disposed affections desires for his last end.

*Reply Obj.* 1. Those who sin turn from that in which their last end really consists: but they do not turn away from the intention of the last end, which intention they mistakenly seek in other things.

*Reply Obj.* 2. Various pursuits in life are found among men by reason of the various things in which men seek to find their last end.

*Reply Obj.* 3. Although actions are of individuals, yet their first principle of action is nature, which tends to one thing, as stated above (A. 5).

## Eighth Article.

### WHETHER OTHER CREATURES CONCUR IN THAT LAST END ?

*We proceed thus to the Eighth Article :—*

*Objection* 1. It would seem that all other creatures concur in man's last end. For the end corresponds to the beginning. But man's beginning—*i.e.*, God—is also the beginning of all else. Therefore all other things concur in man's last end.

*Obj.* 2. Further, Dionysius says (*Div. Nom.* iv.) that *God turns all things to Himself as to their last end.* But He is also man's last end; because He alone is to be enjoyed by man, as Augustine says (*De Doctr. Christ.* i. 5, 22.) Therefore other things, too, concur in man's last end.

*Obj.* 3. Further, man's last end is the object of the will. But the object of the will is the universal good, which is the end of all. Therefore all must needs concur in man's last end.

*On the contrary*, man's last end is happiness; which all men desire, as Augustine says (*De Trin.* xiii. 3, 4). But *happiness is not possible for animals bereft of reason*, as Augustine says (QQ. LXXXIII., qu. 5). Therefore other things do not concur in man's last end.

*I answer that*, As the Philosopher says (*Phys.* ii. 2), the end is twofold,—the end *for which* and the end *by which ;* viz., the thing itself in which is found the aspect of good, and the use or acquisition of that thing. Thus we say that the end of the movement of a weighty body is either a lower place as *thing*, or to be in a lower place, as *use ;* and the end of the miser is money as *thing*, or possession of money as *use*.

If, therefore, we speak of man's last end as of the thing which is the end, thus all other things concur in man's last end, since God is the last end of man and of all other things. —If, however, we speak of man's last end, as of the acquisition of the end, then irrational creatures do not concur with man in this end. For man and other rational creatures attain to their last end by knowing and loving God: this is not possible to other creatures, which acquire their last end, in so far as they share in the Divine likeness, inasmuch as they are, or live, or even know.

Hence it is evident how the objections are solved: since happiness means the acquisition of the last end.

# QUESTION II.

## OF THOSE THINGS IN WHICH MAN'S HAPPINESS CONSISTS
### (*In Eight Articles.*)

WE have now to consider happiness: and (1) in what it consists; (2) what it is; (3) how we can obtain it.

Concerning the first there are eight points of inquiry: (1) Whether happiness consists in wealth? (2) Whether in honour? (3) Whether in fame or glory? (4) Whether in power? (5) Whether in any good of the body? (6) Whether in pleasure? (7) Whether in any good of the soul? (8) Whether in any created good?

## FIRST ARTICLE.

### WHETHER MAN'S HAPPINESS CONSISTS IN WEALTH?

*We proceed thus to the First Article :—*

*Objection* 1. It would seem that man's happiness consists in wealth. For since happiness is man's last end, it must consist in that which has the greatest hold on man's affections. Now this is wealth: for it is written (Eccles. x. 19): *All things obey money*. Therefore man's happiness consists in wealth.

*Obj.* 2. Further, according to Boethius (*De Consol.* iii.), happiness is *a state of life made perfect by the aggregate of all good things*. Now money seems to be the means of possessing all things: for, as the Philosopher says (*Ethic.* v. 5), money was invented, that it might be a sort of guarantee for the acquisition of whatever man desires. Therefore happiness consists in wealth.

*Obj.* 3. Further, since the desire for the sovereign good

never fails, it seems to be infinite. But this is the case with riches more than anything else; since *a covetous man shall not be satisfied with riches* (Eccles. v. 9). Therefore happiness consists in wealth.

*On the contrary*, Man's good consists in retaining happiness rather than in spreading it. But as Boethius says (*De Consol.* ii.), *wealth shines in giving rather than in hoarding: for the miser is hateful, whereas the generous man is applauded*. Therefore man's happiness does not consist in wealth.

*I answer that*, It is impossible for man's happiness to consist in wealth. For wealth is twofold, as the Philosopher says (*Polit.* i. 3), viz., natural and artificial. Natural wealth is that which serves man as a remedy for his natural wants: such as food, drink, clothing, cars, dwellings, and suchlike, while artificial wealth is that which is not a direct help to nature, as money, but is invented by the art of man, for the convenience of exchange, and as a measure of things saleable.

Now it is evident that man's happiness cannot consist in natural wealth. For wealth of this kind is sought for the sake of something else, viz., as a support of human nature: consequently it cannot be man's last end, rather is it ordained to man as to its end. Wherefore in the order of nature, all such things are below man, and made for him, according to Ps. viii. 8: *Thou hast subjected all things under his feet*.

And as to artificial wealth, it is not sought save for the sake of natural wealth; since man would not seek it except because, by its means, he procures for himself the necessaries of life. Consequently much less can it be considered in the light of the last end. Therefore it is impossible for happiness, which is the last end of man, to consist in wealth.

*Reply Obj.* 1. All material things obey money, so far as the multitude of fools is concerned, who know no other than material goods, which can be obtained for money. But we should take our estimation of human goods not from the foolish but from the wise: just as it is for a person, whose sense of taste is in good order, to judge whether a thing is palatable.

*Reply Obj.* 2. All things saleable can be had for money: not so spiritual things, which cannot be sold. Hence it is written (Prov. xvii. 16): *What doth it avail a fool to have riches, seeing he cannot buy wisdom?*

*Reply Obj.* 3. The desire for natural riches is not infinite: because they suffice for nature in a certain measure. But the desire for artificial wealth is infinite, for it is the servant of disordered concupiscence, which is not curbed, as the Philosopher makes clear (*Polit.* i. 3). Yet this desire for wealth is infinite otherwise than the desire for the sovereign good. For the more perfectly the sovereign good is possessed, the more is it loved, and other things despised: because the more we possess it, the more we know it. Hence it is written (Ecclus. xxiv. 29): *They that eat me shall yet hunger.* Whereas in the desire for wealth and for whatsoever temporal goods, the contrary is the case: for when we already possess them, we despise them, and seek others: which is the sense of Our Lord's words (Jo. iv. 13): *Whosoever drinketh of this water,* by which temporal goods are signified, *shall thirst again.* The reason of this is that we realize more their insufficiency when we possess them: and this very fact shows that they are imperfect, and that the sovereign good does not consist therein.

## Second Article.
### WHETHER MAN'S HAPPINESS CONSISTS IN HONOURS?

*We proceed thus to the Second Article :—*

*Objection* 1. It would seem that man's happiness consists in honours. For happiness or bliss is *the reward of virtue,* as the Philosopher says (*Ethic.* i. 9). But honour more than anything else seems to be that by which virtue is rewarded, as the Philosopher says (*Ethic.* iv. 3). Therefore happiness consists especially in honour.

*Obj.* 2. Further, that which belongs to God and to persons of great excellence seems especially to be happiness, which is the perfect good.  But that is honour, as the Philosopher says (*Ethic*. iv. 3).  Moreover, the Apostle says (1 Tim. i. 17): *To . . . the only God be honour and glory*.  Therefore happiness consists in honour.

*Obj*. 3. Further, that which man desires above all is happiness.  But nothing seems more desirable to man than honour: since man suffers loss in all other things, lest he should suffer loss of honour.  Therefore happiness consists in honour.

*On the contrary*, Happiness is in the happy.  But honour is not in the honoured, but rather in him who honours, and who offers deference to the person honoured, as the Philosopher says (*Ethic*. i. 5).  Therefore happiness does not consist in honour.

*I answer that*, It is impossible for happiness to consist in honour.  For honour is given to a man on account of some excellence in him; and consequently it is a sign and attestation of the excellence that is in the person honoured. Now a man's excellence is in proportion, especially, to his happiness, which is man's perfect good; and to its parts, *i.e.*, those goods by which he has a certain share of happiness. And therefore honour can result from happiness, but happiness cannot principally consist therein.

*Reply Obj*. 1.  As the Philosopher says (*ibid*.), honour is not that reward of virtue, for which the virtuous work: but they receive honour from men by way of reward, *as from those who have nothing greater to offer*.  But virtue's true reward is happiness itself, for which the virtuous work: whereas if they worked for honour, it would no longer be virtue, but ambition.

*Reply Obj*. 2.  Honour is due to God and to persons of great excellence as a sign of attestation of excellence already existing: not that honour makes them excellent.

*Reply Obj*. 3.  That man desires honour above all else, arises from his natural desire for happiness, from which honour results, as stated above.  Wherefore man seeks to be honoured especially by the wise, on whose judgment he believes himself to be excellent or happy.

## THIRD ARTICLE.

### WHETHER MAN'S HAPPINESS CONSISTS IN FAME OR GLORY?

*We proceed thus to the Third Article :—*

*Objection* 1. It would seem that man's happiness consists in glory. For happiness seems to consist in that which is paid to the saints for the trials they have undergone in the world. But this is glory: for the Apostle says (Rom. viii. 18) *The sufferings of this time are not worthy to be compared with the glory to come, that shall be revealed in us.* Therefore happiness consists in glory.

*Obj.* 2. Further, good is diffusive of itself, as stated by Dionysius (*Div. Nom.* iv.). But man's good is spread abroad in the knowledge of others by glory more than by anything else: since, according to Ambrose,* glory consists *in being well known and praised.* Therefore man's happiness consists in glory.

*Obj.* 3. Further, happiness is the most enduring good. Now this seems to be fame or glory; because by this men attain to eternity after a fashion. Hence Boethius says (*De Consol.* ii.): *You seem to beget unto yourselves eternity, when you think of your fame in future time.* Therefore man's happiness consists in fame or glory.

*On the contrary*, Happiness is man's true good. But it happens that fame or glory is false: for as Boethius says (*De Consol.* iii.), *many owe their renown to the lying reports spread among the people. Can anything be more shameful? For those who receive false fame, must needs blush at their own praise.* Therefore man's happiness does not consist in fame or glory.

*I answer that,* Man's happiness cannot consist in human fame or glory. For glory consists *in being well known and praised,* as Ambrose* says. Now the thing known is related to human knowledge otherwise than to God's knowledge: for human knowledge is caused by the things known, whereas God's knowledge is the cause of the things known. Wherefore the perfection of human good, which is

* Augustine,—*Contra Maxim. Arian.* ii. 13.

called happiness, cannot be caused by human knowledge: but rather human knowledge of another's happiness proceeds from, and, in a fashion, is caused by, human happiness itself, inchoate or perfect. Consequently man's happiness cannot consist in fame or glory. On the other hand, man's good depends on God's knowledge as its cause. And therefore man's beatitude depends, as on its cause, on the glory which man has with God; according to Ps. xc. 15, 16: *I will deliver him, and I will glorify him ; I will fill him with length of days, and I will show him my salvation.*

Furthermore, we must observe that human knowledge often fails, especially in contingent singulars, such as are human acts. For this reason human glory is frequently deceptive. But since God cannot be deceived, His glory is always true; hence it is written (2 Cor. x. 18): *He . . . is approved . . . whom God commendeth.*

*Reply Obj.* 1. The Apostle speaks, then, not of the glory which is with men, but of the glory which is from God, with His angels. Hence it is written (Mark viii. 38): *The Son of Man shall confess him in the glory of His Father, before His angels.**

*Reply Obj.* 2. A man's good which, through fame or glory, is in the knowledge of many, if this knowledge be true, must needs be derived from good existing in the man himself: and hence it presupposes perfect or inchoate happiness. But if the knowledge be false, it does not harmonize with the thing: and thus good does not exist in him who is looked upon as famous. Hence it follows that fame can nowise make man happy.

*Reply Obj.* 3. Fame has no stability; in fact, it is easily ruined by false report. And if sometimes it endures, this is by accident. But happiness endures of itself, and for ever.

---

* St. Thomas joins Mark viii. 38 with Luke xii. 8, owing to a possible variant in his text, or to the fact that he was quoting from memory.

### Fourth Article.

#### WHETHER MAN'S HAPPINESS CONSISTS IN POWER?

*We proceed thus to the Fourth Article :—*

*Objection* 1. It would seem that happiness consists in power. For all things desire to become like to God, as to their last end and first beginning. But men who are in power, seem, on account of the similarity of power, to be most like to God: hence also in Scripture they are called *gods* (Exod. xxii. 28),—*Thou shalt not speak ill of the gods*. Therefore happiness consists in power.

*Obj.* 2. Further, happiness is the perfect good. But the highest perfection for man is to be able to rule others; which belongs to those who are in power. Therefore happiness consists in power.

*Obj.* 3. Further, since happiness is supremely desirable, it is contrary to that which is before all to be shunned. But, more than aught else, men shun servitude, which is contrary to power. Therefore happiness consists in power.

*On the contrary,* Happiness is the perfect good. But power is most imperfect. For as Boethius says (*De Consol.* iii.), *the power of man cannot relieve the gnawings of care, nor can it avoid the thorny path of anxiety* : and further on: *Think you a man is powerful who is surrounded by attendants, whom he inspires with fear indeed, but whom he fears still more?* Therefore happiness does not consist in power.

*I answer that,* It is impossible for happiness to consist in power; and this for two reasons. First because power has the nature of principle, as is stated in *Metaph.* v. 12, whereas happiness has the nature of last end.—Secondly, because power has relation to good and evil: whereas happiness is man's proper and perfect good. Wherefore some happiness might consist in the good use of power, which is by virtue, rather than in power itself.

Now four general reasons may be given to prove that happiness consists in none of the foregoing external goods.

First, because, since happiness is man's supreme good, it is
incompatible with any evil.   Now all the foregoing can be
found both in good and in evil men.—Secondly, because,
since it is the nature of happiness to *satisfy of itself*, as
stated in *Ethic*. i. 7, having gained happiness, man cannot
lack any needful good.   But after acquiring any one of the
foregoing, man may still lack many goods that are necessary
to him; for instance, wisdom, bodily health, and suchlike.
Thirdly, because, since happiness is the perfect good, no
evil can accrue to anyone therefrom.   This cannot be
said of the foregoing: for it is written (Eccles. v. 12) that
*riches* are sometimes *kept to the hurt of the owner ;* and the
same may be said of the other three.—Fourthly, because
man is ordained to happiness through principles that are in
him; since he is ordained thereto naturally.   Now the four
goods mentioned above are due rather to external causes,
and in most cases to fortune; for which reason they are
called goods of fortune.   Therefore it is evident that happiness nowise consists in the foregoing.

*Reply Obj.* 1. God's power is His goodness: hence He
cannot use His power otherwise than well.   But it is not
so with men.   Consequently it is not enough for man's
happiness, that he become like God in power, unless he
become like Him in goodness also.

*Reply Obj.* 2. Just as it is a very good thing for a man
to make good use of power in ruling many, so is it a very
bad thing if he makes a bad use of it.   And so it is that
power is towards good and evil.

*Reply Obj.* 3. Servitude is a hindrance to the good use of
power: therefore is it that men naturally shun it; not
because man's supreme good consists in power.

### FIFTH ARTICLE.

WHETHER MAN'S HAPPINESS CONSISTS IN ANY BODILY GOOD ?

*We proceed thus to the Fifth Article :*—

*Objection* 1. It would seem that man's happiness consists
in bodily goods.   For it is written (Ecclus. xxx. 16): *There*

is *no riches above the riches of the health of the body*. But happiness consists in that which is best. Therefore it consists in the health of the body.

*Obj.* 2. Further, Dionysius says (*Div. Nom.* v.), that *to be* is better than *to live*, and *to live* is better than all that follows. But for man's being and living, the health of the body is necessary. Since, therefore, happiness is man's supreme good, it seems that health of the body belongs more than anything else to happiness.

*Obj.* 3. Further, the more universal a thing is, the higher the principle from which it depends; because the higher a cause is, the greater the scope of its power. Now just as the causality of the efficient cause consists in its flowing into something, so the causality of the end consists in its drawing the appetite. Therefore, just as the First Cause is that which flows into all things, so the last end is that which attracts the desire of all. But being itself is that which is most desired by all. Therefore man's happiness consists most of all in things pertaining to his being, such as the health of the body.

*On the contrary*, Man surpasses all other animals in regard to happiness. But in bodily goods he is surpassed by many animals ; for instance, by the elephant in longevity, by the lion in strength, by the stag in fleetness. Therefore man's happiness does not consist in goods of the body.

*I answer that*, It is impossible for man's happiness to consist in the goods of the body; and this for two reasons. First, because, if a thing be ordained to another as to its end, its last end cannot consist in the preservation of its being. Hence a captain does not intend, as a last end, the preservation of the ship entrusted to him, since a ship is ordained to something else as an end, viz., to navigation. Now just as the ship is entrusted to the captain that he may steer its course, so man is given over to his will and reason; according to Ecclus. xv. 14; *God made man from the beginning and left him in the hand of his own counsel*. Now it is evident that man is ordained to something as his end: since man is not the supreme good. Therefore the last end of man's reason and will cannot be the preservation of man's being.

Secondly, because, granted that the end of man's will and reason be the preservation of man's being, it could not be said that the end of man is some good of the body. For man's being consists in soul and body; and though the being of the body depends on the soul, yet the being of the human soul depends not on the body, as shown above (I., Q. LXXV., A. 2); and the very body is for the soul, as matter for its form, and the instruments for the man that puts them into motion, that by their means he may do his work. Wherefore all goods of the body are ordained to the goods of the soul, as to their end. Consequently happiness, which is man's last end, cannot consist in goods of the body.

*Reply Obj.* 1. Just as the body is ordained to the soul, as its end, so are external goods ordained to the body itself. And therefore it is with reason that the good of the body is preferred to external goods, which are signified by *riches*, just as the good of the soul is preferred to all bodily goods.

*Reply Obj.* 2. Being taken simply, as including all perfection of being, surpasses life and all that follows it; for thus being itself includes all these. And in this sense Dionysius speaks. But if we consider being itself as participated in this or that thing, which does not possess the whole perfection of being, but has imperfect being, such as the being of any creature; then it is evident that being itself together with an additional perfection is more excellent. Hence in the same passage Dionysius says that things that live are better than things that exist, and intelligent better than living things.

*Reply Obj.* 3. Since the end corresponds to the beginning, this argument proves that the last end is the first beginning of being, in Whom every perfection of being is: Whose likeness, according to their proportion, some desire as to being only, some as to living being, some as to being which is living, intelligent and happy. And this belongs to few.

## SIXTH ARTICLE.

### WHETHER MAN'S HAPPINESS CONSISTS IN PLEASURE?

*We proceed thus to the Sixth Article :—*

*Objection* 1. It would seem that man's happiness consists in pleasure. For since happiness is the last end, it is not desired for something else, but other things for it. But this answers to pleasure more than to anything else: *for it is absurd to ask anyone what is his motive in wishing to be pleased* (*Ethic.* x. 2). Therefore happiness consists principally in pleasure and delight.

*Obj.* 2. Further, *the first cause goes more deeply into the effect than the second cause* (*De Causis* 1). Now the causality of the end consists in its attracting the appetite. Therefore, seemingly that which moves most the appetite, answers to the notion of the last end. Now this is pleasure: and a sign of this is that delight so far absorbs man's will and reason, that it causes him to despise other goods. Therefore it seems that man's last end, which is happiness, consists principally in pleasure.

*Obj.* 3. Further, since desire is for good, it seems that what all desire is best. But all desire delight; both wise and foolish, and even irrational creatures. Therefore delight is the best of all. Therefore happiness, which is the supreme good, consists in pleasure.

*On the contrary,* Boethius says (*De Consol.* iii.): *Any one that chooses to look back on his past excesses, will perceive that pleasures have a sad ending : and if they can render a man happy, there is no reason why we should not say that the very beasts are happy too.*

*I answer that,* Because bodily delights are more generally known, *the name of pleasure has been appropriated to them* (*Ethic.* vii. 13), although other delights excel them: and yet happiness does not consist in them. Because in every thing, that which pertains to its essence is distinct from its proper accident: thus in man it is one thing that he is a mortal rational animal, and another that he is a risible animal. We must therefore consider that every delight is a proper accident resulting from happiness, or from some part of happiness; since the reason that a man is delighted is that he has some fitting good, either in reality, or in hope, or at least in memory. Now a fitting good, if indeed it be the perfect good, is precisely man's happiness: and if it is imperfect, it is a share of happiness, either proximate, or remote, or at least apparent. Therefore it is evident that neither is delight, which results from the perfect good, the very essence of happiness, but something resulting therefrom as its proper accident.

But bodily pleasure cannot result from the perfect good even in that way. For it results from a good apprehended by sense, which is a power of the soul, which power makes use of the body. Now good pertaining to the body, and apprehended by sense, cannot be man's perfect good. For since the rational soul excels the capacity of corporeal matter, that part of the soul which is independent of a corporeal organ, has a certain infinity in regard to the body and those parts of the soul which are tied down to the body: just as immaterial things are in a way infinite as compared to material things, since a form is, after a fashion, contracted and bounded by matter, so that a form which is independent of matter is, in a way, infinite. Therefore sense, which is a power of the body, knows the singular, which is determinate through matter: whereas the intellect, which is a power independent of matter, knows the universal, which is abstracted from matter, and contains an infinite number of singulars. Consequently it is evident that good which is fitting to the body, and which causes bodily delight through being apprehended by sense, is not man's perfect good, but is quite a trifle as compared with the good of the soul. Hence it is written (Wisd. vii. 9) that *all gold in comparison of her, is as a little sand*. And therefore bodily pleasure is neither happiness itself, nor a proper accident of happiness.

*Reply Obj.* 1. It comes to the same whether we desire good, or desire delight, which is nothing else than the appetite's rest in good: thus it is owing to the same natural force that a weighty body is borne downwards and that it rests there. Consequently just as good is desired for itself, so delight is desired for itself and not for anything else, if the preposition *for* denote the final cause. But if it denote the formal or rather the motive cause, thus delight is desirable for something else, *i.e.*, for the good, which is the object of that delight, and consequently is its principle, and gives it its form: for the reason that delight is desired is that it is rest in the thing desired.

*Reply Obj*. 2. The vehemence of desire for sensible delight arises from the fact that operations of the senses, through being the principles of our knowledge, are more perceptible. And so it is that sensible pleasures are desired by the majority.

*Reply Obj*. 3. All desire delight in the same way as they desire good: and yet they desire delight by reason of the good and not conversely, as stated above (*ad* 1). Consequently it does not follow that delight is the supreme and essential good, but that every delight results from some good, and that some delight results from that which is the essential and supreme good.

## Seventh Article.

### WHETHER SOME GOOD OF THE SOUL CONSTITUTES MAN'S HAPPINESS ?

*We proceed thus to the Seventh Article :—*

*Objection* 1. It would seem that some good of the soul constitutes man's happiness. For happiness is man's good. Now this is threefold, external goods, goods of the body, and goods of the soul. But happiness does not consist in external goods, nor in goods of the body, as shown above (AA. 4, 5). Therefore it consists in goods of the soul.

*Obj*. 2. Further, we love that for which we desire good, more than the good that we desire for it: thus we love a friend for whom we desire money, more than we love money. But whatever good a man desires, he desires it for himself. Therefore he loves himself more than all other goods. Now happiness is what is loved above all: which is evident from the fact that for its sake all else is loved and desired. Therefore happiness consists in some good of man himself: not, however, in goods of the body; therefore, in goods of the soul.

*Obj.* 3. Further, perfection is something belonging to that which is perfected. But happiness is a perfection of man. Therefore happiness is something belonging to man. But it is not something belonging to the body, as shown above (A. 5). Therefore it is something belonging to the soul; and thus it consists in goods of the soul.

*On the contrary,* As Augustine says (*De Doctr. Christ.* i. 22), *that which constitutes the life of happiness is to be loved for its own sake.* But man is not to be loved for his own sake, but whatever is in man is to be loved for God's sake. Therefore happiness consists in no good of the soul.

*I answer that,* As stated above (Q. 1, A. 8), the end is twofold: namely, the thing itself, which we desire to attain, and the use, namely, the attainment or possession of that thing. If, then, we speak of man's last end, as to the thing itself which we desire as last end, it is impossible for man's last end to be the soul itself or something belonging to it. Because the soul, considered in itself, is as something existing in potentiality: for it becomes knowing actually, from being potentially knowing; and actually virtuous, from being potentially virtuous. Now since potentiality is for the sake of act as for its fulfilment, that which in itself is in potentiality cannot be the last end. Therefore the soul itself cannot be its own last end.

In like manner neither can anything belonging to it, whether power, habit, or act. For that good which is the last end, is the perfect good fulfilling the desire. Now man's appetite, otherwise the will, is for the universal good And any good inherent to the soul is a participated good, and consequently a portioned good. Therefore none of them can be man's last end.

But if we speak of man's last end, as to the attainment or possession thereof, or as to any use whatever of the thing itself desired as an end, thus does something of man, in respect of his soul, belong to his last end: since man attains happiness through his soul.   Therefore the thing itself which is desired as end, is that which constitutes happiness, and makes man happy; but the attainment of this thing is called happiness.   Consequently we must say that happiness is something belonging to the soul; but that which constitutes happiness is something outside the soul.

*Reply Obj.* 1. Inasmuch as this division includes all goods that man can desire, thus the good of the soul is not only power, habit, or act, but also the object of these, which is something outside.   And in this way nothing hinders us from saying that what constitutes happiness is a good of the soul.

*Reply Obj.* 2. As far as the proposed objection is concerned, happiness is loved above all, as the good desired; whereas a friend is loved as that for which good is desired; and thus, too, man loves himself.   Consequently it is not the same kind of love in both cases.   As to whether man loves anything more than himself with the love of friendship, there will be occasion to inquire when we treat of Charity.

*Reply Obj.* 3. Happiness itself, since it is a perfection of the soul, is an inherent good of the soul; but that which constitutes happiness, viz., which makes man happy, is something outside his soul, as stated above.

## EIGHTH ARTICLE.

### WHETHER ANY CREATED GOOD CONSTITUTES MAN'S HAPPINESS ?

*We proceed thus to the Eighth Article :—*

*Objection* 1. It would seem that some created good constitutes man's happiness.   For Dionysius says (*Div. Nom.* vii.) that Divine wisdom *unites the ends of first things to the beginnings of second things*, from which we may gather that the summit of a lower nature touches the base of the higher nature.   But man's highest good is happiness.   Since then the angel is above man in the order of nature, as stated in the

First Part (Q. CXI., A. 1), it seems that man's happiness consists in man somehow reaching the angel.

*Obj.* 2. Further, the last end of each thing is that which, in relation to it, is perfect: hence the part is for the whole, as for its end. But the universe of creatures which is called the macrocosm, is compared to man who is called the microcosm (*Phys.* viii. 2), as perfect to imperfect. Therefore man's happiness consists in the whole universe of creatures.

*Obj.* 3. Further, man is made happy by that which lulls his natural desire. But man's natural desire does not reach out to a good surpassing his capacity. Since then man's capacity does not include that good which surpasses the limits of all creation, it seems that man can be made happy by some created good. Consequently some created good constitutes man's happiness.

*On the contrary*, Augustine says (*De Civ. Dei* xix. 26): *As the soul is the life of the body, so God is man's life of happiness : of Whom it is written : ' Happy is that people whose God is the Lord '* (Ps. cxliii. 15).

*I answer that*, It is impossible for any created good to constitute man's happiness. For happiness is the perfect good, which lulls the appetite altogether; else it would not be the last end, if something yet remained to be desired. Now the object of the will, *i.e.*, of man's appetite, is the universal good; just as the object of the intellect is the universal true. Hence it is evident that naught can lull man's will, save the universal good. This is to be found, not in any creature, but in God alone; because every creature has goodness by participation. Wherefore God alone can satisfy the will of man, according to the words of Ps. cii. 5: *Who satisfieth thy desire with good things*. Therefore God alone constitutes man's happiness.

*Reply Obj.* 1. The summit of man does indeed touch the base of the angelic nature, by a kind of likeness; but man does not rest there as in his last end, but reaches out to the universal fount itself of good, which is the common object of happiness of all the blessed, as being the infinite and perfect good.

*Reply Obj.* 2. If a whole be not the last end, but ordained to a further end, then the last end of a part thereof is not the whole itself, but something else. Now the universe of creatures, to which man is compared as part to whole, is not the last end, but is ordained to God, as to its last end. Therefore the last end of man is not the good of the universe, but God himself.

*Reply Obj.* 3. Created good is not less than that good of which man is capable, as of something intrinsic and inherent to him: but it is less than the good of which he is capable, as of an object, and which is infinite. And the participated good which is in an angel, and in the whole universe, is a finite and restricted good.

# QUESTION III.

## WHAT IS HAPPINESS.

### (*In Eight Articles.*)

WE have now to consider (1) what happiness is, and (2) what things are required for it.

Concerning the first there are eight points of inquiry: (1) Whether happiness is something uncreated? (2) If it be something created, whether it is an operation? (3) Whether it is an operation of the sensitive, or only of the intellectual part? (4) If it be an operation of the intellectual part, whether it is an operation of the intellect, or of the will? (5) If it be an operation of the intellect, whether it is an operation of the speculative or of the practical intellect? (6) If it be an operation of the speculative intellect, whether it consists in the consideration of speculative sciences? (7) Whether it consists in the consideration of separate substances, viz., angels? (8) Whether it consists in the sole contemplation of God seen in His Essence?

## FIRST ARTICLE.

### WHETHER HAPPINESS IS SOMETHING UNCREATED?

*We proceed thus to the First Article :—*

*Objection* 1. It would seem that happiness is something uncreated. For Boethius says (*De Consol.* iii.): *We must needs confess that God is happiness itself.*

*Obj.* 2. Further, happiness is the supreme good. But it belongs to God to be the supreme good. Since, then, there are not several supreme goods, it seems that happiness is the same as God.

*Obj.* 3. Further, happiness is the last end, to which man's will tends naturally. But man's will should tend to nothing else as an end, but to God, Who alone is to be enjoyed, as Augustine says (*De Doctr. Christ.* i. 5, 22). Therefore happiness is the same as God.

*On the contrary*, Nothing made is uncreated. But man's happiness is something made; because according to Augustine (*De Doctr. Christ.* i. 3): *Those things are to be enjoyed, which make us happy.* Therefore happiness is not something uncreated.

*I answer that*, As stated above (Q. I., A. 8; Q. II., A. 7), our end is twofold. First, there is the thing itself which we desire to attain: thus for the miser, the end is money. Secondly there is the attainment or possession, the use or enjoyment of the thing desired; thus we may say that the end of the miser is the possession of money; and the end of the intemperate man is to enjoy something pleasurable. In the first sense, then, man's last end is the uncreated good, namely God, Who alone by His infinite goodness can perfectly satisfy man's will. But in the second way, man's last end is something created, existing in him, and this is nothing else than the attainment or enjoyment of the last end. Now the last end is called happiness. If, therefore, we consider man's happiness in its cause or object, then it is something uncreated; but if we consider it as to the very essence of happiness, then it is something created.

*Reply Obj.* 1. God is happiness by His Essence: for He is happy not by acquisition or participation of something else, but by His Essence. On the other hand, men are happy, as Boethius says (*loc. cit.*), by participation; just as they are called *gods*, by participation. And this participation of happiness, in respect of which man is said to be happy, is something created.

*Reply Obj.* 2. Happiness is called man's supreme good, because it is the attainment or enjoyment of the supreme good.

*Reply Obj.* 3. Happiness is said to be the last end, in the same way as the attainment of the end is called the end.

## SECOND ARTICLE.

### WHETHER HAPPINESS IS AN OPERATION?

*We proceed thus to the Second Article:—*

*Objection* 1. It would seem that happiness is not an operation. For the Apostle says (Rom. vi. 22): *You have your fruit unto sanctification, and the end, life everlasting.* But life is not an operation, but the very being of living things. Therefore the last end, which is happiness, is not an operation.

*Obj.* 2. Further, Boethius says (*De Consol.* iii.) that happiness is *a state made perfect by the aggregate of all good things.* But state does not indicate operation. Therefore happiness is not an operation.

*Obj.* 3. Further, happiness signifies something existing in the happy one: since it is man's final perfection. But the meaning of operation does not imply anything existing in the operator, but rather something proceeding therefrom. Therefore happiness is not an operation.

*Obj.* 4. Further, happiness remains in the happy one. Now operation does not remain, but passes. Therefore happiness is not an operation.

*Obj.* 5. Further, to one man there is one happiness. But operations are many. Therefore happiness is not an operation.

*Obj.* 6. Further, happiness is in the happy one uninterruptedly. But human operation is often interrupted; for instance, by sleep, or some other occupation, or by cessation. Therefore happiness is not an operation.

*On the contrary*, The Philosopher says (*Ethic.* i. 13) that *happiness is an operation according to perfect virtue.*

*I answer that,* In so far as man's happiness is something created, existing in him, we must needs say that it is an operation. For happiness is man's supreme perfection. Now each thing is perfect in so far as it is actual; since potentiality without act is imperfect. Consequently happiness must consist in man's last act. But it is evident that operation is the last act of the operator, wherefore the

Philosopher calls it *second act* (*De Anima* ii. 1): because that which has a form can be potentially operating, just as he who knows is potentially considering. And hence it is that in other things, too, each one is said to be *for its operation* (*De Cœlo* ii. 3). Therefore man's happiness must of necessity consist in an operation.

*Reply Obj.* 1. Life is taken in two senses. First for the very being of the living. And thus happiness is not life: since it has been shown (Q. II., A. 5) that the being of a man, no matter in what it may consist, is not that man's happiness; for of God alone is it true that His Being is His Happiness. Secondly, life means the operation of the living, by which operation the principle of life is made actual: thus we speak of active and contemplative life, or of a life of pleasure. And in this sense eternal life is said to be the last end, as is clear from Jo. xvii. 3: *This is eternal life, that they may know Thee, the only true God.*

*Reply Obj.* 2. Boethius, in defining happiness, considered happiness in general: for considered thus it is the perfect common good; and he signified this by saying that happiness is *a state made perfect by the aggregate of all good things*, thus implying that the state of a happy man consists in possessing the perfect good. But Aristotle expressed the very essence of happiness, showing by what man is established in this state, and that it is by some kind of operation. And so it is that he proves happiness to be *the perfect good* (*Ethic.* i. 7).

*Reply Obj.* 3. As stated in *Metaph.* ix. 7 action is twofold. One proceeds from the agent into outward matter, such as *to burn* and *to cut*. And such an operation cannot be happiness: for such an operation is an action and a perfection, not of the agent, but rather of the patient, as is stated in the same passage. The other is an action that remains in the agent, such as to feel, to understand, and to will: and such an action is a perfection and an act of the agent. And such an operation can be happiness.

*Reply Obj.* 4. Since happiness signifies some final perfection; according as various things capable of happiness can attain to various degrees of perfection, so must there

be various meanings applied to happiness. For in God
there is happiness essentially; since His very Being is His
operation, whereby He enjoys no other than Himself.   In
the happy angels, the final perfection is in respect of some
operation, by which they are united to the Uncreated Good:
and this operation of theirs is one only and everlasting.
But in men, according to their present state of life, the final
perfection is in respect of an operation whereby man is united
to God: but this operation neither can be continual, nor,
consequently, is it one only, because operation is multiplied
by being discontinued.   And for this reason in the present
state of life, perfect happiness cannot be attained by man.
Wherefore the Philosopher, in placing man's happiness in
this life (*Ethic.* i. 10), says that it is imperfect, and after a long
discussion, concludes: *We call men happy, but only as men.*
But God has promised us perfect happiness, when we shall
be *as the angels . . . in heaven* (Matth. xxii. 30).

Consequently in regard to this perfect happiness, the
objection fails: because in that state of happiness, man's
mind will be united to God by one, continual, everlasting
operation.   But in the present life, in as far as we fall short
of the unity and continuity of that operation, so do we fall
short of perfect happiness.   Nevertheless it is a participation of happiness: and so much the greater, as the operation
can be more continuous and more one.   Consequently the
active life, which is busy with many things, has less of
happiness than the contemplative life, which is busied with
one thing, *i.e.*, the contemplation of truth.   And if at any
time man is not actually engaged in this operation, yet since
he can always easily turn to it, and since he ordains the
very cessation, by sleeping or occupying himself otherwise,
to the aforesaid occupation, the latter seems, as it were,
continuous.   From these remarks the replies to Objections 5
and 6 are evident.

## Third Article.

### WHETHER HAPPINESS IS AN OPERATION OF THE SENSITIVE PART, OR OF THE INTELLECTIVE PART ONLY?

*We proceed thus to the Third Article :—*

*Objection* 1. It would seem that happiness consists in an operation of the senses also. For there is no more excellent operation in man than that of the senses, except the intellective operation. But in us the intellective operation depends on the sensitive: since *we cannot understand without a phantasm* (*De Anima* iii. 7). Therefore happiness consists in an operation of the senses also.

*Obj.* 2. Further, Boethius says (*De Consol.* iii.) that happiness is *a state made perfect by the aggregate of all good things.* But some goods are sensible, which we attain by the operation of the senses. Therefore it seems that the operation of the senses is needed for happiness.

*Obj.* 3. Further, happiness is the perfect good, as we find proved in *Ethic.* i. 7: which would not be true, were not man perfected thereby in all his parts. But some parts of the soul are perfected by sensitive operations. Therefore sensitive operation is required for happiness.

*On the contrary*, Irrational animals have the sensitive operation in common with us: but they have not happiness in common with us. Therefore happiness does not consist in a sensitive operation.

*I answer that*, A thing may belong to happiness in three ways: (1) essentially, (2) antecedently, (3) consequently. Now the operation of sense cannot belong to happiness essentially. For man's happiness consists essentially in his being united to the Uncreated Good, Which is his last end, as shown above (A. 1): to Which man cannot be united by an operation of his senses. Again, in like manner, because, as shown above (Q. II., A. 5), man's happiness does not consist in goods of the body, which goods alone, however, we attain through the operation of the senses.

Nevertheless the operations of the senses can belong to

happiness, both antecedently and consequently: antecedently, in respect of imperfect happiness, such as can be had in this life, since the operation of the intellect demands a previous operation of the sense;—consequently, in that perfect happiness which we await in heaven; because at the resurrection, *from the very happiness of the soul*, as Augustine says (*Ep. ad Dioscor.*) *the body and the bodily senses will receive a certain overflow, so as to be perfected in their operations ;* a point which will be explained farther on when we treat of the resurrection (Suppl. QQ. LXXXII.—LXXXV.). But then the operation whereby man's mind is united to God will not depend on the senses.

*Reply Obj.* 1. This objection proves that the operation of the senses is required antecedently for imperfect happiness, such as can be had in this life.

*Reply Obj.* 2. Perfect happiness, such as the angels have, includes the aggregate of all good things, by being united to the universal source of all good; not that it requires each individual good. But in this imperfect happiness, we need the aggregate of those goods that suffice for the most perfect operation of this life.

*Reply Obj.* 3. In perfect happiness the entire man is perfected, in the lower part of his nature, by an overflow from the higher. But in the imperfect happiness of this life, it is otherwise; we advance from the perfection of the lower part to the perfection of the higher part.

## Fourth Article.

### WHETHER, IF HAPPINESS IS IN THE INTELLECTIVE PART, IT IS AN OPERATION OF THE INTELLECT OR OF THE WILL ?

*We proceed thus to the Fourth Article :—*

*Objection* 1. It would seem that happiness consists in an act of the will. For Augustine says (*De Civ. Dei* xix. 10, 11), that man's happiness consists in peace; wherefore it is written (Ps. cxlvii. 3): *Who hath placed peace in thy end* (Douay,—*borders*). But peace pertains to the will. Therefore man's happiness is in the will.

*Obj.* 2. Further, happiness is the supreme good. But good is the object of the will. Therefore happiness consists in an operation of the will.

*Obj.* 3. Further, the last end corresponds to the first mover: thus the last end of the whole army is victory, which is the end of the general, who moves all the men. But the first mover in regard to operations is the will: because it moves the other powers, as we shall state further on (Q. IX., AA. 1, 3). Therefore happiness regards the will.

*Obj.* 4. Further, if happiness be an operation, it must needs be man's most excellent operation. But the love of God, which is an act of the will, is a more excellent operation than knowledge, which is an operation of the intellect, as the Apostle declares (1 Cor. xiii.). Therefore it seems that happiness consists in an act of the will.

*Obj.* 5. Further, Augustine says (*De Trin.* xiii. 5) that *happy is he who has whatever he desires, and desires nothing amiss.* And a little further on (6) he adds: *He is almost happy who desires well, whatever he desires : for good things make a man happy, and such a man already possesses some good— i.e., a good will.* Therefore happiness consists in an act of the will.

*On the contrary,* Our Lord said (Jo. xvii. 3): *This is eternal life : that they may know Thee, the only true God.* Now eternal life is the last end, as stated above (A. 2 *ad* 1). Therefore man's happiness consists in the knowledge of God, which is an act of the intellect.

*I answer that,* As stated above (Q. II., A. 6) two things are needed for happiness: one, which is the essence of happiness: the other, that is, as it were, its proper accident, *i.e.,* the delight connected with it. I say, then, that as to the very essence of happiness, it is impossible for it to consist in an act of the will. For it is evident from what has been said (AA. 1, 2; Q. II., A. 7) that happiness is the attainment of the last end. But the attainment of the end does not consist in the very act of the will. For the will is directed to the end, both absent, when it desires it; and present, when it is delighted by resting therein. Now it is evident that the desire itself of the end is not the attainment of the end, but is a movement towards the end: while delight comes to the will from the end being present; and not conversely, is a thing made present, by the fact that the will delights in it. Therefore, that the end be present to him who desires it, must be due to something else than an act of the will.

This is evidently the case in regard to sensible ends. For if the acquisition of money were through an act of the will, the covetous man would have it from the very moment that he wished for it. But at that moment it is far from him; and he attains it, by grasping it in his hand, or in some like manner; and then he delights in the money got. And so it is with an intelligible end. For at first we desire to attain an intelligible end; we attain it, through its being made present to us by an act of the intellect; and then the delighted will rests in the end when attained.

So, therefore, the essence of happiness consists in an act of the intellect: but the delight that results from happiness pertains to the will. In this sense Augustine says (*Conf.* x. 23) that happiness is *joy in truth*, because, to wit, joy itself is the consummation of happiness.

*Reply Obj.* 1. Peace pertains to man's last end, not as though it were the very essence of happiness; but because it is antecedent and consequent thereto: antecedent, in so far as all those things are removed which disturb and hinder man in attaining the last end: consequent, inasmuch as, when man has attained his last end, he remains at peace, his desire being at rest.

*Reply Obj.* 2. The will's first object is not its act: just as neither is the first object of the sight, vision, but a visible thing. Wherefore, from the very fact that happiness belongs to the will, as the will's first object, it follows that it does not belong to it as its act.

*Reply Obj.* 3. The intellect apprehends the end before the will does: yet motion towards the end begins in the will. And therefore to the will belongs that which last of all follows the attainment of the end, viz., delight or enjoyment.

*Reply Obj.* 4. Love ranks above knowledge in moving,

but knowledge precedes love in attaining: for *naught is loved save what is known*, as Augustine says (*De Trin.* x. 1). Consequently we first attain an intelligible end by an act of the intellect; just as we first attain a sensible end by an act of sense.

*Reply Obj.* 5. He who has whatever he desires, is happy, because he has what he desires: and this indeed is by something other than the act of his will. But to desire nothing amiss is needed for happiness, as a necessary disposition thereto. And a good will is reckoned among the good things which make a man happy, forasmuch as it is an inclination of the will: just as a movement is reduced to the genus of its terminus, for instance, *alteration* to the genus *quality*.

## Fifth Article.

### WHETHER HAPPINESS IS AN OPERATION OF THE SPECULATIVE, OR OF THE PRACTICAL INTELLECT?

*We proceed thus to the Fifth Article :—*

*Objection* 1. It would seem that happiness is an operation of the practical intellect. For the end of every creature consists in becoming like God. But man is like God, by his practical intellect, which is the cause of things understood, rather than by his speculative intellect, which derives its knowledge from things. Therefore man's happiness consists in an operation of the practical intellect rather than of the speculative.

*Obj.* 2. Further, happiness is man's perfect good. But the practical intellect is ordained to the good rather than the speculative intellect, which is ordained to the true. Hence we are said to be good, in reference to the perfection of the practical intellect, but not in reference to the perfection of the speculative intellect, according to which we are said to be knowing or understanding. Therefore man's happiness consists in an act of the practical intellect rather than of the speculative.

*Obj.* 3. Further, happiness is a good of man himself. But the speculative intellect is more concerned with things outside man; whereas the practical intellect is concerned with things belonging to man himself, viz., his operations and passions. Therefore man's happiness consists in an operation of the practical intellect rather than of the speculative.

*On the contrary*, Augustine says (*De Trin.* i. 8) that *contemplation is promised us, as being the goal of all our actions, and the everlasting perfection of our joys.*

*I answer that,* Happiness consists in an operation of the speculative rather than of the practical intellect. This is evident for three reasons. First because if man's happiness is an operation, it must needs be man's highest operation. Now man's highest operation is that of his highest power in respect of its highest object: and his highest power is the intellect, whose highest object is the Divine Good, which is the object, not of the practical, but of the speculative intellect. Consequently happiness consists principally in such an operation, viz., in the contemplation of Divine things. And since that *seems to be each man's self, which is best in him,* according to *Ethic.* ix. 8, and x. 7, therefore such an operation is most proper to man and most delightful to him.

Secondly, it is evident from the fact that contemplation is sought principally for its own sake. But the act of the practical intellect is not sought for its own sake but for the sake of action: and these very actions are ordained to some end. Consequently it is evident that the last end cannot consist in the active life, which pertains to the practical intellect.

Thirdly, it is again evident, from the fact that in the contemplative life man has something in common with things above him, viz., with God and the angels, to whom he is made like by happiness. But in things pertaining to the active life, other animals also have something in common with man, although imperfectly.

Therefore the last and perfect happiness, which we await in the life to come, consists entirely in contemplation. But imperfect happiness, such as can be had here, consists first and principally in contemplation, but secondarily, in an operation of the practical intellect directing human actions and passions, as stated in *Ethic.* x. 7, 8.

*Reply Obj.* 1. The asserted likeness of the practical intellect to God is one of proportion; that is to say, by reason of its standing in relation to what it knows, as God does to what He knows. But the likeness of the speculative intellect to God is one of union and *information ;* which is a much greater likeness.—And yet it may be answered that, in regard to the principal thing known, which is His Essence, God has not practical but merely speculative knowledge.

*Reply Obj.* 2. The practical intellect is ordained to good which is outside of it: but the speculative intellect has good within it, viz., the contemplation of truth. And if this good be perfect, the whole man is perfected and made good thereby: such a good the practical intellect has not; but it directs man thereto.

*Reply Obj.* 3. This argument would hold, if man himself were his own last end; for then the consideration and direction of his actions and passions would be his happiness. But since man's last end is something outside of him, to wit, God, to Whom we reach out by an operation of the speculative intellect; therefore man's happiness consists in an operation of the speculative intellect rather than of the practical intellect.

## SIXTH ARTICLE.

### WHETHER HAPPINESS CONSISTS IN THE CONSIDERATION OF SPECULATIVE SCIENCES ?

*We proceed thus to the Sixth Article :—*

*Objection* 1. It would seem that man's happiness consists in the consideration of speculative sciences. For the Philosopher says (*Ethic.* i. 13) that *happiness is an operation according to perfect virtue.* And in distinguishing the virtues, he gives no more than three speculative virtues—*knowledge, wisdom* and *understanding,* which all belong to the consideration of speculative sciences. Therefore man's final happiness consists in the consideration of speculative sciences.

*Obj.* 2. Further, that which all desire for its own sake,

seems to be man's final happiness.   Now such is the consideration of speculative sciences; because, as stated in *Metaph.* i. 1, *all men naturally desire to know ;* and, a little farther on (2), it is stated that speculative sciences are sought for their own sakes.   Therefore happiness consists in the consideration of speculative sciences.

*Obj.* 3. Further, happiness is man's final perfection.   Now everything is perfected, according as it is reduced from potentiality to act.   But the human intellect is reduced to act by the consideration of speculative sciences.   Therefore it seems that in the consideration of these sciences, man's final happiness consists.

*On the contrary,* It is written (Jer. ix. 23): *Let not the wise man glory in his wisdom :* and this is said in reference to speculative sciences.   Therefore man's final happiness does not consist in the consideration of these.

*I answer that,* As stated above (A. 2 *ad* 4), man's happiness is twofold, one perfect, the other imperfect.   And by perfect happiness we are to understand that which attains to the true notion of happiness; and by imperfect happiness that which does not attain thereto, but partakes of some particular likeness of happiness.   Thus perfect prudence is in man, with whom is the idea of things to be done; while imperfect prudence is in certain irrational animals, who are possessed of certain particular instincts in respect of works similar to works of prudence.

Accordingly perfect happiness cannot consist essentially in the consideration of speculative sciences.   To prove this, we must observe that the consideration of a speculative science does not extend beyond the scope of the principles of that science: since the entire science is virtually contained in its principles.   Now the first principles of speculative sciences are received through the senses, as the Philosopher clearly states at the beginning of the *Metaphysics* (i. 1), and at the end of the *Posterior Analytics* (ii. 15).   Wherefore the entire consideration of speculative sciences cannot extend farther than knowledge of sensibles can lead.   Now man's final happiness, which is his final perfection, cannot consist in the knowledge of sensibles. For a thing is not perfected by something lower, except in so far as the lower partakes of something higher. Now it is evident that the form of a stone or of any sensible, is lower than man. Consequently the intellect is not perfected by the form of a stone, as such, but inasmuch as it partakes of a certain likeness to that which is above the human intellect, viz., the intelligible light, or something of the kind. Now whatever is by something else is reduced to that which is of itself. Therefore man's final perfection must needs be through knowledge of something above the human intellect. But it has been shown (Part I., Q. LXXXVIII., A. 2), that man cannot acquire through sensibles, the knowledge of separate substances, which are above the human intellect. Consequently it follows that man's happiness cannot consist in the consideration of speculative sciences. However, just as in sensible forms there is a participation of the higher substances, so the consideration of speculative sciences is a certain participation of true and perfect happiness.

*Reply Obj.* 1. In his book on *Ethics* the Philosopher treats of imperfect happiness, such as can be had in this life, as stated above (A. 2 *ad* 4).

*Reply Obj.* 2. Not only is perfect happiness naturally desired, but also any likeness or participation thereof.

*Reply Obj.* 3. Our intellect is reduced to act, in a fashion, by the consideration of speculative sciences, but not to its final and perfect act.

## Seventh Article.

### WHETHER HAPPINESS CONSISTS IN THE KNOWLEDGE OF SEPARATE SUBSTANCES, NAMELY, ANGELS?

*We proceed thus to the Seventh Article :—*

*Objection* 1. It would seem that man's happiness consists in the knowledge of separate substances, namely, angels. For Gregory says in a homily (xxvi. *in Ev.*): *It avails nothing to take part in the feasts of men, if we fail to take part in the feasts of angels ;* by which he means final happiness. But we can take part in the feasts of the angels by contemplating them. Therefore it seems that man's final happiness consists in contemplating the angels.

*Obj.* 2. Further, the final perfection of each thing is for it to be united to its principle: wherefore a circle is said to be a perfect figure, because its beginning and end coincide. But the beginning of human knowledge is from the angels, by whom men are enlightened, as Dionysius says (*Cœl. Hier.* iv.). Therefore the perfection of the human intellect consists in contemplating the angels.

*Obj.* 3. Further, each nature is perfect, when united to a higher nature; just as the final perfection of a body is to be united to the spiritual nature. But above the human intellect, in the natural order, are the angels. Therefore the final perfection of the human intellect is to be united to the angels by contemplation.

*On the contrary*, It is written (Jerem. ix. 24): *Let him that glorieth, glory in this, that he understandeth and knoweth Me.* Therefore man's final glory or happiness consists only in the knowledge of God.

*I answer that*, As stated above (A. 6), man's perfect happiness consists not in that which perfects the intellect by some participation, but in that which is so by its essence. Now it is evident that whatever is the perfection of a power is so in so far as the proper formal object of that power belongs to it. Now the proper object of the intellect is the true. Therefore the contemplation of whatever has participated truth, does not perfect the intellect with its final perfection. Since, therefore, the order of things is the same in being and in truth (*Metaph.* ii. 1); whatever are beings by participation, are true by participation. Now angels have being by participation: because in God alone is His Being His Essence, as shown in the First Part (Q. XLIV., A. 1). It follows that God alone is truth by His Essence, and that contemplation of Him makes man perfectly happy. However, there is no reason why we should not admit a certain imperfect happiness in the contemplation of the angels; and higher indeed than in the consideration of speculative science.

*Reply Obj.* 1. We shall take part in the feasts of the angels, by contemplating not only the angels, but, together with them, also God Himself.

*Reply Obj.* 2. According to those that hold human souls to be created by the angels, it seems fitting enough, that man's happiness should consist in the contemplation of the angels, in the union, as it were, of man with his beginning. But this is erroneous, as stated in the First Part (Q. XC., A. 3). Wherefore the final perfection of the human intellect is by union with God, Who is the first principle both of the creation of the soul and of its enlightenment. Whereas the angel enlightens as a minister, as stated in the First Part (Q. CXI., A. 2 *ad* 2). Consequently, by his ministration he helps man to attain to happiness; but he is not the object of man's happiness.

*Reply Obj.* 3. The lower nature may reach the higher in two ways. First, according to a degree of the participating power: and thus man's final perfection will consist in his attaining to a contemplation such as that of the angels. Secondly, as the object is attained by the power: and thus the final perfection of each power is to attain that in which is found the fulness of its formal object.

## EIGHTH ARTICLE.

### WHETHER MAN'S HAPPINESS CONSISTS IN THE VISION OF THE DIVINE ESSENCE ?

*We proceed thus to the Eighth Article :—*

*Objection* 1. It would seem that man's happiness does not consist in the vision of the Divine Essence. For Dionysius says (*Myst. Theol.* i.) that by that which is highest in his intellect, man is united to God as to something altogether unknown. But that which is seen in its essence is not altogether unknown. Therefore the final perfection of the intellect, namely, happiness, does not consist in God being seen in His Essence.

*Obj.* 2. Further, the higher perfection belongs to the higher nature. But to see His own Essence is the perfection proper to the Divine intellect. Therefore the final perfection of the human intellect does not reach to this, but consists in something less.

*On the contrary*, It is written (1 Jo. iii. 2): *When He shall appear, we shall be like to Him; and* (Vulg., *because*) *we shall see Him as He is.*

*I answer that*, Final and perfect happiness can consist in nothing else than the vision of the Divine Essence. To make this clear, two points must be observed. First, that man is not perfectly happy, so long as something remains for him to desire and seek: secondly, that the perfection of any power is determined by the nature of its object. Now the object of the intellect is *what a thing is, i.e.*, the essence of a thing, according to *De Anima* iii. 6. Wherefore the intellect attains perfection, in so far as it knows the essence of a thing. If therefore an intellect know the essence of some effect, whereby it is not possible to know the essence of the cause, *i.e.*, to know of the cause *what it is;* that intellect cannot be said to reach that cause simply, although it may be able to gather from the effect the knowledge that the cause is. Consequently, when man knows an effect, and knows that it has a cause, there naturally remains in man the desire to know about that cause, *what it is*. And this desire is one of wonder, and causes inquiry, as is stated in the beginning of the *Metaphysics* (i. 2). For instance, if a man, knowing the eclipse of the sun, consider that it must be due to some cause, and know not what that cause is, he wonders about it, and from wondering proceeds to inquire. Nor does this inquiry cease until he arrive at a knowledge of the essence of the cause.

If therefore the human intellect, knowing the essence of some created effect, knows no more of God than *that He is;* the perfection of that intellect does not yet reach simply the First Cause, but there remains in it the natural desire to seek the cause. Wherefore it is not yet perfectly happy. Consequently, for perfect happiness the intellect needs to reach the very Essence of the First Cause. And thus it will have its perfection through union with God as with that object, in which alone man's happiness consists, as stated above (AA. 1, 7; Q. II., A. 8).

*Reply Obj.* 1. Dionysius speaks of the knowledge of wayfarers journeying towards happiness.

*Reply Obj.* 2. As stated above (Q. I., A. 8), the end has a twofold acceptation. First, as to the thing itself which is desired: and in this way, the same thing is the end of the higher and of the lower nature, and indeed of all things, as stated above (*ibid.*). Secondly, as to the attainment of this thing; and thus the end of the higher nature is different from that of the lower, according to their respective habitudes to that thing. So then the happiness of God, Who, in understanding his Essence, comprehends It, is higher than that of a man or angel who sees It indeed, but comprehends It not.

# QUESTION IV.

## OF THOSE THINGS THAT ARE REQUIRED FOR HAPPINESS.

### (*In Eight Articles.*)

WE have now to consider those things that are required for happiness: and concerning this there are eight points of inquiry: (1) Whether delight is required for happiness? (2) Which is of greater account in happiness, delight or vision? (3) Whether comprehension is required? (4) Whether rectitude of the will is required? (5) Whether the body is necessary for man's happiness? (6) Whether any perfection of the body is necessary? (7) Whether any external goods are necessary? (8) Whether the fellowship of friends is necessary?

## FIRST ARTICLE.

### WHETHER DELIGHT IS REQUIRED FOR HAPPINESS?

*We proceed thus to the First Article :—*

*Objection* 1. It would seem that delight is not required for happiness. For Augustine says (*De Trin.* i. 8) that *vision is the entire reward of faith.* But the prize or reward of virtue is happiness, as the Philosopher clearly states (*Ethic.* i. 9). Therefore nothing besides vision is required for happiness.

*Obj.* 2. Further, happiness is *the most self-sufficient of all goods*, as the Philosopher declares (*Ethic.* i. 7). But that which needs something else is not self-sufficient. Since then the essence of happiness consists in seeing God, as stated above (Q. III., A. 8); it seems that delight is not necessary for happiness.

*Obj.* 3. Further, the *operation of bliss or happiness should*

*be unhindered* (*Ethic*. vii. 13).   But delight hinders the operation of the intellect: since it destroys the estimate of prudence (*Ethic*. vi. 5).   Therefore delight is not necessary for
happiness.

*On the contrary*, Augustine says (*Conf.* x. 23) that happiness
is *joy in truth*.

*I answer that*, One thing may be necessary for another in
four ways.   First, as a preamble and preparation to it:
thus instruction is necessary for science.   Secondly, as perfecting it: thus the soul is necessary for the life of the body.
Thirdly, as helping it from without: thus friends are necessary for some undertaking.   Fourthly, as something attend-
dant on it: thus we might say that heat is necessary for fire.
And in this way delight is necessary for happiness.   For it
is caused by the appetite being at rest in the good attained.
Wherefore, since happiness is nothing else but the attainment of the Sovereign Good, it cannot be without concomitant delight.

*Reply Obj.* 1. From the very fact that a reward is given
to anyone, the will of him who deserves it is at rest, and in
this consists delight.   Consequently, delight is included in
the very notion of reward.

*Reply Obj.* 2. The very sight of God causes delight.   Consequently, he who sees God cannot need delight.

*Reply Obj.* 3. Delight that is attendant upon the operation of the intellect does not hinder it, rather does it perfect it, as stated in *Ethic*. x. 4: since what we do with delight,
we do with greater care and perseverance.   On the other
hand, delight which is extraneous to the operation is a
hindrance thereto:—sometimes by distracting the attention; because, as already observed, we are more attentive
to those things that delight us; and when we are very attentive to one thing, we must needs be less attentive to another:
—sometimes on account of opposition; thus a sensual delight that is contrary to reason, hinders the estimate of
prudence more than it hinders the estimate of the speculative intellect.

## SECOND ARTICLE.

### WHETHER IN HAPPINESS VISION RANKS BEFORE DELIGHT?

*We proceed thus to the Second Article :—*

*Objection* 1. It would seem that in happiness, delight ranks before vision. For *delight is the perfection of operation* (*Ethic.* x. 4).   But perfection ranks before the thing perfected. Therefore delight ranks before the operation of the intellect, *i.e.*, vision.

*Obj.* 2. Further, that by reason of which a thing is desirable, is yet more desirable.   But operations are desired on account of the delight they afford: hence, too, nature has adjusted delight to those operations which are necessary for the preservation of the individual and of the species, lest animals should disregard such operations.   Therefore, in happiness, delight ranks before the operation of the intellect, which is vision.

*Obj.* 3. Further, vision corresponds to faith; while delight or enjoyment corresponds to charity.   But charity ranks before faith, as the Apostle says (1 Cor. xiii. 13).   Therefore delight or enjoyment ranks before vision.

*On the contrary*, The cause is greater than its effect.   But vision is the cause of delight.   Therefore vision ranks before delight.

*I answer that*, The Philosopher discusses this question (*Ethic.* x. 4), and leaves it unsolved.   But if one consider the matter carefully, the operation of the intellect which is vision, must needs rank before delight.   For delight consists in a certain repose of the will.   Now that the will finds rest in anything, can only be on account of the goodness of that thing in which it reposes.   If therefore the will reposes in an operation, the will's repose is caused by the goodness of the operation.   Nor does the will seek good for the sake of repose; for thus the very act of the will would be the end, which has been disproved above (Q. I., A. 1 *ad* 2; Q. III., A. 4): but it seeks to be at rest in the operation, because that operation is its good.   Consequently it is evident that the operation in which the will reposes ranks before the resting of the will therein.

*Reply Obj.* 1. As the Philosopher says (*ibid.*) *delight perfects operation as vigour perfects youth*, because it is a result of youth. Consequently delight is a perfection attendant upon vision; but not a perfection whereby vision is made perfect in its own species.

*Reply Obj.* 2. The apprehension of the senses does not attain to the universal good, but to some particular good which is delightful. And consequently, according to the sensitive appetite which is in animals, operations are sought for the sake of delight. But the intellect apprehends the universal good, the attainment of which results in delight: wherefore its purpose is directed to good rather than to delight. Hence it is that the Divine intellect, which is the Author of nature, adjusted delights to operations on account of the operations. And we should form our estimate of things not simply according to the order of the sensitive appetite, but rather according to the order of the intellectual appetite.

*Reply Obj.* 3. Charity does not seek the beloved good for the sake of delight: it is for charity a consequence that it delights in the good gained which it loves. Thus delight does not answer to charity as its end, but vision does, whereby the end is first made present to charity.

### THIRD ARTICLE.

#### WHETHER COMPREHENSION IS NECESSARY FOR HAPPINESS?

*We proceed thus to the Third Article :—*

*Objection* 1. It would seem that comprehension is not necessary for happiness. For Augustine says (*Ad Paulinam de Videndo Deum*) :* *To reach God with the mind is happiness, to comprehend Him is impossible.* Therefore happiness is without comprehension.

*Obj.* 2. Further, happiness is the perfection of man as to his intellective part, wherein there are no other powers than the intellect and will, as stated in the First Part

* Cf. *Serm.* xxxviii. *de Verb. Dom.*

(QQ. LXXIX. *and foll.*).   But the intellect is sufficiently perfected by seeing God, and the will by enjoying Him. Therefore there is no need for comprehension as a third.

*Obj.* 3. Further, happiness consists in an operation.   But operations are determined by their objects: and there are two universal objects, the true and the good: of which the true corresponds to vision, and good to delight.   Therefore there is no need for comprehension as a third.

*On the contrary*, The Apostle says (1 Cor. ix. 24): *So run that you may comprehend* (Douay,—*obtain*).   But happiness is the goal of the spiritual race: hence he says (2 Tim. iv. 7, 8): *I have fought a good fight, I have finished my course, I have kept the faith ; as to the rest there is laid up for me a crown of justice.*   Therefore comprehension is necessary for Happiness.

*I answer that*, Since Happiness consists in gaining the last end, those things that are required for Happiness must be gathered from the way in which man is ordered to an end. Now man is ordered to an intelligible end partly through his intellect, and partly through his will:—through his intellect, in so far as a certain imperfect knowledge of the end pre-exists in the intellect:—through the will, first by love which is the will's first movement towards anything; secondly, by a real relation of the lover to the thing beloved, which relation may be threefold.   For sometimes the thing beloved is present to the lover: and then it is no longer sought for. Sometimes it is not present, and it is impossible to attain it: and then, too, it is not sought for.   But sometimes it is possible to attain it, yet it is raised above the capability of the attainer, so that he cannot have it forthwith; and this is the relation of one that hopes, to that which he hopes for, and this relation alone causes a search for the end.   To these three, there are a corresponding three in Happiness itself. For perfect knowledge of the end corresponds to imperfect knowledge; presence of the end corresponds to the relation of hope; but delight in the end now present results from love, as already stated (A. 2 *ad* 3).   And therefore these three must concur in Happiness; to wit, vision, which is perfect knowledge of the intelligible end; comprehension, which implies presence of the end; and delight or enjoyment, which implies repose of the lover in the object beloved.

*Reply Obj.* 1. Comprehension is twofold. First, inclusion of the comprehended in the comprehensor; and thus whatever is comprehended by the finite, is itself finite. Wherefore God cannot be thus comprehended by a created intellect. Secondly, comprehension means nothing but the holding of something already present and possessed: thus one who runs after another is said to comprehend* him when he lays hold on him. And in this sense comprehension is necessary for Happiness.

*Reply Obj.* 2. Just as hope and love pertain to the will, because it is the same one that loves a thing, and that tends towards it while not possessed, so, too, comprehension and delight belong to the will, since it is the same that possesses a thing and reposes therein.

*Reply Obj.* 3. Comprehension is not a distinct operation from vision; but a certain relation to the end already gained. Wherefore even vision itself, or the thing seen, inasmuch as it is present, is the object of comprehension.

## FOURTH ARTICLE.

### WHETHER RECTITUDE OF THE WILL IS NECESSARY FOR HAPPINESS ?

*We proceed thus to the Fourth Article :—*

*Objection* 1. It would seem that rectitude of the will is not necessary for Happiness. For Happiness consists essentially in an operation of the intellect, as stated above (Q. III., A. 4). But rectitude of the will, by reason of which men are said to be clean of heart, is not necessary for the perfect operation of the intellect: for Augustine says (*Retract.* i. 4): *I do not approve of what I said in a prayer : O God, Who didst will none but the clean of heart to know the truth. For it can be answered that many who are not clean of heart, know many truths.* Therefore rectitude of the will is not necessary for Happiness.

* In English we should say ' *catch.*'

*Obj.* 2. Further, what precedes does not depend on what follows. But the operation of the intellect precedes the operation of the will. Therefore Happiness, which is the perfect operation of the intellect, does not depend on rectitude of the will.

*Obj.* 3. Further, that which is ordained to another as its end, is not necessary, when the end is already gained; as a ship, for instance, after arrival in port. But rectitude of the will, which is by reason of virtue, is ordained to Happiness as its end. Therefore, Happiness once obtained, rectitude of the will is no longer necessary.

*On the contrary,* It is written (Matth. v. 8): *Blessed are the clean of heart ; for they shall see God :* and (Heb. xii. 14): *Follow peace with all men, and holiness ; without which no man shall see God.*

*I answer that,* Rectitude of the will is necessary for Happiness both antecedently and concomitantly. Antecedently, because rectitude of the will consists in being duly ordered to the last end. Now the end in comparison to what is ordained to the end is as form compared to matter. Wherefore, just as matter cannot receive a form, unless it be duly disposed thereto, so nothing gains an end, except it be duly ordained thereto. And therefore none can obtain Happiness, without rectitude of the will. Concomitantly, because as stated above (Q. III., A. 8), final Happiness consists in the vision of the Divine Essence, Which is the very essence of goodness. So that the will of him who sees the Essence of God, of necessity, loves, whatever he loves, in subordination to God; just as the will of him who sees not God's Essence, of necessity, loves whatever he loves, under that common notion of good which he knows. And this is precisely what makes the will right. Wherefore it is evident that Happiness cannot be without a right will.

*Reply Obj.* 1. Augustine is speaking of the knowledge of that truth which is not the very Essence of goodness.

*Reply Obj.* 2. Every act of the will is preceded by an act of the intellect: but a certain act of the will precedes a certain act of the intellect. For the will tends to the final act of the intellect which is happiness. And consequently right inclination of the will is required antecedently for happiness, just as the arrow must take a right course in order to strike the target.

*Reply Obj.* 3. Not everything that is ordained to the end, ceases with the getting of the end: but only that which involves imperfection, such as movement. Hence the instruments of movement are no longer necessary, when the end has been gained: but the due order to the end is necessary.

## FIFTH ARTICLE.

### WHETHER THE BODY IS NECESSARY FOR MAN'S HAPPINESS?

*We proceed thus to the Fifth Article :—*

*Objection* 1. It would seem that the body is necessary for Happiness. For the perfection of virtue and grace pre-supposes the perfection of nature. But Happiness is the perfection of virtue and grace. Now the soul, without the body, has not the perfection of nature; since it is naturally a part of human nature, and every part is imperfect while separated from its whole. Therefore the soul cannot be happy without the body.

*Obj.* 2. Further, Happiness is a perfect operation, as stated above (Q. III., AA. 2, 5). But perfect operation follows perfect being: since nothing operates except in so far as it is an actual being. Since, therefore, the soul has not perfect being, while it is separated from the body, just as neither has a part, while separate from its whole; it seems that the soul cannot be happy without the body.

*Obj.* 3. Further, Happiness is the perfection of man. But the soul, without the body, is not man. Therefore Happiness cannot be in the soul separated from the body.

*Obj.* 4. Further, according to the Philosopher (*Ethic.* vii. 13) *the operation of bliss*, in which operation happiness consists, is *not hindered*. But the operation of the separate soul is hindered; because, as Augustine says (*Gen. ad lit.*, xii. 35), the soul *has a natural desire to rule the body, the result of which is that it is held back, so to speak, from tending with all its might to the heavenward journey, i.e.,* to the vision of the Divine Essence. Therefore the soul cannot be happy without the body.

*Obj.* 5. Further, Happiness is the sufficient good and lulls desire. But this cannot be said of the separated soul; for it yet desires to be united to the body, as Augustine says (*ibid.*). Therefore the soul is not happy while separated from the body.

*Obj.* 6. Further, in Happiness man is equal to the angels. But the soul without the body is not equal to the angels, as Augustine says (*ibid.*). Therefore it is not happy.

*On the contrary,* It is written (Apoc. xiv. 13): *Happy* (Douay,—*blessed*) *are the dead who die in the Lord.*

*I answer that,* Happiness is twofold; the one is imperfect and is had in this life; the other is perfect, consisting in the vision of God. Now it is evident that the body is necessary for the happiness of this life. For the happiness of this life consists in an operation of the intellect, either speculative or practical. And the operation of the intellect in this life cannot be without a phantasm, which is only in a bodily organ, as was shown in the First Part (Q. LXXXIV., AA. 6, 7). Consequently that happiness which can be had in this life, depends, in a way, on the body.

But as to perfect Happiness, which consists in the vision of God, some have maintained that it is not possible to the soul separated from the body; and have said that the souls of saints, when separated from their bodies, do not attain to that Happiness until the Day of Judgment, when they will receive their bodies back again. And this is shown to be false, both by authority and by reason. By authority, since the Apostle says (2 Cor. v. 6): *While we are in the body, we are absent from the Lord ;* and he points out the reason of this absence, saying: *For we walk by faith and not by sight.* Now from this it is clear that so long as we walk by faith and not by sight, bereft of the vision of the Divine Essence, we are not present to the Lord. But the souls of the saints, separated from their bodies, are in God's presence; wherefore the text continues: *But we are confident and have a good will*

*to be absent . . . from the body, and to be present with the Lord.*
Whence it is evident that the souls of the saints, separated
from their bodies, *walk by sight*, seeing the Essence of God,
wherein is true Happiness.

Again this is made clear by reason. For the intellect
needs not the body, for its operation, save on account of the
phantasms, wherein it looks on the intelligible truth, as
stated in the First Part (Q. LXXXIV., A. 7). Now it is
evident that the Divine Essence cannot be seen by means of
phantasms, as stated in the First Part (Q. XII., A. 3).
Wherefore, since man's perfect Happiness consists in the
vision of the Divine Essence, it does not depend on the body.
Consequently, without the body the soul can be happy.

We must, however, notice that something may belong to
a thing's perfection in two ways. First, as constituting the
essence thereof; thus the soul is necessary for man's perfection. Secondly, as necessary for its well-being: thus,
beauty of body and keenness of perception belong to man's
perfection. Wherefore though the body does not belong in
the first way to the perfection of human Happiness, yet it
does in the second way. For since operation depends on a
thing's nature, the more perfect is the soul in its nature, the
more perfectly it has its proper operation, wherein its happiness consists. Hence Augustine, after inquiring (*Gen. ad lit.*
xii. 35) *whether that perfect Happiness can be ascribed to the
souls of the dead separated from their bodies,* answers *that they
cannot see the Unchangeable Substance, as the blessed angels
see It ; either for some other more hidden reason, or because
they have a natural desire to rule the body.*

*Reply Obj.* 1. Happiness is the perfection of the soul on the
part of the intellect, in respect of which the soul transcends
the organs of the body; but not according as the soul is the
natural form of the body. Wherefore the soul retains that
natural perfection in respect of which happiness is due to it,
though it does not retain that natural perfection in respect
of which it is the form of the body.

*Reply Obj.* 2. The relation of the soul to being is not the
same as that of other parts: for the being of the whole is not

that of any individual part: wherefore, either the part ceases altogether to be, when the whole is destroyed, just as the parts of an animal, when the animal is destroyed; or, if they remain, they have another actual being, just as a part of a line has another being from that of the whole line.   But the human soul retains the being of the composite after the destruction of the body: and this because the being of the form is the same as that of its matter, and this is the being of the composite.   Now the soul subsists in its own being, as stated in the First Part (Q. LXXV., A. 2).   It follows, therefore, that after being separated from the body it has perfect being, and that consequently it can have a perfect operation; although it has not the perfect specific nature.

*Reply Obj.* 3. Happiness belongs to man in respect of his intellect: and, therefore, since the intellect remains, it can have Happiness.   Thus the teeth of an Ethiopian, in respect of which he is said to be white, can retain their whiteness, even after extraction.

*Reply Obj.* 4. One thing is hindered by another in two ways.   First, by way of opposition; thus cold hinders the action of heat: and such a hindrance to operation is repugnant to Happiness.   Secondly, by way of some kind of defect, because, to wit, that which is hindered has not all that is necessary to make it perfect in every way: and such a hindrance to operation is not incompatible with Happiness, but prevents it from being perfect in every way.   And thus it is that separation from the body is said to hold the soul back from tending with all its might to the vision of the Divine Essence.   For the soul desires to enjoy God in such a way that the enjoyment also may overflow into the body, as far as possible.   And therefore, as long as it enjoys God, without the fellowship of the body, its appetite is at rest in that which it has, in such a way, that it would still wish the body to attain to its share.

*Reply Obj.* 5. The desire of the separated soul is entirely at rest, as regards the thing desired; since, to wit, it has that which suffices its appetite.   But it is not wholly at rest, as regards the desirer, since it does not possess that good in every way that it would wish to possess it. Consequently, after the body has been resumed, Happiness increases not in intensity, but in extent.

*Reply Obj.* 6. The statement made (*ibid.*) to the effect that *the souls of the departed see not God as the angels do*, is not to be understood as referring to inequality of quantity; because even now some souls of the Blessed are raised to the higher orders of angels, thus seeing God more clearly than the lower angels. But it refers to inequality of proportion: because the angels, even the lowest, have every perfection of Happiness that they ever will have, whereas the separated souls of the saints have not.

## SIXTH ARTICLE.

### WHETHER PERFECTION OF THE BODY IS NECESSARY FOR HAPPINESS ?

*We proceed thus to the Sixth Article :—*

*Objection* 1. It would seem that perfection of the body is not necessary for man's perfect Happiness. For perfection of the body is a bodily good. But it has been shown above (Q. II.) that Happiness does not consist in bodily goods. Therefore no perfect disposition of the body is necessary for man's Happiness.

*Obj.* 2. Further, man's Happiness consists in the vision of the Divine Essence, as shown above (Q. III., A. 8). But the body has no part in this operation, as shown above (A. 5). Therefore no disposition of the body is necessary for Happiness.

*Obj.* 3. Further, the more the intellect is abstracted from the body, the more perfectly it understands. But Happiness consists in the most perfect operation of the intellect. Therefore the soul should be abstracted from the body in every way. Therefore, in no way is a disposition of the body necessary for Happiness.

*On the contrary*, Happiness is the reward of virtue; wherefore it is written (Jo. xiii. 17): *You shall be blessed, if you do them.* But the reward promised to the saints is not only that they shall see and enjoy God, but also that their bodies shall be well-disposed; for it is written (Isa. lxvi. 14): *You shall see and your heart shall rejoice, and your bones shall flourish like a herb.* Therefore good disposition of the body is necessary for Happiness.

*I answer that,* If we speak of that happiness which man can acquire in this life, it is evident that a well-disposed body is of necessity required for it. For this happiness consists, according to the Philosopher (*Ethic.* i. 13) in *an operation according to perfect virtue ;* and it is clear that man can be hindered, by indisposition of the body, from every operation of virtue.

But speaking of perfect Happiness, some have maintained that no disposition of body is necessary for Happiness; indeed, that it is necessary for the soul to be entirely separated from the body. Hence Augustine (*De Civ Dei.* xxii. 26) quotes the words of Porphyry who said that *for the soul to be happy, it must be severed from everything corporeal.* But this is unreasonable. For since it is natural to the soul to be united to the body; it is not possible for the perfection of the soul to exclude its natural perfection.

Consequently, we must say that perfect disposition of the body is necessary, both antecedently and consequently, for that Happiness which is in all ways perfect.—Antecedently, because, as Augustine says (*Gen. ad lit.* xii. 35), *if the body be such, that the governance thereof is difficult and burdensome, like unto flesh which is corruptible and weighs upon the soul, the mind is turned away from that vision of the highest heaven.* Whence he concludes that, *when this body will no longer be ' natural,' but ' spiritual,' then will it be equalled to the angels, and that will be its glory, which erstwhile was its burden.* —Consequently, because from the Happiness of the soul there will be an overflow on to the body, so that this too will obtain its perfection. Hence Augustine says (*Ep. ad Dioscor.*) that *God gave the soul such a powerful nature that from its exceeding fulness of happiness the vigour of incorruption overflows into the lower nature.*

*Reply Obj.* 1. Happiness does not consist in bodily good as its object: but bodily good can add a certain charm and perfection to Happiness.

*Reply Obj.* 2. Although the body has no part in that operation of the intellect whereby the Essence of God is seen, yet it might prove a hindrance thereto. Consequently, perfection of the body is necessary, lest it hinder the mind from being lifted up.

*Reply Obj.* 3. The perfect operation of the intellect requires indeed that the intellect be abstracted from this corruptible body which weighs upon the soul; but not from the spiritual body, which will be wholly subject to the spirit. On this point we shall treat in the Third Part of this work (Suppl., Q. LXXXII., *seqq.*).

## Seventh Article.

### WHETHER ANY EXTERNAL GOODS ARE NECESSARY FOR HAPPINESS ?

*We proceed thus to the Seventh Article :—*

*Objection* 1. It would seem that external goods also are necessary for Happiness. For that which is promised the saints for reward, belongs to Happiness. But external goods are promised the saints; for instance, food and drink, wealth, and a kingdom: for it is said (Luke xxii. 30): *That you may eat and drink at My table in My kingdom :* and (Matth. vi. 20): *Lay up to yourselves treasures in heaven :* and (Matth. xxv. 34): *Come, ye blessed of My Father, possess you the kingdom.* Therefore external goods are necessary for Happiness.

*Obj.* 2. Further, according to Boethius (*De Consol.* iii.): happiness is *a state made perfect by the aggregate of all good things.* But some of man's goods are external, although they be of least account, as Augustine says (*De Lib. Arb.* ii. 19). Therefore they too are necessary for Happiness.

*Obj.* 3. Further, Our Lord said (Matth. v. 12): *Your reward is very great in heaven.* But to be in heaven implies being in a place. Therefore at least external place is necessary for Happiness.

*On the contrary,* It is written (Ps. lxxii. 25): *For what have*

*I in heaven ? and besides Thee what do I desire upon earth ?*
As though to say: ' I desire nothing but this,—*It is good
for me to adhere to my God*.' Therefore nothing further
external is necessary for Happiness.

*I answer that*, For imperfect happiness, such as can be had
in this life, external goods are necessary, not as belonging
to the essence of happiness, but by serving as instruments
to happiness, which consists in an operation of virtue, as
stated in *Ethic*. i. 13. For man needs, in this life, the necessaries of the body, both for the operation of contemplative
virtue, and for the operation of active virtue, for which
latter he needs also many other things by means of which
to perform its operations.

On the other hand, such goods as these are nowise necessary for perfect Happiness, which consists in seeing God.
The reason of this is that all suchlike external goods are
requisite either for the support of the animal body; or for
certain operations which belong to human life, which we
perform by means of the animal body: whereas that perfect
Happiness which consists in seeing God, will be either in
the soul separated from the body, or in the soul united to
the body then no longer animal but spiritual. Consequently
these external goods are nowise necessary for that Happiness, since they are ordained to the animal life.—And since,
in this life, the felicity of contemplation, as being more
God-like, approaches nearer than that of action to the likeness of that perfect Happiness, therefore it stands in less
need of these goods of the body, as stated in *Ethic*. x. 8.

*Reply Obj*. 1. All those material promises contained in
Holy Scripture, are to be understood metaphorically, inasmuch as Scripture is wont to express spiritual things under
the form of things corporeal, in order *that from things we
know, we may rise to the desire of things unknown*, as Gregory
says (*Hom*. xi. *in Ev*.). Thus food and drink signify the
delight of Happiness: wealth, the sufficiency of God for man;
the kingdom, the lifting up of man to union with God.

*Reply Obj*. 2. These goods that serve for the animal life,
are incompatible with that spiritual life wherein perfect

Happiness consists. Nevertheless in that Happiness there will be the aggregate of all good things, because whatever good there be in these things, we shall possess it all in the Supreme Fount of goodness.

*Reply Obj.* 3. According to Augustine (*De Serm. Dom. in Monte* i. 5), it is not a material heaven that is described as the reward of the saints, but a heaven raised on the height of spiritual goods. Nevertheless a bodily place, viz., the empyrean heaven, will be appointed to the Blessed, not as a need of Happiness, but by reason of a certain fitness and adornment.

### Eighth Article.

#### WHETHER THE FELLOWSHIP OF FRIENDS IS NECESSARY FOR HAPPINESS ?

*We proceed thus to the Eighth Article :—*

*Objection* 1. It would seem that friends are necessary for Happiness. For future Happiness is frequently designated by Scripture under the name of *glory*. But glory consists in man's good being brought to the notice of many. Therefore the fellowship of friends is necessary for Happiness.

*Obj.* 2. Further, Boethius* says that *there is no delight in possessing any good whatever, without someone to share it with us*. But delight is necessary for Happiness. Therefore fellowship of friends is also necessary.

*Obj.* 3. Further, charity is perfected in Happiness. But charity includes the love of God and of our neighbour. Therefore it seems that fellowship of friends is necessary for Happiness.

*On the contrary*, It is written (Wisd. vii. 11): *All good things came to me together with her, i.e.*, with divine wisdom, which consists in contemplating God. Consequently nothing else is necessary for Happiness.

*I answer that*, If we speak of the happiness of this life, the happy man needs friends, as the Philosopher says (*Ethic.* ix. 9), not, indeed, to make use of them, since he suffices himself; nor to delight in them, since he possesses

* Seneca, *Ep.* 6.

perfect delight in the operation of virtue; but for the purpose of a good operation, viz., that he may do good to them; that he may delight in seeing, them do good; and again that he may be helped by them in his good work. For in order that man may do well, whether in the works of the active life, or in those of the contemplative life, he needs the fellowship of friends.

But if we speak of perfect Happiness which will be in our heavenly Fatherland, the fellowship of friends is not essential to Happiness; since man has the entire fulness of his perfection in God. But the fellowship of friends conduces to the well-being of Happiness. Hence Augustine says (*Gen. ad lit.* viii. 25) that *the spiritual creatures receive no other interior aid to happiness than the eternity, truth, and charity of the Creator. But if they can be said to be helped from without, perhaps it is only by this that they see one another and rejoice in God, at their fellowship.*

*Reply Obj.* 1. That glory which is essential to Happiness, is that which man has, not with man but with God.

*Reply Obj.* 2. This saying is to be understood of the possession of good that does not fully satisfy. This does not apply to the question under consideration; because man possesses in God a sufficiency of every good.

*Reply Obj.* 3. Perfection of charity is essential to Happiness, as to the love of God, but not as to the love of our neighbour. Wherefore if there were but one soul enjoying God, it would be happy, though having no neighbour to love. But supposing one neighbour to be there, love of him results from perfect love of God. Consequently, friendship is, as it were, concomitant with perfect Happiness.

# QUESTION V.

## OF THE ATTAINMENT OF HAPPINESS.

### (*In Eight Articles.*)

WE must now consider the attainment of Happiness. Under this heading there are eight points of inquiry: (1) Whether man can attain Happiness? (2) Whether one man can be happier than another? (3) Whether any man can be happy in this life? (4) Whether Happiness once had can be lost? (5) Whether man can attain Happiness by means of his natural powers? (6) Whether man attains Happiness through the action of some higher creature? (7) Whether any actions of man are necessary in order that man may obtain Happiness of God? (8) Whether every man desires Happiness?

## FIRST ARTICLE.

### WHETHER MAN CAN ATTAIN HAPPINESS?

*We proceed thus to the First Article :—*

*Objection* 1. It would seem that man cannot attain happiness. For just as the rational is above the sensible nature, so the intellectual is above the rational, as Dionysius declares (*Div. Nom.* iv., vi., vii.) in several passages. But irrational animals that have the sensitive nature only, cannot attain the end of the rational nature. Therefore neither can man, who is of rational nature, attain the end of the intellectual nature, which is Happiness.

*Obj.* 2. Further, True Happiness consists in seeing God, Who is pure Truth. But from his very nature, man considers truth in material things: wherefore *he understands*

*the intelligible species in the phantasm* (*De Anima* iii. 7).
Therefore he cannot attain Happiness.

*Obj.* 3. Further, Happiness consists in attaining the Sovereign Good.   But we cannot arrive at the top without sur-
mounting the middle.   Since, therefore, the angelic nature
through which man cannot mount is midway between God
and human nature; it seems that he cannot attain Happiness.

*On the contrary,* It is written (Ps. xciii. 12): *Blessed is the*
*man whom Thou shalt instruct, O Lord.*

*I answer that,* Happiness is the attainment of the Perfect
Good.   Whoever, therefore, is capable of the Perfect Good
can attain Happiness.   Now, that man is capable of the
Perfect Good, is proved both because his intellect can apprehend the universal and perfect good, and because his will
can desire it.   And therefore man can attain Happiness.—
This can be proved again from the fact that man is capable
of seeing God, as stated in the First Part (Q. XII., A. 1):
in which vision, as we stated above (Q. III., A. 8) man's
perfect Happiness consists.

*Reply Obj.* 1. The rational exceeds the sensitive nature,
otherwise than the intellectual surpasses the rational.   For
the rational exceeds the sensitive nature in respect of the
object of its knowledge: since the senses have no knowledge
whatever of the universal, whereas the reason has knowledge thereof.   But the intellectual surpasses the rational
nature, as to the mode of knowing the same intelligible
truth: for the intellectual nature grasps forthwith the truth
which the rational nature reaches by the inquiry of reason,
as was made clear in the First Part (Q. LVIII., A. 3;
Q. LXXIX., A. 8).   Therefore reason arrives by a kind of
movement at that which the intellect grasps.   Consequently
the rational nature can attain Happiness, which is the perfection of the intellectual nature: but otherwise than the
angels.   Because the angels attained it forthwith after the
beginning of their creation: whereas man attains it after a
time.   But the sensitive nature can nowise attain this end.

*Reply Obj.* 2. To man in the present state of life the
natural way of knowing intelligible truth is by means of

phantasms. But after this state of life, he has another natural way, as was stated in the First Part (Q. LXXXIV., A. 7; Q. LXXXIX., A. 1).

*Reply Obj.* 3. Man cannot surmount the angels in the degree of nature, so as to be above them naturally. But he can surmount them by an operation of the intellect, by understanding that there is above the angels something that makes men happy; and when he has attained it, he will be perfectly happy.

## SECOND ARTICLE.

### WHETHER ONE MAN CAN BE HAPPIER THAN ANOTHER?

*We proceed thus to the Second Article :—*

*Objection* 1. It would seem that one man cannot be happier than another. For Happiness is *the reward of virtue*, as the Philosopher says (*Ethic.* i. 9). But equal reward is given for all the works of virtue; because it is written (Matth. xx. 10) that all who laboured in the vineyard *received every man a penny ;* for, as Gregory says (*Hom.* xix. *in Evang.*), *each was equally rewarded with eternal life.* Therefore one man cannot be happier than another.

*Obj.* 2. Further, Happiness is the supreme good. But nothing can surpass the supreme. Therefore one man's Happiness cannot be surpassed by another's.

*Obj.* 3. Further, since Happiness is *the perfect and sufficient good* (*Ethic.* i. 7) it brings rest to man's desire. But his desire is not at rest, if he yet lacks some good that can be got. And if he lack nothing that he can get, there can be no still greater good. Therefore either man is not happy; or, if he be happy, no other Happiness can be greater.

*On the contrary*, It is written (Jo. xiv. 2): *In My Father's house there are many mansions ;* which, according to Augustine (*Tract.* lxvii. *in Joan.*) signify *the diverse dignities of merits in the one eternal life.* But the dignity of eternal life which is given according to merit, is Happiness itself. Therefore there are diverse degrees of Happiness, and Happiness is not equally in all.

*I answer that*, As stated above (Q. I., A. 8; Q. II., A. 7), Happiness implies two things, to wit, the last end itself, *i.e.*, the Sovereign Good; and the attainment or enjoyment of that same Good.   As to that Good itself, Which is the object and cause of Happiness, one Happiness cannot be greater than another, since there is but one Sovereign Good, namely, God, by enjoying Whom, men are made happy.— But as to the attainment or enjoyment of this Good, one man can be happier than another; because the more a man enjoys this Good the happier he is.   Now, that one man enjoys God more than another, happens through his being better disposed or ordered to the enjoyment of Him.   And in this sense one man can be happier than another.

*Reply Obj.* 1.  The one penny signifies that Happiness is one in its object.   But the many mansions signify the manifold Happiness in the divers degrees of enjoyment.

*Reply Obj.* 2.  Happiness is said to be the supreme good, inasmuch as it is the perfect possession or enjoyment of the Supreme Good.

*Reply Obj.* 3.  None of the Blessed lacks any desirable good; since they have the Infinite Good Itself, Which is *the good of all good*, as Augustine says (*Enarr. in* Ps. cxxxiv.). But one is said to be happier than another, by reason of diverse participation of the same good.   And the addition of other goods does not increase Happiness, hence Augustine says (*Conf.* v. 4): *He who knows Thee, and others besides, is not the happier for knowing them, but is happy for knowing Thee alone.*

### THIRD ARTICLE.

#### WHETHER ONE CAN BE HAPPY IN THIS LIFE ?

*We proceed thus to the Third Article :—*

*Objection* 1.  It would seem that Happiness can be had in this life.   For it is written (Ps. cxviii. 1): *Blessed are the undefiled in the way, who walk in the law of the Lord.*   But this happens in this life.   Therefore one can be happy in this life.

*Obj.* 2.  Further, imperfect participation in the Sovereign Good does not destroy the nature of Happiness, otherwise one would not be happier than another. But men can participate in the Sovereign Good in this life, by knowing and loving God, albeit imperfectly. Therefore man can be happy in this life.

*Obj.* 3. Further, what is said by many cannot be altogether false: since what is in many, comes, apparently, from nature; and nature does not fail altogether. Now many say that Happiness can be had in this life, as appears from Ps. cxliii. 15: *They have called the people happy that hath these things*, to wit, the good things of this life. Therefore one can be happy in this life.

*On the contrary*, It is written (Job xiv. 1): *Man born of a woman, living for a short time, is filled with many miseries.* But Happiness excludes misery. Therefore man cannot be happy in this life.

*I answer that*, A certain participation of Happiness can be had in this life: but perfect and true Happiness cannot be had in this life. This may be seen from a twofold consideration.

First, from the general notion of happiness. For since happiness is a *perfect and sufficient good*, it excludes every evil, and fulfils every desire. But in this life every evil cannot be excluded. For this present life is subject to many unavoidable evils; to ignorance on the part of the intellect; to inordinate affection on the part of the appetite, and to many penalties on the part of the body; as Augustine sets forth in *De Civ. Dei* xix. 4. Likewise neither can the desire for good be satiated in this life. For man naturally desires the good, which he has, to be abiding. Now the goods of the present life pass away; since life itself passes away, which we naturally desire to have, and would wish to hold abidingly, for man naturally shrinks from death. Wherefore it is impossible to have true Happiness in this life.

Secondly, from a consideration of the specific nature of Happiness, viz., the vision of the Divine Essence, which man cannot obtain in this life, as was shown in the First Part (Q. XII., A. 11). Hence it is evident that none can attain true and perfect Happiness in this life.

*Reply Obj.* 1. Some are said to be happy in this life, either on account of the hope of obtaining Happiness in the life to come, according to Rom. viii. 24: *We are saved by hope ;* or on account of a certain participation of Happiness, by reason of a kind of enjoyment of the Sovereign Good.

*Reply Obj.* 2. The imperfection of participated Happiness is due to one of two causes.  First, on the part of the object of Happiness, which is not seen in Its Essence: and this imperfection destroys the nature of true Happiness. Secondly, the imperfection may be on the part of the participator, who indeed attains the object of Happiness, in itself, namely God: imperfectly, however, in comparison with the way in which God enjoys Himself.  This imperfection does not destroy the true nature of Happiness; because, since Happiness is an operation, as stated above (Q. III., A. 2), the true nature of Happiness is taken from the object, which specifies the act, and not from the subject.

*Reply Obj.* 3. Men esteem that there is some kind of happiness to be had in this life, on account of a certain likeness to true Happiness.  And thus they do not fail altogether in their estimate.

## FOURTH ARTICLE.
### WHETHER HAPPINESS ONCE HAD CAN BE LOST ?

*We proceed thus to the Fourth Article :—*

*Objection* 1. It would seem that Happiness can be lost. For Happiness is a perfection.  But every perfection is in the thing perfected according to the mode of the latter.  Since then man is, by his nature, changeable, it seems that Happiness is participated by man in a changeable manner.  And consequently it seems that man can lose Happiness.

*Obj.* 2. Further, Happiness consists in an act of the intellect; and the intellect is subject to the will.  But the will can be directed to opposites.  Therefore it seems that it can desist from the operation whereby man is made happy: and thus man will cease to be happy.

*Obj.* 3. Further, the end corresponds to the beginning. But man's Happiness has a beginning, since man was not always happy. Therefore it seems that it has an end.

*On the contrary*, It is written (Matth. xxv. 46) of the righteous that *they shall go . . . into life everlasting*, which, as above stated (A. 2), is the Happiness of the saints. Now what is eternal ceases not. Therefore Happiness cannot be lost.

*I answer that*, If we speak of imperfect happiness, such as can be had in this life, in this sense it can be lost. This is clear of contemplative happiness, which is lost either by forgetfulness, for instance, when knowledge is lost through sickness; or again by certain occupations, whereby a man is altogether withdrawn from contemplation.

This is also clear of active happiness: since man's will can be changed so as to fall to vice from the virtue, in whose act that happiness principally consists. If, however, the virtue remain unimpaired, outward changes can indeed disturb suchlike happiness, in so far as they hinder many acts of virtue; but they cannot take it away altogether, because there still remains an act of virtue, whereby man bears these trials in a praiseworthy manner.—And since the happiness of this life can be lost, a circumstance that appears to be contrary to the nature of happiness, therefore did the Philosopher state (*Ethic.* i. 10) that some are happy in this life, not simply, but *as men*, whose nature is subject to change.

But if we speak of that perfect Happiness which we await after this life, it must be observed that Origen (*Peri Archon*, ii. 3), following the error of certain Platonists, held that man can become unhappy after the final Happiness.

This, however, is evidently false, for two reasons. First, from the general notion of happiness. For since happiness is the *perfect and sufficient good*, it must needs set man's desire at rest and exclude every evil. Now man naturally desires to hold to the good that he has, and to have the surety of his holding: else he must of necessity be troubled with the fear of losing it, or with the sorrow of knowing that he will lose it.

Therefore it is necessary for true Happiness that man have the assured opinion of never losing the good that he possesses. If this opinion be true, it follows that he never will lose happiness: but if it be false, it is in itself an evil that he should have a false opinion: because the false is the evil of the intellect, just as the true is its good, as stated in *Ethic.* vi. 2. Consequently he will no longer be truly happy, if evil be in him.

Secondly, it is again evident if we consider the specific nature of Happiness.   For it has been shown above (Q. III., A. 8) that man's perfect Happiness consists in the vision of the Divine Essence.   Now it is impossible for anyone seeing the Divine Essence, to wish not to see It.   Because every good that one possesses and yet wishes to be without, is either insufficient, something more sufficing being desired in its stead; or else has some inconvenience attached to it, by reason of which it becomes wearisome.   But the vision of the Divine Essence fills the soul with all good things, since it unites it to the source of all goodness; hence it is written (Ps. xvi. 15): *I shall be satisfied when Thy glory shall appear ;* and (Wisd. vii. 11): *All good things came to me together with her, i.e.*, with the contemplation of wisdom.   In like manner neither has it any inconvenience attached to it; because it is written of the contemplation of wisdom (Wisd. viii. 16): *Her conversation hath no bitterness, nor her company any tediousness.*   It is thus evident that the happy man cannot forsake Happiness of his own accord.—Moreover, neither can he lose Happiness, through God taking it away from him. Because, since the withdrawal of Happiness is a punishment, it cannot be enforced by God, the just Judge, except for some fault; and he that sees God cannot fall into a fault, since rectitude of the will, of necessity, results from that vision as was shown above (Q. IV., A. 4).—Nor again can it be withdrawn by any other agent.   Because the mind that is united to God is raised above all other things: and consequently no other agent can sever the mind from that union. Therefore it seems unreasonable that as time goes on, man should pass from happiness to misery, and *vice versa ;* because suchlike vicissitudes of time can only be for such things as are subject to time and movement.

*Reply Obj.* 1. Happiness is consummate perfection, which excludes every defect from the happy. And therefore whoever has happiness has it altogether unchangeably: this is done by the Divine power, which raises man to the participation of eternity which transcends all change.

*Reply Obj.* 2. The will can be directed to opposites, in things which are ordained to the end; but it is ordained, of natural necessity, to the last end. This is evident from the fact that man is unable not to wish to be happy.

*Reply Obj.* 3. Happiness has a beginning owing to the condition of the participator: but it has no end by reason of the condition of the good, the participation of which makes man happy. Hence the beginning of happiness is from one cause, its endlessness is from another

## FIFTH ARTICLE.

### WHETHER MAN CAN ATTAIN HAPPINESS BY HIS NATURAL POWERS ?

*We proceed thus to the Fifth Article :—*

*Objection* 1. It would seem that man can attain Happiness by his natural powers. For nature does not fail in necessary things. But nothing is so necessary to man as that by which he attains the last end. Therefore this is not lacking to human nature. Therefore man can attain Happiness by his natural powers.

*Obj.* 2. Further, since man is more noble than irrational creatures, it seems that he must be better equipped than they. But irrational creatures can attain their end by their natural powers. Much more therefore can man attain Happiness by his natural powers.

*Obj.* 3. Further, Happiness is a *perfect operation*, according to the Philosopher (*Ethic*. vii. 13). Now the beginning of a thing belongs to the same principle as the perfecting thereof. Since, therefore, the imperfect operation, which is as the beginning in human operations, is subject to man's natural power, whereby he is master of his own actions; it seems that he can attain to perfect operation, *i.e.*, Happiness, by his natural powers.

*On the contrary*, Man is naturally the principle of his action, by his intellect and will.   But final Happiness prepared for the saints, surpasses the intellect and will of man; for the Apostle says (1 Cor. ii. 9): *Eye hath not seen, nor ear heard, neither hath it entered into the heart of man, what things God hath prepared for them that love Him*.   Therefore man cannot attain Happiness by his natural powers.

*I answer that*, Imperfect happiness that can be had in this life, can be acquired by man by his natural powers, in the same way as virtue, in whose operation it consists: on this point we shall speak further on (Q. LXIII.).   But man's perfect Happiness, as stated above (Q. III., A. 8), consists in the vision of the Divine Essence.   Now the vision of God's Essence surpasses the nature not only of man, but also of every creature, as was shown in the First Part (Q. XII., A. 4).   For the natural knowledge of every creature is in keeping with the mode of its substance: thus it is said of the intelligence (*De Causis ; Prop.* viii.) that *it knows things that are above it, and things that are below it, according to the mode of its substance*.   But every knowledge that is according to the mode of created substance, falls short of the vision of the Divine Essence, which infinitely surpasses all created substance.   Consequently neither man, nor any creature, can attain final Happiness by his natural powers.

*Reply Obj.* 1.   Just as nature does not fail man in necessaries, although it has not provided him with weapons and clothing, as it provided other animals, because it gave him reason and hands, with which he is able to get these things for himself; so neither did it fail man in things necessary, although it gave him not the wherewithal to attain Happiness: since this it could not do.   But it did give him freewill, with which he can turn to God, that He may make him happy.   *For what we do by means of our friends, is done, in a sense, by ourselves* (*Ethic.* iii. 3).

*Reply Obj.* 2.   The nature that can attain perfect good,

although it needs help from without in order to attain it, is of more noble condition than a nature which cannot attain perfect good, but attains some imperfect good, although it need no help from without in order to attain it, as the Philosopher says (*De Cœlo* ii. 12). Thus he is better disposed to health who can attain perfect health, albeit by means of medicine, than he who can attain but imperfect health, without the help of medicine. And therefore the rational creature, which can attain the perfect good of happiness, but needs the Divine assistance for the purpose, is more perfect than the irrational creature, which is not capable of attaining this good, but attains some imperfect good by its natural powers.

*Reply Obj.* 3. When imperfect and perfect are of the same species, they can be caused by the same power. But this does not follow of necessity, if they be of different species: for not everything, that can cause the disposition of matter, can produce the final perfection. Now the imperfect operation, which is subject to man's natural power, is not of the same species as that perfect operation which is man's happiness: since operation takes its species from its object. Consequently the argument does not prove.

## SIXTH ARTICLE.

### WHETHER MAN ATTAINS HAPPINESS THROUGH THE ACTION OF SOME HIGHER CREATURE ?

*We proceed thus to the Sixth Article :—*

*Objection* 1. It would seem that man can be made happy through the action of some higher creature, viz., an angel. For since we observe a twofold order in things—one, of the parts of the universe to one another, the other, of the whole universe to a good which is outside the universe; the former order is ordained to the second as to its end (*Metaph.* xii. 10). Thus the mutual order of the parts of an army is dependent on the order of the whole army to the general. But the mutual order of the parts of the universe consists in the higher creatures acting on the lower, as stated in the First

Part (Q. CIX., A. 2): while happiness consists in the order of man to a good which is outside the universe, *i.e.*, God. Therefore man is made happy, through a higher creature, viz., an angel, acting on him.

*Obj.* 2. Further, that which is such in potentiality, can be reduced to act, by that which is such actually: thus what is potentially hot, is made actually hot, by something that is actually hot. But man is potentially happy. Therefore he can be made actually happy by an angel who is actually happy.

*Obj.* 3. Further, Happiness consists in an operation of the intellect, as stated above (Q. III., A. 4). But an angel can enlighten man's intellect, as shown in the First Part (Q. CXI., A. 1). Therefore an angel can make a man happy.

*On the contrary*, It is written (Ps. lxxxiii. 12): *The Lord will give grace and glory*.

*I answer that*, Since every creature is subject to the laws of nature, from the very fact that its power and action are limited: that which surpasses created nature, cannot be done by the power of any creature. Consequently if anything need to be done that is above nature, it is done by God immediately; such as raising the dead to life, restoring sight to the blind, and suchlike. Now it has been shown above (A. 5) that Happiness is a good surpassing created nature. Therefore it is impossible that it be bestowed through the action of any creature: but by God alone is man made happy,—if we speak of perfect Happiness. If, however, we speak of imperfect happiness, the same is to be said of it as of the virtue, in whose act it consists.

*Reply Obj.* 1. It often happens in the case of active powers ordained to one another, that it belongs to the highest power to reach the last end, while the lower powers contribute to the attainment of that last end, by causing a disposition thereto: thus to the art of sailing, which commands the art of ship-building, it belongs to use a ship for the end for which it was made. Thus, too, in the order of the universe, man is indeed helped by angels in the attainment of his last end, in respect of certain preliminary dispositions thereto: whereas he attains the last end itself through the First Agent, which is God.

*Reply Obj.* 2. When a form exists perfectly and naturally in something, it can be the principle of action on something else: for instance, a hot thing heats through heat. But if a form exist in something imperfectly and not naturally, it cannot be the principle whereby it is communicated to something else: thus the *intention* of colour which is in the pupil, cannot make a thing white; nor indeed can everything enlightened or heated give heat or light to something else; for if they could, enlightening and heating would go on to infinity. But the light of glory, whereby God is seen, is in God perfectly and naturally; whereas in any creature, it is imperfectly and by likeness or participation. Consequently no creature can communicate its Happiness to another.

*Reply Obj.* 3. A happy angel enlightens the intellect of a man or of a lower angel, as to certain notions of the Divine works: but not as to the vision of the Divine Essence, as was stated in the First Part (Q. CVI., A. 1): since in order to see this, all are immediately enlightened by God.

## Seventh Article.

### WHETHER ANY GOOD WORKS ARE NECESSARY THAT MAN MAY RECEIVE HAPPINESS FROM GOD?

*We proceed thus to the Seventh Article:—*

*Objection* 1. It would seem that no works of man are necessary that he may obtain Happiness from God. For since God is an agent of infinite power, He requires before acting, neither matter, nor disposition of matter, but can forthwith produce the whole effect. But man's works, since they are not required for Happiness, as the efficient cause thereof, as stated above (A. 6), can be required only as dispositions thereto. Therefore God Who does not require dispositions before acting, bestows Happiness, without any previous works.

*Obj.* 2. Further, just as God is the immediate cause of Happiness, so is He the immediate cause of nature. But when God first established nature, He produced creatures without any previous disposition or action on the part of the creature, but made each one perfect forthwith in its species. Therefore it seems that He bestows Happiness on man without any previous works.

*Obj.* 3. Further, the Apostle says (Rom. iv. 6) that Happiness is of the man *to whom God reputeth justice without works.* Therefore no works of man are necessary for attaining Happiness.

*On the contrary,* It is written (Jo. xiii. 17): *If you know these things, you shall be blessed if you do them.* Therefore Happiness is obtained through works.

*I answer that,* Rectitude of the will, as stated above (Q. IV., A. 4), is necessary for Happiness; since it is nothing else than the right order of the will to the last end; and it is therefore necessary for obtaining the end, just as the right disposition of matter, in order to receive the form. But this does not prove that any work of man need precede his Happiness: for God could make a will having a right tendency to the end, and at the same time attaining the end; just as sometimes He disposes matter and at the same time introduces the form. But the order of Divine wisdom demands that it should not be thus; for as it is stated in *De Cælo* ii. 12, *of those things that have a natural capacity for the perfect good, one has it without movement, some by one movement, some by several.* Now to possess the perfect good without movement, belongs to that which has it naturally: and to have Happiness naturally belongs to God alone. Therefore it belongs to God alone not to be moved towards Happiness by any previous operation. Now since Happiness surpasses every created nature, no pure creature can becomingly gain Happiness, without the movement of operation, whereby it tends thereto. But the angel, who is above man in the natural order, obtained it, according to the order of Divine wisdom, by one movement of a meritorious work, as was explained in the First Part (Q. LXII., A. 5); whereas man obtains it by many movements of works which are called merits. Wherefore also according to the Philosopher (*Ethic.* i. 9), happiness is the reward of works of virtue.

*Reply Obj.* 1. Works are necessary to man in order to gain Happiness; not on account of the insufficiency of the Divine power which bestows Happiness, but that the order in things be observed.

*Reply Obj.* 2. God produced the first creatures so that they were perfect forthwith, without any previous disposition or operation of the creature; because He instituted the first individuals of the various species, that through them nature might be propagated to their progeny. In like manner, because Happiness was to be bestowed on others through Christ, who is God and Man, *Who*, according to Heb. ii. 10, *had brought many children into glory ;* therefore, from the very beginning of His conception, His soul was happy, without any previous meritorious operation. But this is peculiar to Him: for Christ's merit avails baptized children for the gaining of Happiness, though they have no merits of their own; because by Baptism they are made members of Christ.

*Reply Obj.* 3. The Apostle is speaking of the Happiness of Hope, which is bestowed on us by sanctifying grace, which is not given on account of previous works. For grace is not a term of movement, as Happiness is; rather is it the principle of the movement that tends towards Happiness.

## Eighth Article.

### WHETHER EVERY MAN DESIRES HAPPINESS ?

*We proceed thus to the Eighth Article :—*

*Objection* 1. It would seem that not all desire Happiness. For no man can desire what he knows not; since the apprehended good is the object of the appetite (*De Anima* iii. 10). But many know not what Happiness is. This is evident from the fact that, as Augustine says (*De Trin.* xiii. 4), *some thought that Happiness consists in pleasures of the body ; some, in a virtue of the soul ; some, in other things.* Therefore not all desire Happiness.

*Obj.* 2. Further, the essence of Happiness is the vision of the Divine Essence, as stated above (Q. III., A. 8). But some consider it impossible for man to see the Divine Essence; wherefore they desire it not. Therefore all men do not desire Happiness.

*Obj.* 3. Further, Augustine says (*De Trin.* xiii. 5) that *happy is he who has all he desires, and desires nothing amiss.* But all do not desire this; for some desire certain things amiss, and yet they wish to desire such things. Therefore all do not desire Happiness.

*On the contrary,* Augustine says (*De Trin.* xiii. 3): *If that actor had said : ' You all wish to be happy ; you do not wish to be unhappy,' he would have said that which none would have failed to acknowledge in his will.* Therefore everyone desires to be happy.

*I answer that,* Happiness can be considered in two ways. First according to the general notion of happiness: and thus, of necessity, every man desires happiness. For the general notion of happiness consists in the perfect good, as stated above (AA. 3, 4). But since good is the object of the will, the perfect good of a man is that which entirely satisfies his will. Consequently to desire happiness is nothing else than to desire that one's will be satisfied. And this everyone desires. Secondly we may speak of Happines according to its specific notion, as to that in which it consists. And thus all do not know Happiness; because they know not in what thing the general notion of happiness is found. And consequently, in this respect, not all desire it. Wherefore the reply to the first Objection is clear.

*Reply Obj.* 2. Since the will follows the apprehension of the intellect or reason; just as it happens that where there is no real distinction, there may be a distinction according to the consideration of reason; so does it happen that one and the same thing is desired in one way, and not desired in another. So that happiness may be considered as the final and perfect good, which is the general notion of happiness: and thus the will naturally and of necessity tends thereto, as stated above. Again it can be considered under other special aspects, either on the part of the operation itself, or on the part of the operating power, or on the part of the object; and thus the will does not tend thereto of necessity.

*Reply Obj.* 3. This definition of Happiness given by some,—*Happy is the man that has all he desires*, or, *whose every wish is fulfilled*, is a good and adequate definition, if it be understood in a certain way; but an inadequate definition if understood in another. For if we understand it simply of all that man desires by his natural appetite, thus it is true that he who has all that he desires, is happy: since nothing satisfies man's natural desire, except the perfect good which is Happiness. But if we understand it of those things that man desires according to the apprehension of the reason, thus it does not belong to Happiness, to have certain things that man desires; rather does it belong to unhappiness, in so far as the possession of such things hinders man from having all that he desires naturally; thus it is that reason sometimes accepts as true things that are a hindrance to the knowledge of truth. And it was through taking this into consideration that Augustine added so as to include perfect Happiness,—that he *desires nothing amiss*: although the first part suffices if rightly understood, to wit, that *happy is he who has all he desires*.

# QUESTION VI.

## OF THE VOLUNTARY AND THE INVOLUNTARY.

### (*In Eight Articles.*)

SINCE therefore Happiness is to be gained by means of certain acts, we must in due sequence consider human acts, in order to know by what acts we may obtain Happiness, and by what acts we are prevented from obtaining it. But because operations and acts are concerned with things singular, consequently all practical knowledge is incomplete unless it take account of things in detail. The study of Morals, therefore, since it treats of human acts, should consider first the general principles; and secondly matters of detail.

In treating of the general principles, the points that offer themselves for our consideration are—(1) human acts themselves; (2) their principles. Now of human acts some are proper to man; others are common to man and animals. And since Happiness is man's proper good, those acts which are proper to man have a closer connection with Happiness than have those which are common to man and the other animals. First, then, we must consider those acts which are proper to man; secondly, those acts which are common to man and the other animals, and are called Passions. The first of these points offers a twofold consideration: (1) What makes a human act? (2) What distinguishes human acts?

And since those acts are properly called human, which are voluntary, because the will is the rational appetite, which is proper to man; we must consider acts in so far as they are voluntary.

First, then, we must consider the voluntary and involuntary in general; secondly, those acts which are voluntary, as being elicited by the will, and as issuing from the will immediately; thirdly, those acts which are voluntary, as being commanded by the will, which issue from the will through the medium of the other powers.

And because voluntary acts have certain circumstances, according to which we form our judgment concerning them, we must first consider the voluntary and the involuntary, and afterwards, the circumstances of those acts which are found to be voluntary or involuntary. Under the first head there are eight points of inquiry: (1) Whether there is anything voluntary in human acts? (2) Whether in irrational animals? (3) Whether there can be voluntariness without any action? (4) Whether violence can be done to the will? (5) Whether violence causes involuntariness? (6) Whether fear causes involuntariness? (7) Whether concupiscence causes involuntariness? (8) Whether ignorance causes involuntariness?

## First Article.

### Whether there is anything voluntary in human acts?

*We proceed thus to the First Article :—*

*Objection* 1. It would seem that there is nothing voluntary in human acts. For that is voluntary *which has its principle within itself*, as Gregory of Nyssa,* Damascene (*De Fide Orthod.* ii. 24), and Aristotle (*Ethic.* iii. 1) declare. But the principle of human acts is not in man himself, but outside him: since man's appetite is moved to act, by the appetible object which is outside him, and is as a *mover unmoved* (*De Anima* iii. 10). Therefore there is nothing voluntary in human acts.

*Obj.* 2. Further, the Philosopher (*Phys.* viii. 2) proves that in animals no new movement arises that is not preceded by a motion from without. But all human acts are new, since none is eternal. Consequently, the principle of all human

* Nemesius, *De Natura Hom.* xxxii.

acts is from without: and therefore there is nothing voluntary in them.

*Obj.* 3. Further, he that acts voluntarily, can act of himself. But this is not true of man; for it is written (Jo. xv. 5): *Without Me you can do nothing.* Therefore there is nothing voluntary in human acts.

*On the contrary*, Damascene says (*De Fide Orthod.* ii.) that *the voluntary is an act consisting in a rational operation.* Now such are human acts. Therefore there is something voluntary in human acts.

*I answer that*, There must needs be something voluntary in human acts. In order to make this clear, we must take note that the principle of some acts or movements is within the agent, or that which is moved; whereas the principle of some movements or acts is outside. For when a stone is moved upwards, the principle of this movement is outside the stone: whereas when it is moved downwards, the principle of this movement is in the stone. Now of those things that are moved by an intrinsic principle, some move themselves, some not. For since every agent or thing moved, acts or is moved for an end, as stated above (Q. I., A. 2); those are perfectly moved by an intrinsic principle, whose intrinsic principle is one not only of movement but of movement for an end. Now in order for a thing to be done for an end, some knowledge of the end is necessary. Therefore, whatever so acts or is so moved by an intrinsic principle, that it has some knowledge of the end, has within itself the principle of its act, so that it not only acts, but acts for an end. On the other hand, if a thing has no knowledge of the end, even though it have an intrinsic principle of action or movement, nevertheless the principle of acting or being moved for an end is not in that thing, but in something else, by which the principle of its action towards an end is imprinted on it. Wherefore suchlike things are not said to move themselves, but to be moved by others. But those things which have a knowledge of the end are said to move themselves because there is in them a principle by which they not only act but also act for an end. And consequently, since both are from an intrinsic principle, to wit, that they act and that they act for an end, the movements of such things are said to be voluntary: for the word *voluntary* implies that their movements and acts are from their own inclination.   Hence it is that, according to the definitions of Aristotle, Gregory of Nyssa, and Damascene,* the voluntary is defined not only as having *a principle within* the agent, but also as implying *knowledge*.   Therefore, since man especially knows the end of his work, and moves himself, in his acts especially is the voluntary to be found.

*Reply Obj.* 1. Not every principle is a first principle. Therefore, although it is essential to the voluntary act that its principle be within the agent, nevertheless it is not contrary to the nature of the voluntary act that this intrinsic principle be caused or moved by an extrinsic principle: because it is not essential to the voluntary act that its intrinsic principle be a first principle.—Yet again it must be observed that a principle of movement may happen to be first in a genus, but not first simply: thus in the genus of things subject to alteration, the first principle of alteration is a heavenly body, which nevertheless is not the first mover simply, but is moved locally by a higher mover.   And so the intrinsic principle of the voluntary act, *i.e.*, the cognitive and appetitive power, is the first principle in the genus of appetitive movement, although it is moved by an extrinsic principle according to other species of movement.

*Reply Obj.* 2. New movements in animals are indeed preceded by a motion from without; and this in two respects. First, in so far as by means of an extrinsic motion an animal's senses are confronted with something sensible, which, on being apprehended, moves the appetite.   Thus a lion, on seeing a stag in movement and coming towards him, begins to be moved towards the stag.—Secondly, in so far as some extrinsic motion produces a physical change in an animal's body, as in the case of cold or heat; and through the body being thus affected by the motion of an outward body, the sensitive appetite which is the power of a bodily

* See objection 1.

organ, is also moved indirectly; thus it happens that through some alteration in the body the appetite is roused to the desire of something. But this is not contrary to the nature of voluntariness, as stated above (*ad* 1), for such movements caused by an extrinsic principle are of another genus of movement.

*Reply Obj.* 3. God moves man to act, not only by proposing the appetible to the senses, or by effecting a change in his body, but also by moving the will itself; because every movement either of the will or of nature, proceeds from God as the First Mover. And just as it is not incompatible with nature that the natural movement be from God as the First Mover, inasmuch as nature is an instrument of God moving it: so it is not contrary to the essence of a voluntary act, that it proceed from God, inasmuch as the will is moved by God. Nevertheless both natural and voluntary movements have this in common, that it is essential that they should proceed from a principle within the agent.

## SECOND ARTICLE.

### WHETHER THERE IS ANYTHING VOLUNTARY IN IRRATIONAL ANIMALS?

*We proceed thus to the Second Article :—*

*Objection* 1. It would seem that there is nothing voluntary in irrational animals. For a thing is called *voluntary* from *voluntas* (*will*). Now since the will is in the reason (*De Anima* iii. 9), it cannot be in irrational animals. Therefore neither is there anything voluntary in them.

*Obj.* 2. Further, according as human acts are voluntary, man is said to be master of his actions. But irrational animals are not masters of their actions; for *they act not ; rather are they acted upon*, as Damascene says (*De Fide Orthod.* ii. 27). Therefore there is no such thing as a voluntary act in irrational animals.

*Obj.* 3. Further, Damascene says (*ibid.*, 24) that *voluntary acts lead to praise and blame*. But neither praise nor blame is due to the acts of irrational animals. Therefore such acts are not voluntary.

*On the contrary,* The Philosopher says (*Ethic.* iii. 2) that *both children and irrational animals participate in the voluntary.* The same is said by Damascene (*loc. cit.*) and Gregory of Nyssa.*

*I answer that,* As stated above (A. 1), it is essential to the voluntary act that its principle be within the agent, together with some knowledge of the end. Now knowledge of the end is twofold; perfect and imperfect. Perfect knowledge of the end consists in not only apprehending the thing which is the end, but also in knowing it under the aspect of end, and the relationship of the means to that end. And such knowledge belongs to none but the rational nature.— But imperfect knowledge of the end consists in mere apprehension of the end, without knowing it under the aspect of end, or the relationship of an act to the end. Such knowledge of the end is exercised by irrational animals, through their senses and their natural estimative power.

Consequently perfect knowledge of the end leads to the perfect voluntary; inasmuch as, having apprehended the end, a man can, from deliberating about the end and the means thereto, be moved, or not, to gain that end.—But imperfect knowledge of the end leads to the imperfect voluntary; inasmuch as the agent apprehends the end, but does not deliberate, and is moved to the end at once. Wherefore the voluntary in its perfection belongs to none but the rational nature: whereas the imperfect voluntary is within the competency of even irrational animals.

*Reply Obj.* 1. The will is the name of the rational appetite; and consequently it cannot be in things devoid of reason. But the word *voluntary* is derived from *voluntas* (*will*), and can be extended to those things in which there is some participation of will, by way of likeness thereto. It is thus that voluntary action is attributed to irrational animals, in so far as they are moved to an end, through some kind of knowledge.

*Reply Obj.* 2. The fact that man is master of his actions, is due to his being able to deliberate about them: for since the deliberating reason is indifferently disposed to opposite

* Nemesius, *De Nat. Hom.* xxxii.

things, the will can be inclined to either. But it is not thus that voluntariness is in irrational animals, as stated above.

*Reply Obj.* 3. Praise and blame are the result of the voluntary act, wherein is the perfect voluntary; such as is not to be found in irrational animals.

THIRD ARTICLE.

WHETHER THERE CAN BE VOLUNTARINESS WITHOUT
ANY ACT ?

*We proceed thus to the Third Article :—*

*Objection* 1. It would seem that voluntariness cannot be without any act. For that is voluntary which proceeds from the will. But nothing can proceed from the will, except through some act, at least an act of the will. Therefore there cannot be voluntariness without act.

*Obj.* 2. Further, just as one is said to wish by an act of the will, so when the act of the will ceases, one is said not to wish. But not to wish implies involuntariness, which is contrary to voluntariness. Therefore there can be nothing voluntary when the act of the will ceases.

*Obj.* 3. Further, knowledge is essential to the voluntary, as stated above (AA. 1, 2). But knowledge involves an act. Therefore voluntariness cannot be without some act.

*On the contrary*, The word *voluntary* is applied to that of which we are masters. Now we are masters in respect of to act and not to act, to will and not to will. Therefore just as to act and to will are voluntary, so also are not to act and not to will.

*I answer that*, Voluntary is what proceeds from the will. Now one thing proceeds from another in two ways. First, directly; in which sense something proceeds from another inasmuch as this other acts; for instance, heating from heat. Secondly, indirectly; in which sense something proceeds from another through this other not acting; thus the sinking of a ship is set down to the helmsman, from his having ceased to steer.—But we must take note that the cause of what follows from want of action is not always the agent as not acting; but only then when the agent can and ought to act. For if the helmsman were unable to steer the ship or if the ship's helm be not entrusted to him, the sinking of the ship would not be set down to him, although it might be due to his absence from the helm.

Since, then, the will by willing and acting, is able, and sometimes ought, to hinder not-willing and not-acting; this not-willing and not-acting is imputed to, as though proceeding from, the will. And thus it is that we can have the voluntary without an act; sometimes without outward act, but with an interior act; for instance, when one wills not to act; and sometimes without even an interior act, as when one does not will to act.

*Reply Obj.* 1. We apply the word *voluntary* not only to that which proceeds from the will directly, as from its action; but also to that which proceeds from it indirectly as from its inaction.

*Reply Obj.* 2. *Not to wish* is said in two senses. First, as though it were one word, and the infinitive of *I-do-not-wish.* Consequently just as when I say *I do not wish to read*, the sense is, *I wish not to read ;* so *not to wish to read* is the same as *to wish not to read*, and in this sense *not to wish* implies involuntariness.—Secondly it is taken as a sentence: and then no act of the will is affirmed. And in this sense *not to wish* does not imply involuntariness.

*Reply Obj.* 3. Voluntariness requires an act of knowledge in the same way as it requires an act of will; namely, in order that it be in one's power to consider, to wish and to act. And then, just as not to wish, and not to act, when it is time to wish and to act, is voluntary, so is it voluntary not to consider.

### FOURTH ARTICLE.

#### WHETHER VIOLENCE CAN BE DONE TO THE WILL ?

*We proceed thus to the Fourth Article :—*

*Objection* 1. It would seem that violence can be done to the will. For everything can be compelled by that which is more powerful. But there is something, namely, God, that is more powerful than the human will. Therefore it can be compelled, at least by Him.

*Obj.* 2. Further, every passive subject is compelled by its active principle, when it is changed by it. But the will is a passive force: for it is a *mover moved* (*De Anima* iii. 10). Therefore, since it is sometimes moved by its active principle, it seems that sometimes it is compelled.

*Obj.* 3. Further, violent movement is that which is contrary to nature. But the movement of the will is sometimes contrary to nature; as is clear of the will's movement to sin, which is contrary to nature, as Damascene says (*De Fide Orthod.* iv. 20). Therefore the movement of the will can be compelled.

*On the contrary*, Augustine says (*De Civ. Dei* v. 10) that what is done by the will is not done of necessity. Now, whatever is done under compulsion is done of necessity: consequently what is done by the will, cannot be compelled. Therefore the will cannot be compelled to act.

*I answer that*, The act of the will is twofold: one is its immediate act, as it were, elicited by it, namely, *to wish ;* the other is an act of the will commanded by it, and put into execution by means of some other power, such as *to walk* and *to speak*, which are commanded by the will to be executed by means of the motive power.

As regards the commanded acts of the will, then, the will can suffer violence, in so far as violence can prevent the exterior members from executing the will's command. But as to the will's own proper act, violence cannot be done to the will.

The reason of this is that the act of the will is nothing else than an inclination proceeding from the interior principle of knowledge: just as the natural appetite is an inclination proceeding from an interior principle without knowledge. Now what is compelled or violent is from an exterior principle. Consequently it is contrary to the nature of the will's own act, that it should be subject to compulsion or violence: just as it is also contrary to the nature of a natural inclination or movement. For a stone may have an upward movement from violence, but that this violent movement be from its natural inclination is impossible. In like manner a man may be dragged by force: but it is contrary to the very notion of violence, that he be thus dragged of his own will.

*Reply Obj.* 1. God Who is more powerful than the human will, can move the will of man, according to Prov. xxi. 1: *The heart of the king is in the hand of the Lord ; whithersoever He will He shall turn it.* But if this were by compulsion, it would no longer be by an act of the will, nor would the will itself be moved, but something else against the will.

*Reply Obj.* 2. It is not always a violent movement, when a passive subject is moved by its active principle; but only when this is done against the interior inclination of the passive subject. Otherwise every alteration and generation of simple bodies would be unnatural and violent: whereas they are natural by reason of the natural interior aptitude of the matter or subject to such a disposition. In like manner when the will is moved, according to its own inclination, by the appetible object, this movement is not violent but voluntary.

*Reply Obj.* 3. That to which the will tends by sinning, although in reality it is evil and contrary to the rational nature, nevertheless is apprehended as something good and suitable to nature, in so far as it is suitable to man by reason of some pleasurable sensation or some vicious habit.

## Fifth Article.

### WHETHER VIOLENCE CAUSES INVOLUNTARINESS ?

*We proceed thus to the Fifth Article :—*

*Objection* 1. It would seem that violence does not cause involuntariness. For we speak of voluntariness and involuntariness in respect of the will. But violence cannot be done to the will, as shown above (A. 4). Therefore violence cannot cause involuntariness.

*Obj.* 2. Further, that which is done involuntarily is done with grief, as Damascene (*De Fide Orthod.* ii. 24) and the

Philosopher (*Ethic*. iii. 5) say.  But sometimes a man suffers compulsion without being grieved thereby.  Therefore violence does not cause involuntariness.

*Obj*. 3. Further, what is from the will cannot be involuntary.  But some violent actions proceed from the will: for instance, when a man with a heavy body goes upwards; or when a man contorts his limbs in a way contrary to their natural flexibility.  Therefore violence does not cause involuntariness.

*On the contrary*, The Philosopher (*Ethic*. iii. 1) and Damascene (*loc. cit.*) say that *things done under compulsion are involuntary*.

*I answer that*, Violence is directly opposed to the voluntary, as likewise to the natural.  For the voluntary and the natural have this in common, that both are from an intrinsic principle; whereas violence is from an extrinsic principle.  And for this reason, just as in things devoid of knowledge, violence effects something against nature: so in things endowed with knowledge, it effects something against the will.  Now that which is against nature is said to be *unnatural ;* and in like manner that which is against the will is said to be *involuntary*.  Therefore violence causes involuntariness.

*Reply Obj*. 1. The involuntary is opposed to the voluntary.  Now it has been said (A. 4) that not only the act, which proceeds immediately from the will, is called voluntary, but also the act commanded by the will.  Consequently, as to the act which proceeds immediately from the will, violence cannot be done to the will, as stated above (*ibid*.): wherefore violence cannot make that act involuntary.  But as to the commanded act, the will can suffer violence: and consequently in this respect violence causes involuntariness.

*Reply Obj*. 2. As that is said to be natural, which is according to the inclination of nature; so that is said to be voluntary, which is according to the inclination of the will.  Now a thing is said to be natural in two ways.  First, because it is from nature as from an active principle: thus it is natural for fire to produce heat.  Secondly, according to a passive principle; because, to wit, there is in nature an inclination to receive an action from an extrinsic principle: thus the movement of the heavens is said to be natural, by reason of the natural aptitude in a heavenly body to receive such movement; although the cause of that movement is a voluntary agent. In like manner an act is said to be voluntary in two ways. First, in regard to action, for instance, when one wishes to act: secondly, in regard to passion, as when one wishes to be passive to another. Hence when action is brought to bear on something, by an extrinsic agent, as long as the will to suffer that action remains in the passive subject, there is not violence simply: for although the patient does nothing by way of action, he does something by being willing to suffer. Consequently this cannot be called involuntary.

*Reply Obj.* 3. As the Philosopher says (*Phys.* viii. 4) the movement of an animal, whereby at times an animal is moved against the natural inclination of the body, although it is not natural to the body, is nevertheless somewhat natural to the animal, to which it is natural to be moved according to its appetite. Accordingly this is violent, not simply but in a certain respect.—The same remark applies in the case of one who contorts his limbs in a way that is contrary to their natural disposition. For this is violent in a certain respect, *i.e.*, as to that particular limb; but not simply, *i.e.*, as to the man himself.


### Sixth Article.

#### WHETHER FEAR CAUSES INVOLUNTARINESS SIMPLY ?

*We proceed thus to the Sixth Article :—*

*Objection* 1. It would seem that fear causes involuntariness simply. For just as violence regards that which is contrary to the will at the time, so fear regards a future evil which is repugnant to the will. But violence causes involuntariness simply. Therefore fear too causes involuntariness simply.

*Obj.* 2. Further, that which is such of itself, remains such, whatever be added to it: thus what is hot of itself, as long

II. i.

7

as it remains, is still hot, whatever be added to it. But that which is done through fear, is involuntary in itself. Therefore, even with the addition of fear, it is involuntary.

*Obj.* 3. Further, that which is such, subject to a condition, is such in a certain respect; whereas what is such, without any condition, is such simply: thus what is necessary, subject to a condition, is necessary in some respect: but what is necessary absolutely, is necessary simply. But that which is done through fear, is absolutely involuntary; and is not voluntary, save under a condition, namely, in order that the evil feared may be avoided. Therefore that which is done through fear, is involuntary simply.

*On the contrary*, Gregory of Nyssa* and the Philosopher (*Ethic*. iii. I) say that such things as are done through fear are *voluntary rather than involuntary*.

*I answer that*, As the Philosopher says (*Ethic*. iii.) and likewise Gregory of Nyssa in his book on Man (Nemesius, *loc. cit.*), such things as are done through fear *are of a mixed character*, being partly voluntary and partly involuntary. For that which is done through fear, considered in itself, is not voluntary; but it becomes voluntary in this particular case, in order, namely, to avoid the evil feared.

But if the matter be considered aright, such things are voluntary rather than involuntary; for they are voluntary simply, but involuntary in a certain respect. For a thing is said to be simply, according as it is in act; but according as it is only in the apprehension, it is not simply, but in a certain respect. Now that which is done through fear, is in act in so far as it is done. For, since acts are concerned with singulars; and the singular, as such, is here and now; that which is done is in act, in so far as it is here and now and under other individuating circumstances. And that which is done through fear, is voluntary, inasmuch as it is here and now, that is to say, in so far as, under the circumstances, it hinders a greater evil which was feared; thus the throwing of the cargo into the sea becomes voluntary during the storm, through fear of the danger: wherefore it

* Nemesius, *De Nat. Hom.* xxx.

is clear that it is voluntary simply. And hence it is that what is done out of fear is essentially voluntary, because its principle is within.—But if we consider what is done through fear, as outside this particular case, and inasmuch as it is repugnant to the will, this is merely a consideration of the mind. And consequently what is done through fear is involuntary, considered in that respect, that is to say, outside the actual circumstances of the case.

*Reply Obj.* 1. Things done through fear and compulsion, differ not only according to present and future time, but also in this, that the will does not consent, but is moved entirely counter to that which is done through compulsion: whereas what is done through fear, becomes voluntary, because the will is moved towards it, albeit not for its own sake, but on account of something else, that is, in order to avoid an evil which is feared. For the conditions of a voluntary act are satisfied, if it be done on account of something else voluntary: since the voluntary is not only what we wish, for its own sake, as an end, but also what we wish for the sake of something else, as an end. It is clear therefore that in what is done from compulsion, the will does nothing inwardly; whereas in what is done through fear, the will does something. Accordingly, as Gregory of Nyssa* says, in order to exclude things done through fear, a violent action is defined as not only one, *the principle whereof is from without*, but with the addition, *in which he that suffers violence concurs not at all ;* because the will of him that is in fear, does concur somewhat in that which he does through fear.

*Reply Obj.* 2. Things that are such absolutely, remain such, whatever be added to them; for instance, a cold thing, or a white thing: but things that are such relatively, vary according as they are compared with different things. For what is big in comparison with one thing, is small in comparison with another. Now a thing is said to be voluntary, not only for its own sake, as it were absolutely; but also for the sake of something else, as it were relatively. Accord-

* Nemesius, *loc. cit.*

ngly, nothing prevents a thing which was not voluntary in comparison with one thing, from becoming voluntary when compared with another.

*Reply Obj.* 3. That which is done through fear, is voluntary without any condition, that is to say, according as it is actually done: but it is involuntary, under a certain condition, that is to say, if such a fear were not threatening. Consequently, this argument proves rather the opposite.

SEVENTH ARTICLE.

WHETHER CONCUPISCENCE CAUSES INVOLUNTARINESS?

*We proceed thus to the Seventh Article :—*

*Objection* 1. It would seem that concupiscence causes involuntariness. For just as fear is a passion, so is concupiscence. But fear causes involuntariness to a certain extent. Therefore concupiscence does so too.

*Obj.* 2. Further, just as the timid man through fear acts counter to that which he proposed, so does the incontinent, through concupiscence. But fear causes involuntariness to a certain extent. Therefore concupiscence does so also.

*Obj.* 3. Further, knowledge is necessary for voluntariness. But concupiscence impairs knowledge; for the Philosopher says (*Ethic.* vi. 5) that *delight*, or the lust of pleasure, *destroys the judgment of prudence.* Therefore concupiscence causes involuntariness.

*On the contrary,* Damascene says (*De Fide Orthod.* ii. 24): *The involuntary act deserves mercy or indulgence, and is done with regret.* But neither of these can be said of that which is done out of concupiscence. Therefore concupiscence does not cause involuntariness.

*I answer that,* Concupiscence does not cause involuntariness, but on the contrary makes something to be voluntary. For a thing is said to be voluntary, from the fact that the will is moved to it. Now concupiscence inclines the will to desire the object of concupiscence. Therefore the effect of concupiscence is to make something to be voluntary rather than involuntary.

*Reply Obj.* 1. Fear regards evil, but concupiscence regards good. Now evil of itself is counter to the will, whereas good harmonizes with the will. Therefore fear has a greater tendency than concupiscence to cause involuntariness.

*Reply Obj.* 2. He who acts from fear retains the repugnance of the will to that which he does, considered in itself. But he that acts from concupiscence, *e.g.*, an incontinent man, does not retain his former will whereby he repudiated the object of his concupiscence; for his will is changed so that he desires that which previously he repudiated. Accordingly, that which is done out of fear is involuntary, to a certain extent, but that which is done from concupiscence is nowise involuntary. For the man who yields to concupiscence acts counter to that which he purposed at first, but not counter to that which he desires now; whereas the timid man acts counter to that which in itself he desires now.

*Reply Obj.* 3. If concupiscence were to destroy knowledge altogether, as happens with those whom concupiscence has rendered mad, it would follow that concupiscence would take away voluntariness. And yet properly speaking it would not result in the act being involuntary, because in things bereft of reason, there is neither voluntary nor involuntary. But sometimes in those actions which are done from concupiscence, knowledge is not completely destroyed, because the power of knowing is not taken away entirely, but only the actual consideration in some particular possible act. Nevertheless, this itself is voluntary, according as by voluntary we mean that which is in the power of the will, for example, *not to act* or *not to will*, and in like manner *not to consider ;* for the will can resist the passion, as we shall state later on (Q. X., A. 3; Q. LXXVII., A. 7).

## EIGHTH ARTICLE.

### WHETHER IGNORANCE CAUSES INVOLUNTARINESS ?

*We proceed thus to the Eighth Article :—*

*Objection* 1. It would seem that ignorance does not cause involuntariness. For *the involuntary act deserves pardon*, as

Damascene says (*De Fide Orthod*. ii. 24).  But sometimes that which is done through ignorance does not deserve pardon, according to 1 Cor. xiv. 38 : *If any man know not, he shall not be known*.  Therefore ignorance does not cause involuntariness.

*Obj*. 2. Further, every sin implies ignorance; according to Prov. xiv. 22: *They err, that work evil*.  If, therefore, ignorance causes involuntariness, it would follow that every sin is involuntary: which is opposed to the saying of Augustine, that *every sin is voluntary* (*De Vera Relig*. xiv.).

*Obj*. 3. Further, *involuntariness is not without sadness*, as Damascene says (*loc. cit.*).  But some things are done out of ignorance, but without sadness: for instance, a man may kill a foe, whom he wishes to kill, thinking at the time that he is killing a stag.  Therefore ignorance does not cause involuntariness.

*On the contrary*, Damascene (*loc. cit.*) and the Philosopher (*Ethic*. iii. 1) say that *what is done through ignorance is involuntary*.

*I answer that*, If ignorance cause involuntariness, it is in so far as it deprives one of knowledge, which is a necessary condition of voluntariness, as was declared above (A. 1). But it is not every ignorance that deprives one of this knowledge.  Accordingly, we must take note that ignorance has a threefold relationship to the act of the will: in one way, *concomitantly* ; in another, *consequently* ; in a third way, *antecedently*.—*Concomitantly*, when there is ignorance of what is done; but, so that even if it were known, it would be done.  For then, ignorance does not induce one to wish this to be done, but it just happens that a thing is at the same time done and not known: thus in the example given (*Obj*. 3) a man did indeed wish to kill his foe, but killed him in ignorance, thinking to kill a stag.  And ignorance of this kind, as the Philosopher states (*Ethic*. iii. 1), does not cause involuntariness, since it is not the cause of anything that is repugnant to the will: but it causes *non-voluntariness*, since that which is unknown cannot be actually willed. Ignorance is *consequent* to the act of the will, in so far as ignorance itself is voluntary: and this happens in two ways, in accordance with the two aforesaid modes of voluntary (A. 3). First, because the act of the will is brought to bear on the ignorance: as when a man wishes not to know, that he may have an excuse for sin, or that he may not be withheld from sin; according to Job xxi. 14: *We desire not the knowledge of Thy ways*. And this is called *affected ignorance*.—Secondly, ignorance is said to be voluntary, when it regards that which one can and ought to know: for in this sense *not to act* and *not to will* are said to be voluntary, as stated above (A. 3). And ignorance of this kind happens, either when one does not actually consider what one can and ought to consider;—this is called *ignorance of evil choice*, and arises from some passion or habit: or when one does not take the trouble to acquire the knowledge which one ought to have; in which sense, ignorance of the general principles of law, which one ought to know, is voluntary, as being due to negligence.— Accordingly, if in either of these ways, ignorance is voluntary, it cannot cause involuntariness simply. Nevertheless it causes involuntariness in a certain respect, inasmuch as it precedes the movement of the will towards the act, which movement would not be, if there were knowledge. Ignorance is *antecedent* to the act of the will, when it is not voluntary, and yet is the cause of man's willing what he would not will otherwise. Thus a man may be ignorant of some circumstance of his act, which he was not bound to know, the result being that he does that which he would not do, if he knew of that circumstance; for instance, a man, after taking proper precaution, may not know that someone is coming along the road, so that he shoots an arrow and slays a passer-by. Such ignorance causes involuntariness simply.

From this may be gathered the solution of the objections. For the first objection deals with ignorance of what a man is bound to know. The second, with ignorance of choice, which is voluntary to a certain extent, as stated above. The third, with that ignorance which is concomitant with the act of the will.

# QUESTION VII.

## OF THE CIRCUMSTANCES OF HUMAN ACTS.

### (*In Four Articles.*)

WE must now consider the circumstances of human acts: under which head there are four points of inquiry: (1) What is a circumstance ? (2) Whether a theologian should take note of the circumstances of human acts ? (3) How many circumstances are there ? (4) Which are the most important of them ?

### FIRST ARTICLE.

#### WHETHER A CIRCUMSTANCE IS AN ACCIDENT OF A HUMAN ACT ?

*We proceed thus to the First Article :—*

*Objection* 1. It would seem that a circumstance is not an accident of a human act. For Tully says (*De Invent. Rhetor.* i.) that a circumstance is that from *which an orator adds authority and strength to his argument.* But oratorical arguments are derived principally from things pertaining to the essence of a thing, such as the definition, the genus, the species, and the like, from which also Tully declares that an orator should draw his arguments. Therefore a circumstance is not an accident of a human act.

*Obj.* 2. Further, *to be in* is proper to an accident. But that which surrounds (*circumstat*) is rather out than in. Therefore the circumstances are not accidents of human acts.

*Obj.* 3. Further, an accident has no accident. But human acts themselves are accidents. Therefore the circumstances are not accidents of acts.

*On the contrary*, The particular conditions of any singular thing are called its individuating accidents. But the Philosopher (*Ethic.* iii. 1) calls the circumstances particular things,* *i.e.*, the particular conditions of each act. Therefore the circumstances are individual accidents of human acts.

*I answer that*, Since, according to the Philosopher (*Peri Herm.* i.), *words are the signs of what we understand*, it must needs be that in naming things we follow the process of intellectual knowledge. Now our intellectual knowledge proceeds from the better known to the less known. Accordingly with us, names of more obvious things are transferred so as to signify things less obvious: and hence it is that, as stated in *Metaph.* x. 4, *the notion of distance has been transferred from things that are apart locally, to all kinds of opposition :* and in like manner words that signify local movement are employed to designate all other movements, because bodies which are circumscribed by place, are best known to us. And hence it is that the word *circumstance* has passed from located things to human acts.

Now in things located, that is said to surround something, which is outside it, but touches it, or is placed near it. Accordingly, whatever conditions are outside the substance of an act, and yet in some way touch the human act, are called circumstances. Now what is outside a thing's substance, while it belongs to that thing, is called its accident. Wherefore the circumstances of human acts should be called their accidents.

*Reply Obj.* 1. The orator gives strength to his argument, in the first place, from the substance of the act; and, secondly, from the circumstances of the act. Thus a man becomes indictable, first, through being guilty of murder; secondly, through having done it fraudulently, or from motives of greed, or at a holy time or place, and so forth. And so in the passage quoted, it is said pointedly that the orator *adds strength to his argument*, as though this were something secondary.

*Reply Obj.* 2. A thing is said to be an accident of something in two ways. First, from being in that thing: thus,

* τα καθ' ἕκαστα.

whiteness is said to be an accident of Socrates. Secondly, because it is together with that thing in the same subject: thus, whiteness is an accident of the art of music, inasmuch as they meet in the same subject, so as to touch one another, as it were. And in this sense circumstances are said to be the accidents of human acts.

*Reply Obj*. 3. As stated above (*ad* 2), an accident is said to be the accident of an accident, from the fact that they meet in the same subject. But this happens in two ways. First, in so far as two accidents are both related to the same subject, without any relation to one another; as whiteness and the art of music in Socrates. Secondly, when such accidents are related to one another; as when the subject receives one accident by means of the other; for instance, a body receives colour by means of its surface. And thus also is one accident said to be in another; for we speak of colour as being in the surface.

Accordingly, circumstances are related to acts in both these ways. For some circumstances that have a relation to acts, belong to the agent otherwise than through the act; as place and condition of person: whereas others belong to the agent by reason of the act, as the manner in which the act is done.

## SECOND ARTICLE.

### WHETHER THEOLOGIANS SHOULD TAKE NOTE OF THE CIRCUMSTANCES OF HUMAN ACTS ?

*We proceed thus to the Second Article :—*

*Objection* 1. It would seem that theologians should not take note of the circumstances of human acts. Because theologians do not consider human acts otherwise than according to their quality of good or evil. But it seems that circumstances cannot give quality to human acts; for a thing is never qualified, formally speaking, by that which is outside it; but by that which is in it. Therefore theologians should not take note of the circumstances of acts.

*Obj*. 2. Further, circumstances are the accidents of acts.

But one thing may be subject to an infinity of accidents; hence the Philosopher says (*Metaph.* vi. 2) that *no art or science considers accidental being, except only the art of sophistry*. Therefore the theologian has not to consider circumstances.

*Obj.* 3. Further, the consideration of circumstances belongs to the orator. But oratory is not a part of theology. Therefore it is not a theologian's business to consider circumstances.

*On the contrary*, Ignorance of circumstances causes an act to be involuntary, according to Damascene (*De Fide Orthod.* ii. 24) and Gregory of Nyssa.\* But involuntariness excuses from sin, the consideration of which belongs to the theologian. Therefore circumstances also should be considered by the theologian.

*I answer that*, Circumstances come under the consideration of the theologian, for a threefold reason. First, because the theologian considers human acts, inasmuch as man is thereby directed to Happiness. Now, everything that is directed to an end should be proportionate to that end. But acts are made proportionate to an end by means of a certain commensurateness, which results from the due circumstances. Hence the theologian has to consider the circumstances.—Secondly, because the theologian considers human acts according as they are found to be good or evil, better or worse: and this diversity depends on circumstances, as we shall see further on (Q. XVIII., AA. 10, 11; Q. LXXIII., A. 7).—Thirdly, because the theologian considers human acts under the aspect of merit and demerit, which is proper to human acts; and for this it is requisite that they be voluntary. Now a human act is deemed to be voluntary or involuntary, according to knowledge or ignorance of circumstances, as stated above (*cf.* Q. VI., A. 8). Therefore the theologian has to consider circumstances.

*Reply Obj.* 1. Good directed to the end is said to be useful; and this implies some kind of relation: wherefore the Philosopher says (*Ethic.* i. 6) that *the good in the genus 'relation'*

* Nemesius, *De Nat. Hom.* xxxi.

*is the useful,*  Now, in the genus *relation* a thing is denominated not only according to that which is inherent in the thing, but also according to that which is extrinsic to it: as may be seen in the expressions *right* and *left*, *equal* and *unequal*, and suchlike.  Accordingly, since the goodness of acts consists in their utility to the end, nothing hinders their being called good or bad according to their proportion to extrinsic things that are adjacent to them.

*Reply Obj.* 2. Accidents which are altogether accidental are neglected by every art, by reason of their uncertainty and infinity.  But suchlike accidents are not what we call circumstances; because circumstances, although, as stated above (A. 1), they are extrinsic to the act, nevertheless are in a kind of contact with it, by being related to it.  Proper accidents, however, come under the consideration of art.

*Reply Obj.* 3. The consideration of circumstances belongs to the moralist, the politician, and the orator.  To the moralist, in so far as with respect to circumstances we find or lose the mean of virtue in human acts and passions.  To the politician and to the orator, in so far as circumstances make acts to be worthy of praise or blame, of excuse or indictment.  In different ways, however: because where the orator persuades, the politician judges.  To the theologian this consideration belongs, in all the aforesaid ways: since to him all the other arts are subservient: for he has to consider virtuous and vicious acts, just as the moralist does; and with the orator and politician he considers acts according as they are deserving of reward or punishment.

## Third Article.

### WHETHER THE CIRCUMSTANCES ARE PROPERLY SET FORTH IN THE THIRD BOOK OF ETHICS?

*We proceed thus to the Third Article :—*

*Objection* 1. It would seem that the circumstances are not properly set forth in *Ethic.* iii. 1.  For a circumstance of an act is described as something outside the act.  Now time and place answer to this description. Therefore there are only two circumstances, to wit, *when* and *where*.

*Obj.* 2. Further, we judge from the circumstances whether a thing is well or ill done. But this belongs to the mode of an act. Therefore all the circumstances are included under one, which is the *mode of acting*.

*Obj.* 3. Further, circumstances are not part of the substance of an act. But the causes of an act seem to belong to its substance. Therefore no circumstance should be taken from the cause of the act itself. Accordingly, neither *who*, nor *why*, nor *about what*, are circumstances: since *who* refers to the efficient cause, *why* to the final cause, and *about what* to the material cause.

*On the contrary* is the authority of the Philosopher in *Ethic.* iii. 1.

*I answer that,* Tully, in his Rhetoric (*De Invent. Rhetor.* i.), gives seven circumstances, which are contained in this verse:

> *Quis, quid, ubi, quibus auxiliis, cur, quomodo, quando—*
> *Who, what, where, by what aids, why, how,* and *when.*

For in acts we must take note of *who* did it, *by what aids* or *instruments* he did it, *what* he did, *where* he did it, *why* he did it, *how* and *when* he did it. But Aristotle in *Ethic.* iii. 1 adds yet another, to wit, *about what*, which Tully includes in the circumstance *what*.

The reason of this enumeration may be set down as follows. For a circumstance is described as something outside the substance of the act, and yet in a way touching it. Now this happens in three ways: first, inasmuch as it touches the act itself; secondly, inasmuch as it touches the cause of the act; thirdly, inasmuch as it touches the effect. It touches the act itself, either by way of measure, as *time* and *place;* or by qualifying the act, as the *mode of acting*. It touches the effect, when we consider *what* is done. It touches the cause of the act, as to the final cause, by the circumstance *why;* as to the material cause, or object, in the circumstance *about what;* as to the principal efficient cause, in the circumstance *who ;* and as to the instrumental efficient cause, in the circumstance *by what aids.*

*Reply Obj.* 1. Time and place surround (*circumstant*) the act by way of measure; but the others surround the act by touching it in any other way, while they are extrinsic to the substance of the act.

*Reply Obj.* 2. This mode *well* or *ill* is not a circumstance, but results from all the circumstances. But the mode which refers to a quality of the act is a special circumstance; for instance, that a man walk fast or slowly; that he strike hard or gently, and so forth.

*Reply Obj.* 3. A condition of the cause, on which the substance of the act depends, is not a circumstance; it must be an additional condition. Thus, in regard to the object, it is not a circumstance of theft that the object is another's property, for this belongs to the substance of the act; but that it be great or small. And the same applies to the other circumstances which are considered in reference to the other causes. For the end that specifies the act is not a circumstance, but some additional end. Thus, that a valiant man act *valiantly for the sake of* the good of the virtue of fortitude, is not a circumstance; but if he act valiantly for the sake of the delivery of the state, or of Christendom, or some such purpose. The same is to be said with regard to the circumstance *what ;* for that a man by pouring water on someone should happen to wash him, is not a circumstance of the washing; but that in doing so he give him a chill, or scald him; heal him or harm him, these are circumstances.

## FOURTH ARTICLE.

### WHETHER THE MOST IMPORTANT CIRCUMSTANCES ARE "WHY" AND "IN WHAT THE ACT CONSISTS"?

*We proceed thus to the Fourth Article :—*

*Objection* 1. It would seem that these are not the most important circumstances, namely, *why* and those *in which the act is,** as stated in *Ethic.* iii. 1. For those in which the act

* ἐν οἷς ἡ πρᾶξις.

is seem to be place and time: and these do not seem to be the most important of the circumstances, since, of them all, they are the most extrinsic to the act. Therefore those things in which the act is are not the most important circumstances.

*Obj.* 2. Further, the end of a thing is extrinsic to it. Therefore it is not the most important circumstance.

*Obj.* 3. Further, that which holds the foremost place in regard to each thing, is its cause and its form. But the cause of an act is the person that does it; while the form of an act is the manner in which it is done. Therefore these two circumstances seem to be of the greatest importance.

*On the contrary*, Gregory of Nyssa* says that *the most important circumstances* are *why it is done* and *what is done*.

*I answer that*, As stated above (Q. I., A. 1), acts are properly called human, inasmuch as they are voluntary. Now, the motive and object of the will is the end. Therefore that circumstance is the most important of all which touches the act on the part of the end, viz., the circumstance *why*: and the second in importance, is that which touches the very substance of the act, viz., the circumstance *what he did*. As to the other circumstances, they are more or less important, according as they more or less approach to these.

*Reply Obj.* 1. By those things *in which the act is* the Philosopher does not mean time and place, but those circumstances that are affixed to the act itself. Wherefore Gregory of Nyssa,* as though he were explaining the dictum of the Philosopher, instead of the latter's term,—*in which the act is*, said, *what is done*.

*Reply Obj.* 2. Although the end is not part of the substance of the act, yet it is the most important cause of the act, inasmuch as it moves the agent to act. Wherefore the moral act is specified chiefly by the end.

*Reply Obj.* 3. The person that does the act is the cause of that act, inasmuch as he is moved thereto by the end; and it is chiefly in this respect that he is directed to the

* Nemesius, *De Nat. Hom.* xxxi.

act; while other conditions of the person have not such an important relation to the act.—As to the mode, it is not the substantial form of the act, for in an act the substantial form depends on the object and term or end; but it is, as it were, a certain accidental quality of the act.

# QUESTION VIII.

## OF THE WILL, IN REGARD TO WHAT IT WILLS.
### (*In Three Articles.*)

WE must now consider the different acts of the will; and in the first place, those acts which belong to the will itself immediately, as being elicited by the will; secondly, those acts which are commanded by the will.

Now the will is moved to the end, and to the means to the end; we must therefore consider—(1) Those acts of the will whereby it is moved to the end; and (2) those whereby it is moved to the means. And since it seems that there are three acts of the will in reference to the end; viz., *volition, enjoyment,* and *intention;* we must consider—(1) Volition; (2) enjoyment; (3) intention.—Concerning the first, three things must be considered: (1) Of what things is the will? (2) By what is the will moved? (3) How is it moved?

Under the first head there are three points of inquiry: (1) Whether the will is of good only? (2) Whether it is of the end only, or also of the means? (3) If in any way it be of the means, whether it be moved to the end and to the means, by the same movement?

## FIRST ARTICLE.

### WHETHER THE WILL IS OF GOOD ONLY?

*We proceed thus to the First Article :—*

*Objection* 1. It would seem that the will is not of good only. For the same power regards opposites; for instance, sight regards white and black. But good and evil are opposites. Therefore the will is not only of good, but also of evil.

*Obj.* 2. Further, rational powers can be directed to opposite purposes, according to the Philosopher (*Metaph.* ix. 2). But the will is a rational power, since it is *in the reason*, as is stated in *De Anima* iii. 9. Therefore the will can be directed to opposites; and consequently its volition is not confined to good, but extends to evil.

*Obj.* 3. Further, good and being are convertible. But volition is directed not only to beings, but also to non-beings. For sometimes we wish *not to walk*, or *not to speak ;* and again at times we wish for future things, which are not actual beings. Therefore the will is not of good only.

*On the contrary*, Dionysius says (*Div. Nom.* iv.) that *evil is outside the scope of the will*, and that *all things desire good*.

*I answer that*, The will is a rational appetite. Now every appetite is only of something good. The reason of this is that the appetite is nothing else than an inclination of a person desirous of a thing towards that thing. Now every inclination is to something like and suitable to the thing inclined. Since, therefore, everything, inasmuch as it is being and substance, is a good, it must needs be that every inclination is to something good. And hence it is that the Philosopher says (*Ethic.* i. 1) that *the good is that which all desire*.

But it must be noted that, since every inclination results from a form, the natural appetite results from a form existing in the nature of things: while the sensitive appetite, as also the intellective or rational appetite, which we call the will, follows from an apprehended form. Therefore, just as the natural appetite tends to good existing in a thing; so the animal or voluntary appetite tends to a good which is apprehended. Consequently, in order that the will tend to anything, it is requisite, not that this be good in very truth, but that it be apprehended as good. Wherefore the Philosopher says (*Phys.* ii. 3) that *the end is a good, or an apparent good*.

*Reply Obj.* 1. The same power regards opposites, but it is

not referred to them in the same way. Accordingly, the will is referred both to good and to evil: but to good, by desiring it: to evil, by shunning it. Wherefore the actual desire of good is called *volition*,\* meaning thereby the act of the will; for it is in this sense that we are now speaking of the will. On the other hand, the shunning of evil is better described as *nolition* : wherefore, just as volition is of good, so nolition is of evil.

*Reply Obj.* 2. A rational power is not to be directed to all opposite purposes, but to those which are contained under its proper object: for no power seeks other than its proper object. Now, the object of the will is good. Wherefore the will can be directed to such opposite purposes as are contained under good, such as to be moved or to be at rest, to speak or to be silent, and suchlike: for the will can be directed to either under the aspect of good.

*Reply Obj.* 3. That which is not a being in nature, is considered as a being in the reason, wherefore negations and privations are said to be *beings of reason*. In this way, too, future things, in so far as they are apprehended, are beings. Accordingly, in so far as suchlike are beings, they are apprehended under the aspect of good; and it is thus that the will is directed to them. Wherefore the Philosopher says (*Ethic.* v. 1) that *to lack evil is considered as a good*.

### Second Article.

#### WHETHER VOLITION IS OF THE END ONLY, OR ALSO OF THE MEANS ?

*We proceed thus to the Second Article :—*

*Objection* 1. It would seem that volition is not of the means, but of the end only. For the Philosopher says (*Ethic.* iii. 2) that *volition is of the end, while choice is of the means*.

*Obj.* 2. Further, *For objects differing in genus there are corresponding different powers of the soul* (*Ethic.* vi. 1). Now,

---

\* In Latin,—*voluntas*. To avoid confusion with *voluntas* (the will) St. Thomas adds a word of explanation, which in the translation may appear superfluous.

the end and the means are in different genera of good: because the end, which is a good either of rectitude or of pleasure, is in the genus *quality*, or *action*, or *passion;* whereas the good which is useful, and is directed to an end, is in the genus *relation* (*Ethic.* i. 6). Therefore, if volition is of the end, it is not of the means.

*Obj.* 3. Further, habits are proportionate to powers, since they are perfections thereof. But in those habits which are called practical arts, the end belongs to one, and the means to another art; thus the use of a ship, which is its end, belongs to the (art of the) helmsman; whereas the building of the ship, which is directed to the end, belongs to the art of the shipwright. Therefore, since volition is of the end, it is not of the means.

*On the contrary,* In natural things, it is by the same power that a thing passes through the middle space, and arrives at the terminus. But the means are a kind of middle space, through which one arrives at the end or terminus. Therefore, if volition is of the end, it is also of the means.

*I answer that,* The word *voluntas* sometimes designates the power of the will, sometimes its act.* Accordingly, if we speak of the will as a power, thus it extends both to the end and to the means. For every power extends to those things in which may be considered the aspect of the object of that power in any way whatever: thus the sight extends to all things whatsoever that are in any way coloured. Now the aspect of good, which is the object of the power of will, may be found not only in the end, but also in the means.

If, however, we speak of the will in regard to its act, then, properly speaking, volition is of the end only. Because every act denominated from a power, designates the simple act of that power: thus *to understand* designates the simple act of the understanding. Now the simple act of a power is referred to that which is in itself the object of that power. But that which is good and willed in itself is the end. Wherefore volition, properly speaking, is of the end itself. On the

* See note on p. 115.

other hand, the means are good and willed, not in themselves, but as referred to the end. Wherefore the will is directed to them, only in so far as it is directed to the end: so that what it wills in them, is the end. Thus, to understand, is properly directed to things that are known in themselves, *i.e.*, first principles: but we do not speak of understanding with regard to things known through first principles, except in so far as we see the principles in those things. For in morals the end is what principles are in speculative science (*cf. Ethic.* vii. 8).

*Reply Obj.* 1. The Philosopher is speaking of the will in reference to the simple act of the will; not in reference to the power of the will.

*Reply Obj.* 2. There are different powers for objects that differ in genus and are on an equality; for instance, sound and colour are different genera of sensibles, to which are referred hearing and sight. But the useful and the righteous are not on an equality, but are as that which is of itself, and that which is in relation to another. Now suchlike objects are always referred to the same power; for instance, the power of sight perceives both colour and light by which colour is seen.

*Reply Obj.* 3. Not everything that diversifies habits, diversifies the powers: since habits are certain determinations of powers to certain special acts. Moreover, every practical art considers both the end and the means. For the art of the helmsman does indeed consider the end, as that which it effects; and the means, as that which it commands. On the other hand, the ship-building art considers the means as that which it effects; but it considers that which is the end, as that to which it refers what it effects. And again, in every practical art there is an end proper to it and means that belong properly to that art.

### Third Article.

#### WHETHER THE WILL IS MOVED BY THE SAME ACT TO THE END AND TO THE MEANS?

*We proceed thus to the Third Article :—*

*Objection* 1. It would seem that the will is moved by the same act, to the end and to the means. Because according to the Philosopher (*Topic.* iii. 2) *where one thing is on account of another there is only one.* But the will does not will the means save on account of the end. Therefore it is moved to both by the same act.

*Obj.* 2. Further, the end is the reason for willing the means, just as light is the reason of seeing colours. But light and colours are seen by the same act. Therefore it is the same movement of the will, whereby it wills the end and the means.

*Obj.* 3. Further, it is one and the same natural movement which tends through the middle space to the terminus. But the means are in comparison to the end, as the middle space is to the terminus. Therefore it is the same movement of the will whereby it is directed to the end and to the means.

*On the contrary,* Acts are diversified according to their objects. But the end is a different species of good from the means, which are a useful good. Therefore the will is not moved to both by the same act.

*I answer that,* Since the end is willed in itself, whereas the means, as such, are only willed for the end, it is evident that the will can be moved to the end, without being moved to the means; whereas it cannot be moved to the means, as such, unless it is moved to the end. Accordingly the will is moved to the end in two ways: first, to the end absolutely and in itself; secondly, as the reason for willing the means. Hence it is evident that the will is moved by one and the same movement,—to the end, as the reason for willing the means; and to the means themselves. But it is another act whereby the will is moved to the end absolutely. And sometimes this act precedes the other in time; for example when a man first wills to have health, and afterwards deliberating by what means to be healed, wills to send for the doctor to heal him. The same happens in regard to the intellect: for at first a man understands the principles in themselves; but afterwards he understands them in the conclusions, inasmuch as he assents to the conclusions on account of the principles.

*Reply Obj.* 1. This argument holds in respect of the will being moved to the end as the reason for willing the means.

*Reply Obj.* 2. Whenever colour is seen, by the same act the light is seen; but the light can be seen without the colour being seen. In like manner whenever a man wills the means, by the same act he wills the end; but not conversely.

*Reply Obj.* 3. In the execution of a work, the means are as the middle space, and the end, as the terminus. Wherefore just as natural movement sometimes stops in the middle and does not reach the terminus; so sometimes one is busy with the means, without gaining the end. But in willing it is the reverse: for the will through (willing) the end comes to will the means; just as the intellect arrives at the conclusions through the principles which are called *means*. Hence it is that sometimes the intellect understands a mean, and does not proceed thence to the conclusion. And in like manner the will sometimes wills the end, and yet does not proceed to will the means.

The solution to the argument in the contrary sense is clear from what has been said above (A. 2 *ad* 2). For the useful and the righteous are not species of good in an equal degree, but are as that which is for its own sake and that which is for the sake of something else: wherefore the act of the will can be directed to one and not to the other; but not conversely.

# QUESTION IX.

## OF THAT WHICH MOVES THE WILL

### (*In Six Articles.*)

WE must now consider what moves the will: and under this head there are six points of inquiry: (1) Whether the will is moved by the intellect? (2) Whether it is moved by the sensitive appetite? (3) Whether the will moves itself? (4) Whether it is moved by an extrinsic principle? (5) Whether it is moved by a heavenly body? (6) Whether the will is moved by God alone as by an extrinsic principle?

## FIRST ARTICLE.

### WHETHER THE WILL IS MOVED BY THE INTELLECT?

*We proceed thus to the First Article :—*

*Objection* 1. It would seem that the will is not moved by the intellect. For Augustine says on Ps. cxviii. 20: *My soul hath coveted to long for Thy justifications :—The intellect flies ahead, the desire follows sluggishly or not at all : we know what is good, but deeds delight us not.* But it would not be so, if the will were moved by the intellect: because movement of the moveable results from motion of the mover. Therefore the intellect does not move the will.

*Obj.* 2. Further, the intellect in presenting the appetible object to the will, stands in relation to the will, as the imagination in representing the appetible object to the sensitive appetite. But the imagination, in presenting the appetible object, does not move the sensitive appetite: indeed sometimes our imagination affects us no more than what is set before us in a picture, and moves us not at all (*De Anima* ii. 3). Therefore neither does the intellect move the will.

*Obj.* 3. Further, the same is not mover and moved in respect of the same thing. But the will moves the intellect; for we exercise the intellect when we will. Therefore the intellect does not move the will.

*On the contrary,* The Philosopher says (*De Anima* iii. 10) that *the appetible object is a mover not moved, whereas the will is a mover moved.*

*I answer that,* A thing requires to be moved by something in so far as it is in potentiality to several things; for that which is in potentiality needs to be reduced to act by something actual; and to do this is to move. Now a power of the soul is seen to be in potentiality to different things in two ways: first, with regard to acting and not acting; secondly, with regard to this or that action. Thus the sight sometimes sees actually, and sometimes sees not: and sometimes it sees white, and sometimes black. It needs therefore a mover in two respects: viz., as to the exercise or use of the act, and as to the determination of the act. The first of these is on the part of the subject, which is sometimes acting, sometimes not acting: while the other is on the part of the object, by reason of which the act is specified.

The motion of the subject itself is due to some agent. And since every agent acts for an end, as was shown above (Q. I., A. 2), the principle of this motion lies in the end. And hence it is that the art which is concerned with the end, by its command moves the art which is concerned with the means; just as the *art of sailing commands the art of ship-building* (*Phys.* ii. 2). Now good in general, which has the nature of an end, is the object of the will. Consequently, in this respect, the will moves the other powers of the soul to their acts, for we make use of the other powers when we will. For the end and perfection of every other power, is included under the object of the will as some particular good: and always the art or power to which the universal end belongs, moves to their acts the arts or powers to which belong the particular ends included in the universal end. Thus the leader of an army, who intends the common good— *i.e.*, the order of the whole army—by his command moves one of the captains, who intends the order of one company.

On the other hand, the object moves, by determining the act, after the manner of a formal principle, whereby in natural things actions are specified, as heating by heat. Now the first formal principle is universal *being* and *truth*, which is the object of the intellect. And therefore by this kind of motion the intellect moves the will, as presenting its object to it.

*Reply Obj.* 1. The passage quoted proves, not that the intellect does not move, but that it does not move of necessity.

*Reply Obj.* 2. Just as the imagination of a form without estimation of fitness or harmfulness, does not move the sensitive appetite; so neither does the apprehension of the true without the aspect of goodness and desirability. Hence it is not the speculative intellect that moves, but the practical intellect (*De Anima* iii. 9).

*Reply Obj.* 3. The will moves the intellect as to the exercise of its act; since even the true itself which is the perfection of the intellect, is included in the universal good, as a particular good. But as to the determination of the act, which the act derives from the object, the intellect moves the will; since the good itself is apprehended under a special aspect as contained in the universal true. It is therefore evident that the same is not mover and moved in the same respect.

## SECOND ARTICLE.

### WHETHER THE WILL IS MOVED BY THE SENSITIVE APPETITE ?

*We proceed thus to the Second Article :*—

*Objection* 1. It would seem that the will cannot be moved by the sensitive appetite. For *to move and to act is more excellent than to be passive*, as Augustine says (*Gen. ad lit.* xii. 16).

But the sensitive appetite is less excellent than the will which is the intellectual appetite; just as sense is less excellent than intellect. Therefore the sensitive appetite does not move the will.

*Obj.* 2. Further, no particular power can produce a universal effect. But the sensitive appetite is a particular power, because it follows the particular apprehension of sense. Therefore it cannot cause the movement of the will, which movement is universal, as following the universal apprehension of the intellect.

*Obj.* 3. Further, as is proved in *Phys.* viii. 5, the mover is not moved by that which it moves, in such a way that there be reciprocal motion. But the will moves the sensitive appetite, inasmuch as the sensitive appetite obeys the reason. Therefore the sensitive appetite does not move the will.

*On the contrary*, It is written (James i. 14): *Every man is tempted by his own concupiscence, being drawn away and allured*. But man would not be drawn away by his concupiscence, unless his will were moved by the sensitive appetite, wherein concupiscence resides. Therefore the sensitive appetite moves the will.

*I answer that*, As stated above (A. 1), that which is apprehended as good and fitting, moves the will by way of object. Now, that a thing appear to be good and fitting, happens from two causes: namely, from the condition, either of the thing proposed, or of the one to whom it is proposed. For fitness is spoken of by way of relation; hence it depends on both extremes. And hence it is that taste, according as it is variously disposed, takes to a thing in various ways, as being fitting or unfitting. Wherefore as the Philosopher says (*Ethic.* iii. 5): *According as a man is, such does the end seem to him*.

Now it is evident that according to a passion of the sensitive appetite man is changed to a certain disposition. Wherefore according as man is affected by a passion, something seems to him fitting, which does not seem so when he is not so affected: thus that seems good to a man when angered, which does not seem good when he is calm. And in this way, the sensitive appetite moves the will, on the part of the object.

*Reply Obj.* 1. Nothing hinders that which is better simply and in itself, from being less excellent in a certain respect. Accordingly the will is simply more excellent than the sensitive appetite: but in respect of the man in whom a passion is predominant, in so far as he is subject to that passion, the sensitive appetite is more excellent.

*Reply Obj.* 2. Men's acts and choices are in reference to singulars. Wherefore from the very fact that the sensitive appetite is a particular power, it has great influence in disposing man so that something seems to him such or otherwise, in particular cases.

*Reply Obj.* 3. As the Philosopher says (*Polit.* i. 2), the reason, in which resides the will, moves, by its command, the irascible and concupiscible powers, not, indeed, *by a despotic sovereignty*, as a slave is moved by his master, but by a *royal and politic sovereignty*, as free men are ruled by their governor, and can nevertheless act counter to his commands. Hence both irascible and concupiscible can move counter to the will: and accordingly nothing hinders the will from being moved by them at times.

## THIRD ARTICLE.

### WHETHER THE WILL MOVES ITSELF ?

*We proceed thus to the Third Article :—*

*Objection* 1. It would seem that the will does not move itself. For every mover, as such, is in act: whereas what is moved, is in potentiality; since *movement is the act of that which is in potentiality, as such.** Now the same is not in potentiality and in act, in respect of the same. Therefore nothing moves itself. Neither, therefore, can the will move itself.

*Obj.* 2. Further, the movable is moved on the mover being present. But the will is always present to itself. If, therefore, it moved itself, it would always be moving itself, which is clearly false.

* Aristotle, *Phys.* iii. 1.

*Obj.* 3. Further, the will is moved by the intellect, as stated above (A. 1). If, therefore, the will move itself, it would follow that the same thing is at once moved immediately by two movers; which seems unreasonable. Therefore the will does not move itself.

*On the contrary,* The will is mistress of its own act, and to it belongs to will and not to will. But this would not be so, had it not the power to move itself to will. Therefore it moves itself.

*I answer that,* As stated above (A. 1), it belongs to the will to move the other powers, by reason of the end which is the will's object. Now, as stated above (Q. VIII., A. 2), the end is in things appetible, what the principle is in things intelligible. But it is evident that the intellect, through its knowledge of the principle, reduces itself from potentiality to act, as to its knowledge of the conclusions; and thus it moves itself. And, in like manner, the will, through its volition of the end, moves itself to will the means.

*Reply Obj.* 1. It is not in respect of the same that the will moves itself and is moved: wherefore neither is it in act and in potentiality in respect of the same. But forasmuch as it actually wills the end, it reduces itself from potentiality to act, in respect of the means, so as, in a word, to will them actually.

*Reply Obj.* 2. The power of the will is always actually present to itself; but the act of the will, whereby it wills an end, is not always in the will. But it is by this act that it moves itself. Accordingly it does not follow that it is always moving itself.

*Reply Obj.* 3. The will is moved by the intellect, otherwise than by itself. By the intellect it is moved on the part of the object: whereas it is moved by itself, as to the exercise of its act, in respect of the end.

## FOURTH ARTICLE.

### WHETHER THE WILL IS MOVED BY AN EXTERIOR PRINCIPLE ?

*We proceed thus to the Fourth Article :—*

*Objection* 1. It would seem that the will is not moved by anything exterior. For the movement of the will is voluntary. But it is essential to the voluntary act that it be from an intrinsic principle, just as it is essential to the natural act. Therefore the movement of the will is not from anything exterior.

*Obj.* 2. Further, the will cannot suffer violence, as was shown above (Q. VI., A. 4). But the violent act is one *the principle of which is outside the agent.** Therefore the will cannot be moved by anything exterior.

*Obj.* 3. Further, that which is sufficiently moved by one mover, needs not to be moved by another. But the will moves itself sufficiently. Therefore it is not moved by anything exterior.

*On the contrary*, The will is moved by the object, as stated above (A. 1). But the object of the will can be something exterior, offered to the sense. Therefore the will can be moved by something exterior.

*I answer that*, As far as the will is moved by the object, it is evident that it can be moved by something exterior. But in so far as it is moved in the exercise of its act, we must again hold it to be moved by some exterior principle.

For everything that is at one time an agent actually, and at another time an agent in potentiality, needs to be moved by a mover. Now it is evident that the will begins to will something, whereas previously it did not will it. Therefore it must, of necessity, be moved by something to will it. And, indeed, it moves itself, as stated above (A. 3), in so far as through willing the end it reduces itself to the act of willing the means. Now it cannot do this without the aid of counsel: for when a man wills to be healed, he begins to reflect how this can be attained, and through this reflexion

* Aristotle, *Ethic.* iii. 1.

he comes to the conclusion that he can be healed by a physician: and this he wills. But since he did not always actually will to have health, he must, of necessity, have begun, through something moving him, to will to be healed. And if the will moved itself to will this, it must, of necessity, have done this with the aid of counsel following some previous volition. But this process could not go on to infinity. Wherefore we must, of necessity, suppose that the will advanced to its first movement in virtue of the instigation of some exterior mover, as Aristotle concludes in a chapter of the *Eudemian Ethics* (vii. 14).

*Reply Obj.* 1. It is essential to the voluntary act that its principle be within the agent: but it is not necessary that this inward principle be the first principle unmoved by another. Wherefore though the voluntary act has an inward proximate principle, nevertheless its first principle is from without. Thus, too, the first principle of the natural movement is from without, that, to wit, which moves nature.

*Reply Obj.* 2. For an act to be violent it is not enough that its principle be extrinsic, but we must add *without the concurrence of him that suffers violence*. This does not happen when the will is moved by an exterior principle: for it is the will that wills, though moved by another. But this movement would be violent, if it were counter to the movement of the will: which in the present case is impossible; since then the will would will and not will the same thing.

*Reply Obj.* 3. The will moves itself sufficiently in one respect, and in its own order, that is to say as proximate agent; but it cannot move itself in every respect, as we have shown. Wherefore it needs to be moved by another as first mover.

### FIFTH ARTICLE.

#### WHETHER THE WILL IS MOVED BY A HEAVENLY BODY?

*We proceed thus to the Fifth Article:—*

*Objection* 1. It would seem that the human will is moved by a heavenly body. For all various and multiform movements are reduced, as to their cause, to a uniform movement which is that of the heavens, as is proved in *Phys.* viii. 9. But human movements are various and multiform, since they begin to be, whereas previously they were not. Therefore they are reduced, as to their cause, to the movement of the heavens, which is uniform according to its nature.

*Obj.* 2. Further, according to Augustine (*De Trin.* iii. 4) *the lower bodies are moved by the higher.* But the movements of the human body, which are caused by the will, could not be reduced to the movement of the heavens, as to their cause, unless the will too were moved by the heavens. Therefore the heavens move the human will.

*Obj.* 3. Further, by observing the heavenly bodies astrologers foretell the truth about future human acts, which are caused by the will. But this would not be so, if the heavenly bodies could not move man's will. Therefore the human will is moved by a heavenly body.

*On the contrary,* Damascene says (*De Fide Orthod.* ii. 7) that *the heavenly bodies are not the causes of our acts.* But they would be, if the will, which is the principle of human acts, were moved by the heavenly bodies. Therefore the will is not moved by the heavenly bodies.

*I answer that,* It is evident that the will can be moved by the heavenly bodies in the same way as it is moved by its object: that is to say, in so far as exterior bodies, which move the will, through being offered to the senses, and also the organs themselves of the sensitive powers, are subject to the movements of the heavenly bodies.

But some have maintained that heavenly bodies have an influence on the human will, in the same way as some exterior agent moves the will, as to the exercise of its act.—But this is impossible. For the *will,* as stated in *De Anima* iii. 9, *is in the reason.* Now the reason is a power of the soul, not bound to a bodily organ: wherefore it follows that the will is a power absolutely incorporeal and immaterial. But it is evident that no body can act on what is incorporeal, but rather the reverse: because things incorporeal and immaterial have a power more formal and more universal than any corporeal things whatever. Therefore it is impossible for a heavenly body to act directly on the intellect or the will.—For this reason Aristotle (*De Anima* iii. 3) ascribed to those who held that intellect differs not from sense, the theory that *such is the will of men, as is the day which the father of men and of gods brings on** (referring to Jupiter, by whom they understand the entire heavens). For all the sensitive powers, since they are acts of bodily organs, can be moved accidentally, by the heavenly bodies—*i.e.,* through those bodies being moved, whose acts they are.

But since it has been stated (A. 2) that the intellectual appetite is moved, in a fashion, by the sensitive appetite, the movements of the heavenly bodies have an indirect bearing on the will; in so far as the will happens to be moved by the passions of the sensitive appetite.

*Reply Obj.* 1. The multiform movements of the human will are reduced to some uniform cause, which, however, is above the intellect and will. This can be said, not of any body, but of some superior immaterial substance. Therefore there is no need for the movement of the will to be referred to the movement of the heavens, as to its cause.

*Reply Obj.* 2. The movements of the human body are reduced, as to their cause, to the movement of a heavenly body, in so far as the disposition suitable to a particular movement, is somewhat due to the influence of heavenly bodies;—also, in so far as the sensitive appetite is stirred by the influence of heavenly bodies;—and again, in so far as exterior bodies are moved in accordance with the movement of heavenly bodies, at whose presence, the will begins to will or not to will something; for instance, when the body is chilled, we begin to wish to make the fire. But this movement of the will is on the part of the object offered from without: not on the part of an inward instigation.

*Reply Obj.* 3. As stated above (*cf.* P. I., Q. LXXXIV., AA. 6, 7) the sensitive appetite is the act of a bodily organ. Wherefore there is no reason why man should not be prone to anger or concupiscence, or some like passion, by reason

* *Odyssey* xviii. 135.

of the influence of heavenly bodies, just as by reason of his natural complexion. But the majority of men are led by the passions, which the wise alone resist. Consequently, in the majority of cases predictions about human acts, gathered from the observation of heavenly bodies, are fulfilled. Nevertheless, as Ptolemy says (*Centiloquium* v.), *the wise man governs the stars :* which is as though to say that by resisting his passions, he opposes his will, which is free and nowise subject to the movement of the heavens, to suchlike effects of the heavenly bodies.

Or, as Augustine says (*Gen. ad lit.* ii. 17): *We must confess that when the truth is foretold by astrologers, this is due to some most hidden inspiration, to which the human mind is subject without knowing it. And since this is done in order to deceive man, it must be the work of the lying spirits.*

### Sixth Article.

#### WHETHER THE WILL IS MOVED BY GOD ALONE, AS EXTERIOR PRINCIPLE ?

*We proceed thus to the Sixth Article :—*

*Objection* 1. It would seem that the will is not moved by God alone as exterior principle. For it is natural that the inferior be moved by its superior: thus the lower bodies are moved by the heavenly bodies. But there is something which is higher than the will of man and below God, namely, the angel. Therefore man's will can be moved by an angel also, as exterior principle.

*Obj.* 2. Further, the act of the will follows the act of the intellect. But man's intellect is reduced to act, not by God alone, but also by the angel who enlightens it, as Dionysius says (*Cæl. Hier.* iv.). For the same reason, therefore, the will also is moved by an angel.

*Obj.* 3. Further, God is not cause of other than good things, according to Gen. i. 31: *God saw all the things that He had made, and they were very good.* If, therefore, man's will were moved by God alone, it would never be moved to evil: and yet it is the will whereby *we sin and whereby we do right*, as Augustine says (*Retract.* i. 9).

On the *contrary*, It is written (Phil. ii. 13): *It is God Who worketh in us* (Vulg.,—*you*) *both to will and to accomplish.*

*I answer that,* The movement of the will is from within, as also is the movement of nature. Now although it is possible for something to move a natural thing, without being the cause of the thing moved, yet that alone, which is in some way the cause of a thing's nature, can cause a natural movement in that thing. For a stone is moved upwards by a man, who is not the cause of the stone's nature, but this movement is not natural to the stone; but the natural movement of the stone is caused by no other than the cause of its nature. Wherefore it is said in *Phys.* viii. 4, that the generator moves locally heavy and light things. Accordingly man endowed with a will is sometimes moved by something that is not his cause; but that his voluntary movement be from an exterior principle that is not the cause of his will, is impossible.

Now the cause of the will can be none other than God. And this is evident for two reasons. First, because the will is a power of the rational soul, which is caused by God alone, by creation, as was stated in the First Part (Q. XC., A. 2).—Secondly, it is evident from the fact that the will is ordained to the universal good. Wherefore nothing else can be the cause of the will, except God Himself, Who is the universal good: while every other good is good by participation, and is some particular good; and a particular cause does not give a universal inclination. Hence neither can primary matter, which is potentiality to all forms, be created by some particular agent.

*Reply Obj.* 1. An angel is not above man in such a way as to be the cause of his will, as the heavenly bodies are the causes of natural forms, from which result the natural movements of natural bodies.

*Reply Obj.* 2. Man's intellect is moved by an angel, on the part of the object, which by the power of the angelic light is proposed to man's knowledge. And in this way the will also can be moved by a creature from without, as stated above (A. 4).

*Reply Obj.* 3. God moves man's will, as the Universal Mover, to the universal object of the will, which is good. And without this universal motion, man cannot will anything. But man determines himself by his reason to will this or that, which is true or apparent good.—Nevertheless, sometimes God moves some specially to the willing of something determinate, which is good; as in the case of those whom He moves by grace, as we shall state later on (Q. CIX., A. 2).

# QUESTION X.

## OF THE MANNER IN WHICH THE WILL IS MOVED.
### (*In Four Articles.*)

WE must now consider the manner in which the will is moved. Under this head there are four points of inquiry: (1) Whether the will is moved to anything naturally? (2) Whether it is moved of necessity by its object? (3) Whether it is moved of necessity by the lower appetite? (4) Whether it is moved of necessity by the exterior mover which is God?

## FIRST ARTICLE.

### WHETHER THE WILL IS MOVED TO ANYTHING NATURALLY?

*We proceed thus to the First Article :—*

*Objection* 1. It would seem that the will is not moved to anything naturally. For the natural agent is condivided with the voluntary agent, as stated at the beginning of *Phys.* ii. 1. Therefore the will is not moved to anything naturally.

*Obj.* 2. Further, that which is natural is in a thing always: as *being hot* is in fire. But no movement is always in the will. Therefore no movement is natural to the will.

*Obj.* 3. Further, nature is determinate to one thing: whereas the will is referred to opposites. Therefore the will wills nothing naturally.

*On the contrary*, The movement of the will follows the movement of the intellect. But the intellect understands some things naturally. Therefore the will, too, wills some things naturally.

*I answer that*, As Boethius says (*De Duabus Nat.*) and the Philosopher also (*Metaph.* v. 4) the word *nature* is used in a manifold sense.   For sometimes it stands for the intrinsic principle in movable things.   In this sense nature is either matter or the material form, as stated in *Phys.* ii. 1.—In another sense nature stands for any substance, or even for any being.   And in this sense, that is said to be natural to a thing which befits it in respect of its substance.   And this is that which of itself is in a thing.   Now all things that do not of themselves belong to the thing in which they are, are reduced to something which belongs of itself to that thing, as to their principle.   Wherefore, taking nature in this sense, it is necessary that the principle of whatever belongs to a thing, be a natural principle.   This is evident in regard to the intellect: for the principles of intellectual knowledge are naturally known.   In like manner the principle of voluntary movements must be something naturally willed.

Now this is good in general, to which the will tends naturally, as does each power to its object; and again it is the last end, which stands in the same relation to things appetible, as the first principles of demonstrations to things intelligible: and, speaking generally, it is all those things which belong to the willer according to his nature.   For it is not only things pertaining to the will that the will desires, but also that which pertains to each power, and to the entire man.   Wherefore man wills naturally not only the object of the will, but also other things that are appropriate to the other powers; such as the knowledge of truth, which befits the intellect; and to be and to live and other like things which regard the natural well-being; all of which are included in the object of the will, as so many particular goods.

*Reply Obj.* 1.   The will is distinguished from nature as one kind of cause from another; for some things happen naturally and some are done voluntarily.   There is, however, another manner of causing that is proper to the will, which is mistress of its act, besides the manner proper to nature, which is determinate to one thing.   But since the will is founded on some nature, it is necessary that the movement proper to nature be shared by the will, to some extent: just as what belongs to a previous cause is shared by a subsequent cause. Because in every thing, being itself, which is from nature, precedes volition, which is from the will. And hence it is that the will wills something naturally.

*Reply Obj.* 2. In the case of natural things, that which is natural, as a result of the form only, is always in them actually, as heat is in fire. But that which is natural as a result of matter, is not always in them actually, but sometimes only in potentiality: because form is act, whereas matter is potentiality. Now movement is *the act of that which is in potentiality* (Aristotle, *Phys*. iii. 1). Wherefore that which belongs to, or results from, movement, in regard to natural things, is not always in them. Thus fire does not always move upwards, but only when it is outside its own place.* And in like manner it is not necessary that the will (which is reduced from potentiality to act, when it wills something), should always be in the act of volition; but only when it is in a certain determinate disposition. But God's will, which is pure act, is always in the act of volition.

*Reply Obj.* 3. To every nature there is one thing corresponding, proportionate, however, to that nature. For to nature considered as a genus, there corresponds something one generically; and to nature as species there corresponds something one specifically; and to the individualized nature there corresponds some one individual. Since, therefore, the will is an immaterial power like the intellect, some one general thing corresponds to it, naturally which is the good; just as to the intellect there corresponds some one general thing, which is the true, or being, or *what a thing is*. And under good in general are included many particular goods, to none of which is the will determined.

* The Aristotelian theory was that fire's proper place is the fiery heaven, *i.e.*, the *Empyrean*.

## Second Article.

### WHETHER THE WILL IS MOVED, OF NECESSITY, BY ITS OBJECT?

*We proceed thus to the Second Article :—*

*Objection* 1. It seems that the will is moved, of necessity, by its object. For the object of the will is compared to the will as mover to movable, as stated in *De Anima* iii. 10. But a mover, if it be sufficient, moves the movable of necessity, Therefore the will can be moved of necessity by its object.

*Obj.* 2. Further, just as the will is an immaterial power, so is the intellect: and both powers are ordained to a universal object, as stated above (A. 1 *ad* 3). But the intellect is moved, of necessity, by its object: therefore the will also, by its object.

*Obj.* 3. Further, whatever one wills, is either the end, or something ordained to an end. But, seemingly, one wills an end necessarily: because it is like the principle in speculative matters, to which principle one assents of necessity. Now the end is the reason for willing the means; and so it seems that we will the means also necessarily. Therefore the will is moved of necessity by its object.

*On the contrary*, The rational powers, according to the Philosopher (*Metaph*. ix. 2) are directed to opposites. But the will is a rational power, since it is in the reason, as stated in *De Anima* iii. 9. Therefore the will is directed to opposites. Therefore it is not moved, of necessity, to either of the opposites.

*I answer that*, The will is moved in two ways: first, as to the exercise of its act; secondly, as to the specification of its act, derived from the object. As to the first way, no object moves the will necessarily, for no matter what the object be, it is in man's power not to think of it, and consequently not to will it actually. But as to the second manner of motion, the will is moved by one object necessarily, by another not. For in the movement of a power by its object, we must consider under what aspect the object moves the power. For the visible moves the sight, under the aspect of colour actually visible. Wherefore if colour be offered to the sight, it moves the sight necessarily: unless one turns one's eyes away; which belongs to the exercise of the act. But if the sight were confronted with something not in all respects coloured actually, but only so in some respects, and in other respects not, the sight would not of necessity see such an object: for it might look at that part of the object which is not actually coloured, and thus it would not see it. Now just as the actually coloured is the object of sight, so is good the object of the will. Wherefore if the will be offered an object which is good universally and from every point of view, the will tends to it of necessity, if it wills anything at all; since it cannot will the opposite. If, on the other hand, the will is offered an object that is not good from every point of view, it will not tend to it of necessity.— And since lack of any good whatever, is a non-good, consequently, that good alone which is perfect and lacking in nothing, is such a good that the will cannot not-will it: and this is Happiness. Whereas any other particular goods, in so far as they are lacking in some good, can be regarded as non-goods: and from this point of view, they can be set aside or approved by the will, which can tend to one and the same thing from various points of view.

*Reply Obj.* 1. The sufficient mover of a power is none but that object that in every respect presents the aspect of the mover of that power. If, on the other hand, it is lacking in any respect, it will not move of necessity, as stated above.

*Reply Obj.* 2. The intellect is moved, of necessity, by an object, which is such as to be always and necessarily true: but not by that which may be either true or false—viz., by that which is contingent: as we have said of the good.

*Reply Obj.* 3. The last end moves the will necessarily, because it is the perfect good. In like manner whatever is ordained to that end, and without which the end cannot be attained, such as *to be* and *to live*, and the like. But other things without which the end can be gained, are not necessarily willed by one who wills the end : just as he who assents to the principle, does not necessarily assent to the conclusions, without which the principles can still be true.

### Third Article.

#### WHETHER THE WILL IS MOVED, OF NECESSITY, BY THE LOWER APPETITE ?

*We proceed thus to the Third Article :—*

*Objection* 1. It would seem that the will is moved of necessity by a passion of the lower appetite.   For the Apostle says (Rom. vii. 19) : *The good which I will I do not ; but the evil which I will not, that I do :* and this is said by reason of concupiscence, which is a passion.   Therefore the will is moved of necessity by a passion.

*Obj.* 2. Further, as stated in *Ethic.* iii. 5, *according as a man is, such does the end seem to him.*   But it is not in man's power to cast aside a passion at once.   Therefore it is not in man's power not to will that to which the passion inclines him.

*Obj.* 3. Further, a universal cause is not applied to a particular effect, except by means of a particular cause : wherefore the universal reason does not move save by means of a particular estimation, as stated in *De Anima* iii. 11.   But as the universal reason is to the particular estimation, so is the will to the sensitive appetite. Therefore the will is not moved to will something particular, except through the sensitive appetite.   Therefore, if the sensitive appetite happen to be disposed to something, by reason of a passion, the will cannot be moved in a contrary sense.

*On the contrary,* It is written (Gen. iv. 7) : *Thy lust* (Vulg.,—*The lust thereof*) *shall be under thee, and thou shalt have dominion over it.*   Therefore man's will is not moved of necessity by the lower appetite.

*I answer that,* As stated above (Q. IX., A. 2), the passion of the sensitive appetite moves the will, in so far as the will is moved by its object : inasmuch as, to wit, man through being disposed in such and such a way by a passion, judges something to be fitting and good, which he would not judge thus were it not for the passion. Now this influence of a passion on man occurs in two ways. First, so that his reason is wholly bound, so that he has not the use of reason: as happens in those who through a violent access of anger or concupiscence become furious or insane, just as they may from some other bodily disorder; since suchlike passions do not take place without some change in the body. And of such the same is to be said as of irrational animals, which follow, of necessity, the impulse of their passions: for in them there is neither movement of reason, nor, consequently, of will.

Sometimes, however, the reason is not entirely engrossed by the passion, so that the judgment of reason retains, to a certain extent, its freedom: and thus the movement of the will remains in a certain degree. Accordingly in so far as the reason remains free, and not subject to the passion, the will's movement, which also remains, does not tend of necessity to that whereto the passion inclines it. Consequently, either there is no movement of the will in that man, and the passion alone holds its sway: or if there be a movement of the will, it does not necessarily follow the passion.

*Reply Obj.* 1. Although the will cannot prevent the movement of concupiscence from arising, of which the Apostle says: *The evil which I will not, that I do—i.e., I desire ;* yet it is in the power of the will not to will to desire, or not to consent to concupiscence. And thus it does not necessarily follow the movement of concupiscence.

*Reply Obj.* 2. Since there is in man a twofold nature, intellectual and sensitive; sometimes man is such and such uniformly in respect of his whole soul: either because the sensitive part is wholly subject to his reason, as in the virtuous; or because reason is entirely engrossed by passion, as in a madman. But sometimes, although reason is clouded by passion, yet something of the reason remains free. And in respect of this, man can either repel the passion entirely, or at least hold himself in check so as not to be led away by the passion. For when thus disposed, since man is variously disposed according to the various parts of the soul, a thing appears to him otherwise according to his reason, than it does according to a passion.

*Reply Obj.* 3. The will is moved not only by the universal good apprehended by the reason, but also by good apprehended by sense. Wherefore he can be moved to some particular good independently of a passion of the sensitive appetite. For we will and do many things without passion, and through choice alone; as is most evident in those cases wherein reason resists passion.

## FOURTH ARTICLE.

### WHETHER THE WILL IS MOVED OF NECESSITY BY THE EXTERIOR MOVER WHICH IS GOD ?

*We proceed thus to the Fourth Article :—*

*Objection* 1. It would seem that the will is moved of necessity by God. For every agent that cannot be resisted moves of necessity. But God cannot be resisted, because His power is infinite; wherefore it is written (Rom. ix. 19): *Who resisteth His will?* Therefore God moves the will of necessity.

*Obj.* 2. Further, the will is moved of necessity to whatever it wills naturally, as stated above (A. 2 *ad* 3). But *whatever God does in a thing is natural to it*, as Augustine says (*Contra Faust.* xxvi. 3). Therefore the will wills of necessity everything to which God moves it.

*Obj.* 3. Further, a thing is possible, if nothing impossible follows from its being supposed. But something impossible follows from the supposition that the will does not will that to which God moves it: because in that case God's operation would be ineffectual. Therefore it is not possible for the will not to will that to which God moves it. Therefore it wills it of necessity.

*On the contrary,* It is written (Ecclus. xv. 14): *God made man from the beginning, and left him in the hand of his own counsel.* Therefore He does not of necessity move man's will.

*I answer that*, As Dionysius says (*Div. Nom.* iv.) *it belongs to Divine providence, not to destroy but to preserve the nature of things.* Wherefore it moves all things in accordance with their conditions; so that from necessary causes through the Divine motion, effects follow of necessity ; but from contingent causes, effects follow contingently. Since, therefore, the will is an active principle, not determinate to one thing, but having an indifferent relation to many things, God so moves it, that He does not determine it of necessity to one thing, but its movement remains contingent and not necessary, except in those things to which it is moved naturally.

*Reply Obj.* 1. The Divine will extends not only to the doing of something by the thing which He moves, but also to its being done in a way which is fitting to the nature of that thing. And therefore it would be more repugnant to the Divine motion, for the will to be moved of necessity, which is not fitting to its nature; than for it to be moved freely, which is becoming to its nature.

*Reply Obj.* 2. That is natural to a thing, which God so works in it that it may be natural to it : for thus is something becoming to a thing, according as God wishes it to be becoming. Now He does not wish that whatever He works in things should be natural to them, for instance, that the dead should rise again. But this He does wish to be natural to each thing,—that it be subject to the Divine power.

*Reply Obj.* 3. If God moves the will to anything, it is incompatible with this supposition, that the will be not moved thereto. But it is not impossible simply. Consequently it does not follow that the will is moved by God necessarily.

# QUESTION XI.

## OF ENJOYMENT,* WHICH IS AN ACT OF THE WILL.

### (*In Four Articles.*)

WE must now consider enjoyment: concerning which there are four points of inquiry: (1) Whether to enjoy is an act of the appetitive power? (2) Whether it belongs to the rational creature alone, or also to irrational animals? (3) Whether enjoyment is only of the last end? (4) Whether it is only of the end possessed?

### FIRST ARTICLE.

#### WHETHER TO ENJOY IS AN ACT OF THE APPETITIVE POWER?

*We proceed thus to the First Article :—*

*Objection* 1. It would seem that to enjoy belongs not only to the appetitive power. For to enjoy seems nothing else than to receive the fruit. But it is the intellect, in whose act Happiness consists, as shown above (Q. III., A. 4), that receives the fruit of human life, which is Happiness. Therefore to enjoy is not an act of the appetitive power, but of the intellect.

*Obj.* 2. Further, each power has its proper end, which is its perfection: thus the end of sight is to know the visible; of the hearing, to perceive sounds; and so forth. But the end of a thing is its fruit. Therefore to enjoy belongs to each power, and not only to the appetite.

*Obj.* 3. Further, enjoyment implies a certain delight. But sensible delight belongs to sense, which delights in its object: and for the same reason, intellectual delight

* Or, Fruition.

belongs to the intellect.   Therefore enjoyment belongs to
the apprehensive, and not to the appetitive power.

*On the contrary*, Augustine says (*De Doctr. Christ.*, i. 4 and
*De Trin.* x. 10, 11) : *To enjoy is to adhere lovingly to something
for its own sake.*   But love belongs to the appetitive power·
Therefore also to enjoy is an act of the appetitive power.

*I answer that, Fruitio* (enjoyment) and *fructus* (fruit) seem
to refer to the same, one being derived from the other;
which from which, matters not for our purpose; though it
seems probable that the one which is more clearly known,
was first named.   Now those things are most manifest to
us which appeal most to the senses: wherefore it seems that
the word ' fruition ' is derived from sensible fruits.   But
sensible fruit is that which we expect the tree to produce
in the last place, and in which a certain sweetness is to be
perceived.   Hence fruition seems to have relation to love,
or to the delight which one has in realizing the longed-for
term, which is the end.   Now the end and the good is the
object of the appetitive power.   Wherefore it is evident that
fruition is the act of the appetitive power.

*Reply Obj.* 1. Nothing hinders one and the same thing
from belonging, under different aspects, to different powers.
Accordingly the vision of God, as vision, is an act of the
intellect, but as a good and an end, is the object of the will.
And as such is the fruition thereof: so that the intellect
attains this end, as the executive power, but the will as the
motive power, moving (the powers) towards the end and
enjoying the end attained.

*Reply Obj.* 2. The perfection and end of every other power
is contained in the object of the appetitive power, as the
proper is contained in the common, as stated above (Q. IX.,
A. 1).   Hence the perfection and end of each power, in so
far as it is a good, belongs to the appetitive power.   Wherefore the appetitive power moves the other powers to their
ends; and itself realizes the end, when each of them reaches
the end.

*Reply Obj.* 3. In delight there are two things: perception
of what is becoming; and this belongs to the apprehensive

power; and complacency in that which is offered as becoming: and this belongs to the appetitive power, in which power delight is formally completed.

## SECOND ARTICLE.

### WHETHER TO ENJOY BELONGS TO THE RATIONAL CREATURE ALONE, OR ALSO TO IRRATIONAL ANIMALS ?

*We proceed thus to the Second Article :—*

*Objection* 1. It would seem that to enjoy belongs to men alone. For Augustine says (*De Doctr. Christ.* i. 22) that *it is given to us men to enjoy and to use.* Therefore other animals cannot enjoy.

*Obj.* 2. Further, to enjoy relates to the last end. But irrational animals cannot obtain the last end. Therefore it is not for them to enjoy.

*Obj.* 3. Further, just as the sensitive appetite is beneath the intellectual appetite, so is the natural appetite beneath the sensitive. If, therefore, to enjoy belongs to the sensitive appetite, it seems that for the same reason it can belong to the natural appetite. But this is evidently false, since the latter cannot delight in anything. Therefore the sensitive appetite cannot enjoy: and accordingly enjoyment is not possible for irrational animals.

*On the contrary,* Augustine says (QQ. LXXXIII, qu. 30): *It is not so absurd to suppose that even beasts enjoy their food and any bodily pleasure.*

*I answer that,* As was stated above (A. 1) to enjoy is not the act of the power that achieves the end as executor, but of the power that commands the achievement; for it has been said to belong to the appetitive power. Now things void of reason have indeed a power of achieving an end by way of execution, as that by which a heavy body has a downward tendency, whereas a light body has an upward tendency. Yet the power of command in respect of the end is not in them, but in some higher nature, which moves all nature by its command, just as in things endowed with knowledge, the appetite moves the other powers to their acts.    Wherefore it is clear that things void of knowledge, although they attain an end, have no enjoyment of the end: this is only for those that are endowed with knowledge.

Now knowledge of the end is twofold: perfect and imperfect.    Perfect knowledge of the end, is that whereby not only is that known which is the end and the good, but also the universal formality of the end and the good; and such knowledge belongs to the rational nature alone.    On the other hand, imperfect knowledge is that by which the end and the good are known in the particular.    Such knowledge is in irrational animals: whose appetitive powers do not command with freedom, but are moved according to a natural instinct to whatever they apprehend.    Consequently, enjoyment belongs to the rational nature, in a perfect degree; to irrational animals, imperfectly; to other creatures, not at all.

*Reply Obj.* 1. Augustine is speaking there of perfect enjoyment.

*Reply Obj.* 2. Enjoyment need not be of the last end simply; but of that which each one chooses for his last end.

*Reply Obj.* 3. The sensitive appetite follows some knowledge; not so the natural appetite, especially in things void of knowledge.

*Reply Obj.* 4. Augustine is speaking there of imperfect enjoyment.   This is clear from his way of speaking: for he says that *it is not so absurd to suppose that even beasts enjoy*, that is, as it would be, if one were to say that they *use*.


## Third Article.

### whether enjoyment is only of the last end ?

*We proceed thus to the Third Article:—*

*Objection* 1. It would seem that enjoyment is not only of the last end.   For the Apostle says (*Philem.* 20): *Yea, brother, may I enjoy thee in the Lord*.   But it is evident that Paul had not placed his last end in a man.   Therefore to enjoy is not only of the last end.

*Obj.* 2. Further, What we enjoy is the fruit.   But the

ii. i.                                                         10

Apostle says (Gal. v. 22): *The fruit of the Spirit is charity, joy, peace,* and other like things, which are not in the nature of the last end. Therefore enjoyment is not only of the last end.

*Obj.* 3. Further, the acts of the will reflect on one another; for I will to will, and I love to love. But to enjoy is an act of the will: since *it is the will with which we enjoy,* as Augustine says (*De Trin.* x. 10). Therefore a man enjoys his enjoyment. But the last end of man is not enjoyment, but the uncreated good alone, which is God. Therefore enjoyment is not only of the last end.

*On the contrary,* Augustine says (*De Trin.* x. 11): *A man does not enjoy that which he desires for the sake of something else.* But the last end alone is that which man does not desire for the sake of something else. Therefore enjoyment is of the last end alone.

*I answer that,* As stated above (A. 1) the notion of fruit implies two things: first that it should come last; second, that it should calm the appetite with a certain sweetness and delight. Now a thing is last either simply or relatively; simply, if it be referred to nothing else; relatively, if it is the last in a particular series. Therefore that which is last simply, and in which one delights as in the last end, is properly called fruit; and this it is that one is properly said to enjoy.—But that which is delightful not in itself, but is desired, only as referred to something else, *e.g.,* a bitter potion for the sake of health, can nowise be called fruit.— And that which has something delightful about it, to which a number of preceding things are referred, may indeed be called fruit in a certain manner; but we cannot be said to enjoy it properly or as though it answered perfectly to the notion of fruit. Hence Augustine says (*De Trin.* x. 10) that *we enjoy what we know, when the delighted will is at rest therein.* But its rest is not absolute save in the possession of the last end: for as long as something is looked for, the movement of the will remains in suspense, although it has reached something. Thus in local movement, although any point between the two terms is a beginning and an end, yet it is not considered as an actual end, except when the movement stops there.

*Reply Obj.* 1. As Augustine says (*De Doctr. Christ.* i. 33), *if he had said, ' May I enjoy thee,' without adding ' in the Lord,' he would seem to have set the end of his love in him. But since he added that he set his end in the Lord, he implied his desire to enjoy Him :* as if we were to say that he expressed his enjoyment of his brother not as a term but as a means.

*Reply Obj.* 2. Fruit bears one relation to the tree that bore it, and another to man that enjoys it. To the tree indeed that bore it, it is compared as effect to cause; to the one enjoying it, as the final object of his longing and the consummation of his delight. Accordingly these fruits mentioned by the Apostle are so called because they are certain effects of the Holy Ghost in us, wherefore they are called *fruits of the Spirit :* but not as though we are to enjoy them as our last end. Or we may say with Ambrose that they are called fruits because *we should desire them for their own sake*: not indeed as though they were not ordained to the last end; but because they are such that we ought to find pleasure in them.

*Reply Obj.* 3. As stated above (Q. I., A. 8; Q. II., A. 7), we speak of an end in a twofold sense: first, as being the thing itself; secondly, as the attainment thereof. These are not, of course, two ends, but one end, considered in itself, and in its relation to something else. Accordingly God is the last end, as that which is ultimately sought for: while the enjoyment is as the attainment of this last end. And so, just as God is not one end, and the enjoyment of God, another: so it is the same enjoyment whereby we enjoy God, and whereby we enjoy our enjoyment of God. And the same applies to created happiness which consists in enjoyment.

## FOURTH ARTICLE.

### WHETHER ENJOYMENT IS ONLY OF THE END POSSESSED?

*We proceed thus to the Fourth Article :—*

*Objection* 1. It would seem that enjoyment is only of the end possessed. For Augustine says (*De Trin.* x. 11) that *to enjoy is to use joyfully, with the joy, not of hope, but of possession.* But so long as a thing is not had, there is joy, not of possession but of hope. Therefore enjoyment is only of the end possessed.

*Obj.* 2. Further, as stated above (A. 3), enjoyment is not properly otherwise than of the last end: because this alone gives rest to the appetite. But the appetite has no rest save in the possession of the end. Therefore enjoyment, properly speaking, is only of the end possessed.

*Obj.* 3. Further, to enjoy is to lay hold of the fruit. But one does not lay hold of the fruit until one is in possession of the end. Therefore enjoyment is only of the end possessed.

*On the contrary, To enjoy is to adhere lovingly to something for its own sake*, as Augustine says (*De Doctr. Christ.* i. 4). But this is possible, even in regard to a thing which is not in our possession. Therefore it is possible to enjoy the end even though it be not possessed.

*I answer that*, To enjoy implies a certain relation of the will to the last end, according as the will has something by way of last end. Now an end is possessed in two ways; perfectly and imperfectly. Perfectly, when it is possessed not only in intention but also in reality; imperfectly, when it is possessed in intention only. Perfect enjoyment, therefore, is of the end already possessed: but imperfect enjoyment is also of the end possessed not really, but only in intention.

*Reply Obj.* 1. Augustine speaks there of perfect enjoyment.

*Reply Obj.* 2. The will is hindered in two ways from being at rest. First on the part of the object; by reason of its not being the last end, but ordained to something else: secondly on the part of the one who desires the end, by reason of his not being yet in possession of it. Now it is the object that specifies an act: but on the agent depends the manner of acting, so that the act be perfect or imperfect, as compared with the actual circumstances of the agent. Therefore enjoyment of anything but the last end is not enjoyment properly speaking, as falling short of the nature of enjoyment. But enjoyment of the last end, not yet possessed, is enjoyment properly speaking, but imperfect, on account of the imperfect way in which it is possessed.

*Reply Obj.* 3. One is said to lay hold of or to have an end, not only in reality, but also in intention, as stated above.

# QUESTION XII.

## OF INTENTION.

### (*In Five Articles.*)

WE must now consider Intention: concerning which there are five points of inquiry: (1) Whether intention is an act of the intellect or of the will? (2) Whether it is only of the last end? (3) Whether one can intend two things at the same time? (4) Whether intention of the end is the same act as volition of the means? (5) Whether intention is within the competency of irrational animals?

### FIRST ARTICLE.

#### WHETHER INTENTION IS AN ACT OF THE INTELLECT OR OF THE WILL?

*We proceed thus to the First Article :—*

*Objection* 1. It would seem that intention is an act of the intellect, and not of the will. For it is written (Matth. vi. 22): *If thy eye be single, thy whole body shall be lightsome :* where, according to Augustine (*De Serm. Dom. in Monte* ii. 13) the eye signifies intention. But since the eye is the organ of sight, it signifies the apprehensive power. Therefore intention is not an act of the appetitive but of the apprehensive power.

*Obj.* 2. Further, Augustine says (*ibid.*) that Our Lord spoke of intention as a light, when He said (Matth. vi. 23): *If the light that is in thee be darkness*, etc. But light pertains to knowledge. Therefore intention does too.

*Obj.* 3. Further, intention implies a kind of ordaining to an end. But to ordain is an act of reason. Therefore intention belongs not to the will but to the reason.

*Obj.* 4. Further, an act of the will is either of the end or of the means. But the act of the will in respect of the end is called volition, or enjoyment; with regard to the means, it is choice, from which intention is distinct. Therefore it is not an act of the will.

*On the contrary*, Augustine says (*De Trin.* xi. 4, 8, 9) that *the intention of the will unites the sight to the object seen; and the images retained in the memory, to the penetrating gaze of the soul's inner thought.* Therefore intention is an act of the will.

*I answer that*, Intention, as the very word denotes, signifies, *to tend to something.* Now both the action of the mover and the movement of the thing moved, tend to something. But that the movement of the thing moved tends to anything, is due to the action of the mover. Consequently intention belongs first and principally to that which moves to the end: hence we say that an architect or anyone who is in authority, by his command moves others to that which he intends. Now the will moves all the other powers of the soul to the end, as shown above (Q. IX., A. 1). Wherefore it is evident that intention, properly speaking, is an act of the will.

*Reply Obj.* 1. The eye designates intention figuratively, not because intention has reference to knowledge, but because it presupposes knowledge, which proposes to the will the end to which the latter moves; thus we foresee with the eye whither we should tend with our bodies.

*Reply Obj.* 2. Intention is called a light because it is manifest to him who intends. Wherefore works are called darkness, because a man knows what he intends, but knows not what the result may be, as Augustine expounds (*loc. cit.*).

*Reply Obj.* 3. The will does not ordain, but tends to something according to the order of reason. Consequently this word *intention* indicates an act of the will, presupposing the act whereby the reason orders something to the end.

*Reply Obj.* 4. Intention is an act of the will in regard to the end. Now the will stands in a threefold relation to the end. First, absolutely; and thus we have *volition*, whereby we will absolutely to have health and so forth. Secondly, it considers the end, as its place of rest; and thus *enjoyment* regards the end.  Thirdly, it considers the end as the term towards which something is ordained; and thus *intention* regards the end.  For when we speak of intending to have health, we mean not only that we will to have it, but that we will to have it by means of something else.

### Second Article.

#### WHETHER INTENTION IS ONLY OF THE LAST END?

*We proceed thus to the Second Article :—*

*Objection* 1.  It would seem that intention is only of the last end.  For it is said in the book of Prosper's *Sentences* (*Sent.* 100): *The intention of the heart is a cry to God*.  But God is the last end of the human heart.  Therefore intention always regards the last end.

*Obj.* 2.  Further, intention regards the end as the terminus, as stated above (A. 1 *ad* 4).  But a terminus is something last.  Therefore intention always regards the last end.

*Obj.* 3. Further, just as intention regards the end, so does enjoyment.  But enjoyment is always of the last end. Therefore intention is too.

*On the contrary*, There is but one last end of human wills, viz., Happiness, as stated above (Q. I., A. 7).  If, therefore, intentions were only of the last end, men would not have different intentions: which is evidently false.

*I answer that*, As stated above (A. 1 *ad* 4), intention regards the end as a terminus of the movement of the will. Now a terminus of movement may be taken in two ways. First, the very last terminus, when the movement comes to a stop; this is the terminus of the whole movement. Secondly, some point midway, which is the beginning of one part of the movement, and the end or terminus of the other. Thus in the movement from A to C through B, C is the last terminus, while B is a terminus, but not the last.  And intention can be of both.  Consequently though intention is always of the end, it need not be always of the last end.

*Reply Obj.* 1.  The intention of the heart is called a cry to God, not that God is always the object of intention, but because He sees our intention.—Or because, when we pray, we direct our intention to God, which intention has the force of a cry.

*Reply Obj.* 2. A terminus is something last, not always in respect of the whole, but sometimes in respect of a part.

*Reply Obj.* 3. Enjoyment implies rest in the end; and this belongs to the last end alone. But intention implies movement towards an end, not rest. Wherefore the comparison proves nothing.

### THIRD ARTICLE.

#### WHETHER ONE CAN INTEND TWO THINGS AT THE SAME TIME?

*We proceed thus to the Third Article :—*

*Objection* 1. It would seem that one cannot intend several things at the same time. For Augustine says (*De Serm. Dom. in Monte* ii. 14, 16, 17) that man's intention cannot be directed at the same time to God and to bodily benefits. Therefore, for the same reason, neither to any other two things.

*Obj.* 2. Further, intention designates a movement of the will towards a terminus. Now there cannot be several termini in the same direction of one movement. Therefore the will cannot intend several things at the same time.

*Obj.* 3. Further, intention presupposes an act of reason or of the intellect. But *it is not possible to understand several things at the same time*, according to the Philosopher (*Topic.* ii. 10). Therefore neither is it possible to intend several things at the same time.

*On the contrary,* Art imitates nature. Now nature intends two purposes by means of one instrument: thus *the tongue is for the purpose of taste and speech* (*De Anima* ii. 8). Therefore, for the same reason, art or reason can at the same time direct one thing to two ends: so that one can intend several ends at the same time.

*I answer that,* The expression *two things* may be taken in two ways: they may be ordained to one another or not so ordained. And if they be ordained to one another, it is evident, from what has been said, that a man can intend

several things at the same time.   For intention is not only of
the last end, as stated above (A. 2), but also of an inter-
mediary end.   Now a man intends at the same time, both
the proximate and the last end; as the mixing of a medicine
and the giving of health.

But if we take two things that are not ordained to one
another, thus also a man can intend several things at the
same time.   This is evident from the fact that a man prefers
one thing to another because it is the better of the two.   Now
one of the reasons for which one thing is better than another
is that it is available for more purposes: wherefore one thing
can be chosen in preference to another, because of the greater
number of purposes for which it is available: so that evidently a man can intend several things at the same time.

*Reply Obj.* 1. Augustine means to say that man cannot
at the same time direct his intention to God and to bodily
benefits, as to two last ends: since, as stated above (Q. I.,
A. 5), one man cannot have several last ends.

*Reply Obj.* 2. There can be several termini ordained to
one another, of the same movement and in the same direction;
but not unless they be ordained to one another.   At the same
time it must be observed that what is not one in reality may
be taken as one by the reason.   Now intention is a movement of the will to something already ordained by the
reason, as stated above (A. 1 *ad* 3).   Wherefore where we
have many things in reality, we may take them as one term
of intention, in so far as the reason takes them as one:
either because two things concur in the integrity of one
whole, as a proper measure of heat and cold conduce to
health: or because two things are included in one which may
be intended.   For instance, the acquiring of wine and clothing
is included in wealth, as in something common to both;
wherefore nothing hinders the man who intends to acquire
wealth, from intending both the others.

*Reply Obj.* 3. As stated in the First Part (Q. XII., A. 10;
Q. LVIII., A. 2; Q. LXXXV., A. 4), it is possible to understand several things at the same time, in so far as, in some
way, they are one.

## FOURTH ARTICLE.

### WHETHER INTENTION OF THE END IS THE SAME ACT AS THE VOLITION OF THE MEANS?

*We proceed thus to the Fourth Article :—*

*Objection* 1. It would seem that the intention of the end and the volition of the means are not one and the same movement. For Augustine says (*De Trin.* xi. 6) that *the will to see the window, has for its end the seeing of the window ; and is another act from the will to see, through the window, the passers-by.* But that I should will to see the passers-by, through the window, belongs to intention; whereas that I will to see the window, belongs to the volition of the means. Therefore intention of the end and the willing of the means are distinct movements of the will.

*Obj.* 2. Further, acts are distinct according to their objects. But the end and the means are distinct objects. Therefore the intention of the end and the willing of the means are distinct movements of the will.

*Obj.* 3. Further, the willing of the means is called choice. But choice and intention are not the same. Therefore intention of the end and the willing of the means are not the same movement of the will.

*On the contrary,* The means in relation to the end, are as the mid-space to the terminus. Now it is all the same movement that passes through the mid-space to the terminus, in natural things. Therefore in things pertaining to the will, the intention of the end is the same movement as the willing of the means.

*I answer that,* The movement of the will to the end and to the means can be considered in two ways. First, according as the will is moved to each of the aforesaid absolutely and in itself. And thus there are really two movements of the will to them. Secondly, it may be considered accordingly as the will is moved to the means for the sake of the end: and thus the movement of the will to the end and its movement to the means are one and the same thing. For when I say:

*I wish to take medicine for the sake of health,* I signify no more than one movement of my will. And this is because the end is the reason for willing the means. Now the object, and that by reason of which it is an object, come under the same act; thus it is the same act of sight that perceives colour and light, as stated above (Q. VIII., A. 3 *ad* 2). And the same applies to the intellect; for if it consider principle and conclusion absolutely, it considers each by a distinct act; but when it assents to the conclusion on account of the principles, there is but one act of the intellect.

*Reply Obj.* 1. Augustine is speaking of seeing the window and of seeing, through the window, the passers-by, according as the will is moved to either absolutely.

*Reply Obj.* 2. The end, considered as a thing, and the means to that end, are distinct objects of the will. But in so far as the end is the formal object in willing the means, they are one and the same object.

*Reply Obj.* 3. A movement which is one as to the subject, may differ, according to our way of looking at it, as to its beginning and end, as in the case of ascent and descent (*Physic.* iii. 3). Accordingly, in so far as the movement of the will is to the means, as ordained to the end, it is called *choice :* but the movement of the will to the end as acquired by the means, is called *intention.* A sign of this is that we can have intention of the end without having determined the means which are the object of choice.

### Fifth Article.

#### WHETHER INTENTION IS WITHIN THE COMPETENCY OF IRRATIONAL ANIMALS ?

*We proceed thus to the Fifth Article :—*

*Objection* 1. It would seem that irrational animals intend the end. For in things void of reason nature stands further apart from the rational nature, than does the sensitive nature in irrational animals. But nature intends the end even in things void of reason, as is proved in *Phys.* ii. 8.

Much more, therefore, do irrational animals intend the end.

*Obj.* 2. Further, just as intention is of the end, so is enjoyment. But enjoyment is in irrational animals, as stated above (Q. XI., A. 2). Therefore intention is too.

*Obj.* 3. Further, to intend an end belongs to one who acts for an end; since to intend is nothing else than to tend to something. But irrational animals act for an end; for an animal is moved either to seek food, or to do something of the kind. Therefore irrational animals intend an end.

*On the contrary*, Intention of an end implies ordaining something to an end: which belongs to reason. Since therefore irrational animals are void of reason, it seems that they do not intend an end.

*I answer that*, As stated above (A. 1), to intend is to tend to something; and this belongs to the mover and to the moved. According, therefore, as that which is moved to an end by another is said to intend the end, thus nature is said to intend an end, as being moved to its end by God, as the arrow is moved by the archer. And in this way, irrational animals intend an end, inasmuch as they are moved to something by natural instinct.—The other way of intending an end belongs to the mover; according as he ordains the movement of something, either his own or another's, to an end. This belongs to reason alone. Wherefore irrational animals do not intend an end in this way, which is to intend properly and principally, as stated above (A. 1).

*Reply Obj.* 1. This argument takes intention in the sense of being moved to an end.

*Reply Obj.* 2. Enjoyment does not imply the ordaining of one thing to another, as intention does, but absolute repose in the end.

*Reply Obj.* 3. Irrational animals are moved to an end, not as though they thought that they can gain the end by this movement; this belongs to one that intends; but through desiring the end by natural instinct, they are moved to an end, moved, as it were, by another, like other things that are moved naturally.

# QUESTION XIII.

## OF CHOICE, WHICH IS AN ACT OF THE WILL WITH REGARD TO THE MEANS.

### (*In Six Articles.*)

WE must now consider the acts of the will with regard to the means. There are three of them: to choose, to consent, and to use. And choice is preceded by counsel. First of all, then, we must consider choice; secondly, counsel; thirdly, consent; fourthly, use.

Concerning choice there are six points of inquiry: (1) Of what power is it the act; of the will or of the reason? (2) Whether choice is to be found in irrational animals? (3) Whether choice is only of the means, or sometimes also of the end? (4) Whether choice is only of things that we do ourselves? (5) Whether choice is only of possible things? (6) Whether man chooses of necessity or freely?

## FIRST ARTICLE.

### WHETHER CHOICE IS AN ACT OF WILL OR OF REASON?

*Objection* 1. It would seem that choice is an act, not of will but of reason. For choice implies comparison, whereby one is given preference to another. But to compare is an act of reason. Therefore choice is an act of reason.

*Obj.* 2. Further, it is for the same faculty to form a syllogism, and to draw the conclusion. But, in practical matters, it is the reason that forms syllogisms. Since therefore choice is a kind of conclusion in practical matters, as stated in *Ethic.* vii. 3, it seems that it is an act of reason.

*Obj.* 3. Further, ignorance does not belong to the will but to the cognitive power. Now there is an *ignorance of choice*, as is stated in *Ethic.* iii. 1. Therefore it seems that choice does not belong to the will but to the reason.

*On the contrary*, The Philosopher says (*Ethic.* iii. 3) that choice is *the desire of things in our power*. But desire is an act of will. Therefore choice is too.

*I answer that*, The word choice implies something belonging to the reason or intellect, and something belonging to the will: for the Philosopher says (*Ethic.* vi. 2) that choice is either *intellect influenced by appetite or appetite influenced by intellect*. Now whenever two things concur to make one, one of them is formal in regard to the other. Hence Gregory of Nyssa* says that choice *is neither desire only, nor counsel only, but a combination of the two. For just as we say that an animal is composed of soul and body, and that it is neither a mere body, nor a mere soul, but both ; so is it with choice.*

Now we must observe, as regards the acts of the soul, that an act belonging essentially to some power or habit, receives a form or species from a higher power or habit, according as an inferior is ordained by a superior: for if a man were to perform an act of fortitude for the love of God, that act is materially an act of fortitude, but formally, an act of charity. Now it is evident that, in a sense, reason precedes the will and ordains its act: in so far as the will tends to its object, according to the order of reason, since the apprehensive power presents the object to the appetite. Accordingly, that act whereby the will tends to something proposed to it as being good, through being ordained to the end by the reason, is materially an act of the will, but formally an act of the reason. Now in suchlike matters the substance of the act is as the matter in comparison to the order imposed by the higher power. Wherefore choice is substantially not an act of the reason but of the will: for choice is accomplished in a certain movement of the soul towards the good which is chosen. Consequently it is evidently an act of the appetitive power.

*Reply Obj.* 1. Choice implies a previous comparison; not that it consists in the comparison itself.

* Nemesius, *De Nat. Hom.* xxxiii.

*Reply Obj.* 2. It is quite true that it is for the reason to draw the conclusion of a practical syllogism; and it is called *a decision* or *judgment*, to be followed by *choice*. And for this reason the conclusion seems to belong to the act of choice, as to that which results from it.

*Reply Obj.* 3. In speaking *of ignorance of choice*, we do not mean that choice is a sort of knowledge, but that there is ignorance of what ought to be chosen.

### SECOND ARTICLE.

#### WHETHER CHOICE IS TO BE FOUND IN IRRATIONAL ANIMALS?

*Objection* 1. It would seem that irrational animals are able to choose. For choice *is the desire of certain things on account of an end*, as stated in *Ethic.* iii. 2, 3. But irrational animals desire something on account of an end: since they act for an end, and from desire. Therefore choice is in irrational animals.

*Obj.* 2. Further, the very word *electio* (choice) seems to signify the taking of something in preference to others. But irrational animals take something in preference to others: thus we can easily see for ourselves that a sheep will eat one grass and refuse another. Therefore choice is in irrational animals.

*Obj.* 3. Further, according to *Ethic.* vi. 12, *it is from prudence that a man makes a good choice of means*. But prudence is found in irrational animals: hence it is said in the beginning of *Metaph.* (i., 1) that *those animals which, like bees, cannot hear sounds, are prudent by instinct*. We see this plainly, in wonderful cases of sagacity manifested in the works of various animals, such as bees, spiders, and dogs. For a hound in following a stag, on coming to a cross road, tries by scent whether the stag has passed by the first or the second road: and if he find that the stag has not passed there, being thus assured, takes to the third road without trying the scent; as though he were reasoning by way of exclusion, arguing that the stag must have passed by this way, since he did not pass by the others, and there is no other road. Therefore it seems that irrational animals are able to choose.

*On the contrary*, Gregory of Nyssa* says that *children and irrational animals act willingly but not from choice.* Therefore choice is not in irrational animals.

*I answer that*, Since choice is the taking of one thing in preference to another, it must of necessity be in respect of several things that can be chosen. Consequently in those things which are altogether determinate to one there is no place for choice. Now the difference between the sensitive appetite and the will is that, as stated above (Q. I., A. 2 *ad* 3), the sensitive appetite is determinate to one particular thing, according to the order of nature; whereas the will, although determinate to one thing in general, viz., the good, according to the order of nature, is nevertheless indeterminate in respect of particular goods. Consequently choice belongs properly to the will, and not to the sensitive appetite which is all that irrational animals have. Wherefore irrational animals are not competent to choose.

*Reply Obj.* 1. Not every desire of one thing on account of an end is called choice: there must be a certain discrimination of one thing from another. And this cannot be except when the appetite can be moved to several things.

*Reply Obj.* 2. An irrational animal takes one thing in preference to another, because its appetite is naturally determinate to that thing. Wherefore as soon as an animal, whether by its sense or by its imagination, is offered something to which its appetite is naturally inclined, it is moved to that alone, without making any choice. Just as fire is moved upwards and not downwards, without its making any choice.

*Reply Obj.* 3. As stated in *Phys.* iii. 3 *movement is the act of the movable, caused by a mover.* Wherefore the power of the mover appears in the movement of that which it moves. Accordingly, in all things moved by reason, the order of reason which moves them is evident, although the things

* Nemesius, *De Nat. Hom.* xxxiii.

themselves are without reason: for an arrow through the motion of the archer goes straight towards the target, as though it were endowed with reason to direct its course. The same may be seen in the movements of clocks and all engines put together by the art of man. Now as artificial things are in comparison to human art, so are all natural things in comparison to the Divine art. And accordingly order is to be seen in things moved by nature, just as in things moved by reason, as is stated in *Phys.* ii. And thus it is that in the works of irrational animals we notice certain marks of sagacity, in so far as they have a natural inclination to set about their actions in a most orderly manner through being ordained by the Supreme art. For which reason, too, certain animals are called prudent or sagacious; and not because they reason or exercise any choice about things. This is clear from the fact that all that share in one nature, invariably act in the same way.

## Third Article.

### WHETHER CHOICE IS ONLY OF THE MEANS, OR SOMETIMES ALSO OF THE END ?

*We proceed thus to the Third Article :—*

*Objection* 1. It would seem that choice is not only of the means. For the Philosopher says (*Ethic.* vi. 12) that *virtue makes us choose aright ; but it is not the part of virtue, but of some other power to direct aright those things which are to be done for its sake.* But that for the sake of which something is done is the end. Therefore choice is of the end.

*Obj.* 2. Further, choice implies preference of one thing to another. But just as there can be preference of means, so can there be preference of ends. Therefore choice can be of ends, just as it can be of means.

*On the contrary,* The Philosopher says (*Ethic.* iii. 2) that *volition is of the end, but choice of the means.*

*I answer that,* As already stated (A. 1 *ad* 2), choice results from the decision or judgment which is, as it were, the conclusion of a practical syllogism. Hence that which is the conclusion of a practical syllogism, is the matter of choice. Now in practical things the end stands in the position of a principle, not of a conclusion, as the Philosopher says (*Phys*. ii. 9). Wherefore the end, as such, is not a matter of choice.

But just as in speculative knowledge nothing hinders the principle of one demonstration or of one science, from being the conclusion of another demonstration or science; while the first indemonstrable principle cannot be the conclusion of any demonstration or science; so too that which is the end in one operation, may be ordained to something as an end. And in this way it is a matter of choice. Thus in the work of a physician health is the end: wherefore it is not a matter of choice for a physician, but a matter of principle. Now the health of the body is ordained to the good of the soul, consequently with one who has charge of the soul's health, health or sickness may be a matter of choice; for the Apostle says (2 Cor. xii. 10): *For when I am weak, then am I powerful.* But the last end is nowise a matter of choice.

*Reply Obj.* 1. The proper ends of virtues are ordained to Happiness as to their last end. And thus it is that they can be a matter of choice.

*Reply Obj.* 2. As stated above (Q. I., A. 5), there is but one last end. Accordingly wherever there are several ends, they can be the subject of choice, in so far as they are ordained to a further end.

# FOURTH ARTICLE.

## WHETHER CHOICE IS OF THOSE THINGS ONLY THAT ARE DONE BY US?

*We proceed thus to the Fourth Article :—*

*Objection* 1. It would seem that choice is not only in respect of human acts. For choice regards the means. Now, not only acts, but also the organs, are means (*Phys*. ii. 3). Therefore choice is not only concerned with human acts.

*Obj.* 2. Further, action is distinct from contemplation. But choice has a place even in contemplation; in so far as one opinion is preferred to another. Therefore choice is not concerned with human acts alone.

*Obj.* 3. Further, men are chosen for certain posts, whether secular or ecclesiastical, by those who exercise no action in their regard. Therefore choice is not concerned with human acts alone.

*On the contrary*, The Philosopher says (*Ethic*. iii. 2) that *no man chooses save what he thinks he can do himself.*

*I answer that*, Just as intention regards the end, so does choice regard the means. Now the end is either an action or a thing. And when the end is a thing, some human action must intervene; either in so far as man produces the thing which is the end, as the physician produces health (wherefore the production of health is said to be the end of the physician); or in so far as man, in some fashion, uses or enjoys the thing which is the end; thus for the miser, money or the possession of money is the end. The same is to be said of the means. For the means must needs be either an action; or a thing, with some action intervening whereby man either makes the thing which is the means, or puts it to some use. And thus it is that choice is always in regard to human acts.

*Reply Obj.* 1. The organs are ordained to the end, inasmuch as man makes use of them for the sake of the end.

*Reply Obj.* 2. In contemplation itself there is the act of the intellect assenting to this or that opinion. It is exterior action that is put in contradistinction to contemplation.

*Reply Obj.* 3. When a man chooses someone for a bishopric or some high position in the state, he chooses to name that man to that post. Else, if he had no right to act in the appointment of the bishop or official, he would have no right to choose. Likewise, whenever we speak of one thing being chosen in preference to another, it is in conjunction with some action of the chooser.

## Fifth Article.

### WHETHER CHOICE IS ONLY OF POSSIBLE THINGS?

*We proceed thus to the Fifth Article :—*

*Objection* 1. It would seem that choice is not only of possible things. For choice is an act of the will, as stated above (A. 1). Now *there is a willing of impossibilities* (*Ethic.* iii. 2). Therefore there is also a choice of impossibilities.

*Obj.* 2. Further, choice is of things done by us, as stated above (A. 4). Therefore it matters not, as far as the act of choosing is concerned, whether one choose that which is impossible in itself, or that which is impossible to the chooser. Now it often happens that we are unable to accomplish what we choose: so that this proves to be impossible to us. Therefore choice is of the impossible.

*Obj.* 3. Further, to try to do a thing is to choose to do it. But the Blessed Benedict says (*Regula*, lxviii.) that if the superior command what is impossible, it should be attempted. Therefore choice can be of the impossible.

*On the contrary*, The Philosopher says (*Ethic.* iii. *loc. cit.*) that *there is no choice of impossibilities.*

*I answer that*, As stated above (A. 4), our choice is always concerned with our actions. Now whatever is done by us, is possible to us. Therefore we must needs say that choice is only of possible things.

Moreover, the reason for choosing a thing is that it conduces to an end. But what is impossible cannot conduce to an end. A sign of this is that when men in taking counsel together come to something that is impossible to them, they depart, as being unable to proceed with the business.

Again, this is evident if we examine the previous process of the reason. For the means, which are the object of choice, are to the end, as the conclusion is to the principle. Now it is clear that an impossible conclusion does not follow from a possible principle. Wherefore an end cannot be possible, unless the means be possible. Now no one is moved to the impossible. Consequently no one would tend to the end, save for the fact that the means appear to be possible. Therefore the impossible is not the object of choice.

*Reply Obj.* 1. The will stands between the intellect and the external action: for the intellect proposes to the will its object, and the will causes the external action. Hence the principle of the movement in the will is to be found in the intellect, which apprehends something under the universal notion of good: but the term or perfection of the will's act is to be observed in its relation to the action whereby a man tends to the attainment of a thing; for the movement of the will is from the soul to the thing. Consequently the perfect act of the will is in respect of something that is good for one to do. Now this cannot be something impossible. Wherefore the complete act of the will is only in respect of what is possible and good for him that wills. But the incomplete act of the will is in respect of the impossible; and by some is called *velleity*, because, to wit, one would will (*vellet*) such a thing, were it possible. But choice is an act of the will, fixed on something to be done by the chooser. And therefore it is by no means of anything but what is possible.

*Reply Obj.* 2. Since the object of the will is the apprehended good, we must judge of the object of the will according as it is apprehended. And so, just as sometimes the will tends to something which is apprehended as good, and yet is not really good; so is choice sometimes made of something apprehended as possible to the chooser, and yet impossible to him.

*Reply Obj.* 3. The reason for this is that the subject should not rely on his own judgment to decide whether a certain thing is possible ; but in each case should stand by his superior's judgment.

## SIXTH ARTICLE.

### WHETHER MAN CHOOSES OF NECESSITY OR FREELY?

*We proceed thus to the Sixth Article :—*

*Objection* 1. It would seem that man chooses of necessity. For the end stands in relation to the object of choice, as the principle to that which follows from the principles, as declared in *Ethic.* vii. 8. But conclusions follow of necessity from their principles. Therefore man is moved of necessity from (willing) the end to the choice (of the means).

*Obj.* 2. Further, as stated above (A. 1 *ad* 2), choice follows the reason's judgment of what is to be done. But reason judges of necessity about some things: on account of the necessity of the premises. Therefore it seems that choice also follows of necessity.

*Obj.* 3. Further, if two things are absolutely equal, man is not moved to one more than to the other; thus if a hungry man, as Plato says (*cf. De Cælo* ii. 13), be confronted on either side with two portions of food equally appetizing and at an equal distance, he is not moved towards one more than to the other; and he finds the reason of this in the immobility of the earth in the middle of the world. Now, if that which is equally (eligible) with something else cannot be chosen, much less can that be chosen which appears as less (eligible). Therefore if two or more things are available, of which one appears to be more (eligible), it is impossible to choose any of the others. Therefore that which appears to hold the first place is chosen of necessity. But every act of choosing is in regard to something that seems in some way better. Therefore every choice is made necessarily.

*On the contrary*, Choice is an act of a rational power; which according to the Philosopher (*Metaph.* ix. 2) stands in relation to opposites.

*I answer that*, Man does not choose of necessity. And this is because that which is possible not to be, is not of necessity. Now the reason why it is possible not to choose, or to choose, may be gathered from a twofold power in man. For man can will and not will, act and not act; again, he can

will this or that, and do this or that.   The reason of this
is seated in the very power of the reason.   For the will can
tend to whatever the reason can apprehend as good.   Now
the reason can apprehend as good, not only this, viz., *to will*
or *to act*, but also this, viz., *not to will* or *not to act*.   Again,
in all particular goods, the reason can consider an aspect of
some good, and the lack of some good, which has the aspect
of evil: and in this respect, it can apprehend any single one
of such goods as to be chosen or to be avoided.   The perfect good alone, which is Happiness, cannot be apprehended
by the reason as an evil, or as lacking in any way.   Consequently man wills Happiness of necessity, nor can he will
not to be happy, or to be unhappy.   Now since choice is not
of the end, but of the means, as stated above (A. 3); it is not
of the perfect good, which is Happiness, but of other particular goods.   Therefore man chooses not of necessity, but
freely.

*Reply Obj.* 1.   The conclusion does not always of necessity
follow from the principles, but only when the principles
cannot be true if the conclusion is not true.   In like manner,
the end does not always necessitate in man the choosing of
the means, because the means are not always such that the
end cannot be gained without them; or, if they be such, they
are not always considered in that light.

*Reply Obj.* 2.   The reason's decision or judgment of what
is to be done is about things that are contingent and possible
to us.   In such matters the conclusions do not follow of
necessity from principles that are absolutely necessary, but
from such as are so conditionally; as, for instance, *If he runs,
he is in motion.*

*Reply Obj.* 3.   If two things be proposed as equal under
one aspect, nothing hinders us from considering in one of
them some particular point of superiority, so that the will
has a bent towards that one rather than towards the other.

# QUESTION XIV.

## OF COUNSEL, WHICH PRECEDES CHOICE.

### (*In Six Articles.*)

WE must now consider counsel; concerning which there are six points of inquiry: (1) Whether counsel is an inquiry? (2) Whether counsel is of the end or of the means? (3) Whether counsel is only of things that we do? (4) Whether counsel is of all things that we do? (5) Whether the process of counsel is one of analysis? (6) Whether the process of counsel is indefinite?

### FIRST ARTICLE.

#### WHETHER COUNSEL IS AN INQUIRY?

*We proceed thus to the First Article :—*

*Objection* 1. It would seem that counsel is not an inquiry. For Damascene says (*De Fide Orthod.* ii. 22) that counsel is *an act of the appetite.* But inquiry is not an act of the appetite. Therefore counsel is not an inquiry.

*Obj.* 2. Further, inquiry is a discursive act of the intellect: for which reason it is not found in God, Whose knowledge is not discursive, as we have shown in the First Part (Q. XIV., A. 7). But counsel is ascribed to God: for it is written (Eph. i. 11) that *He worketh all things according to the counsel of His will.* Therefore counsel is not inquiry.

*Obj.* 3. Further, inquiry is of doubtful matters. But counsel is given in matters that are certainly good; thus the Apostle says (1 Cor. vii. 25): *Now concerning virgins I have no commandment of the Lord : but I give counsel.* Therefore, counsel is not an inquiry.

169

*On the contrary,* Gregory of Nyssa* says: *Every counsel is an inquiry ; but not every inquiry is a counsel.*

*I answer that,* Choice, as stated above (Q. XIII., A. 1 *ad* 2; A. 3), follows the judgment of the reason about what is to be done. Now there is much uncertainty in things that have to be done; because actions are concerned with contingent singulars, which by reason of their vicissitude, are uncertain. Now in things doubtful and uncertain the reason does not pronounce judgment, without previous inquiry: wherefore the reason must of necessity institute an inquiry before deciding on the objects of choice; and this inquiry is called counsel. Hence the Philosopher says (*Ethic.* iii. 2) that choice is the *desire of what has been already counselled.*

*Reply Obj.* 1. When the acts of two powers are ordained to one another, in each of them there is something belonging to the other power: consequently each act can be denominated from either power. Now it is evident that the act of the reason giving direction as to the means, and the act of the will tending to these means according to the reason's direction, are ordained to one another. Consequently there is to be found something of the reason, viz., order, in that act of the will, which is choice: and in counsel, which is an act of reason, something of the will,—both as matter (since counsel is of what man wills to do),—and as motive (because it is from willing the end, that man is moved to take counsel in regard to the means). And therefore, just as the Philosopher says (*Ethic.* vi. 2) that choice is *intellect influenced by appetite,* thus pointing out that both concur in the act of choosing; so Damascene says (*loc. cit.*) that counsel is *appetite based on inquiry,* so as to show that counsel belongs, in a way, both to the will, on whose behalf and by whose impulsion the inquiry is made, and to the reason that executes the inquiry.

*Reply Obj.* 2. The things that we say of God must be understood without any of the defects which are to be found in us: thus in us science is of conclusions derived by reason-

* Nemesius, *De Nat. Hom.* xxxiv.

ing from causes to effects: but science when said of God, means sure knowledge of all effects in the First Cause, without any reasoning process. In like manner we ascribe counsel to God, as to the certainty of His knowledge or judgment, which certainty in us arises from the inquiry of counsel. But such inquiry has no place in God; wherefore in this respect it is not ascribed to God: in which sense Damascene says (*loc. cit.*): *God takes not counsel: those only take counsel who lack knowledge.*

*Reply Obj.* 3. It may happen that things which are most certainly good in the opinion of wise and spiritual men are not certainly good in the opinion of many, or at least of carnal-minded men. Consequently in such things counsel may be given.

## SECOND ARTICLE.

### WHETHER COUNSEL IS OF THE END, OR ONLY OF THE MEANS?

*We proceed thus to the Second Article :—*

*Objection* 1. It would seem that counsel is not only of the means but also of the end. For whatever is doubtful, can be the subject of inquiry. Now in things to be done by man there happens sometimes a doubt as to the end and not only as to the means. Since therefore inquiry as to what is to be done is counsel, it seems that counsel can be of the end.

*Obj.* 2. Further, the matter of counsel is human actions. But some human actions are ends, as stated in *Ethic.* i. 1. Therefore counsel can be of the end.

*On the contrary*, Gregory of Nyssa* says that *counsel is not of the end, but of the means.*

*I answer that,* The end is the principle in practical matters: because the reason of the means is to be found in the end. Now the principle cannot be called in question, but must be presupposed in every inquiry. Since therefore counsel is an inquiry, it is not of the end, but only of the means. Nevertheless it may happen that what is the end in regard to some things, is ordained to something else; just as also what is the principle of one demonstration, is the conclusion of

* Nemesius, *De Nat. Hom.* xxxiv.

another: and consequently that which is looked upon as the end in one inquiry, may be looked upon as the means in another; and thus it will become an object of counsel.

*Reply Obj.* 1. That which is looked upon as an end, is already fixed: consequently as long as there is any doubt about it, it is not looked upon as an end. Wherefore if counsel is taken about it, it will be counsel not about the end, but about the means.

*Reply Obj.* 2. Counsel is about operations, in so far as they are ordained to some end. Consequently if any human act be an end, it will not, as such, be the matter of counsel.

## THIRD ARTICLE.

### WHETHER COUNSEL IS ONLY OF THINGS THAT WE DO?

*We proceed thus to the Third Article :—*

*Objection* 1. It would seem that counsel is not only of things that we do. For counsel implies some kind of conference. But it is possible for many to confer about things that are not subject to movement, and are not the result of our actions, such as the natures of various things. Therefore counsel is not only of things that we do.

*Obj.* 2. Further, men sometimes seek counsel about things that are laid down by law; hence we speak of counsel at law. And yet those who seek counsel thus, have nothing to do in making the laws. Therefore counsel is not only of things that we do.

*Obj.* 3. Further, some are said to take consultation about future events; which, however, are not in our power. Therefore counsel is not only of things that we do.

*Obj.* 4. Further, if counsel were only of things that we do, no one would take counsel about what another does. But this is clearly untrue. Therefore counsel is not only of things that we do.

*On the contrary*, Gregory of Nyssa* says: *We take counsel of things that are within our competency and that we are able to do.*

* Nemesius, *De Nat. Hom.* xxxiv.

*I answer that,* Counsel properly implies a conference held between several; the very word (*consilium*) denotes this, for it means a sitting together (*considium*), from the fact that many sit together in order to confer with one another. Now we must take note that in contingent particular cases, in order that anything be known for certain, it is necessary to take several conditions or circumstances into consideration, which it is not easy for one to consider, but are considered by several with greater certainty, since what one takes note of, escapes the notice of another; whereas in necessary and universal things, our view is brought to bear on matters much more absolute and simple, so that one man by himself may be sufficient to consider these things. Wherefore the inquiry of counsel is concerned, properly speaking, with contingent singulars. Now the knowledge of the truth in such matters does not rank so high as to be desirable of itself, as is the knowledge of things universal and necessary; but it is desired as being useful towards action, because actions bear on things singular and contingent. Consequently, properly speaking, counsel is about things done by us.

*Reply Obj.* 1. Counsel implies conference, not of any kind, but about what is to be done, for the reason given above.

*Reply Obj.* 2. Although that which is laid down by the law is not due to the action of him who seeks counsel, nevertheless it directs him in his action: since the mandate of the law is one reason for doing something.

*Reply Obj.* 3. Counsel is not only about what is done, but also about whatever has relation to what is done. And for this reason we speak of consulting about future events, in so far as man is induced to do or omit something, through the knowledge of future events.

*Reply Obj.* 4. We seek counsel about the actions of others, in so far as they are, in some way, one with us; either by union of affection—thus a man is solicitous about what concerns his friend, as though it concerned himself; or after the manner of an instrument, for the principal agent and the instrument are, in a way, one cause, since one acts through the other; thus the master takes counsel about what he would do through his servant.

## FOURTH ARTICLE.

### WHETHER COUNSEL IS ABOUT ALL THINGS THAT WE DO ?

*We proceed thus to the Fourth Article :—*

*Objection* 1. It would seem that counsel is about all things that we have to do.   For choice is the *desire of what is counselled* as stated above (A. 1).   But choice is about all things that we do.   Therefore counsel is too.

*Obj.* 2. Further, counsel implies the reason's inquiry.   But, whenever we do not act through the impulse of passion, we act in virtue of the reason's inquiry.   Therefore there is counsel about everything that we do.

*Obj.* 3. Further, the Philosopher says (*Ethic.* iii. 3) that *if it appears that something can be done by more means than one, we take counsel by inquiring whereby it may be done most easily and best ; but if it can be accomplished by one means, how it can be done by this*.   But whatever is done, is done by one means or by several.   Therefore counsel takes place in all things that we do.

*On the contrary*, Gregory of Nyssa* says that *counsel has no place in things that are done according to science or art*.

*I answer that*, Counsel is a kind of inquiry, as stated above (A. 1).   But we are wont to inquire about things that admit of doubt; hence the process of inquiry, which is called an argument, *is a reason that attests something that admitted of doubt*.†   Now, that something in relation to human acts admits of no doubt, arises from a twofold source.   First, because certain determinate ends are gained by certain determinate means: as happens in the arts which are governed by certain fixed rules of action; thus a writer does not take counsel how to form his letters, for this is determined by art.—Secondly, from the fact that it little matters whether it is done this or that way; this occurs in minute matters,

* Nemesius, *De Nat. Hom.* xxxiv.       † Cicero, *Topic. ad Trebat.*

which help or hinder but little with regard to the end aimed at; and reason looks upon small things as mere nothings. Consequently there are two things of which we do not take counsel, although they conduce to the end, as the Philosopher says (*Ethic.* iii. 3): namely, minute things, and those which have a fixed way of being done, as in works produced by art, with the exception of those arts that admit of conjecture such as medicine, commerce, and the like, as Gregory of Nyssa* says.

*Reply Obj.* 1. Choice presupposes counsel by reason of its judgment or decision. Consequently when the judgment or decision is evident without inquiry, there is no need for the inquiry of counsel.

*Reply Obj.* 2. In matters that are evident, the reason makes no inquiry, but judges at once. Consequently there is no need of counsel in all that is done by reason.

*Reply Obj.* 3. When a thing can be accomplished by one means, but in different ways, doubt may arise, just as when it can be accomplished by several means: hence the need of counsel. But when not only the means, but also the way of using the means, is fixed, then there is no need of counsel.

## FIFTH ARTICLE.

### WHETHER THE PROCESS OF COUNSEL IS ONE OF ANALYSIS?

*We proceed thus to the Fifth Article :—*

*Objection* 1. It would seem that the process of counsel is not one of analysis. For counsel is about things that we do. But the process of our actions is not one of analysis, but rather one of synthesis, viz., from the simple to the composite. Therefore counsel does not always proceed by way of analysis.

*Obj.* 2. Further, counsel is an inquiry of the reason. But reason proceeds from things that precede to things that follow, according to the more appropriate order. Since then, the past precedes the present, and the present precedes the future, it seems that in taking counsel one should pro-

* Nemesius, *loc. cit.*

ceed from the past and present to the future: which is not
an analytical process.   Therefore the process of counsel is
not one of analysis.

*Obj.* 3. Further, counsel is only of such things as are possible to us, according to *Ethic.* iii. 3.   But the question as to
whether a certain thing is possible to us, depends on what
we are able or unable to do, in order to gain such and such
an end. Therefore the inquiry of counsel should begin
from things present.

*On the contrary*, The Philosopher says (*Ethic.* iii. 3) that *he
who takes counsel seems to inquire and analyze.*

*I answer that*, In every inquiry one must begin from some
principle.   And if this principle precedes both in knowledge
and in being, the process is not analytic, but synthetic:
because to proceed from cause to effect is to proceed syntheti-
cally, since causes are more simple than effects.   But if that
which precedes in knowledge is later in the order of being,
the process is one of analysis, as when our judgment deals
with effects, which by analysis we trace to their simple
causes. Now the principle in the inquiry of counsel is the
end, which precedes indeed in intention, but comes afterwards into execution.   Hence the inquiry of counsel must
needs be one of analysis, beginning, that is to say, from
that which is intended in the future, and continuing until it
arrives at that which is to be done at once.

*Reply Obj.* 1. Counsel is indeed about action.   But actions
take their reason from the end; and consequently the order
of reasoning about actions is contrary to the order of actions.

*Reply Obj.* 2. Reason begins with that which is first
according to reason; but not always with that which is first
in point of time.

*Reply Obj.* 3. We should not want to know whether something to be done for an end be possible, if it were not suitable
for gaining that end.   Hence we must first inquire whether
it be conducive to the end, before considering whether it be
possible.

## Sixth Article.

#### WHETHER THE PROCESS OF COUNSEL IS INDEFINITE ?

*We proceed thus to the Sixth Article :—*

*Objection* 1. It would seem that the process of counsel is indefinite. For counsel is an inquiry about the particular things with which action is concerned. But singulars are infinite. Therefore the process of counsel is indefinite.

*Obj.* 2. Further, the inquiry of counsel has to consider not only what is to be done, but how to avoid obstacles. But every human action can be hindered, and an obstacle can be removed by some human reason. Therefore the inquiry about removing obstacles can go on indefinitely.

*Obj.* 3. Further, the inquiry of demonstrative science does not go on indefinitely, because one can come to principles that are self-evident, which are absolutely certain. But suchlike certainty is not to be had in contingent singulars, which are variable and uncertain. Therefore the inquiry of counsel goes on indefinitely.

*On the contrary,* No one is moved to that which he cannot possibly reach (*De Cœlo* i. 7). But it is impossible to pass through the infinite. If therefore the inquiry of counsel is infinite, no one would begin to take counsel. Which is clearly untrue.

*I answer that,* The inquiry of counsel is actually finite on both sides, on that of its principle and on that of its term. For a twofold principle is available in the inquiry of counsel. One is proper to it, and belongs to the very genus of things pertaining to operation: this is the end which is not the matter of counsel, but is taken for granted as its principle, as stated above (A. 2). The other principle is taken from another genus, so to speak; thus in demonstrative sciences one science postulates certain things from another, without inquiring into them. Now these principles which are taken for granted in the inquiry of counsel are any facts received through the senses—for instance, that this is bread or iron: and also any general statements known either through speculative or through practical science; for instance, that adultery is forbidden by God, or that man cannot live without suitable nourishment. Of such things counsel makes no inquiry.—But the term of inquiry is that which we are able to do at once. For just as the end is considered in the light of a principle, so the means are considered in the light of a conclusion. Wherefore that which presents itself as to be done first, holds the position of an ultimate conclusion whereat the inquiry comes to an end.—Nothing however prevents counsel from being infinite potentially, for as much as an infinite number of things may present themselves to be inquired into by means of counsel.

*Reply Obj.* 1. Singulars are infinite, not actually, but only potentially.

*Reply Obj.* 2. Although human action can be hindered, the hindrance is not always at hand. Consequently it is not always necessary to take counsel about removing the obstacle.

*Reply Obj.* 3. In contingent singulars, something may be taken for certain, not simply, indeed, but for the time being, and as far as it concerns the work to be done. Thus that Socrates is sitting is not a necessary statement; but that he is sitting, as long as he continues to sit, is necessary; and this can be taken for a certain fact.

# QUESTION XV.

## OF CONSENT, WHICH IS AN ACT OF THE WILL IN REGARD TO THE MEANS.

### (*In Four Articles.*)

WE must now consider consent; concerning which there are four points of inquiry: (1) Whether consent is an act of the appetitive or of the apprehensive power? (2) Whether it is to be found in irrational animals? (3) Whether it is directed to the end or to the means? (4) Whether consent to an act belongs to the higher part of the soul only?

## FIRST ARTICLE.

### WHETHER CONSENT IS AN ACT OF THE APPETITIVE OR OF THE APPREHENSIVE POWER?

*We proceed thus to the First Article :—*

*Objection* 1. It would seem that consent belongs only to the apprehensive part of the soul. For Augustine (*De Trin.* xii. 12) ascribes consent to the higher reason. But the reason is an apprehensive power. Therefore consent belongs to an apprehensive power.

*Obj.* 2. Further, consent is *co-sense*. But sense is an apprehensive power. Therefore consent is the act of an apprehensive power.

*Obj.* 3. Further, just as assent is an application of the intellect to something, so is consent. But assent belongs to the intellect, which is an apprehensive power. Therefore consent also belongs to an apprehensive power.

*On the contrary*, Damascene says (*De Fide Orthod.* ii. 22) that *if a man judge without affection for that of which he judges,*

179

*there is no sentence, i.e.* consent. But affection belongs to the appetitive power. Therefore consent does also.

*I answer that*, Consent implies application of sense to something. Now it is proper to sense to take cognizance of things present; for the imagination apprehends the similitude of corporeal things, even in the absence of the things of which they bear the likeness; while the intellect apprehends universal ideas, which it can apprehend indifferently, whether the singulars be present or absent. And since the act of an appetitive power is a kind of inclination to the thing itself, the application of the appetitive power to the thing, in so far as it cleaves to it, gets by a kind of similitude, the name of sense, since, as it were, it acquires direct knowledge of the thing to which it cleaves, in so far as it takes complacency in it. Hence it is written (Wisd. i. 1): *Think of (Sentite) the Lord in goodness.* And on these grounds consent is an act of the appetitive power.

*Reply Obj.* 1. As stated in *De Anima* iii. 9, *the will is in the reason.* Hence, when Augustine ascribes consent to the reason, he takes reason as including the will.

*Reply Obj.* 2. Sense, properly speaking, belongs to the apprehensive faculty; but by way of similitude, in so far as it implies seeking acquaintance, it belongs to the appetitive power, as stated above.

*Reply Obj.* 3. *Assentire (to assent)* is, so to speak, *ad aliud sentire (to feel towards something)*; and thus it implies a certain distance from that to which assent is given. But *consentire* (to consent) is *to feel with*, and this implies a certain union to the object of consent. Hence the will, to which it belongs to tend to the thing itself, is more properly said to consent: whereas the intellect, whose act does not consist in a movement towards the thing, but rather the reverse, as we have stated in the First Part (Q. XVI., A. 1 Q. XXVII., A. 4; Q. LIX., A. 2), is more properly said to assent: although one word is wont to be used for the other.* We may also say that the intellect assents, in so far as it is moved by the will.

* In Latin rather than in English.

## SECOND ARTICLE.

### WHETHER CONSENT IS TO BE FOUND IN IRRATIONAL ANIMALS?

*We proceed thus to the Second Article :—*

*Objection* 1. It would seem that consent is to be found in irrational animals. For consent implies a determination of the appetite to one thing. But the appetite of irrational animals is determinate to one thing. Therefore consent is to be found in irrational animals.

*Obj.* 2. Further, if you remove what is first, you remove what follows. But consent precedes the accomplished act. If therefore there were no consent in irrational animals, there would be no act accomplished; which is clearly false.

*Obj.* 3. Further, men are sometimes said to consent to do something, through some passion; desire, for instance, or anger. But irrational animals act through passion. Therefore they consent.

*On the contrary,* Damascene says (*De Fide Orthod.* ii. 22) that *after judging, man approves and embraces the judgment of his counselling, and this is called the sentence, i.e.,* consent. But counsel is not in irrational animals. Therefore neither is consent.

*I answer that,* Consent, properly speaking, is not in irrational animals. The reason of this is that consent implies an application of the appetitive movement to something as to be done. Now to apply the appetitive movement to the doing of something, belongs to the subject in whose power it is to move the appetite: thus to touch a stone is an action suitable to a stick, but to apply the stick so that it touch the stone, belongs to one who has the power of moving the stick. But irrational animals have not the command of the appetitive movement; for this is in them through natural instinct. Hence in the irrational animal, there is indeed the movement of appetite, but it does not apply that movement to some particular thing. And hence it is that the irrational animal is not properly said to consent: this is proper to the rational nature, which has the command of the appetitive movement, and is able to apply or not to apply it to this or that thing.

*Reply Obj.* 1. In irrational animals the determination of the appetite to a particular thing is merely passive: whereas consent implies a determination of the appetite, which is active rather than merely passive.

*Reply Obj.* 2. If the first be removed, then what follows is removed, provided that, properly speaking, it follow from that only. But if something can follow from several things, it is not removed by the fact that one of them is removed; thus if hardening is the effect of heat and of cold (since bricks are hardened by fire, and frozen water is hardened by the cold), then by removing heat it does not follow that there is no hardening. Now the accomplishment of an act follows not only from consent, but also from the impulse of the appetite, such as is found in irrational animals.

*Reply Obj.* 3. The man who acts through passion is able not to follow the passion: whereas irrational animals have not that power. Hence the comparison fails.

## Third Article.

### WHETHER CONSENT IS DIRECTED TO THE END OR TO THE MEANS ?

*We proceed thus to the Third Article :—*

*Objection* 1. It would seem that consent is directed to the end. Because that on account of which a thing is such is still more such. But it is on account of the end that we consent to the means. Therefore, still more do we consent to the end.

*Obj.* 2. Further, the act of the intemperate man is his end, just as the act of the virtuous man is his end. But the intemperate man consents to his own act. Therefore consent can be directed to the end.

*Obj.* 3. Further, desire of the means is choice, as stated above (Q. XIII., A. 1). If therefore consent were only directed to the means it would nowise differ from choice. And this is proved to be false by the authority of Damascene who says (*De Fide Orthod.* ii. 22) that *after the approval* which

to the speculative reason; which seems to be altogether distinct from the will, which is the principle of human acts. Therefore use is not an act of the will.

*On the contrary,* Augustine says (*De Trin.* x. 11): *To use is to apply something to the purpose of the will.*

*I answer that,* The use of a thing implies the application of that thing to an operation: hence the operation to which we apply a thing is called its use; thus the use of a horse is to ride, and the use of a stick is to strike. Now we apply to an operation not only the interior principles of action, viz., the powers of the soul or the members of the body; as the intellect, to understand; and the eye, to see; but also external things, as a stick, to strike. But it is evident that we do not apply external things to an operation save through the interior principles which are either the powers of the soul, or the habits of those powers, or the organs which are parts of the body. Now it has been shown above (Q. IX., A. 1) that it is the will which moves the soul's powers to their acts, and this is to apply them to operation. Hence it is evident that first and principally use belongs to the will as first mover; to the reason, as directing; and to the other powers as executing the operation, which powers are compared to the will which applies them to act, as the instruments are compared to the principal agent. Now action is properly ascribed, not to the instrument, but to the principal agent, as building is ascribed to the builder, but not to his tools. Hence it is evident that use is, properly speaking, an act of the will.

*Reply Obj.* 1. Reason does indeed refer one thing to another; but the will tends to that which is referred by the reason to something else. And in this sense to use is to refer one thing to another.

*Reply Obj.* 2. Damascene is speaking of use in so far as it belongs to the executive powers.

*Reply Obj.* 3. Even the speculative reason is applied by the will to the act of understanding or judging. Consequently the speculative reason is said to use, in so far as it is moved by the will, in the same way as the other powers.

## Second Article.

#### WHETHER USE IS TO BE FOUND IN IRRATIONAL ANIMALS ?

*We proceed thus to the Second Article :—*

*Objection* 1. It would seem that use is to be found in irrational animals. For it is better to enjoy than to use, because, as Augustine says (*De Trin.* x. 10): *We use things by referring them to something else which we are to enjoy.* But enjoyment is to be found in irrational animals, as stated above (Q. XI., A. 2). Much more, therefore, is it possible for them to use.

*Obj.* 2. Further, to apply the members to action is to use them. But irrational animals apply their members to action; for instance, their feet, to walk; their horns, to strike. Therefore it is possible for irrational animals to use.

*On the contrary*, Augustine says (QQ. LXXXIII, qu. 30): *None but a rational animal can make use of a thing.*

*I answer that*, as stated above (A. 1), to use is to apply an active principle to action: thus to consent is to apply the appetitive movement to the desire of something, as stated above (Q. XV., AA. 1, 2, 3). Now he alone who has the disposal of a thing, can apply it to something else; and this belongs to him alone who knows how to refer it to something else, which is an act of the reason. And therefore none but a rational animal consents and uses.

*Reply Obj.* 1. To enjoy implies the absolute movement of the appetite to the appetible: whereas to use implies a movement of the appetite to something as directed to something else. If therefore we compare use and enjoyment in respect of their objects, enjoyment is better than use; because that which is appetible absolutely is better than that which is appetible only as directed to something else. But if we compare them in respect of the apprehensive power that precedes them, greater excellence is required on the part of use: because to direct one thing to another is an act of reason; whereas to apprehend something absolutely is within the competency even of sense.

*Reply Obj.* 2. Animals by means of their members do something from natural instinct; not through knowing the relation of their members to these operations. Wherefore, properly speaking, they do not apply their members to action, nor do they use them.

### Third Article.
#### WHETHER USE REGARDS ALSO THE LAST END?

*We proceed thus to the Third Article :—*

*Objection* 1. It would seem that use can regard also the last end. For Augustine says (*De Trin.* x. 11): *Whoever enjoys, uses.* But man enjoys the last end. Therefore he uses the last end.

*Obj.* 2. Further, *to use is to apply something to the purpose of the will* (*ibid.*). But the last end, more than anything else, is the object of the will's application. Therefore it can be the object of use.

*Obj.* 3. Further, Hilary says (*De Trin.* ii.) that *Eternity is in the Father, Likeness in the Image, i.e.,* in the Son, *Use in the Gift, i.e.,* in the Holy Ghost. But the Holy Ghost, since He is God, is the last end. Therefore the last end can be the object of use.

*On the contrary,* Augustine says (QQ. LXXXIII., qu. 30): *No one rightly uses God, but one enjoys Him.* But God alone is the last end. Therefore we cannot use the last end.

*I answer that,* Use, as stated above (A. 1), implies the application of one thing to another. Now that which is applied to another is regarded in the light of means to an end; and consequently use always regards the means. For this reason things that are adapted to a certain end are said to be *useful;* in fact their very usefulness is sometimes called use.

It must, however, be observed that the last end may be taken in two ways: first, simply; secondly, in respect of an individual. For since the end, as stated above (Q. I., A. 8; Q. II., A. 7), signifies sometimes the thing itself, and sometimes the attainment or possession of that thing (thus the miser's end is either money or the possession of it); it is evident that, simply speaking, the last end is the thing itself; for the possession of money is good only inasmuch as there is some good in money. But in regard to the individual, the obtaining of money is the last end; for the miser would not seek for money, save that he might have it. Therefore, simply and properly speaking, a man enjoys money, because he places his last end therein; but in so far as he seeks to possess it, he is said to use it.

*Reply Obj.* 1. Augustine is speaking of use in general, in so far as it implies the relation of an end to the enjoyment which a man seeks in that end.

*Reply Obj.* 2. The end is applied to the purpose of the will, that the will may find rest in it. Consequently this rest in the end, which is the enjoyment thereof, is in this sense called use of the end. But the means are applied to the will's purpose, not only in being used as means, but as ordained to something else in which the will finds rest.

*Reply Obj.* 3. The words of Hilary refer to use as applicable to rest in the last end; just as, speaking in a general sense, one may be said to use the end for the purpose of attaining it, as stated above. Hence Augustine says (*De Trin.* vi. 10) that *this love, delight, felicity, or happiness, is called use by him*.

### FOURTH ARTICLE.

#### WHETHER USE PRECEDES CHOICE ?

*We proceed thus to the Fourth Article :—*

*Objection* 1. It would seem that use precedes choice. For nothing follows after choice, except execution. But use, since it belongs to the will, precedes execution. Therefore it precedes choice also.

*Obj.* 2. Further, the absolute precedes the relative. Therefore the less relative precedes the more relative. But choice implies two relations: one, of the thing chosen, in relation to the end; the other, of the thing chosen, in respect of that to which it is preferred; whereas use implies relation to the end only. Therefore use precedes choice.

*Obj.* 3. Further, the will uses the other powers in so far as it moves them. But the will moves itself too, as stated above (Q. IX., A. 3). Therefore it uses itself, by applying itself to act. But it does this when it consents. Therefore there is use in consent. But consent precedes choice as stated above (Q. XV., A. 3 *ad* 3). Therefore use does also.

*On the contrary,* Damascene says (*De Fide Orthod.* ii. 22) that *the will after choosing has an impulse to the operation, and afterwards it uses* (*the powers*). Therefore use follows choice.

*I answer that,* The will has a twofold relation to the thing willed. One, according as the thing willed is, in a way, in the willing subject, by a kind of proportion or order to the thing willed. Wherefore those things that are naturally proportionate to a certain end, are said to desire that end naturally.—Yet to have an end thus is to have it imperfectly. Now every imperfect thing tends to perfection. And therefore both the natural and the voluntary appetite tend to have the end in reality; and this is to have it perfectly. This is the second relation of the will to the thing willed.

Now the thing willed is not only the end, but also the means. And the last act that belongs to the first relation of the will to the means, is choice; for there the will becomes fully proportionate, by willing the means fully. Use, on the other hand, belongs to the second relation of the will, in respect of which it tends to the realization of the thing willed. Wherefore it is evident that use follows choice; provided that by use we mean the will's use of the executive power in moving it. But since the will, in a way, moves the reason also, and uses it, we may take the use of the means, as consisting in the consideration of the reason, whereby it refers the means to the end. In this sense use precedes choice.

*Reply Obj.* 1. The motion of the will to the execution of the work, precedes execution, but follows choice. And so, since use belongs to that very motion of the will, it stands between choice and execution.

*Reply Obj.* 2. What is essentially relative is after the absolute; but the thing to which relation is referred need

not come after.   Indeed, the more a cause precedes, the
more numerous the effects to which it has relation.

*Reply Obj.* 3. Choice precedes use, if they be referred to
the same object.   But nothing hinders the use of one thing
preceding the choice of another.   And since the acts of the
will react on one another, in each act of the will we can find
both consent and choice and use; so that we may say that
the will consents to choose, and consents to consent, and
uses itself in consenting and choosing.   And such acts as are
ordained to that which precedes, precede also.

# QUESTION XVII.

## OF THE ACTS COMMANDED BY THE WILL.

### (*In Nine Articles.*)

WE must now consider the acts commanded by the will; under which head there are nine points of inquiry: (1) Whether command is an act of the will or of the reason? (2) Whether command belongs to irrational animals? (3) Of the order between command and use. (4) Whether command and the commanded act are one act or distinct? (5) Whether the act of the will is commanded? (6) Whether the act of the reason is commanded? (7) Whether the act of the sensitive appetite is commanded? (8) Whether the act of the vegetal soul is commanded? (9) Whether the acts of the external members are commanded?

### FIRST ARTICLE.

#### WHETHER COMMAND IS AN ACT OF THE REASON OR OF THE WILL?

*We proceed thus to the First Article :—*

*Objection* 1. It would seem that command is not an act of the reason but of the will. For command is a kind of motion; because Avicenna says that there are four ways of moving, *by perfecting, by disposing, by commanding, and by counselling.* But it belongs to the will to move all the other powers of the soul, as stated above (Q. IX., A. 1). Therefore command is an act of the will.

*Obj.* 2. Further, just as to be commanded belongs to that which is subject, so, seemingly, to command belongs to that which is most free. But the root of liberty is especially in the will. Therefore to command belongs to the will.

*Obj.* 3. Further, command is followed at once by act. But the act of the reason is not followed at once by act: for he who judges that a thing should be done, does not do it at once.   Therefore command is not an act of the reason, but of the will.

*On the contrary*, Gregory of Nyssa* and the Philosopher (*Ethic.* i. 13) say that *the appetite obeys reason*.   Therefore command is an act of the reason.

*I answer that*, Command is an act of the reason, presupposing, however, an act of the will.   In proof of this, we must take note that, since the acts of the reason and of the will can be brought to bear on one another, in so far as the reason reasons about willing, and the will wills to reason, the result is that the act of the reason precedes the act of the will, and conversely.   And since the power of the preceding act continues in the act that follows, it happens sometimes that there is an act of the will in so far as it retains in itself something of an act of the reason, as we have stated in reference to use and choice; and conversely, that there is an act of the reason in so far as it retains in itself something of an act of the will.

Now, command is essentially indeed an act of the reason: for the commander orders the one commanded to do something, by way of intimation or declaration; and to order thus by intimating or declaring is an act of the reason.   Now the reason can intimate or declare something in two ways. First, absolutely: and this intimation is expressed by a verb in the indicative mood, as when one person says to another *This is what you should do*.   Sometimes, however, the reason intimates something to a man by moving him thereto; and this intimation is expressed by a verb in the imperative mood; as when it is said to someone: *Do this*.   Now the first mover, among the powers of the soul, to the doing of an act is the will, as stated above (Q. IX., A. 1).   Since, therefore, the second mover does not move, save in virtue of the first mover, it follows that the very fact that the reason moves by commanding, is due to the power of the will.   Com-

* Nemesius, *De Nat. Hom.* xvi.

sequently it follows that command is an act of the reason, presupposing an act of the will, in virtue of which the reason, by its command, moves (the power) to the execution of the act.

*Reply Obj.* 1. To command is to move, not anyhow, but by intimating and declaring to another; and this is an act of the reason.

*Reply Obj.* 2. The root of liberty is the will as the subject thereof; but it is the reason as its cause. For the will can tend freely towards various objects, precisely because the reason can have various perceptions of good. Hence philosophers define the free-will as being *a free judgment arising from reason*, implying that reason is the root of liberty.

*Reply Obj.* 3. This argument proves that command is an act of reason not absolutely, but with a kind of motion, as stated above.

## SECOND ARTICLE.

### WHETHER COMMAND BELONGS TO IRRATIONAL ANIMALS?

*We proceed thus to the Second Article :—*

*Objection* 1. It would seem that command belongs to irrational animals. Because, according to Avicenna, *the power that commands movement is the appetite ; and the power that executes movement is in the muscles and nerves*. But both powers are in irrational animals. Therefore command is to be found in irrational animals.

*Obj.* 2. Further, the condition of a slave is that of one who receives commands. But the body is compared to the soul as a slave to his master, as the Philosopher says (*Polit.* i. 2). Therefore the body is commanded by the soul, even in irrational animals, since they are composed of soul and body.

*Obj.* 3. Further, by commanding, man has an impulse towards an action. But impulse to action is to be found in irrational animals, as Damascene says (*De Fide Orthod.* ii. 22). Therefore command is to be found in irrational animals.

*On the contrary*, Command is an act of reason, as stated above (A. 1). But in irrational animals there is no reason. Neither, therefore, is there command.

*I answer that,* To command is nothing else than to direct someone to do something, by a certain motion of intimation. Now to direct is the proper act of the reason. Wherefore it is impossible that irrational animals should command in any way, since they are devoid of reason.

*Reply Obj.* 1. The appetitive power is said to command movement, in so far as it moves the commanding reason. But this is only in man. In irrational animals the appetitive power is not, properly speaking, a commanding faculty, unless command be taken loosely for motion.

*Reply Obj.* 2. The body of the irrational animal is competent to obey; but its soul is not competent to command, because it is not competent to direct. Consequently there is no ratio there of commander and commanded; but only of mover and moved.

*Reply Obj.* 3. Impulse to action is in irrational animals otherwise than in man. For the impulse of man to action arises from the directing reason; wherefore his impulse is one of command. On the other hand, the impulse of the irrational animal arises from natural instinct; because as soon as they apprehend the fitting or the unfitting, their appetite is moved naturally to pursue or to avoid. Wherefore they are directed by another to act; and they themselves do not direct themselves to act. Consequently in them is impulse but not command.

## THIRD ARTICLE.

### WHETHER USE PRECEDES COMMAND ?

*We proceed thus to the Third Article :—*

*Objection* 1. It would seem that use precedes command. For command is an act of the reason presupposing an act of the will, as stated above (A. 1). But, as we have already shown (Q. XVI., A. 1), use is an act of the will. Therefore use precedes command.

*Obj.* 2. Further, command is one of those things that are ordained to the end. But use is of those things that are ordained to the end. Therefore it seems that use precedes command.

*Obj.* 3. Further, every act of a power moved by the will is called use; because the will uses the other powers, as stated above (Q. XVI., A. 1). But command is an act of the reason as moved by the will, as stated above (A. 1). Therefore command is a kind of use. Now the common precedes the proper. Therefore use precedes command.

*On the contrary,* Damascene says (*De Fide Orthod.* ii. 22) that impulse to action precedes use. But impulse to operation is given by command. Therefore command precedes use.

*I answer that,* use of that which is directed to the end, in so far as it is in the reason referring this to the end, precedes choice, as stated above (Q. XVI., A. 4). Wherefore still more does it precede command.—On the other hand, use of that which is directed to the end, in so far as it is subject to the executive power, follows command; because use in the user is united to the act of the thing used; for one does not use a stick before doing something with the stick. But command is not simultaneous with the act of the thing to which the command is given: for it naturally precedes its fulfilment, sometimes, indeed, by priority of time. Consequently it is evident that command precedes use.

*Reply Obj.* 1. Not every act of the will precedes this act of the reason which is command; but an act of the will precedes, viz., choice; and an act of the will follows, viz., use. Because after counsel's decision, which is reason's judgment, the will chooses; and after choice, the reason commands that power which has to do what was chosen; and then, last of all, someone's will begins to use, by executing the command of reason; sometimes it is another's will, when one commands another; sometimes the will of the one that commands, when he commands himself to do something.

*Reply Obj.* 2. Just as act ranks before power, so does the object rank before the act. Now the object of use is that which is directed to the end. Consequently, from the fact that command is directed to the end, one should conclude that command precedes, rather than that it follows use.

*Reply Obj.* 3. Just as the act of the will in using the reason for the purpose of command, precedes the command; so also we may say that this act whereby the will uses the reason, is preceded by a command of reason; since the acts of these powers react on one another.

## FOURTH ARTICLE.

### WHETHER COMMAND AND THE COMMANDED ACT ARE ONE ACT, OR DISTINCT ?

*We proceed thus to the Fourth Article :—*

*Objection* 1. It would seem that the commanded act is not one with the command itself. For the acts of different powers are themselves distinct. But the commanded act belongs to one power, and the command to another; since one is the power that commands, and the other is the power that receives the command. Therefore the commanded act is not one with the command.

*Obj.* 2. Further, whatever things can be separate from one another, are distinct: for nothing is severed from itself. But sometimes the commanded act is separate from the command: for sometimes the command is given, and the commanded act follows not. Therefore command is a distinct act from the act commanded.

*Obj.* 3. Further, whatever things are related to one another as precedent and consequent, are distinct. But command naturally precedes the commanded act. Therefore they are distinct.

*On the contrary,* The Philosopher says (*Topic.* iii. 2) that *where one thing is by reason of another, there is but one.* But there is no commanded act unless by reason of the command. Therefore they are one.

*I answer that,* Nothing prevents certain things being distinct in one respect, and one in another respect. Indeed every multitude is one in some respect, as Dionysius says (*Div. Nom.* xiii.). But a difference is to be observed in this, that some are simply many, and one in a particular respect, while with others it is the reverse. Now *one* is predicated in the same way as *being.* And substance is being simply, whereas accident or being *of reason* is a being only in a certain respect. Wherefore those things that are one in substance are one simply, though many in a certain respect. Thus, in the genus substance, the whole composed of its integral or essential parts, is one simply: because the whole is being and substance simply, and the parts are beings and substances in the whole. But those things which are distinct in substance, and one according to an accident, are distinct simply, and one in a certain respect: thus many men are one people, and many stones are one heap; which is unity of composition or order. In like manner also many individuals that are one in genus or species are many simply, and one in a certain respect: since to be one in genus or species is to be one according to the consideration of the reason.

Now just as in the genus of natural things, a whole is composed of matter and form (*e.g.*, man, who is one natural being, though he has many parts, is composed of soul and body); so, in human acts, the act of a lower power is in the position of matter in regard to the act of a higher power, in so far as the lower power acts in virtue of the higher power moving it: for thus also the act of the first mover is as the form in regard to the act of its instrument. Hence it is evident that command and the commanded act are one human act, just as a whole is one, yet in its parts, many.

*Reply Obj.* 1. If the distinct powers are not ordained to one another, their acts are diverse simply. But when one power is the mover of the other, then their acts are, in a way, one: since *the act of the mover and the act of the thing moved are one act* (*Phys.* iii. 3).

*Reply Obj.* 2. The fact that command and the commanded act can be separated from one another shows that they are different parts. Because the parts of a man can be separated from one another, and yet they form one whole.

*Reply Obj.* 3. In those things that are many in parts, but one as a whole, nothing hinders one part from preceding another. Thus the soul, in a way, precedes the body; and the heart, the other members.

### FIFTH ARTICLE.

#### WHETHER THE ACT OF THE WILL IS COMMANDED?

*We proceed thus to the Fifth Article :—*

*Objection* 1. It would seem that the act of the will is not commanded. For Augustine says (*Conf.* viii. 9): *The mind commands the mind to will, and yet it does not.* But to will is the act of the will. Therefore the act of the will is not commanded.

*Obj.* 2. Further, to receive a command belongs to one who can understand the command. But the will cannot understand the command; for the will differs from the intellect, to which it belongs to understand. Therefore the act of the will is not commanded.

*Obj.* 3. Further, if one act of the will is commanded, for the same reason all are commanded. But if all the acts of the will are commanded, we must needs proceed to infinity; because the act of the will precedes the act of reason commanding, as stated above (A. 1); for if that act of the will be also commanded, this command will be preceded by another act of the reason, and so on to infinity. But to proceed to infinity is not possible. Therefore the act of the will is not commanded.

*On the contrary*, Whatever is in our power, is subject to our command. But the acts of the will, most of all, are in our power; since all our acts are said to be in our power, in so far as they are voluntary. Therefore the acts of the will are commanded by us.

*I answer that*, As stated above (A. 1), command is nothing else than the act of the reason directing, with a certain motion, something to act. Now it is evident that the reason can direct the act of the will: for just as it can judge it to be good to will something so it can direct by commanding man to will. From this it is evident that an act of the will can be commanded.

*Reply Obj.* 1. As Augustine says (*ibid.*) when the mind commands itself perfectly to will, then already it wills: but that sometimes it commands and wills not, is due to the fact that it commands imperfectly. Now imperfect command arises from the fact that the reason is moved by opposite motives to command or not to command: wherefore it fluctuates between the two, and fails to command perfectly.

*Reply Obj.* 2. Just as each of the members of the body works not for itself alone but for the whole body; thus it is for the whole body that the eye sees; so is it with the powers of the soul. For the intellect understands, not for itself alone, but for all the powers; and the will wills not only for itself, but for all the powers too. Wherefore man, in so far as he is endowed with intellect and will, commands the act of the will for himself.

*Reply Obj.* 3. Since command is an act of the reason, that act is commanded which is subject to reason. Now the first act of the will is not due to the direction of the reason but to the instigation of nature, or of a higher cause, as stated above (Q. IX., A. 4). Therefore there is no need to proceed to infinity.

## SIXTH ARTICLE.

### WHETHER THE ACT OF THE REASON IS COMMANDED?

*We proceed thus to the Sixth Article :—*

*Objection* 1. It would seem that the act of the reason cannot be commanded. For it seems impossible for a thing to command itself. But it is the reason that commands, as stated above (A. 1). Therefore the act of the reason is not commanded.

*Obj.* 2. Further, that which is essential is different from that which is by participation. But the power whose act is commanded by reason, is rational by participation, as stated in *Ethic.* i. 13. Therefore the act of that power, which is essentially rational, is not commanded.

*Obj.* 3. Further, that act is commanded, which is in our power. But to know and judge the truth, which is the act of reason, is not always in our power. Therefore the act of the reason cannot be commanded.

*On the contrary,* That which we do of our free-will, can be done by our command. But the acts of the reason are accomplished through the free-will: for Damascene says (*De Fide Orthod*. ii. 22) that *by his free-will man inquires, considers, judges, approves*. Therefore the acts of the reason can be commanded.

*I answer that*, Since the reason re-acts on itself, just as it directs the acts of other powers, so can it direct its own act. Consequently its act can be commanded.

But we must take note that the act of the reason may be considered in two ways. First, as to the exercise of the act. And considered thus, the act of the reason can always be commanded: as when one is told to be attentive, and to use one's reason. Secondly, as to the object; in respect of which two acts of the reason have to be noticed. One is the act whereby it apprehends the truth about something. This act is not in our power: because it happens in virtue of a natural or supernatural light. Consequently in this respect, the act of the reason is not in our power, and cannot be commanded. The other act of the reason is that whereby it assents to what it apprehends. If, therefore, that which the reason apprehends is such that it naturally assents thereto, *e.g.*, the first principles, it is not in our power to assent or dissent to the like: assent follows naturally, and consequently, properly speaking, is not subject to our command. But some things which are apprehended do not convince the intellect to such an extent as not to leave it free to assent or dissent, or at least suspend its assent or dissent, on account of some cause or other; and in such things assent or dissent is in our power, and is subject to our command.

*Reply Obj*. 1. Reason commands itself, just as the will moves itself, as stated above (Q. IX., A. 3), that is to say, in so far as each power reacts on its own act, and from one thing tends to another.

*Reply Obj*. 2. On account of the diversity of objects subject to the act of the reason, nothing prevents the reason from participating in itself: thus the knowledge of principles is participated in the knowledge of the conclusions.

The reply to the third objection is evident from what has been said.

## SEVENTH ARTICLE.

### WHETHER THE ACT OF THE SENSITIVE APPETITE IS COMMANDED ?

*We proceed thus to the Seventh Article :—*

*Objection* 1. It would seem that the act of the sensitive appetite is not commanded. For the Apostle says (*Rom.* vii. 15): *For I do not that good which I will :* and a gloss explains this by saying that man lusts, although he wills not to lust. But to lust is an act of the sensitive appetite. Therefore the act of the sensitive appetite is not subject to our command.

*Obj.* 2. Further, corporeal matter obeys God alone, to the effect of formal transmutation, as was shown in the First Part (Q. LXV., A. 4; Q. XCI., A. 2; Q. CX., A. 2). But the act of the sensitive appetite is accompanied by a formal transmutation of the body, consisting in heat or cold. Therefore the act of the sensitive appetite is not subject to man's command.

*Obj.* 3. Further, the proper motive principle of the sensitive appetite is something apprehended by sense or imagination. But it is not always in our power to apprehend something by sense or imagination. Therefore the act of the sensitive appetite is not subject to our command.

*On the contrary,* Gregory of Nyssa* says: *That which obeys reason is twofold, the concupiscible and the irascible,* which belong to the sensitive appetite. Therefore the act of the sensitive appetite is subject to the command of reason.

*I answer that,* An act is subject to our command, in so far as it is in our power, as stated above (A. 5). Consequently in order to understand in what manner the act of the sensitive appetite is subject to the command of reason, we must consider in what manner it is in our power. Now it must be observed that the sensitive appetite differs from the intellective appetite, which is called the will, in the fact that the sensitive appetite is a power of a corporeal organ,

* Nemesius, *De Nat. Hom.* xvi.

whereas the will is not. Again, every act of a power that
uses a corporeal organ, depends not only on a power of the
soul, but also on the disposition of that corporeal organ:
thus the act of vision depends on the power of sight, and
on the condition of the eye, which condition is a help or a
hindrance to that act. Consequently the act of the sensitive
appetite depends not only on the appetitive power, but also
on the disposition of the body.

Now whatever part the power of the soul takes in the act,
follows apprehension. And the apprehension of the imagination, being a particular apprehension, is regulated by
the apprehension of reason, which is universal; just as a
particular active power is regulated by a universal active
power. Consequently in this respect the act of the sensitive
appetite is subject to the command of reason.—On the other
hand, condition or disposition of the body is not subject to
the command of reason: and consequently in this respect,
the movement of the sensitive appetite is hindered from being
wholly subject to the command of reason.

Moreover it happens sometimes that the movement of the
sensitive appetite is aroused suddenly in consequence of an
apprehension of the imagination or sense. And then such
movement occurs without the command of reason: although
reason could have prevented it, had it foreseen. Hence the
Philosopher says (*Polit*. i. 2) that the reason governs the
irascible and concupiscible not by a *despotic supremacy*,
which is that of a master over his slave; but by a *politic
and royal supremacy*, whereby the free are governed, who
are not wholly subject to command.

*Reply Obj.* 1. That man lusts, although he wills not to lust,
is due to a disposition of the body, whereby the sensitive
appetite is hindered from perfect compliance with the command of reason. Hence the Apostle adds (*ibid.*): *I see
another law in my members, fighting against the law of my
mind.*—This may also happen through a sudden movement
of concupiscence, as stated above.

*Reply Obj.* 2. The condition of the body stands in a twofold relation to the act of the sensitive appetite. First, as

preceding it: thus a man may be disposed in one way or another, in respect of his body, to this or that passion. Secondly, as consequent to it: thus a man becomes heated through anger. Now the condition that precedes, is not subject to the command of reason: since it is due either to nature, or to some previous movement, which cannot cease at once. But the condition that is consequent, follows the command of reason: since it results from the local movement of the heart, which has various movements according to the various acts of the sensitive appetite.

*Reply Obj.* 3. Since the external sensible is necessary for the apprehension of the senses, it is not in our power to apprehend anything by the senses, unless the sensible be present; which presence of the sensible is not always in our power. For it is then that man can use his senses if he will so to do; unless there be some obstacle on the part of the organ.—On the other hand, the apprehension of the imagination is subject to the ordering of reason, in proportion to the strength or weakness of the imaginative power. For that man is unable to imagine the things that reason considers, is either because they cannot be imagined, such as incorporeal things; or because of the weakness of the imaginative power, due to some organic indisposition.

### EIGHTH ARTICLE.

#### WHETHER THE ACT OF THE VEGETAL SOUL IS COMMANDED ?

*We proceed thus to the Eighth Article :—*

*Objection* 1. It would seem that the acts of the vegetal soul are subject to the command of reason. For the sensitive powers are of higher rank than the vegetal powers. But the powers of the sensitive soul are subject to the command of reason. Much more, therefore, are the powers of the vegetal soul.

*Obj.* 2. Further, man is called a *little world*,* because the soul is in the body, as God is in the world. But God is in

* Aristotle, *Phys.* viii. 2.

the world in such a way, that everything in the world obeys His command. Therefore all that is in man, even the powers of the vegetal soul, obey the command of reason.

*Obj.* 3. Further, praise and blame are awarded only to such acts as are subject to the command of reason. But in the acts of the nutritive and generative power, there is room for praise and blame, virtue and vice: as in the case of gluttony and lust, and their contrary virtues. Therefore the acts of these powers are subject to the command of reason.

*On the contrary*, Gregory of Nyssa* says that *the nutritive and generative power is one over which the reason has no control.*

*I answer that*, Some acts proceed from the natural appetite, others from the animal, or from the intellectual appetite: for every agent desires an end in some way. Now the natural appetite does not follow from some apprehension, as do the animal and the intellectual appetite. But the reason commands by way of an apprehensive power. Wherefore those acts that proceed from the intellective or the animal appetite, can be commanded by the reason: but not those acts that proceed from the natural appetite. And such are the acts of the vegetal soul; wherefore Gregory of Nyssa (Nemesius,—*loc. cit.*) says that *generation and nutrition belong to what are called natural powers.* Consequently the acts of the vegetal soul are not subject to the command of reason.

*Reply Obj.* 1. The more immaterial an act is, the more noble it is, and the more is it subject to the command of reason. Hence the very fact that the acts of the vegetal soul do not obey reason, shows that they rank lowest.

*Reply Obj.* 2. The comparison holds in a certain respect: because, to wit, as God moves the world, so the soul moves the body. But it does not hold in every respect: for the soul did not create the body out of nothing, as God created the world; for which reason the world is wholly subject to His command.

*Reply Obj.* 3. Virtue and vice, praise and blame do not affect the acts themselves of the nutritive and generative

* Nemesius, *De Nat. Hom.* xxii.

power, *i.e.*, digestion, and formation of the human body; but they affect the acts of the sensitive part, that are ordained to the acts of generation and nutrition; for example the desire for pleasure in the act of taking food or in the act of generation, and the right or wrong use thereof.

## NINTH ARTICLE.

### WHETHER THE ACTS OF THE EXTERNAL MEMBERS ARE COMMANDED ?

*We proceed thus to the Ninth Article :—*

*Objection* 1. It would seem that the members of the body do not obey reason as to their acts. For it is evident that the members of the body are more distant from the reason, than the powers of the vegetal soul. But the powers of the vegetal soul do not obey reason, as stated above (A. 8). Therefore much less do the members of the body obey.

*Obj.* 2. Further, the heart is the principle of animal movement. But the movement of the heart is not subject to the command of reason: for Gregory of Nyssa* says that *the pulse is not controlled by reason.* Therefore the movement of the bodily members is not subject to the command of reason.

*Obj.* 3. Further, Augustine says (*De Civ. Dei* xiv. 16) that *the movement of the genital members is sometimes inopportune and not desired ; sometimes when sought it fails, and whereas the heart is warm with desire, the body remains cold.* Therefore the movements of the members are not obedient to reason.

*On the contrary,* Augustine says (*Conf.* viii. 9): *The mind commands a movement of the hand, and so ready is the hand to obey, that scarcely can one discern obedience from command.*

*I answer that,* The members of the body are organs of the soul's powers. Consequently according as the powers of the soul stand in respect of obedience to reason, so do the members of the body stand in respect thereof. Since then the sensitive powers are subject to the command of reason,

* Nemesius, *De Nat. Hom.* xxii.

whereas the natural powers are not; therefore all movements of members, that are moved by the sensitive powers, are subject to the command of reason; whereas those movements of members, that arise from the natural powers, are not subject to the command of reason.

*Reply Obj.* 1. The members do not move themselves, but are moved through the powers of the soul; of which powers, some are in closer contact with the reason than are the powers of the vegetal soul.

*Reply Obj.* 2. In things pertaining to intellect and will, that which is according to nature stands first, whence all other things are derived: thus from the knowledge of principles that are naturally known, is derived knowledge of the conclusions; and from volition of the end naturally desired, is derived the choice of the means. So also in bodily movements the principle is according to nature. Now the principle of bodily movements begins with the movement of the heart. Consequently the movement of the heart is according to nature, and not according to the will: for like a proper accident, it results from life, which follows from the union of soul and body. Thus the movement of heavy and light things results from their substantial form: for which reason they are said to be moved by their generator, as the Philosopher states (*Phys.* viii. 4). Wherefore this movement is called *vital*. For which reason Gregory of Nyssa (Nemesius,—*loc. cit.*) says that, just as the movement of generation and nutrition does not obey reason, so neither does the pulse which is a vital movement. By the pulse he means the movement of the heart which is indicated by the pulse veins.

*Reply Obj.* 3. As Augustine says (*De Civ. Dei* xiv. 17, 20) it is in punishment of sin that the movement of these members does not obey reason: in this sense, that the soul is punished for its rebellion against God, by the insubmission of that member whereby original sin is transmitted to posterity.

But because, as we shall state later on, the effect of the sin of our first parent was that his nature was left to itself, through the withdrawal of the supernatural gift which God had bestowed on man, we must consider the natural cause of this particular member's insubmission to reason. This is stated by Aristotle (*De Causis Mot. Animal.*) who says that *the movements of the heart and of the organs of generation are involuntary*, and that the reason of this is as follows. These members are stirred at the occasion of some apprehension; in so far as the intellect and imagination represent such things as arouse the passions of the soul, of which passions these movements are a consequence. But they are not moved at the command of the reason or intellect, because these movements are conditioned by a certain natural change of heat and cold, which change is not subject to the command of reason. This is the case with these two organs in particular, because each is as it were a separate animal being, in so far as it is a principle of life; and the principle is virtually the whole. For the heart is the principle of the senses; and from the organ of generation proceeds the seminal virtue, which is virtually the entire animal. Consequently they have their proper movements naturally: because principles must needs be natural, as stated above (*Reply Obj. 2*).

# QUESTION XVIII.

## OF THE GOOD AND EVIL OF HUMAN ACTS, IN GENERAL.

### (*In Eleven Articles.*)

WE must now consider the good and evil of human acts. First, how a human act is good or evil; secondly, what results from the good or evil of a human act, as merit or demerit, sin and guilt.

Under the first head there will be a threefold consideration: the first will be of the good and evil of human acts, in general; the second, of the good and evil of internal acts; the third, of the good and evil of external acts.

Concerning the first there are eleven points of inquiry: (1) Whether every human action is good, or are there evil actions? (2) Whether the good or evil of a human action is derived from its object? (3) Whether it is derived from a circumstance? (4) Whether it is derived from the end? (5) Whether a human action is good or evil in its species? (6) Whether an action has the species of good or evil from its end? (7) Whether the species derived from the end is contained under the species derived from the object, as under its genus, or conversely? (8) Whether any action is indifferent in its species? (9) Whether an individual action can be indifferent? (10) Whether a circumstance places a moral action in the species of good or evil? (11) Whether every circumstance that makes an action better or worse, places the moral action in the species of good or evil?

## First Article.

### WHETHER EVERY HUMAN ACTION IS GOOD, OR ARE THERE EVIL ACTIONS ?

*We proceed thus to the First Article :—*

*Objection* 1. It would seem that every human action is good, and that none is evil. For Dionysius says (*Div. Nom.* iv.) that evil acts not, save in virtue of the good. But no evil is done in virtue of the good. Therefore no action is evil.

*Obj.* 2. Further, nothing acts except in so far as it is in act. Now a thing is evil, not according as it is in act, but according as its potentiality is void of act; whereas in so far as its potentiality is perfected by act, it is good, as stated in *Metaph.* ix. 9. Therefore nothing acts in so far as it is evil, but only according as it is good. Therefore every action is good, and none is evil.

*Obj.* 3. Further, evil cannot be a cause, save accidentally, as Dionysius declares (*Div. Nom.* iv.). But every action has some effect which is proper to it. Therefore no action is evil, but every action is good.

*On the contrary*, Our Lord said (Jo. iii. 20): *Every one that doth evil, hateth the light.* Therefore some actions of man are evil.

*I answer that*, We must speak of good and evil in actions as of good and evil in things: because such as everything is, such is the act that it produces. Now in things, each one has so much good as it has being: since good and being are convertible, as was stated in the First Part (Q. V., AA. 1, 3). But God alone has the whole plenitude of His Being in a certain unity: whereas every other thing has its proper fulness of being in a certain multiplicity. Wherefore it happens with some things, that they have being in some respect, and yet they are lacking in the fulness of being due to them. Thus the fulness of human being requires a compound of soul and body, having all the powers and instruments of knowledge and movement: wherefore if any man be lacking in any of these, he is lacking in something due to the fulness of his being. So that as much as he has of being, so much has he of goodness: while so far as he is lacking in the fulness of his being, so far is he lacking in goodness, and is said to be evil: thus a blind man is possessed of goodness inasmuch as he lives; and of evil, inasmuch as he lacks sight. That, however, which has nothing of being or goodness, could not be said to be either evil or good. But since this same fulness of being is of the very essence of good, if a thing be lacking in its due fulness of being, it is not said to be good simply, but in a certain respect, inasmuch as it is a being; although it can be called a being simply, and a non-being in a certain respect, as was stated in the First Part (Q. V., A. 1 *ad* 1). We must therefore say that every action has goodness, in so far as it has being: whereas it is lacking in goodness, in so far as it is lacking in something that is due to its fulness of being; and thus it is said to be evil: for instance if it lacks the quantity determined by reason, or its due place, or something of the kind.

*Reply Obj*. 1. Evil acts in virtue of deficient goodness. For if there were nothing of good there, there would be neither being nor possibility of action. On the other hand if good were not deficient, there would be no evil. Consequently the action done is a deficient good, which is good in a certain respect, but simply evil.

*Reply Obj*. 2. Nothing hinders a thing from being in act in a certain respect, so that it can act; and in a certain respect deficient in act, so as to cause a deficient act. Thus a blind man has in act the power of walking, whereby he is able to walk; but inasmuch as he is deprived of sight he suffers a defect in walking by stumbling when he walks.

*Reply Obj*. 3. An evil action can have a proper effect, according to the goodness and being that it has. Thus adultery is the cause of human generation, inasmuch as it implies union of male and female, but not inasmuch as it lacks the order of reason.

## SECOND ARTICLE.

### WHETHER THE GOOD OR EVIL OF A MAN'S ACTION IS DERIVED FROM ITS OBJECT?

*We proceed thus to the Second Article :—*

*Objection* 1. It would seem that the good or evil of an action is not derived from its object. For the object of any action is a thing. But *evil is not in things, but in the sinner's use of them*, as Augustine says (*De Doctr. Christ.* iii. 12). Therefore the good or evil of a human action is not derived from its object.

*Obj.* 2. Further, the object is compared to the action as its matter. But the goodness of a thing is not from its matter, but rather from the form, which is an act. Therefore good and evil in actions is not derived from their object.

*Obj.* 3. Further, the object of an active power is compared to the action as effect to cause. But the goodness of a cause does not depend on its effect; rather is it the reverse. Therefore good or evil in actions is not derived from their object.

*On the contrary*, It is written (Osee ix. 10): *They became abominable as those things which they loved.* Now man becomes abominable to God on account of the malice of his action. Therefore the malice of his action is according to the evil objects that man loves. And the same applies to the goodness of his action.

*I answer that*, as stated above (A. 1) the good or evil of an action, as of other things, depends on its fulness of being or its lack of that fulness. Now the first thing that belongs to the fulness of being seems to be that which gives a thing its species. And just as a natural thing has its species from its form, so an action has its species from its object, as movement from its term. And therefore, just as the primary goodness of a natural thing is derived from its form, which gives it its species, so the primary goodness of a moral action is derived from its suitable object: hence some call such an action *good in its genus ;* for instance, *to make use of what is one's own.* And just as, in natural things, the primary evil is when a generated thing does not realize its specific form (for instance, if instead of a man, something else be generated); so the primary evil in moral actions is that which is from the object, for instance, *to take what belongs to another*. And this action is said to be *evil in its genus*, genus here standing for species, just as we apply the term *mankind* to the whole human species.

*Reply Obj.* 1. Although external things are good in themselves, nevertheless they have not always a due proportion to this or that action. And so, inasmuch as they are considered as objects of such actions, they have not the quality of goodness.

*Reply Obj.* 2. The object is not the matter *of which* (a thing is made), but the matter *about which* (something is done); and stands in relation to the act as its form, as it were, through giving it its species.

*Reply Obj.* 3. The object of the human action is not always the object of an active power. For the appetitive power is, in a way, passive; in so far as it is moved by the appetible object; and yet it is a principle of human actions.—Nor again have the objects of the active powers always the nature of an effect, but only when they are already transformed: thus food when transformed is the effect of the nutritive power; whereas food before being transformed stands in relation to the nutritive power as the matter about which it exercises its operation. Now since the object is in some way the effect of the active power, it follows that it is the term of its action, and consequently that it gives it its form and species, since movement derives its species from its terms.— Moreover, although the goodness of an action is not caused by the goodness of its effect, yet an action is said to be good from the fact that it can produce a good effect. Consequently the very proportion of an action to its effect is the measure of its goodness.

## THIRD ARTICLE.

### WHETHER MAN'S ACTION IS GOOD OR EVIL FROM A CIRCUMSTANCE ?

*We proceed thus to the Third Article :—*

*Objection* 1. It would seem that an action is not good or evil from a circumstance. For circumstances stand around (*circumstant*) an action, as being outside it, as stated above (Q. VII., A. 1). But *good and evil are in things themselves*, as is stated in *Metaph.* vi. 4. Therefore an action does not derive goodness or malice from a circumstance.

*Obj.* 2. Further, the goodness or malice of an action is considered principally in the doctrine of morals. But since circumstances are accidents of actions, it seems that they are outside the scope of art: because *no art takes notice of what is accidental* (*Metaph.* vi. 2). Therefore the goodness or malice of an action is not taken from a circumstance.

*Obj.* 3. Further, that which belongs to a thing, in respect of its substance, is not ascribed to it in respect of an accident. But good and evil belong to an action in respect of its substance; because an action can be good or evil in its genus as stated above (A. 2). Therefore an action is not good or bad from a circumstance.

*On the contrary*, the Philosopher says (*Ethic.* ii. 3) that a virtuous man acts as he should, and when he should, and so on in respect of the other circumstances. Therefore, on the other hand, the vicious man, in the matter of each vice, acts when he should not, or where he should not, and so on with the other circumstances. Therefore human actions are good or evil according to circumstances.

*I answer that*, In natural things, it is to be noted that the whole fulness of perfection due to a thing, is not from the mere substantial form, that gives it its species; since a thing derives much from supervening accidents, as man does from shape, colour, and the like; and if any one of these accidents be out of due proportion, evil is the result. So is it with action. For the plenitude of its goodness does not consist wholly in its species, but also in certain additions which accrue to it by reason of certain accidents: and such are its due circumstances. Wherefore if something be wanting that is requisite as a due circumstance the action will be evil.

*Reply Obj.* 1. Circumstances are outside an action, inasmuch as they are not part of its essence; but they are in an action as accidents thereof. Thus, too, accidents in natural substances are outside the essence.

*Reply Obj.* 2. Every accident is not accidentally in its subject; for some are proper accidents; and of these every art takes notice. And thus it is that the circumstances of actions are considered in the doctrine of morals.

*Reply Obj.* 3. Since good and being are convertible; according as being is predicated of substance and of accident, so is good predicated of a thing both in respect of its essential being, and in respect of its accidental being; and this, both in natural things and in moral actions.

## Fourth Article.

### Whether a Human Action is Good or Evil from its End?

*We proceed thus to the Fourth Article :—*

*Objection* 1. It would seem that the good and evil in human actions are not from the end. For Dionysius says (*Div. Nom.* iv.) that *nothing acts with a view to evil.* If therefore an action were good or evil from its end, no action would be evil. Which is clearly false.

*Obj.* 2. Further, the goodness of an action is something in the action. But the end is an extrinsic cause. Therefore an action is not said to be good or bad according to its end.

*Obj.* 3. Further, a good action may happen to be ordained to an evil end, as when a man gives an alms from vainglory; and conversely, an evil action may happen to be ordained to a good end, as a theft committed in order to give something to the poor. Therefore an action is not good or evil from its end.

*On the contrary*, Boethius says (*De Differ. Topic.* ii.) that *if the end is good, the thing is good, and if the end be evil, the thing also is evil.*

*I answer that,* The disposition of things as to goodness is the same as their disposition as to being. Now in some things the being does not depend on another, and in these it suffices to consider their being absolutely. But there are things the being of which depends on something else, and hence in their regard we must consider their being in its relation to the cause on which it depends. Now just as the being of a thing depends on the agent and the form, so the goodness of a thing depends on its end. Hence in the Divine Persons, Whose goodness does not depend on another, the measure of goodness is not taken from the end. Whereas human actions, and other things, the goodness of which depends on something else, have a measure of goodness from the end on which they depend, besides that goodness which is in them absolutely.

Accordingly a fourfold goodness may be considered in a human action. First, that which, as an action, it derives from its genus; because as much as it has of action and being so much has it of goodness, as stated above (A. 1). Secondly, it has goodness according to its species; which is derived from its suitable object. Thirdly, it has goodness from its circumstances, in respect, as it were, of its accidents. Fourthly, it has goodness from its end, to which it is compared as to the cause of its goodness.

*Reply Obj.* 1. The good in view of which one acts is not always a true good; but sometimes it is a true good, sometimes an apparent good. And in the latter event, an evil action results from the end in view.

*Reply Obj.* 2. Although the end is an extrinsic cause, nevertheless due proportion to the end, and relation to the end, are inherent to the action.

*Reply Obj.* 3. Nothing hinders an action that is good in one of the ways mentioned above, from lacking goodness in another way. And thus it may happen that an action which is good in its species or in its circumstances, is ordained to an evil end, or vice versa. However, an action is not good simply, unless it is good in all those ways: since *evil results from any single defect, but good from the complete cause, as* Dionysius says (*Div. Nom.* iv.).

### FIFTH ARTICLE.

#### WHETHER A HUMAN ACTION IS GOOD OR EVIL IN ITS SPECIES ?

*We proceed thus to the Fifth Article :—*

*Objection* 1. It would seem that good and evil in moral actions do not make a difference of species. For the existence of good and evil in actions is in conformity with their existence in things, as stated above (A. 1). But good and evil do not make a specific difference in things; for a good man is specifically the same as a bad man. Therefore neither do they make a specific difference in actions.

*Obj.* 2. Further, since evil is a privation, it is a non-being. But non-being cannot be a difference, according to the Philosopher (*Metaph.* iii. 3). Since therefore the difference constitutes the species, it seems that an action is not constituted in a species through being evil. Consequently good and evil do not diversify the species of human actions.

*Obj.* 3. Further, acts that differ in species produce different effects. But the same specific effect results from a good and from an evil action: thus a man is born of adulterous or of lawful wedlock. Therefore good and evil actions do not differ in species.

*Obj.* 4. Further, actions are sometimes said to be good or bad from a circumstance, as stated above (A. 3). But since a circumstance is an accident, it does not give an action its species. Therefore human actions do not differ in species on account of their goodness or malice.

*On the contrary,* According to the Philosopher (*Ethic.* ii. 1) *like habits produce like actions*. But a good and a bad habit differ in species, as liberality and prodigality. Therefore also good and bad actions differ in species.

*I answer that,* Every action derives its species from its object, as stated above (A. 2). Hence it follows that a difference of object causes a difference of species in actions. Now, it must be observed that a difference of objects causes a difference of species in actions, according as the latter are referred to one active principle, which does not cause a difference in actions, according as they are referred to another active principle. Because nothing accidental constitutes a species, but only that which is essential; and a difference of object may be essential in reference to one active principle, and accidental in reference to another. Thus to know colour and to know sound, differ essentially in reference to sense, but not in reference to the intellect.

Now in human actions, good and evil are predicated in reference to the reason; because as Dionysius says (*Div. Nom.* iv.), *the good of man is to be in accordance with reason*, and evil is *to be against reason.* For that is good for a thing which suits it in regard to its form; and evil, that which is against the order of its form. It is therefore evident that the difference of good and evil considered in reference to the object is an essential difference in relation to reason; that is to say, according as the object is suitable or unsuitable to reason. Now certain actions are called human or moral, inasmuch as they proceed from the reason. Consequently it is evident that good and evil diversify the species in human actions; since essential differences cause a difference of species.

*Reply Obj.* 1. Even in natural things, good and evil, inasmuch as something is according to nature, and something against nature, diversify the natural species; for a dead body and a living body are not of the same species. In like manner, good, inasmuch as it is in accord with reason, and evil, inasmuch as it is against reason, diversify the moral species.

*Reply Obj.* 2. Evil implies privation, not absolute, but affecting some potentiality. For an action is said to be evil in its species, not because it has no object at all; but because it has an object in disaccord with reason, for instance, to appropriate another's property. Wherefore in so far as the object is something positive, it can constitute the species of an evil act.

*Reply Obj.* 3. The conjugal act and adultery, as compared to reason, differ specifically and have effects specifically different; because the one deserves praise and reward, the other, blame and punishment. But as compared to the generative power, they do not differ in species; and thus they have one specific effect.

*Reply Obj.* 4. A circumstance is sometimes taken as the essential difference of the object, as compared to reason; and then it can specify a moral act. And it must needs be so whenever a circumstance transforms an action from good to evil; for a circumstance would not make an action evil, except through being repugnant to reason.

## Sixth Article.

### WHETHER AN ACTION HAS THE SPECIES OF GOOD OR EVIL FROM ITS END ?

*We proceed thus to the Sixth Article :—*

*Objection* 1. It would seem that the good and evil which are from the end do not diversify the species of actions. For actions derive their species from the object. But the end is altogether apart from the object. Therefore the good and evil which are from the end do not diversify the species of an action.

*Obj.* 2. Further, that which is accidental does not constitute the species, as stated above (A. 5). But it is accidental to an action to be ordained to some particular end; for instance, to give alms from vainglory. Therefore actions are not diversified as to species, according to the good and evil which are from the end.

*Obj.* 3. Further, acts that differ in species, can be ordained to the same end: thus to the end of vainglory, actions of various virtues and vices can be ordained. Therefore the good and evil which are taken from the end, do not diversify the species of action.

*On the contrary*, It has been shown above (Q. I., A. 3) that human actions derive their species from the end.

Therefore good and evil in respect of the end diversify the species of actions.

*I answer that,* Certain actions are called human, inasmuch as they are voluntary, as stated above (Q. I., A. 1). Now, in a voluntary action, there is a twofold action, viz., the interior action of the will, and the external action: and each of these actions has its object. The end is properly the object of the interior act of the will: while the object of the external action, is that on which the action is brought to bear. Therefore just as the external action takes its species from the object on which it bears: so the interior act of the will takes its species from the end, as from its own proper object.

Now that which is on the part of the will is formal in regard to that which is on the part of the external action: because the will uses the limbs to act as instruments; nor have external actions any measure of morality, save in so far as they are voluntary. Consequently the species of a human act is considered formally with regard to the end, but materially with regard to the object of the external action. Hence the Philosopher says (*Ethic.* v. 2) that *he who steals that he may commit adultery, is, strictly speaking, more adulterer than thief.*

*Reply Obj.* 1. The end also has the character of an object, as stated above.

*Reply Obj.* 2. Although it is accidental to the external action to be ordained to some particular end, it is not accidental to the interior act of the will, which act is compared to the external act, as form to matter.

*Reply Obj.* 3. When many actions, differing in species, are ordained to the same end, there is indeed a diversity of species on the part of the external actions; but unity of species on the part of the internal action.

## Seventh Article.

### whether the species derived from the end is contained under the species derived from the object, as under its genus, or conversely ?

*We proceed thus to the Seventh Article :—*

*Objection* 1. It would seem that the species of goodness derived from the end is contained under the species of goodness derived from the object, as a species is contained under its genus; for instance, when a man commits a theft in order to give an alms. For an action takes its species from its object, as stated above (AA. 2, 6). But it is impossible for a thing to be contained under another species, if this species be not contained under the proper species of that thing; because the same thing cannot be contained in different species that are not subordinate to one another. Therefore the species which is taken from the end, is contained under the species which is taken from the object.

*Obj.* 2. Further, the last difference always constitutes the most specific species. But the difference derived from the end seems to come after the difference derived from the object: because the end is something last. Therefore the species derived from the end, is contained under the species derived from the object, as its most specific species.

*Obj.* 3. Further, the more formal a difference is, the more specific it is: because difference is compared to genus, as form to matter. But the species derived from the end, is more formal than that which is derived from the object, as stated above (A. 6). Therefore the species derived from the end is contained under the species derived from the object, as the most specific species is contained under the subaltern genus.

*On the contrary*, Each genus has its determinate differences. But an action of one same species on the part of its object, can be ordained to an infinite number of ends: for instance, theft can be ordained to an infinite number of good and bad ends. Therefore the species derived from the end is not contained under the species derived from the object, as under its genus.

*I answer that*, The object of the external act can stand in a twofold relation to the end of the will: first, as being of itself ordained thereto; thus to fight well is of itself ordained to victory; secondly, as being ordained thereto accidentally; thus to take what belongs to another is ordained accidentally to the giving of alms. Now the differences that divide a genus, and constitute the species of that genus, must, as the philosopher says (*Metaph.* vii. 12), divide that genus essentially : and if they divide it accidentally, the division is incorrect: as, if one were to say: *Animals are divided into rational and irrational ; and the irrational into animals with wings, and animals without wings ;* for *winged* and *wingless* are not essential determinations of the irrational being. But the following division would be correct: *Some animals have feet, some have no feet : and of those that have feet, some have two feet, some four, some many :* because the latter division is an essential determination of the former. Accordingly when the object is not of itself ordained to the end, the specific difference derived from the object is not an essential determination of the species derived from the end, nor is the reverse the case. Wherefore one of these species is not under the other; but then the moral action is contained under two species that are disparate, as it were. Consequently we say that he that commits theft for the sake of adultery, is guilty of a twofold malice in one action.—On the other hand, if the object be of itself ordained to the end, one of these differences is an essential determination of the other. Wherefore one of these species will be contained under the other.

It remains to be considered which of the two is contained under the other. In order to make this clear, we must first of all observe that the more particular the form is from which a difference is taken, the more specific is the difference. Secondly, that the more universal an agent is, the more universal a form does it cause. Thirdly, that the more remote an end is, the more universal the agent to which it corresponds; thus victory, which is the last end of the army, is the end intended by the commander in chief; while the right ordering of this or that regiment is the end intended by one of the lower officers. From all this it follows that the specific difference derived from the end, is more general; and that the difference derived from an object which of itself is ordained to that end, is a specific difference in relation to the former. For the will, the proper object of which is the end, is the universal mover in respect of all the powers of the soul, the proper objects of which are the objects of their particular acts.

*Reply Obj.* 1. One and the same thing, considered in its substance, cannot be in two species, one of which is not subordinate to the other. But in respect of those things which are superadded to the substance, one thing can be contained under different species. Thus one and the same fruit, as to its colour, is contained under one species, *i.e.*, a white thing: and, as to its perfume, under the species of sweet-smelling things. In like manner an action which, as to its substance, is in one natural species, considered in respect to the moral conditions that are added to it, can belong to two species, as stated above (Q. I., A. 3 *ad* 3).

*Reply Obj.* 2. The end is last in execution; but first in the intention of the reason, in regard to which moral actions receive their species.

*Reply Obj.* 3. Difference is compared to genus as form to matter, inasmuch as it actualizes the genus. On the other hand, the genus is considered as more formal than the species, inasmuch as it is something more absolute and less contracted. Wherefore also the parts of a definition are reduced to the genus of formal cause, as is stated in *Phys.* ii. 3. And in this sense the genus is the formal cause of the species; and so much the more formal, as it is more universal.

## Eighth Article.

#### WHETHER ANY ACTION IS INDIFFERENT IN ITS SPECIES?

*We proceed thus to the Eighth Article :—*

*Objection* 1. It would seem that no action is indifferent in its species. For evil is the privation of good, according to Augustine (*Enchirid.* xi.). But privation and habit are immediate contraries, according to the Philosopher (*Categor.* viii.). Therefore there is no such thing as an action that is indifferent in its species, as though it were between good and evil.

*Obj.* 2. Further, human actions derive their species from their end or object, as stated above (A. 6; Q. I., A. 3). But every end and every object is either good or bad. Therefore every human action is good or evil according to its species. None, therefore, is indifferent in its species.

*Obj.* 3. Further, as stated above (A. 1), an action is said to be good, when it has its due complement of goodness; and evil, when it lacks that complement. But every action must needs either have the entire plenitude of its goodness, or lack it in some respect. Therefore every action must needs be either good or bad in its species, and none is indifferent.

*On the contrary*, Augustine says (*De Serm. Dom. in Mont.* ii. 18), that *there are certain deeds of a middle kind, which can be done with a good or evil mind, of which it is rash to form a judgment.* Therefore some actions are indifferent according to their species.

*I answer that*, As stated above (AA. 2, 5), every action takes its species from its object; while human action, which is called moral, takes its species from the object, in relation to the principle of human actions, which is the reason. Wherefore if the object of an action includes something in accord with the order of reason, it will be a good action according to its species; for instance, to give alms to a person in want. On the other hand, if it includes something repugnant to the order of reason, it will be an evil act according to its species; for instance, to steal, which is to

appropriate what belongs to another.  But it may happen
that the object of an action does not include something
pertaining to the order of reason; for instance, to pick up a
straw from the ground, to walk in the fields, and the like:
and such actions are indifferent according to their species.

*Reply Obj.* 1. Privation is twofold.  One is privation *as
a result* (*privatum esse*), and this leaves nothing, but takes
all away: thus blindness takes away sight altogether; darkness, light; and death, life.  Between this privation and
the contrary habit, there can be no medium in respect of
the proper subject.—The other is privation *in process*
(*privari*): thus sickness is privation of health; not that it
takes health away altogether, but that it is a kind of road
to the entire loss of health, occasioned by death.  And
since this sort of privation leaves something, it is not always
the immediate contrary of the opposite habit.  In this way
evil is a privation of good, as Simplicius says in his commentary on the Categories: because it does not take away
all good, but leaves some.  Consequently there can be
something between good and evil.

*Reply Obj.* 2. Every object or end has some goodness or
malice, at least natural to it: but this does not imply moral
goodness or malice, which is considered in relation to the
reason, as stated above.  And it is of this that we are here
treating.

*Reply Obj.* 3. Not everything belonging to an action
belongs also to its species.  Wherefore although an action's
specific nature may not contain all that belongs to the full
complement of its goodness, it is not therefore an action
specifically bad; nor is it specifically good.  Thus a man in
regard to his species is neither virtuous nor wicked.

## NINTH ARTICLE.

### WHETHER AN INDIVIDUAL ACTION CAN BE INDIFFERENT ?

*We proceed thus to the Ninth Article :—*

*Objection* 1. It seems that an individual action can be
indifferent.  For there is no species that does not, or cannot,

contain an individual. But an action can be indifferent in its species, as stated above (A. 8). Therefore an individual action can be indifferent.

*Obj.* 2. Further, individual actions cause like habits, as stated in *Ethic.* ii. 1. But a habit can be indifferent: for the Philosopher says (*Ethic.* iv. 1) that those who are of an even temper and prodigal disposition are not evil; and yet it is evident that they are not good, since they depart from virtue; and thus they are indifferent in respect of a habit. Therefore some individual actions are indifferent.

*Obj.* 3. Further, moral good belongs to virtue, while moral evil belongs to vice. But it happens sometimes that a man fails to ordain a specifically indifferent action to a vicious or virtuous end. Therefore an individual action may happen to be indifferent.

*On the contrary*, Gregory says in a homily (vi. *in Evang.*): *An idle word is one that lacks either the usefulness of rectitude or the motive of just necessity or pious utility*. But an idle word is an evil, because *men . . . shall render an account of it in the day of judgment* (Matth. xii. 36):—while if it does not lack the motive of just necessity or pious utility, it is good. Therefore every word is either good or bad. For the same reason every other action is either good or bad. Therefore no individual action is indifferent.

*I answer that*, It sometimes happens that an action is indifferent in its species, but considered in the individual it is good or evil. And the reason of this is because a moral action, as stated above (A. 3), derives its goodness not only from its object, whence it takes its species; but also from the circumstances, which are its accidents, as it were; just as something belongs to a man by reason of his individual accidents, which does not belong to him by reason of his species. And every individual action must needs have some circumstance that makes it good or bad, at least in respect of the intention of the end. For since it belongs to the reason to direct; if an action that proceeds from deliberate reason be not directed to the due end, it is, by that fact alone, repugnant to reason, and has the character of evil.

But if it be directed to a due end it is in accord with reason; wherefore it has the character of good. Now it must needs be either directed or not directed to a due end. Consequently every human action that proceeds from deliberate reason, if it be considered in the individual, must be good or bad.

If, however, it does not proceed from deliberate reason, but from some act of the imagination, as when a man strokes his beard, or moves his hand or foot; such an action, properly speaking, is not moral or human; since this depends on the reason. Hence it will be indifferent, as standing apart from the genus of moral actions.

*Reply Obj.* 1. For an action to be indifferent in its species can be understood in several ways. First in such a way that its species demands that it remain indifferent; and the objection proceeds on this line. But no action can be specifically indifferent thus: since no object of human action is such that it cannot be directed to good or evil, either through its end or through a circumstance.—Secondly, specific indifference of an action may be due to the fact that as far as its species is concerned, it is neither good nor bad. Wherefore it can be made good or bad by something else. Thus man, as far as his species is concerned, is neither white nor black; nor is it a condition of his species that he should not be black or white; but blackness or whiteness is superadded to man by other principles than those of his species.

*Reply Obj.* 2. The Philosopher states that a man is evil, properly speaking, if he be hurtful to others. And accordingly he says that the prodigal is not evil, because he hurts none save himself. And the same applies to all others who are not hurtful to other men. But we say here that evil, in general, is all that is repugnant to right reason. And in this sense every individual action is either good or bad, as stated above.

*Reply Obj.* 3. Whenever an end is intended by deliberate reason, it belongs either to the good of some virtue, or to the evil of some vice. Thus, if a man's action is directed to the support or repose of his body, it is also directed to the good of virtue, provided he direct his body itself to the good of virtue. The same clearly applies to other actions.

## Tenth Article.

### WHETHER A CIRCUMSTANCE PLACES A MORAL ACTION IN THE SPECIES OF GOOD OR EVIL?

*We proceed thus to the Tenth Article :—*

*Objection* 1. It would seem that a circumstance cannot place a moral action in the species of good or evil. For the species of an action is taken from its object. But circumstances differ from the object. Therefore circumstances do not give an action its species.

*Obj.* 2. Further, circumstances are as accidents in relation to the moral action, as stated above (Q. VII., A. 1). But an accident does not constitute the species. Therefore a circumstance does not constitute a species of good or evil.

*Obj.* 3. Further, one thing is not in several species. But one action has several circumstances. Therefore a circumstance does not place a moral action in a species of good or evil.

*On the contrary*, Place is a circumstance. But place makes a moral action to be in a certain species of evil; for theft of a thing from a holy place is a sacrilege. Therefore a circumstance makes a moral action to be specifically good or bad.

*I answer that*, Just as the species of natural things are constituted by their natural forms, so the species of moral actions are constituted by forms as conceived by the reason, as is evident from what was said above (A. 5). But since nature is determinate to one thing, nor can a process of nature go on to infinity, there must needs be some ultimate form, giving a specific difference, after which no further specific difference is possible. Hence it is that in natural things, that which is accidental to a thing, cannot be taken as a difference constituting the species. But the process of reason is not fixed to one particular term, for at any point it can still proceed further.

And consequently that which, in one action, is taken as a circumstance added to the object that specifies the action, can again be taken by the directing reason, as the principal condition of the object that determines the action's species. Thus to appropriate another's property is specified by reason of the property being *another's*, and in this respect it is placed in the species of theft; and if we consider that action also in its bearing on place or time, then this will be an additional circumstance. But since the reason can direct as to place, time, and the like, it may happen that the condition as to place, in relation to the object, is considered as being in disaccord with reason: for instance, reason forbids damage to be done to a holy place. Consequently to steal from a holy place has an additional repugnance to the order of reason. And thus place, which was first of all considered as a circumstance, is considered here as the principal condition of the object, and as itself repugnant to reason. And in this way, whenever a circumstance has a special relation to reason, either for or against, it must needs specify the moral action whether good or bad.

*Reply Obj*. 1. A circumstance, in so far as it specifies an action, is considered as a condition of the object, as stated above, and as being, as it were, a specific difference thereof.

*Reply Obj*. 2. A circumstance, so long as it is but a circumstance, does not specify an action, since thus it is a mere accident: but when it becomes a principal condition of the object, then it does specify the action.

*Reply Obj*. 3. It is not every circumstance that places the moral action in the species of good or evil; since not every circumstance implies accord or disaccord with reason. Consequently, although one action may have many circumstances, it does not follow that it is in many species. Nevertheless there is no reason why one action should not be in several, even disparate, moral species, as said above (A. 7 *ad* 1; Q. I., A. 3 *ad* 3).

## Eleventh Article.

WHETHER EVERY CIRCUMSTANCE THAT MAKES AN ACTION
   BETTER OR WORSE, PLACES A MORAL ACTION IN A
   SPECIES OF GOOD OR EVIL?

*We proceed thus to the Eleventh Article :—*

*Objection* 1. It would seem that every circumstance
relating to good or evil, specifies an action. For good and
evil are specific differences of moral actions. Therefore
that which causes a difference in the goodness or malice of
a moral action, causes a specific difference, which is the
same as to make it differ in species. Now that which makes
an action better or worse, makes it differ in goodness and
malice. Therefore it causes it to differ in species. Therefore every circumstance that makes an action better or
worse, constitutes a species.

*Obj.* 2. Further, an additional circumstance either has in
itself the character of goodness or malice, or it has not. If
not, it cannot make the action better or worse; because what
is not good, cannot make a greater good; and what is not
evil, cannot make a greater evil. But if it has in itself the
character of good or evil, for this very reason it has a certain
species of good or evil. Therefore every circumstance that
makes an action better or worse, constitutes a new species
of good or evil.

*Obj.* 3. Further, according to Dionysius (*Div. Nom.* iv.),
*evil is caused by each single defect*. Now every circumstance
that increases malice, has a special defect. Therefore every
such circumstance adds a new species of sin. And for the
same reason, every circumstance that increases goodness,
seems to add a new species of goodness: just as every unity
added to a number makes a new species of number; since
the good consists in *number, weight, and measure* (P. I.,
Q. V., A. 5).

*On the contrary*, More and less do not change a species.
But more and less is a circumstance of additional goodness or
malice. Therefore not every circumstance that makes a moral
action better or worse, places it in a species of good or evil.

*I answer that,* As stated above (A. 10), a circumstance gives the species of good or evil to a moral action, in so far as it regards a special order of reason. Now it happens sometimes that a circumstance does not regard a special order of reason in respect of good or evil, except on the supposition of another previous circumstance, from which the moral action takes its species of good or evil. Thus to take something in a large or small quantity, does not regard the order of reason in respect of good or evil, except a certain other condition be presupposed, from which the action takes its malice or goodness; for instance, if what is taken belongs to another, which makes the action to be discordant with reason. Wherefore to take what belongs to another in a large or small quantity, does not change the species of the sin. Nevertheless it can aggravate or diminish the sin. The same applies to other evil or good actions. Consequently not every circumstance that makes a moral action better or worse, changes its species.

*Reply Obj.* 1. In things which can be more or less intense, the difference of more or less does not change the species: thus by differing in whiteness through being more or less white a thing is not changed in regard to its species of colour. In like manner that which makes an action to be more or less good or evil, does not make the action differ in species.

*Reply Obj.* 2. A circumstance that aggravates a sin, or adds to the goodness of an action, sometimes has no goodness or malice in itself, but in regard to some other condition of the action, as stated above. Consequently it does not add a new species, but adds to the goodness or malice derived from this other condition of the action.

*Reply Obj.* 3. A circumstance does not always involve a distinct defect of its own; sometimes it causes a defect in reference to something else. In like manner a circumstance does not always add further perfection, except in reference to something else. And, for as much as it does, although it may add to the goodness or malice, it does not always change the species of good or evil.

# QUESTION XIX.

## OF THE GOODNESS AND MALICE OF THE INTERIOR ACT OF THE WILL.

### (*In Ten Articles.*)

WE must now consider the goodness of the interior act of the will; under which head there are ten points of inquiry: (1) Whether the goodness of the will depends on the object? (2) Whether it depends on the object alone? (3) Whether it depends on reason? (4) Whether it depends on the eternal law? (5) Whether erring reason binds? (6) Whether the will is evil if it follows the erring reason against the law of God? (7) Whether the goodness of the will in regard to the means, depends on the intention of the end? (8) Whether the degree of goodness or malice in the will depends on the degree of good or evil in the intention? (9) Whether the goodness of the will depends on its conformity to the Divine Will? (10) Whether it is necessary for the human will, in order to be good, to be conformed to the Divine Will, as regards the thing willed?

## FIRST ARTICLE.

### WHETHER THE GOODNESS OF THE WILL DEPENDS ON THE OBJECT?

*We proceed thus to the First Article :—*

*Objection* 1. It would seem that the goodness of the will does not depend on the object. For the will cannot be directed otherwise than to what is good: since *evil is outside the scope of the will*, as Dionysius says (*Div. Nom.* iv.). If therefore the goodness of the will depended on the object, it would follow that every act of the will is good, and none bad.

*Obj.* 2. Further, good is first of all in the end: wherefore the goodness of the end, as such, does not depend on any other. But, according to the Philosopher (*Ethic.* vi. 5), *goodness of action is the end, but goodness of making is never the end:* because the latter is always ordained to the thing made, as to its end. Therefore the goodness of the act of the will does not depend on any object.

*Obj.* 3. Further, such as a thing is, such does it make a thing to be. But the object of the will is good, by reason of the goodness of nature. Therefore it cannot give moral goodness to the will. Therefore the moral goodness of the will does not depend on the object.

*On the contrary,* the Philosopher says (*Ethic.* v. 1) that justice is that habit *from which men wish for just things:* and accordingly, virtue is a habit from which men wish for good things. But a good will is one which is in accordance with virtue. Therefore the goodness of the will is from the fact that a man wills that which is good.

*I answer that,* Good and evil are essential differences of the act of the will. Because good and evil of themselves regard the will; just as truth and falsehood regard reason; the act of which is divided essentially by the difference of truth and falsehood, for as much as an opinion is said to be true or false. Consequently good and evil will are acts differing in species. Now the specific difference in acts is according to objects, as stated above (Q. XVIII., A. 5). Therefore good and evil in the acts of the will is derived properly from the objects.

*Reply Obj.* 1. The will is not always directed to what is truly good, but sometimes to the apparent good; which has indeed some measure of good, but not of a good that is simply suitable to be desired. Hence it is that the act of the will is not always good, but sometimes evil.

*Reply Obj.* 2. Although an action can, in a certain way, be man's last end; nevertheless such action is not an act of the will, as stated above (Q. I., A. 1 *ad* 2).

*Reply Obj.* 3. Good is presented to the will as its object by the reason: and in so far as it is in accord with reason, it enters the moral order, and causes moral goodness in the act of the will: because the reason is the principle of human and moral acts, as stated above (Q. XVIII., A. 5).

## SECOND ARTICLE.

### WHETHER THE GOODNESS OF THE WILL DEPENDS ON THE OBJECT ALONE ?

*We proceed thus to the Second Article :—*

*Objection* 1. It would seem that the goodness of the will does not depend on the object alone. For the end has a closer relationship to the will than to any other power. But the acts of the other powers derive goodness not only from the object but also from the end, as we have shown above (Q. XVIII., A. 4). Therefore the act also of the will derives goodness not only from the object but also from the end.

*Obj.* 2. Further, the goodness of an action is derived not only from the object but also from the circumstances, as stated above (Q. XVIII., A. 3). But according to the diversity of circumstances there may be diversity of goodness and malice in the act of the will: for instance, if a man will, when he ought, where he ought, as much as he ought, and how he ought, or if he will as he ought not. Therefore the goodness of the will depends not only on the object, but also on the circumstances.

*Obj.* 3. Further, ignorance of circumstances excuses malice of the will, as stated above (Q. VI., A. 8). But it would not be so, unless the goodness or malice of the will depended on the circumstances. Therefore the goodness and malice of the will depend on the circumstances, and not only on the object.

*On the contrary*, An action does not take its species from the circumstances as such, as stated above (Q. XVIII., A. 10 *ad* 2). But good and evil are specific differences of the act of the will, as stated above (A. 1). Therefore the goodness and malice of the will depend, not on the circumstances, but on the object alone.

*I answer that*, In every genus, the more a thing is first, the more simple it is, and the fewer the principles of which it consists: thus primary bodies are simple. Hence it is to be observed that the first things in every genus, are, in some way, simple and consist of one principle. Now the principle of the goodness and malice of human actions is taken from the act of the will. Consequently the goodness and malice of the act of the will depend on some one thing; while the goodness and malice of other acts may depend on several things.

Now that one thing which is the principle in each genus, is not something accidental to that genus, but something essential thereto: because whatever is accidental is reduced to something essential, as to its principle. Therefore the goodness of the will's act depends on that one thing alone, which of itself causes goodness in the act; and that one thing is the object, and not the circumstances, which are accidents, as it were, of the act.

*Reply Obj.* 1. The end is the object of the will, but not of the other powers. Hence, in regard to the act of the will, the goodness derived from the object, does not differ from that which is derived from the end, as they differ in the acts of the other powers; except perhaps accidentally, in so far as one end depends on another, and one act of the will on another.

*Reply Obj.* 2. Given that the act of the will is fixed on some good, no circumstance can make that act bad. Consequently when it is said that a man wills a good when he ought not, or where he ought not, this can be understood in two ways. First, so that this circumstance is referred to the thing willed. And thus the act of the will is not fixed on something good: since to will to do something when it ought not to be done, is not to will something good. Secondly, so that the circumstance is referred to the act of willing. And thus, it is impossible to will something good when one ought not to, because one ought always to will what is good: except, perhaps, accidentally, in so far as a man by willing some particular good, is prevented from willing at the same time another good which he ought to will at that time. And then evil results, not from his willing that particular good, but from his not willing the other. The same applies to the other circumstances.

*Reply Obj.* 3. Ignorance of circumstances excuses malice of the will, in so far as the circumstance affects the thing willed: that is to say, in so far as a man ignores the circumstances of the act which he wills.

### THIRD ARTICLE.

#### WHETHER THE GOODNESS OF THE WILL DEPENDS ON REASON ?

*We proceed thus to the Third Article :—*

*Objection* 1. It would seem that the goodness of the will does not depend on reason. For what comes first does not depend on what follows. But the good belongs to the will before it belongs to reason, as is clear from what has been said above (Q. IX., A. 1). Therefore the goodness of the will does not depend on reason.

*Obj.* 2. Further, the Philosopher says (*Ethic.* vi. 2) that the goodness of the practical intellect is *a truth that is in conformity with right desire.* But right desire is a good will. Therefore the goodness of the practical reason depends on the goodness of the will, rather than conversely.

*Obj.* 3. Further, the mover does not depend on that which is moved, but vice versa. But the will moves the reason and the other powers, as stated above (Q. IX., A. 1). Therefore the goodness of the will does not depend on reason.

*On the contrary*, Hilary says (*De Trin.* x.): *It is an unruly will that persists in its desires in opposition to reason.* But the goodness of the will consists in not being unruly. Therefore the goodness of the will depends on its being subject to reason.

*I answer that*, As stated above (AA. 1, 2), the goodness of the will depends properly on the object. Now the will's object is proposed to it by reason. Because the good understood is the proportionate object of the will; while sensitive or imaginary good is proportionate not to the will but to the sensitive appetite: since the will can tend to the universal good, which reason apprehends; whereas the sensitive appetite tends only to the particular good, apprehended by the sensitive power. Therefore the goodness of the will depends on reason, in the same way as it depends on the object.

*Reply Obj.* 1. The good considered as such, *i.e.*, as appetible, pertains to the will before pertaining to the reason. But considered as true it pertains to the reason, before, under the aspect of goodness, pertaining to the will: because the will cannot desire a good that is not previously apprehended by reason.

*Reply Obj.* 2. The Philosopher speaks there of the practical intellect, in so far as it counsels and reasons about the means: for in this respect it is perfected by prudence. Now in regard to the means, the rectitude of the reason depends on its conformity with the desire of a due end: nevertheless the very desire of the due end presupposes on the part of reason a right apprehension of the end.

*Reply Obj.* 3. The will moves the reason in one way: the reason moves the will in another, viz., on the part of the object, as stated above (Q. IX., A. 1).

## Fourth Article.

### WHETHER THE GOODNESS OF THE WILL DEPENDS ON THE ETERNAL LAW ?

*We proceed thus to the Fourth Article :—*

*Objection* 1. It would seem that the goodness of the human will does not depend on the eternal law. Because to one thing there is one rule and one measure. But the rule of the human will, on which its goodness depends, is right reason. Therefore the goodness of the will does not depend on the eternal law.

*Obj.* 2. Further, *a measure is homogeneous with the thing measured* (*Metaph.* x. 1). But the eternal law is not homogeneous with the human will. Therefore the eternal law cannot be the measure on which the goodness of the human will depends.

*Obj.* 3. Further, a measure should be most certain. But the eternal law is unknown to us. Therefore it cannot be the measure on which the goodness of our will depends.

*On the contrary*, Augustine says (*Contra Faust.* xxii. 27) that *sin is a deed, word or desire against the eternal law*. But malice of the will is the root of sin. Therefore, since malice is contrary to goodness, the goodness of the will depends on the eternal law.

*I answer that*, Wherever a number of causes are subordinate to one another, the effect depends more on the first than on the second cause: since the second cause acts only in virtue of the first. Now it is from the eternal law, which is the Divine Reason, that human reason is the rule of the human will, from which the human will derives its goodness. Hence it is written (Ps. iv. 6, 7): *Many say: Who showeth us good things? The light of Thy countenance, O Lord, is signed upon us:* as though to say: ' The light of our reason is able to show us good things, and guide our will, in so far as it is the light of (*i.e.*, derived from) Thy countenance.' It is therefore evident that the goodness of the human will depends on the eternal law much more than on human reason: and when human reason fails we must have recourse to the Eternal Reason.

*Reply Obj.* 1. To one thing there are not several proximate measures; but there can be several measures if one is subordinate to the other.

*Reply Obj.* 2. A proximate measure is homogeneous with the thing measured; a remote measure is not.

*Reply Obj.* 3. Although the eternal law is unknown to us according as it is in the Divine Mind: nevertheless, it becomes known to us somewhat, either by natural reason which is derived therefrom as its proper image; or by some sort of additional revelation.

## FIFTH ARTICLE.

### WHETHER THE WILL IS EVIL WHEN IT IS AT VARIANCE WITH ERRING REASON ?

*We proceed thus to the Fifth Article :—*

*Objection* 1. It would seem that the will is not evil when it is at variance with erring reason. Because the reason is the rule of the human will, in so far as it is derived from the eternal law, as stated above (A. 4). But erring reason is not derived from the eternal law. Therefore erring reason is not the rule of the human will. Therefore the will is not evil, if it be at variance with erring reason.

*Obj.* 2. Further, according to Augustine, the command of a lower authority does not bind if it be contrary to the command of a higher authority: for instance, if a provincial governor command something that is forbidden by the emperor. But erring reason sometimes proposes what is against the command of a higher power, namely, God Whose power is supreme. Therefore the decision of an erring reason does not bind. Consequently the will is not evil if it be at variance with erring reason.

*Obj.* 3. Further, every evil will is reducible to some species of malice. But the will that is at variance with erring reason is not reducible to some species of malice. For instance, if a man's reason err in telling him to commit fornication, his will in not willing to do so, cannot be reduced to any species of malice. Therefore the will is not evil when it is at variance with erring reason.

*On the contrary*, As stated in the First Part (Q. LXXIX., A. 13), conscience is nothing else than the application of knowledge to some action. Now knowledge is in the reason. Therefore when the will is at variance with erring reason, it is against conscience. But every such will is evil; for it is written (Rom. xiv. 23): *All that is not of faith— i.e.*, all that is against conscience—*is sin*. Therefore the will is evil when it is at variance with erring reason.

*I answer that*, Since conscience is a kind of dictate of the reason (for it is an application of knowledge to action, as was stated in the First Part, Q. LXXIX., A. 13), to inquire whether the will is evil when it is at variance with erring reason, is the same as to inquire *whether an erring conscience binds*. On this matter, some distinguished three kinds of actions: for some are good generically; some are indifferent; some are evil generically. And they say that if reason or conscience tell us to do something which is good generically, there is no error: and in like manner if it tell us not to do something which is evil generically; since it is the same reason that prescribes what is good and forbids what is evil. On the other hand if a man's reason or conscience tell him that he is bound by precept to do what is evil in itself; or that what is good in itself, is forbidden, then his reason or conscience errs. In like manner if a man's reason or conscience tell him, that what is indifferent in itself, for instance to raise a straw from the ground, is forbidden or commanded, his reason or conscience errs. They say, therefore, that reason or conscience when erring in matters of indifference, either by commanding or by forbidding them, binds: so that the will which is at variance with that erring reason is evil and sinful. But they say that when reason or conscience errs in commanding what is evil in itself, or in forbidding what is good in itself and necessary for salvation, it does not bind; wherefore in such cases the will which is at variance with erring reason or conscience is not evil.

But this is unreasonable. For in matters of indifference, the will that is at variance with erring reason or conscience, is evil in some way on account of the object, on which the goodness or malice of the will depends; not indeed on account of the object according as it is in its own nature; but according as it is accidentally apprehended by reason as something evil to do or to avoid. And since the object of the will is that which is proposed by the reason, as stated above (A. 3), from the very fact that a thing is proposed by the reason as being evil, the will by tending thereto becomes evil. And this is the case not only in indifferent matters, but also in those that are good or evil in themselves.

For not only indifferent matters can receive the character of goodness or malice accidentally; but also that which is good, can receive the character of evil, or that which is evil, can receive the character of goodness, on account of the reason apprehending it as such.  For instance, to refrain from fornication is good: yet the will does not tend to this good except in so far as it is proposed by the reason.  If, therefore, the erring reason propose it as an evil, the will tends to it as to something evil.  Consequently the will is evil, because it wills evil, not indeed that which is evil in itself, but that which is evil accidentally, through being apprehended as such by the reason.  In like manner, to believe in Christ is good in itself, and necessary for salvation: but the will does not tend thereto, except inasmuch as it is proposed by the reason.  Consequently if it be proposed by the reason as something evil, the will tends to it as to something evil: not as if it were evil in itself, but because it is evil accidentally, through the apprehension of the reason.  Hence the Philosopher says (*Ethic.* vii. 9) that *properly speaking the incontinent man is one who does not follow right reason ; but accidentally, he is also one who does not follow false reason.*  We must therefore conclude that, absolutely speaking, every will at variance with reason, whether right or erring, is always evil.

*Reply Obj.* 1. Although the judgment of an erring reason is not derived from God, yet the erring reason puts forward its judgment as being true, and consequently as being derived from God, from Whom is all truth.

*Reply Obj.* 2. The saying of Augustine holds good when it is known that the inferior authority prescribes something contrary to the command of the higher authority.  But if a man were to believe the command of the proconsul to be the command of the emperor, in scorning the command of the proconsul he would scorn the command of the emperor. In like manner if a man were to know that human reason was dictating something contrary to God's commandment, he would not be bound to abide by reason: but then reason would not be entirely erroneous.  But when erring reason proposes something as being commanded by God, then to scorn the dictate of reason is to scorn the commandment of God.

*Reply Obj.* 3. Whenever reason apprehends something as evil, it apprehends it under some species of evil; for instance, as being something contrary to a divine precept, or as giving scandal, or for some suchlike reason. And then that evil is reduced to that species of malice.

## SIXTH ARTICLE.

### WHETHER THE WILL IS GOOD WHEN IT ABIDES BY ERRING REASON?

*We proceed thus to the Sixth Article :—*

*Objection* 1. It would seem that the will is good when it abides by erring reason. For just as the will, when at variance with the reason, tends to that which reason judges to be evil; so, when in accord with the reason, it tends to what reason judges to be good. But the will is evil when it is at variance with reason, even when erring. Therefore even when it abides by erring reason, the will is good.

*Obj.* 2. Further, the will is always good, when it abides by the commandment of God and the eternal law. But the eternal law and God's commandment are proposed to us by the apprehension of the reason, even when it errs. Therefore the will is good, even when it abides by erring reason.

*Obj.* 3. Further, the will is evil when it is at variance with erring reason. If, therefore, the will is evil also when it abides by erring reason, it seems that the will is always evil when in conjunction with erring reason: so that in such a case a man would be in a dilemma, and, of necessity, would sin: which is unreasonable. Therefore the will is good when it abides by erring reason.

*On the contrary,* The will of those who slew the apostles was evil. And yet it was in accord with their erring reason, according to Jo. xvi. 2: *The hour cometh, that whosoever killeth you, will think that he doth a service to God.* Therefore the will can be evil, when it abides by erring reason.

*I answer that*, Whereas the previous question is the same as inquiring *whether an erring conscience binds ;* so this question is the same as inquiring *whether an erring conscience excuses*. Now this question depends on what has been said above about ignorance. For it was said (Q. VI., A. 8) that ignorance sometimes causes an act to be involuntary, and sometimes not. And since moral good and evil consist in action in so far as it is voluntary, as was stated above (A. 2); it is evident that when ignorance causes an act to be involuntary, it takes away the character of moral good and evil; but not, when it does not cause the act to be involuntary. Again, it has been stated above (Q. VI., A. 8) that when ignorance is in any way willed, either directly or indirectly, it does not cause the act to be involuntary. And I call that ignorance *directly* voluntary, to which the act of the will tends: and that, *indirectly* voluntary, which is due to negligence, by reason of a man not wishing to know what he ought to know, as stated above (Q. VI., A. 8).

If then reason or conscience err with an error that is voluntary, either directly, or through negligence, so that one errs about what one ought to know; then such an error of reason or conscience does not excuse the will, that abides by that erring reason or conscience, from being evil. But if the error arise from ignorance of some circumstance, and without any negligence, so that it cause the act to be involuntary, then that error of reason or conscience excuses the will, that abides by that erring reason, from being evil. For instance, if erring reason tell a man that he should go to another man's wife, the will that abides by that erring reason is evil; since this error arises from ignorance of the Divine Law, which he is bound to know. But if a man's reason errs in mistaking another for his wife, and if he wish to give her her right when she asks for it, his will is excused from being evil: because this error arises from ignorance of a circumstance, which ignorance excuses, and causes the act to be involuntary.

*Reply Obj*. 1. As Dionysius says (*Div. Nom.* iv.), *good*

*results from the entire cause, evil from each particular defect.*
Consequently, in order that the thing to which the will
tends be called evil, it suffices, either that it be evil in itself,
or that it be apprehended as evil. But in order for it to
be good, it must be good in both ways.

*Reply Obj*. 2. The eternal law cannot err, but human
reason can. Consequently the will that abides by human
reason, is not always right, nor is it always in accord with
the eternal law.

*Reply Obj*. 3. Just as in syllogistic arguments, granted one
absurdity, others must needs follow; so in moral matters,
given one absurdity, others must follow too. Thus suppose
a man to seek vainglory, he will sin, whether he does his
duty for vainglory or whether he omit to do it. Nor is he
in a dilemma about the matter: because he can put aside
his evil intention. In like manner, suppose a man's reason
or conscience to err through inexcusable ignorance, then
evil must needs result in the will. Nor is this man in a
dilemma: because he can lay aside his error, since his
ignorance is vincible and voluntary.

## Seventh Article.

### WHETHER THE GOODNESS OF THE WILL, AS REGARDS THE MEANS, DEPENDS ON THE INTENTION OF THE END ?

*We proceed thus to the Seventh Article :—*

*Objection* 1. It would seem that the goodness of the will
does not depend on the intention of the end. For it has
been stated above (A. 2) that the goodness of the will depends
on the object alone. But as regards the means, the object
of the will is one thing, and the end intended is another.
Therefore in such matters the goodness of the will does not
depend on the intention of the end.

*Obj*. 2. Further, to wish to keep God's commandment,
belongs to a good will. But this can be referred to an evil
end, for instance, to vainglory or covetousness, by willing to
obey God for the sake of temporal gain. Therefore the goodness of the will does not depend on the intention of the end.

*Obj.* 3. Further, just as good and evil diversify the will, so do they diversify the end. But malice of the will does not depend on the malice of the end intended; since a man who wills to steal in order to give alms, has an evil will, although he intends a good end. Therefore neither does the goodness of the will depend on the goodness of the end intended.

*On the contrary*, Augustine says (*Confess.* ix. 3) that God rewards the intention. But God rewards a thing because it is good. Therefore the goodness of the will depends on the intention of the end.

*I answer that*, The intention may stand in a twofold relation to the act of the will; first, as preceding it, secondly as following* it. The intention precedes the act of the will causally, when we will something because we intend a certain end. And then the order to the end is considered as the reason of the goodness of the thing willed: for instance, when a man wills to fast for God's sake; because the act of fasting is specifically good from the very fact that it is done for God's sake. Wherefore, since the goodness of the will depends on the goodness of the thing willed, as stated above (AA. 1, 2), it must, of necessity, depend on the intention of the end.

On the other hand, intention follows the act of the will, when it is added to a preceding act of the will; for instance, a man may will to do something, and may afterwards refer it to God. And then the goodness of the previous act of the will does not depend on the subsequent intention, except in so far as that act is repeated with the subsequent intention.

*Reply Obj.* 1. When the intention is the cause of the act of willing, the order to the end is considered as the reason of the goodness of the object, as stated above.

*Reply Obj.* 2. The act of the will cannot be said to be good, if an evil intention is the cause of willing. For when a man wills to give an alms for the sake of vainglory, he wills that which is good in itself, under a species of evil; and there-

* Leonine ed.—*accompanying.*

fore, as willed by him, it is evil. Wherefore his will is evil. If, however, the intention is subsequent to the act of the will, then the latter may be good: and the intention does not spoil that act of the will which preceded, but that which is repeated.

*Reply Obj.* 3. As we have already stated (A. 6 *ad* 1), *evil results from each particular defect, but good from the whole and entire cause.* Hence, whether the will tend to what is evil in itself, even under the species of good; or to the good under the species of evil, it will be evil in either case. But in order for the will to be good, it must tend to the good under the species of good; in other words, it must will the good for the sake of the good.

### Eighth Article.

#### WHETHER THE DEGREE OF GOODNESS OR MALICE IN THE WILL DEPENDS ON THE DEGREE OF GOOD OR EVIL IN THE INTENTION ?

*We proceed thus to the Eighth Article :—*

*Objection* 1. It would seem that the degree of goodness in the will depends on the degree of good in the intention. Because on Matth. xii. 35, *A good man out of the good treasure of his heart bringeth forth that which is good,* a gloss says: *A man does as much good as he intends.* But the intention gives goodness not only to the external action, but also to the act of the will, as stated above (A. 7). Therefore the goodness of a man's will is according to the goodness of his intention.

*Obj.* 2. Further, if you add to the cause, you add to the effect. But the goodness of the intention is the cause of the good will. Therefore a man's will is good, according as his intention is good.

*Obj.* 3. Further, in evil actions, a man sins in proportion to his intention: for if a man were to throw a stone with a murderous intention, he would be guilty of murder. Therefore, for the same reason, in good actions, the will is good in proportion to the good intended.

*On the contrary*, The intention can be good, while the will is evil. Therefore, for the same reason, the intention can be better, and the will less good.

*I answer that*, In regard to both the act, and the intention of the end, we may consider a twofold quantity: one, on the part of the object, by reason of a man willing or doing a good that is greater; the other, taken from the intensity of the act, according as a man wills or acts intensely; and this is more on the part of the agent.

If then we speak of these respective quantities from the point of view of the object, it is evident that the quantity in the act does not depend on the quantity in the intention. With regard to the external act this may happen in two ways. First, through the object that is ordained to the intended end not being proportionate to that end; for instance, if a man were to give ten pounds, he could not realize his intention, if he intended to buy a thing worth a hundred pounds. Secondly, on account of the obstacles that may supervene in regard to the exterior action, which obstacles we are unable to remove: for instance, a man intends to go to Rome, and encounters obstacles, which prevent him from going.—On the other hand, with regard to the interior act of the will, this happens in only one way: because the interior acts of the will are in our power, whereas the external actions are not. But the will can will an object that is not proportionate to the intended end: and thus the will that tends to that object considered absolutely, is not so good as the intention. Yet because the intention also belongs, in a way, to the act of the will,—inasmuch, to wit, as it is the reason thereof; it comes to pass that the quantity of goodness in the intention redounds upon the act of the will; that is to say, in so far as the will wills some great good for an end, although that by which it wills to gain so great a good, is not proportionate to that good.

But if we consider the quantity in the intention and in the act, according to their respective intensity, then the intensity of the intention redounds upon the interior act and the exterior act of the will: since the intention stands in relation to them as a kind of form, as is clear from what was said above (Q. XII., A. 4; Q. XVIII., A. 6). And yet considered materially, while the intention is intense, the interior or exterior act may be not so intense, materially speaking: for instance, when a man does not will with as much intensity to take medicine as he wills to regain health. Nevertheless the very fact of intending health intensely, redounds, as a formal principle, upon the intense volition of medicine.

We must observe, however, that the intensity of the interior or exterior act, may be referred to the intention as its object: as when a man intends to will intensely, or to do something intensely. And yet it does not follow that he wills or acts intensely; because the quantity of goodness in the interior or exterior act does not depend on the quantity of the good intended, as is shown above. And hence it is that a man does not merit as much as he intends to merit: because the quantity of merit is measured by the intensity of the act, as we shall show later on (Q. XX., A. 4; Q. CXIV., A. 4).

*Reply Obj.* 1. This gloss speaks of good as in the estimation of God, Who considers principally the intention of the end. Wherefore another gloss says on the same passage that *the treasure of the heart is the intention, according to which God judges our works.* For the goodness of the intention, as stated above, redounds, so to speak, upon the goodness of the will, which makes even the external act to be meritorious in God's sight.

*Reply Obj.* 2. The goodness of the intention is not the whole cause of a good will. Hence the argument does not prove.

*Reply Obj.* 3. The mere malice of the intention suffices to make the will evil: and therefore too, the will is as evil as the intention is evil. But the same reasoning does not apply to goodness, as stated above (*ad* 2).

## Ninth Article.

### WHETHER THE GOODNESS OF THE WILL DEPENDS ON ITS CONFORMITY TO THE DIVINE WILL ?

*We proceed thus to the Ninth Article :—*

*Objection* 1. It would seem that the goodness of the human will does not depend on its conformity to the Divine will.   Because it is impossible for man's will to be conformed to the Divine will; as appears from the word of Isaias (lv. 9): *As the heavens are exalted above the earth, so are My ways exalted above your ways, and My thoughts above your thoughts.*   If therefore goodness of the will depended on its conformity to the divine will, it would follow that it is impossible for man's will to be good.   Which is inadmissible.

*Obj.* 2. Further, just as our wills arise from the Divine will, so does our knowledge flow from the Divine knowledge.   But our knowledge does not require to be conformed to God's knowledge; since God knows many things that we know not.   Therefore there is no need for our will to be conformed to the Divine will.

*Obj.* 3. Further, the will is a principle of action.   But our action cannot be conformed to God's.   Therefore neither can our will be conformed to His.

*On the contrary*, It is written (Matth. xxvi. 39): *Not as I will, but as Thou wilt :* which words He said, because *He wishes man to be upright and to tend to God* as Augustine expounds in the *Enchiridion*.*   But the rectitude of the will is its goodness.   Therefore the goodness of the will depends on its conformity to the Divine will.

*I answer that*, As stated above (A. 7), the goodness of the will depends on the intention of the end.   Now the last end of the human will is the Sovereign Good, namely, God, as stated above (Q. I., A. 8; Q. III., A. 1).   Therefore the goodness of the human will requires it to be ordained to the Sovereign Good, that is, to God.

Now this Good is primarily and essentially compared to

* *Enarr. in Ps.* xxxii., *serm.* i.

the Divine will, as its proper object.  Again that which is first in any genus, is the measure and rule of all that belongs to that genus.  Moreover, everything attains to rectitude and goodness, in so far as it is in accord with its proper measure.  Therefore, in order that man's will be good it needs to be conformed to the Divine will.

*Reply Obj.* 1. The human will cannot be conformed to the will of God so as to equal it, but only so as to imitate it. In like manner human knowledge is conformed to the Divine knowledge, in so far as it knows truth: and human action is conformed to the Divine, in so far as it is becoming to the agent:—and this by way of imitation, not by way of equality.

From the above may be gathered the replies to the Second and Third Objections.

## Tenth Article.

### Whether it is necessary for the human will, in order to be good, to be conformed to the divine will, as regards the thing willed ?

*We proceed thus to the Tenth Article :—*

*Objection* 1. It would seem that the human will need not always be conformed to the Divine will, as regards the thing willed.  For we cannot will what we know not: since the apprehended good is the object of the will.  But in many things we know not what God wills.  Therefore the human will cannot be conformed to the Divine will as to the thing willed.

*Obj.* 2. Further, God wills to damn the man whom He foresees about to die in mortal sin.  If therefore man were bound to conform his will to the Divine will, in the point of the thing willed, it would follow that a man is bound to will his own damnation.  Which is inadmissible.

*Obj.* 3. Further, no one is bound to will what is against filial piety.  But if man were to will what God wills, this would sometimes be contrary to filial piety: for instance, when God wills the death of a father: if his son were to will it also, it would be against filial piety.  Therefore man is not bound to conform his will to the Divine will, as to the thing willed.

*On the contrary*, (1) On Ps. xxxii. 1, *Praise becometh the upright*, a gloss says: *That man has an upright heart, who wills what God wills.* But everyone is bound to have an upright heart. Therefore everyone is bound to will what God wills.

(2) Moreover, the will takes its form from the object, as does every act. If therefore man is bound to conform his will to the Divine will, it follows that he is bound to conform it, as to the thing willed.

(3) Moreover, opposition of wills arises from men willing different things. But whoever has a will in opposition to the Divine will, has an evil will. Therefore whoever does not conform his will to the Divine will, as to the thing willed, has an evil will.

*I answer that*, As is evident from what has been said above (AA. 3, 5), the will tends to its object, according as it is proposed by the reason. Now a thing may be considered in various ways by the reason, so as to appear good from one point of view, and not good from another point of view. And therefore if a man's will wills a thing to be, according as it appears to be good, his will is good: and the will of another man, who wills that thing not to be, according as it appears evil, is also good. Thus a judge has a good will, in willing a thief to be put to death, because this is just: while the will of another—*e.g.*, the thief's wife or son, who wishes him not to be put to death, inasmuch as killing is a natural evil, is also good.

Now since the will follows the apprehension of the reason or intellect; the more universal the aspect of the apprehended good, the more universal the good to which the will tends. This is evident in the example given above: because the judge has care of the common good, which is justice, and therefore he wishes the thief's death, which has the aspect of good in relation to the common estate; whereas the thief's wife has to consider the private good of the family, and from this point of view she wishes her husband, the thief, not to be put to death.—Now the good of the whole universe is that which is apprehended by God, Who is the Maker and Governor of all things: hence whatever He wills, He wills it under the aspect of the common good; this is His own Goodness, which is the good of the whole universe. On the other hand, the apprehension of a creature, according to its nature, is of some particular good, proportionate to that nature. Now a thing may happen to be good under a particular aspect, and yet not good under a universal aspect, or vice versa, as stated above. And therefore it comes to pass that a certain will is good from willing something considered under a particular aspect, which thing God wills not, under a universal aspect, and vice versa. And hence too it is, that various wills of various men can be good in respect of opposite things, for as much as, under various aspects, they wish a particular thing to be or not to be.

But a man's will is not right in willing a particular good, unless he refer it to the common good as an end: since even the natural appetite of each part is ordained to the common good of the whole. Now it is the end that supplies the formal reason, as it were, of willing whatever is directed to the end. Consequently, in order that a man will some particular good with a right will, he must will that particular good materially, and the Divine and universal good, formally. Therefore the human will is bound to be conformed to the Divine will, as to that which is willed formally, for it is bound to will the Divine and universal good; but not as to that which is willed materially, for the reason given above.

At the same time in both these respects, the human will is conformed to the Divine, in a certain degree. Because inasmuch as it is conformed to the Divine will in the common aspect of the thing willed, it is conformed thereto in the point of the last end. While, inasmuch as it is not conformed to the Divine will in the thing willed materially, it is conformed to that will considered as efficient cause; since the proper inclination consequent to nature, or to

the particular apprehension of some particular thing, comes
to a thing from God as its efficient cause. Hence it is
customary to say that a man's will, in this respect, is conformed to the Divine will, because it wills what God wishes
him to will.

There is yet another kind of conformity in respect of the
formal cause, consisting in man's willing something from
charity, as God wills it. And this conformity is also reduced
to the formal conformity, that is in respect of the last end,
which is the proper object of charity.

*Reply Obj*. 1. We can know in a general way what God
wills. For we know that whatever God wills, He wills it
under the aspect of good. Consequently whoever wills a
thing under any aspect of good, has a will conformed to the
Divine will, as to the reason of the thing willed. But we
know not what God wills in particular: and in this respect
we are not bound to conform our will to the Divine will.

But in the state of glory, every one will see in each thing
that he wills, the relation of that thing to what God wills
in that particular matter. Consequently he will conform
his will to God in all things not only formally, but also
materially.

*Reply Obj*. 2. God does not will the damnation of a man,
considered precisely as damnation, nor a man's death,
considered precisely as death, because, *He wills all men to
be saved* (1 Tim. ii. 4); but He wills such things under the
aspect of justice. Wherefore in regard to such things it
suffices for man to will the upholding of God's justice and
of the natural order.

Wherefore the reply to the Third Objection is evident.

*To the first argument advanced in a contrary sense*, it
should be said that a man who conforms his will to God's,
in the aspect of reason of the thing willed, wills what God
wills, more than the man, who conforms his will to God's,
in the point of the very thing willed; because the will tends
more to the end, than to that which is on account of the
end.

*To the second*, it must be replied that the species and form of an act are taken from the object considered formally, rather than from the object considered materially.

*To the third*, it must be said that there is no opposition of wills when several people desire different things, but not under the same aspect: but there is opposition of wills, when under one and the same aspect, one man wills a thing which another wills not. But there is no question of this here.

# QUESTION XX.

## OF GOODNESS AND MALICE IN EXTERNAL HUMAN ACTIONS.

### (*In Six Articles.*)

WE must next consider goodness and malice as to external actions: under which head there are six points of inquiry: (1) Whether goodness and malice is first in the act of the will, or in the external action? (2) Whether the whole goodness or malice of the external action depends on the goodness of the will? (3) Whether the goodness and malice of the interior act are the same as those of the external action? (4) Whether the external action adds any goodness or malice to that of the interior act? (5) Whether the consequences of an external action increase its goodness or malice? (6) Whether one and the same external action can be both good and evil?

## FIRST ARTICLE.

### WHETHER GOODNESS OR MALICE IS FIRST IN THE ACT OF THE WILL, OR IN THE EXTERNAL ACTION?

*We proceed thus to the First Article :—*

*Objection* 1. It would seem that good and evil are in the external action prior to being in the act of the will. For the will derives goodness from its object, as stated above (Q. XIX., AA. 1, 2). But the external action is the object of the interior act of the will: for a man is said to will to commit a theft, or to will to give an alms. Therefore good and evil are in the external action, prior to being in the act of the will.

*Obj.* 2. Further, the aspect of good belongs first to the end: since what is directed to the end receives the aspect of good from its relation to the end. Now whereas the act of the will cannot be an end, as stated above (Q. I., A. 1 *ad* 2), the act of another power can be an end. Therefore good is in the act of some other power prior to being in the act of the will.

*Obj.* 3. Further, the act of the will stands in a formal relation to the external action, as stated above (Q. XVIII., A. 6). But that which is formal is subsequent; since form is something added to matter. Therefore good and evil are in the external action, prior to being in the act of the will.

*On the contrary*, Augustine says (*Retract.* i. 9) that *it is by the will that we sin, and that we behave aright.* Therefore moral good and evil are first in the will.

*I answer that*, External actions may be said to be good or bad in two ways. First, in regard to their genus, and the circumstances connected with them: thus the giving of alms, if the required conditions be observed, is said to be good. Secondly, a thing is said to be good or evil, from its relation to the end: thus the giving of alms for vainglory is said to be evil. Now, since the end is the will's proper object, it is evident that this aspect of good or evil, which the external action derives from its relation to the end, is to be found first of all in the act of the will, whence it passes to the external action. On the other hand, the goodness or malice which the external action has of itself, on account of its being about due matter and its being attended by due circumstances, is not derived from the will, but rather from the reason. Consequently, if we consider the goodness of the external action, in so far as it comes from reason's ordination and apprehension, it is prior to the goodness of the act of the will: but if we consider it in so far as it is in the execution of the action done, it is subsequent to the goodness of the will, which is its principle.

*Reply Obj.* 1. The exterior action is the object of the will, inasmuch as it is proposed to the will by the reason, as a good apprehended and ordained by the reason: and thus it

II. i.                                                                    17

is prior to the good in the act of the will.   But inasmuch as
it is found in the execution of the action, it is an effect of the
will, and is subsequent to the will.

*Reply Obj.* 2.  The end precedes in the order of intention,
but follows in the order of execution.

*Reply Obj.* 3.  A form as received into matter, is subsequent
to matter in the order of generation, although it precedes
it in the order of nature: but inasmuch as it is in the active
cause, it precedes in every way.   Now the will is compared
to the exterior action, as its efficient cause.   Wherefore the
goodness of the act of the will, as existing in the active
cause, is the form of the exterior action.

## SECOND ARTICLE.

### WHETHER THE WHOLE GOODNESS AND MALICE OF THE EXTERNAL ACTION DEPEND ON THE GOODNESS OF THE WILL ?

*We proceed thus to the Second Article :—*

*Objection* 1.  It would seem that the whole goodness and
malice of the external action depend on the goodness of the
will.   For it is written (Matth. vii. 18): *A good tree cannot
bring forth evil fruit, neither can an evil tree bring forth good
fruit.*   But, according to the gloss, the tree signifies the will,
and fruit signifies works.   Therefore, it is impossible for the
interior act of the will to be good, and the external action
evil, or vice versa.

*Obj.* 2.  Further, Augustine says (*Retract.* i. 9) that there
is no sin without the will.   If therefore there is no sin in
the will, there will be none in the external action.   And so
the whole goodness or malice of the external action depends
on the will.

*Obj.* 3.  Further, the good and evil of which we are speaking now are differences of the moral act.   Now differences
make an essential division in a genus, according to the
Philosopher (*Metaph.* vii. 12).   Since therefore an act is
moral from being voluntary, it seems that goodness and
malice in an act are derived from the will alone.

*On the contrary,* Augustine says (*Contra Mendac.* vii.

that *there are some actions which neither a good end nor a good will can make good.*

*I answer that,* As stated above (A. 1), we may consider a twofold goodness or malice in the external action: one in respect of due matter and circumstances; the other in respect of the order to the end. And that which is in respect of the order to the end, depends entirely on the will: while that which is in respect of due matter or circumstances, depends on the reason: and on this goodness depends the goodness of the will, in so far as the will tends towards it.

Now it must be observed, as was noted above (Q. XIX., A. 6 *ad* 1), that for a thing to be evil, one single defect suffices, whereas, for it to be good simply, it is not enough for it to be good in one point only, it must be good in every respect. If therefore the will be good, both from its proper object and from its end, it follows that the external action is good. But if the will be good from its intention of the end, this is not enough to make the external action good: and if the will be evil either by reason of its intention of the end, or by reason of the act willed, it follows that the external action is evil.

*Reply Obj.* 1. If the good tree be taken to signify the good will, it must be in so far as the will derives goodness from the act willed and from the end intended.

*Reply Obj.* 2. A man sins by his will, not only when he wills an evil end; but also when he wills an evil act.

*Reply Obj.* 3. Voluntariness applies not only to the interior act of the will, but also to external actions, inasmuch as they proceed from the will and the reason. Consequently the difference of good and evil is applicable to both the interior and external act.

## Third Article.

WHETHER THE GOODNESS AND MALICE OF THE EXTERNAL ACTION ARE THE SAME AS THOSE OF THE INTERIOR ACT ?

*We proceed thus to the Third Article :—*

*Objection* 1. It would seem that the goodness and malice of the interior act of the will are not the same as those of

the external action. For the principle of the interior act i
the interior apprehensive or appetitive power of the soul
whereas the principle of the external action is the powe
that accomplishes the movement. Now where the principle
of action are different, the actions themselves are different
Moreover, it is the action which is the subject of goodnes
or malice: and the same accident cannot be in differen
subjects. Therefore the goodness of the interior act canno
be the same as that of the external action.

*Obj.* 2. Further, *A virtue makes that, which has it, good
and renders its action good also* (*Ethic.* ii. 6). But the intel
lectual virtue in the commanding power is distinct from
the moral virtue in the power commanded, as is declared
in *Ethic.* i. 13. Therefore the goodness of the interior act
which belongs to the commanding power, is distinct from
the goodness of the external action, which belongs to th
power commanded.

*Obj.* 3. Further, the same thing cannot be cause an
effect; since nothing is its own cause. But the goodnes
of the interior act is the cause of the goodness of the ex
ternal action, or vice versa, as stated above (AA. 1, 2)
Therefore it is not the same goodness in each.

*On the contrary,* It was shown above (Q. XVIII., A. 6
that the act of the will is the form, as it were, of the externa
action. Now that which results from the material an
formal element is one thing. Therefore there is but on
goodness of the internal and external act.

*I answer that,* As stated above (Q. XVII., A. 4), the in
terior act of the will, and the external action, considered
morally, are one act. Now it happens sometimes that on
and the same individual act has several aspects of goodnes
or malice, and sometimes that it has but one. Hence w
must say that sometimes the goodness or malice of the in
terior act is the same as that of the external action, an
sometimes not. For as we have already said (AA. 1, 2
these two goodnesses or malices, of the internal and externa
acts, are ordained to one another. Now it may happen
in things that are subordinate to something else, that a thin

is good merely from being subordinate; thus a bitter draught is good merely because it procures health. Wherefore there are not two goodnesses, one the goodness of health, and the other the goodness of the draught; but one and the same. On the other hand it happens sometimes that that which is subordinate to something else, has some aspect of goodness in itself, besides the fact of its being subordinate to some other good: thus a palatable medicine can be considered in the light of a pleasurable good, besides being conducive to health.

We must therefore say that when the external action derives goodness or malice from its relation to the end only, then there is but one and the same goodness of the act of the will which of itself regards the end, and of the external action, which regards the end through the medium of the act of the will. But when the external action has goodness or malice of itself, *i.e.*, in regard to its matter and circumstances, then the goodness of the external action is distinct from the goodness of the will in regarding the end; yet so that the goodness of the end passes into the external action, and the goodness of the matter and circumstances passes into the act of the will, as stated above (AA. 1, 2).

*Reply Obj.* 1. This argument proves that the internal and external actions are different in the physical order: yet distinct as they are in that respect, they combine to form one thing in the moral order, as stated above (Q. XVII., A. 4).

*Reply Obj.* 2. As stated in *Ethic.* vi. 12, a moral virtue is ordained to the act of that virtue, which act is the end, as it were, of that virtue; whereas prudence, which is in the reason, is ordained to things directed to the end. For this reason various virtues are necessary. But right reason in regard to the very end of a virtue has no other goodness than the goodness of that virtue, in so far as the goodness of the reason is participated in each virtue.

*Reply Obj.* 3. When a thing is derived by one thing from another, as from a univocal efficient cause, then it is not the same in both: thus when a hot thing heats, the heat of

the heater is distinct from the heat of the thing heated
although it be the same specifically. But when a thing is
derived by one thing from another, according to analogy
or proportion, then it is one and the same in both: thus
the healthiness which is in medicine or urine is derived from
the healthiness of the animal's body; nor is health as applied
to urine and medicine, distinct from health as applied to
the body of an animal, of which health medicine is the cause
and urine the sign. It is in this way that the goodness of
the external action is derived from the goodness of the will,
and vice versa; viz., according to the order of one to the
other.

## FOURTH ARTICLE.

### WHETHER THE EXTERNAL ACTION ADDS ANY GOODNESS OR MALICE TO THAT OF THE INTERIOR ACT ?

*We proceed thus to the Fourth Article :*—

*Objection* 1. It would seem that the external action does
not add any goodness or malice to that of the interior action.
For Chrysostom says (*Hom.* xix. *in Matth.*): *It is the will
that is rewarded for doing good, or punished for doing evil.*
Now works are the witnesses of the will. Therefore God
seeks for works not on His own account, in order to know
how to judge; but for the sake of others, that all may understand how just He is. But good or evil is to be estimated
according to God's judgment rather than according to the
judgment of man. Therefore the external action adds no
goodness or malice to that of the interior act.

*Obj.* 2. Further, the goodness and malice of the interior
and external acts are one and the same, as stated above
(A. 3). But increase is the addition of one thing to another.
Therefore the external action does not add to the goodness
or malice of the interior act.

*Obj.* 3. Further, the entire goodness of created things
does not add to the Divine Goodness, because it is entirely
derived therefrom. But sometimes the entire goodness
of the external action is derived from the goodness of the
interior act, and sometimes conversely, as stated above

(AA. 1, 2). Therefore neither of them adds to the goodness or malice of the other.

*On the contrary*, Every agent intends to attain good and avoid evil. If therefore by the external action no further goodness or malice be added, it is to no purpose that he who has a good or an evil will, does a good deed or refrains from an evil deed. Which is unreasonable.

*I answer that*, If we speak of the goodness which the external action derives from the will tending to the end, then the external action adds nothing to this goodness, unless it happens that the will in itself is made better in good things, or worse in evil things. This, seemingly, may happen in three ways. First in point of number; if, for instance, a man wishes to do something with a good or an evil end in view, and does not do it then, but afterwards wills and does it, the act of his will is doubled, and a double good, or a double evil is the result.—Secondly, in point of extension: when, for instance, a man wishes to do something for a good or an evil end, and is hindered by some obstacle, whereas another man perseveres in the movement of the will until he accomplish it in deed; it is evident that the will of the latter is more lasting in good or evil, and, in this respect, is better or worse.—Thirdly, in point of intensity: for there are certain external actions, which, in so far as they are pleasurable or painful, are such as naturally to make the will more intense or more remiss; and it is evident that the more intensely the will tends to good or evil, the better or worse it is.

On the other hand, if we speak of the goodness which the external action derives from its matter and due circumstances, thus it stands in relation to the will as its term and end. And in this way it adds to the goodness or malice of the will; because every inclination or movement is perfected by attaining its end or reaching its term. Wherefore the will is not perfect, unless it be such that, given the opportunity, it realizes the operation. But if this prove impossible, as long as the will is perfect, so as to realize the operation if it could; the lack of perfection derived from the external action, is simply involuntary.  Now just as the involuntary deserves neither punishment nor reward in the accomplishment of good or evil deeds, so neither does it lessen reward or punishment, if a man through simple involuntariness fail to do good or evil.

*Reply Obj.* 1. Chrysostom is speaking of the case where a man's will is complete, and does not refrain from the deed save through the impossibility of achievement.

*Reply Obj.* 2. This argument applies to that goodness which the external action derives from the will as tending to the end.  But the goodness which the external action takes from its matter and circumstances, is distinct from that which it derives from the end; but it is not distinct from that which it has from the very act willed, to which it stands in the relation of measure and cause, as stated above (AA. 1, 2).

From this the reply to the Third Objection is evident.

## Fifth Article.

### WHETHER THE CONSEQUENCES OF THE EXTERNAL ACTION INCREASE ITS GOODNESS OR MALICE ?

*We proceed thus to the Fifth Article :—*

*Objection* 1. It would seem that the consequences of the external action increase its goodness or malice.  For the effect pre-exists virtually in its cause.  But the consequences result from the action as an effect from its cause.  Therefore they pre-exist virtually in actions.  Now a thing is judged to be good or bad according to its virtue, since a virtue *makes that which has it to be good* (*Ethic.* ii. 6).  Therefore the consequences increase the goodness or malice of an action.

*Obj.* 2. Further, the good actions of his hearers are consequences resulting from the words of a preacher.  But such goods as these redound to the merit of the preacher, as is evident from Phil. iv. 1: *My dearly beloved brethren, my joy and my crown.*  Therefore the consequences of an action increase its goodness or malice.

*Obj.* 3. Further, punishment is not increased, unless the

fault increases: wherefore it is written (Deut. xxv. 2): *According to the measure of the sin shall the measure also of the stripes be.* But the punishment is increased on account of the consequences; for it is written (Exod. xxi. 29): *But if the ox was wont to push with his horn yesterday and the day before, and they warned his master, and he did not shut him up, and he shall kill a man or a woman, then the ox shall be stoned, and his owner also shall be put to death.* But he would not have been put to death, if the ox, although he had not been shut up, had not killed a man. Therefore the consequences increase the goodness or malice of an action.

*Obj.* 4. Further, if a man do something which may cause death, by striking, or by sentencing, and if death does not ensue, he does not contract irregularity: but he would if death were to ensue. Therefore the consequences of an action increase its goodness or malice.

*On the contrary,* The consequences do not make an action that was evil, to be good; nor one that was good, to be evil. For instance, if a man give an alms to a poor man who makes bad use of the alms by committing a sin, this does not undo the good done by the giver; and, in like manner, if a man bear patiently a wrong done to him, the wrong-doer is not thereby excused. Therefore the consequences of an action do not increase its goodness or malice.

*I answer that,* The consequences of an action are either foreseen or not. If they are foreseen, it is evident that they increase the goodness or malice. For when a man foresees that many evils may follow from his action, and yet does not therefore desist therefrom, this shows his will to be all the more inordinate.

But if the consequences are not foreseen, we must make a distinction. Because if they follow from the nature of the action, and in the majority of cases, in this respect, the consequences increase the goodness or malice of that action: for it is evident that an action is specifically better, if better results can follow from it; and specifically worse, if it is of a nature to produce worse results.—On the other hand, if the consequences follow by accident and seldom, then they do not increase the goodness or malice of the action : because we do not judge of a thing according to that which belongs to it by accident, but only according to that which belongs to it of itself.

*Reply Obj.* 1. The virtue of a cause is measured by the effect that flows from the nature of the cause, not by that which results by accident.

*Reply Obj.* 2. The good actions done by the hearers, result from the preacher's words, as an effect that flows from their very nature. Hence they redound to the merit of the preacher : especially when such is his intention.

*Reply Obj.* 3. The consequences for which that man is ordered to be punished, both follow from the nature of the cause, and are supposed to be foreseen. For this reason they are reckoned as punishable.

*Reply Obj.* 4. This argument would prove if irregularity were the result of the fault. But it is not the result of the fault, but of the fact, and of the obstacle to the reception of a sacrament.

## Sixth Article.

### WHETHER ONE AND THE SAME EXTERNAL ACTION CAN BE BOTH GOOD AND EVIL ?

*We proceed thus to the Sixth Article :—*

*Objection* 1. It would seem that one and the same external action can be both good and evil. For *movement, if continuous, is one and the same* (*Phys.* v. 4). But one continuous movement can be both good and bad : for instance, a man may go to Church continuously, intending at first vainglory, and afterwards the service of God. Therefore one and the same action can be both good and evil.

*Obj.* 2. Further, according to the Philosopher (*Phys.* iii. 3), action and passion are one act. But the passion may be good, as Christ's was ; and the action evil, as that of the Jews. Therefore one and the same act can be both good and evil.

*Obj.* 3. Further, since a servant is an instrument, as it were, of his master, the servant's action is his master's, just as the action of a tool is the workman's action. But it may happen that the servant's action result from his master's good will, and is therefore good: and from the evil will of the servant, and is therefore evil. Therefore the same action can be both good and evil.

*On the contrary*, The same thing cannot be the subject of contraries. But good and evil are contraries. Therefore the same action cannot be both good and evil.

*I answer that*, Nothing hinders a thing from being one, in so far as it is in one genus, and manifold, in so far as it is referred to another genus. Thus a continuous surface is one, considered as in the genus of quantity; and yet it is manifold, considered as to the genus of colour, if it be partly white, and partly black. And accordingly, nothing hinders an action from being one, considered in the natural order; whereas it is not one, considered in the moral order; and vice versa, as we have stated above (A. 3 *ad* 1; Q. XVIII., A. 7 *ad* 1). For continuous walking is one action, considered in the natural order: but it may resolve itself into many actions, considered in the moral order, if a change take place in the walker's will, for the will is the principle of moral actions. If therefore we consider one action in the moral order, it is impossible for it to be morally both good and evil. Whereas if it be one as to natural and not moral unity, it can be both good and evil.

*Reply Obj.* 1. This continual movement which proceeds from various intentions, although it is one in the natural order, is not one in the point of moral unity.

*Reply Obj.* 2. Action and passion belong to the moral order, in so far as they are voluntary. And therefore in so far as they are voluntary in respect of wills that differ, they are two distinct things, and good can be in one of them while evil is in the other.

*Reply Obj.* 3. The action of the servant, in so far as it proceeds from the will of the servant, is not the master's action: but only in so far as it proceeds from the master's command. Wherefore the evil will of the servant does not make the action evil in this respect.

# QUESTION XXI.

## OF THE CONSEQUENCES OF HUMAN ACTIONS BY REASON OF THEIR GOODNESS AND MALICE.

### ( *In Four Articles.*)

WE have now to consider the consequences of human actions by reason of their goodness and malice: and under this head there are four points of inquiry: (1) Whether a human action is right or sinful by reason of its being good or evil ? (2) Whether it thereby deserves praise or blame ? (3) Whether accordingly, it is meritorious or demeritorious ? (4) Whether it is accordingly meritorious or demeritorious before God ?

### FIRST ARTICLE.

#### WHETHER A HUMAN ACTION IS RIGHT OR SINFUL, IN SO FAR AS IT IS GOOD OR EVIL ?

*We proceed thus to the First Article :—*

*Objection* 1. It seems that a human action is not right or sinful, in so far as it is good or evil. For *monsters are the sins of nature* (*Phys.* ii. 8). But monsters are not actions, but things engendered outside the order of nature. Now things that are produced according to art and reason imitate those that are produced according to nature (*ibid.*). Therefore an action is not sinful by reason of its being inordinate and evil.

*Obj.* 2. Further, sin, as stated in *Phys.* ii. (*loc. cit.*), occurs in nature and art, when the end intended by nature or art is not attained. But the goodness or malice of a human action depends, before all, on the intention of the end, and on its achievement. Therefore it seems that the malice of an action does not make it sinful.

*Obj.* 3. Further, if the malice of an action makes it sinful, it follows that wherever there is evil, there is sin. But this is false: since punishment is not a sin, although it is an evil. Therefore an action is not sinful by reason of its being evil.

*On the contrary*, As shown above (Q. XIX., A. 4), the goodness of a human action depends principally on the Eternal Law: and consequently its malice consists in its being in disaccord with the Eternal Law. But this is the very nature of sin; for Augustine says (*Contra Faust.* xxii. 27) that *sin is a word, deed, or desire, in opposition to the Eternal Law*. Therefore a human action is sinful by reason of its being evil.

*I answer that,* Evil is more comprehensive than sin, as also is good than right. For every privation of good, in whatever subject, is an evil: whereas sin consists properly in an action done for a certain end, and lacking due order to that end. Now the due order to an end is measured by some rule. In things that act according to nature, this rule is the natural force that inclines them to that end. When therefore an action proceeds from a natural force, in accord with the natural inclination to an end, then the action is said to be right: since the mean does not exceed its limits, viz., the action does not swerve from the order of its active principle to the end. But when an action strays from this rectitude, it comes under the notion of sin.

Now in those things that are done by the will, the proximate rule is the human reason, while the supreme rule is the Eternal Law. When, therefore, a human action tends to the end, according to the order of reason and of the Eternal Law, then that action is right: but when it turns aside from that rectitude, then it is said to be a sin. Now it is evident from what has been said (Q. XIX., AA. 3, 4) that every voluntary action that turns aside from the order of reason and of the Eternal Law, is evil, and that every good action is in accord with reason and the Eternal Law. Hence it follows that a human action is right or sinful by reason of its being good or evil.

*Reply Obj.* 1. Monsters are called sins, inasmuch as they result from a sin in nature's action.

*Reply Obj.* 2. The end is twofold; the last end, and the proximate end. In the sin of nature, the action does indeed fail in respect of the last end, which is the perfection of the thing generated; but it does not fail in respect of any proximate end whatever; since when nature works it forms something. In like manner, the sin of the will always fails as regards the last end intended, because no voluntary evil action can be ordained to happiness, which is the last end: and yet it does not fail in respect of some proximate end: intended and achieved by the will. Wherefore also, since the very intention of this end is ordained to the last end, this same intention may be right or sinful.

*Reply Obj.* 3. Each thing is ordained to its end by its action: and therefore sin, which consists in straying from the order to the end, consists properly in an action. On the other hand, punishment regards the person of the sinner, as was stated in the First Part (Q. XLVIII., A. 5, *ad* 4; A. 6, *ad* 3).

## SECOND ARTICLE.

### WHETHER A HUMAN ACTION DESERVES PRAISE OR BLAME, BY REASON OF ITS BEING GOOD OR EVIL ?

*We proceed thus to the Second Article :—*

*Objection* 1. It would seem that a human action does not deserve praise or blame by reason of its being good or evil. For *sin happens even in things done by nature* (*Phys.* ii. 8). And yet natural things are not deserving of praise or blame (*Ethic.* iii. 5). Therefore a human action does not deserve blame, by reason of its being evil or sinful; and, consequently, neither does it deserve praise, by reason of its being good.

*Obj.* 2. Further, just as sin occurs in moral actions, so does it happen in the productions of art: because as stated in *Phys.* ii. (*ibid.*), *it is a sin in a grammarian to write badly, and in a doctor to give the wrong medicine.* But the artist is not blamed for making something bad: because the artist's work is such, that he can produce a good or a bad thing, just as he lists. Therefore it seems that neither is there any reason for blaming a moral action, in the fact that it is evil.

*Obj.* 3. Further, Dionysius says (*Div. Nom.* iv.) that evil is *weak and incapable*. But weakness or inability either takes away or diminishes guilt. Therefore a human action does not incur guilt from being evil.

*On the contrary,* The Philosopher says (*De Virt. et Vit.* i.) that *virtuous deeds deserve praise, while deeds that are opposed to virtue deserve censure and blame*. But good actions are virtuous; because *virtue makes that which has it, good, and makes its action good* (*Ethic.* ii. 6): wherefore actions opposed to virtue are evil. Therefore a human action deserves praise or blame, through being good or evil.

*I answer that,* Just as evil is more comprehensive than sin, so is sin more comprehensive than blame. For an action is said to deserve praise or blame, from its being imputed to the agent: since to praise or to blame mean nothing else than to impute to someone the malice or goodness of his action. Now an action is imputed to an agent, when it is in his power, so that he has dominion over it; and this is the case in all voluntary acts: because it is through his will that man has dominion over his actions, as was made clear above (Q. I., AA. 1, 2). Hence it follows that good or evil, in voluntary actions alone, renders them worthy of praise or blame: and in suchlike actions, evil, sin and guilt are one and the same thing.

*Reply Obj.* 1. Natural actions are not in the power of the natural agent: since the action of nature is determinate. And, therefore, although there be sin in natural actions, there is no blame.

*Reply Obj.* 2. Reason stands in different relations to the productions of art, and to moral actions. In matters of art, reason is directed to a particular end, which is something devised by reason: whereas in moral matters, it is directed to the general end of all human life. Now a particular end is subordinate to the general end. Since therefore sin is a departure from the order to the end, as stated above (A. 1), sin may occur in two ways, in a production of art.   First, by a departure from the particular end intended by the artist: and this sin will be proper to the art; for instance, if an artist produce a bad thing, while intending to produce something good; or produce something good, while intending to produce something bad.   Secondly, by a departure from the general end of human life: and then he will be said to sin, if he intend to produce a bad work, and does so in effect, so that another is taken in thereby. But this sin is not proper to the artist as such, but as a man. Consequently for the former sin the artist is blamed as an artist; while for the latter he is blamed as a man.—On the other hand, in moral matters, where we take into consideration the order of reason to the general end of human life, sin and evil are always due to a departure from the order of reason to the general end of human life.   Wherefore man is blamed for such a sin, both as man and as a moral being.   Hence the Philosopher says (*Ethic.* vi. 5) that *in art, he who sins voluntarily is preferable ; but in prudence, as in the moral virtues*, which prudence directs, *he is the reverse.*

*Reply Obj.* 3. Weakness that occurs in voluntary evils, is subject to man's power: wherefore it neither takes away nor diminishes guilt.

### THIRD ARTICLE.

#### WHETHER A HUMAN ACTION IS MERITORIOUS OR DEMERITORIOUS, IN SO FAR AS IT IS GOOD OR EVIL ?

*We proceed thus to the Third Article :—*

*Objection* 1. It would seem that a human action is not meritorious or demeritorious on account of its goodness or malice.   For we speak of merit or demerit in relation to retribution, which has no place save in matters relating to another person.   But good or evil actions are not all related to another person, for some are related to the person of the agent.   Therefore not every good or evil human action is meritorious or demeritorious.

*Obj.* 2. Further, no one deserves punishment or reward

for doing as he chooses with that of which he is master: thus if a man destroys what belongs to him, he is not punished, as if he had destroyed what belongs to another. But man is master of his own actions. Therefore a man does not merit punishment or reward, through putting his action to a good or evil purpose.

*Obj.* 3. Further, if a man acquire some good for himself, he does not on that account deserve to be benefited by another man: and the same applies to evil. Now a good action is itself a kind of good and perfection of the agent: while an inordinate action is his evil. Therefore a man does not merit or demerit, from the fact that he does a good or an evil deed.

*On the contrary*, It is written (Isa. iii. 10, 11): *Say to the just man that it is well ; for he shall eat the fruit of his doings. Woe to the wicked unto evil ; for the reward of his hands shall be given him.*

*I answer that,* We speak of merit and demerit, in relation to retribution, rendered according to justice. Now, retribution according to justice is rendered to a man, by reason of his having done something to another's advantage or hurt. It must, moreover, be observed that every individual member of a society is, in a fashion, a part and member of the whole society. Wherefore, any good or evil, done to the member of a society, redounds on the whole society: thus, who hurts the hand, hurts the man. When, therefore, anyone does good or evil to another individual, there is a twofold measure of merit or demerit in his action: first, in respect of the retribution owed to him by the individual to whom he has done good or harm; secondly, in respect of the retribution owed to him by the whole of society.—Now when a man ordains his action directly for the good or evil of the whole society, retribution is owed to him, before and above all, by the whole society; secondarily, by all the parts of society. Whereas when a man does that which conduces to his own benefit or disadvantage, then again is retribution owed to him, in so far as this too affects the community, forasmuch as he is a part of society: although retribution is not due to him, in so far as it conduces to the good or harm of an individual, who is identical with the agent; unless, perchance, he owe retribution to himself, by a sort of resemblance, in so far as man is said to be just to himself.

It is therefore evident that a good or evil action deserves praise or blame, in so far as it is in the power of the will: that it is right or sinful, according as it is ordained to the end; and that its merit or demerit depends on the recompense for justice or injustice towards another.

*Reply Obj*. 1. A man's good or evil actions, although not ordained to the good or evil of another individual, are nevertheless ordained to the good or evil of another, *i.e.*, the community.

*Reply Obj*. 2. Man is master of his actions; and yet, in so far as he belongs to another, *i.e.*, the community, of which he forms part, he merits or demerits, inasmuch as he disposes his actions well or ill: just as if he were to dispense well or ill other belongings of his, in respect of which he is bound to serve the community.

*Reply Obj*. 3. This very good or evil, which a man does to himself by his action, redounds to the community, as stated above.

## FOURTH ARTICLE.

### WHETHER A HUMAN ACTION IS MERITORIOUS OR DEMERITORIOUS BEFORE GOD, ACCORDING AS IT IS GOOD OR EVIL ?

*We proceed thus to the Fourth Article :—*

*Objection* 1. It would seem that man's actions, good or evil, are not meritorious or demeritorious in the sight of God. Because, as stated above (A. 3), merit and demerit imply relation to retribution for good or harm done to another. But a man's action, good or evil, does no good or harm to God; for it is written (Job xxxv. 6, 7): *If thou sin, what shalt thou hurt Him ? . . . And if thou do justly, what shalt thou give Him ?* Therefore a human action, good or evil, is not meritorious or demeritorious in the sight of God.

*Obj*. 2. Further, an instrument acquires no merit or demerit in the sight of him that uses it; because the entire action of the instrument belongs to the user. Now when man acts he is the instrument of the Divine power which is the principal cause of his action; hence it is written (Isa. x. 15): *Shall the axe boast itself against him that cutteth with it ? Or shall the saw exalt itself against him by whom it is drawn ?* where man while acting is evidently compared to an instrument. Therefore man merits or demerits nothing in God's sight, by good or evil deeds.

*Obj*. 3. Further, a human action acquires merit or demerit through being ordained to someone else. But not all human actions are ordained to God. Therefore not every good or evil action acquires merit or demerit in God's sight.

*On the contrary*, It is written (Eccles. xii. 14): *All things that are done, God will bring into judgment . . . whether it be good or evil.* Now judgment implies retribution, in respect of which we speak of merit and demerit. Therefore every human action, both good and evil, acquires merit or demerit in God's sight.

*I answer that*, A human action, as stated above (A. 3), acquires merit or demerit, through being ordained to someone else, either by reason of himself, or by reason of the community: and in each way, our actions, good and evil, acquire merit or demerit in the sight of God. On the part of God Himself, inasmuch as He is man's last end; and it is our duty to refer all our actions to the last end, as stated above (Q. XIX., A. 10). Consequently, whoever does an evil deed, not referable to God, does not give God the honour due to Him as our last end.—On the part of the whole community of the universe, because in every community, he who governs the community, cares, first of all, for the common good; wherefore it is his business to award retribution for such things as are done well or ill in the community. Now God is the governor and ruler of the whole universe, as stated in the First Part (Q. CIII., A. 5): and especially of rational creatures. Consequently it is evident that human actions acquire merit or demerit in reference to Him: else it would follow that human actions are no business of God's.

*Reply Obj.* 1. God in Himself neither gains nor loses anything by the action of man: but man, for his part, takes something from God, or offers something to Him, when he observes or does not observe the order instituted by God.

*Reply Obj.* 2. Man is so moved, as an instrument, by God, that, at the same time, he moves himself by his free-will, as was explained above (Q. IX., A. 6 *ad* 3). Consequently, by his action, he acquires merit or demerit in God's sight.

*Reply Obj.* 3. Man is not ordained to the body politic, according to all that he is and has; and so it does not follow that every action of his acquires merit or demerit in relation to the body politic. But all that man is, and can, and has, must be referred to God: and therefore every action of man, whether good or bad, acquires merit or demerit in the sight of God, as far as the action itself is concerned.

# QUESTION XXII.

## OF THE SUBJECT OF THE SOUL'S PASSIONS.

### (*In Three Articles.*)

WE must now consider the passions of the soul: first, in general; secondly, in particular. Taking them in general, there are four things to be considered: (1) Their subject: (2) The difference between them: (3) Their mutual relationship: (4) Their malice and goodness.

Under the first head there are three points of inquiry: (1) Whether there is any passion in the soul ? (2) Whether passion is in the appetitive rather than in the apprehensive part ? (3) Whether passion is in the sensitive appetite rather than in the intellectual appetite, which is called the will ?

### FIRST ARTICLE.

#### WHETHER ANY PASSION IS IN THE SOUL ?

*We proceed thus to the First Article :—*

*Objection* 1. It would seem that there is no passion in the soul. Because passivity belongs to matter. But the soul is not composed of matter and form, as stated in the First Part (Q. LXXV., A. 5). Therefore there is no passion in the soul.

*Obj.* 2. Further, passion is movement, as is stated in *Phys.* iii. 3. But the soul is not moved, as is proved in *De Anima* i. 3. Therefore passion is not in the soul.

*Obj.* 3. Further, passion is the road to corruption; since *every passion, when increased, alters the substance*, as is stated in *Topic.* vi. 6. But the soul is incorruptible. Therefore no passion is in the soul.

*On the contrary*, The Apostle says (Rom. vii. 5): *When we were in the flesh, the passions of sins which were by the law, did work in our members.* Now sins are, properly speaking, in the soul. Therefore passions also, which are described as being *of sins*, are in the soul.

*I answer that,* The word *passive* is used in three ways. First, in a general way, according as whatever receives something is passive, although nothing is taken from it: thus we may say that the air is passive when it is lit up. But this is to be perfected rather than to be passive. Secondly, the word *passive* is employed in its proper sense, when something is received, while something else is taken away: and this happens in two ways. For sometimes that which is lost is unsuitable to the thing: thus when an animal's body is healed, it is said to be passive, because it receives health, and loses sickness.—At other times the contrary occurs: thus to ail is to be passive; because the ailment is received and health is lost. And here we have passion in its most proper acceptation. For a thing is said to be passive from its being drawn to the agent: and when a thing recedes from what is suitable to it, then especially does it appear to be drawn to something else. Moreover in *De Generat.* i. 3, it is stated that when a more excellent thing is generated from a less excellent, we have generation simply, and corruption in a particular respect: whereas the reverse is the case, when from a more excellent thing, a less excellent is generated. In these three ways it happens that passions are in the soul. For in the sense of mere reception, we speak of *feeling and understanding as being a kind of passion* (*De Anima* i. 5). But passion, accompanied by the loss of something, is only in respect of a bodily transmutation; wherefore passion properly so called cannot be in the soul, save accidentally, in so far, to wit, as the *composite* is passive. But here again we find a difference; because when this transmutation is for the worse, it has more of the nature of a passion, than when it is for the better: hence sorrow is more properly a passion than joy.

*Reply Obj.* 1. It belongs to matter to be passive in such a way as to lose something and to be transmuted: hence this happens only in those things that are composed of matter and form. But passivity, as implying mere reception, need not be in matter, but can be in anything that is in potentiality. Now, though the soul is not composed of matter and form, yet it has something of potentiality, in respect of which it is competent to receive or to be passive, according as the act of understanding is a kind of passion, as stated in *De Anima* iii. 4.

*Reply Obj.* 2. Although it does not belong to the soul in itself to be passive and to be moved, yet it belongs accidentally, as stated in *De Anima* i. 3.

*Reply Obj.* 3. This argument is true of passion accompanied by transmutation to something worse. And passion, in this sense, is not found in the soul, except accidentally: but the composite, which is corruptible, admits of it by reason of its own nature.

## SECOND ARTICLE.

### WHETHER PASSION IS IN THE APPETITIVE RATHER THAN IN THE APPREHENSIVE PART?

*We proceed thus to the Second Article :—*

*Objection* 1. It would seem that passion is in the apprehensive part of the soul rather than in the appetitive. Because that which is first in any genus, seems to rank first among all things that are in that genus, and to be their cause, as is stated in *Metaph.* ii. 1. Now passion is found to be in the apprehensive, before being in the appetitive part: for the appetitive part is not affected unless there be a previous passion in the apprehensive part. Therefore passion is in the apprehensive part more than in the appetitive.

*Obj.* 2. Further, what is more active is less passive; for action is contrary to passion. Now the appetitive part is more active than the apprehensive. Therefore it seems that passion is more in the apprehensive part.

*Obj.* 3. Further, just as the sensitive appetite is the power of a corporeal organ, so is the power of sensitive apprehension. But passion in the soul occurs, properly speaking, in respect of a bodily transmutation.  Therefore passion is not more in the sensitive appetitive than in the sensitive apprehensive part.

*On the contrary,* Augustine says (*De Civ. Dei* ix. 4) that *the movements of the soul, which the Greeks call* πάθη, *are styled by some of our writers, Cicero\* for instance, disturbances ; by some, affections or emotions ; while others rendering the Greek more accurately, call them passions.*  From this it is evident that the passions of the soul are the same as affections.  But affections manifestly belong to the appetitive, and not to the apprehensive part.  Therefore the passions are in the appetitive rather than in the apprehensive part.

*I answer that,* As we have already stated (A. 1) the word *passion* implies that the patient is drawn to that which belongs to the agent.  Now the soul is drawn to a thing by the appetitive power rather than by the apprehensive power: because the soul has, through its appetitive power, an order to things as they are in themselves: hence the Philosopher says (*Metaph.* vi. 4) that *good and evil, i.e.,* the objects of the appetitive power, *are in things themselves.*  On the other hand the apprehensive power is not drawn to a thing, as it is in itself; but knows it by reason of an *intention* of the thing, which *intention* it has in itself, or receives in its own way.  Hence we find it stated (*ibid.*) that *the true and the false,* which pertain to knowledge, *are not in things, but in the mind.*  Consequently it is evident that the nature of passion is consistent with the appetitive, rather than with the apprehensive part.

*Reply Obj.* 1.  In things relating to perfection the case is the opposite, in comparison to things that pertain to defect.  Because in things relating to perfection, intensity is in proportion to the approach to one first principle; to which the nearer a thing approaches, the more intense it is.  Thus the intensity of a thing possessed of light depends on its approach to something endowed with light in a supreme degree, to which the nearer a thing approaches, the more

---

\* *Those things which the Greeks call* πάθη, *we prefer to call disturbances rather than diseases* (Tusc. iv. 5).

light it possesses. But in things that relate to defect, intensity depends, not on approach to something supreme, but in receding from that which is perfect; because therein consists the very notion of privation and defect. Wherefore the less a thing recedes from that which stands first, the less intense it is: and the result is that at first we always find some small defect, which afterwards increases as it goes on. Now passion pertains to defect, because it belongs to a thing according as it is in potentiality. Wherefore in those things that approach to the Supreme Perfection, *i.e.*, to God, there is but little potentiality and passion: while in other things, consequently, there is more. Hence also, in the supreme, *i.e.*, the apprehensive, power of the soul, passion is found less than in the other powers.

*Reply Obj.* 2. The appetitive power is said to be more active, because it is, more than the apprehensive power, the principle of the exterior action: and this for the same reason that it is more passive, namely, its being related to things as existing in themselves: since it is through the external action that we come into contact with things.

*Reply Obj.* 3. As stated in the First Part (Q. LXXVIII., A. 3), the organs of the soul can be changed in two ways. First, by a spiritual change, in respect of which the organ receives an *intention* of the object. And this is essential to the act of the sensitive apprehension: thus is the eye changed by the object visible, not by being coloured, but by receiving an intention of colour. But the organs are receptive of another and natural change, which affects their natural disposition; for instance, when they become hot or cold, or undergo some similar change. And whereas this kind of change is accidental to the act of the sensitive apprehension; for instance, if the eye be wearied through gazing intently at something, or be overcome by the intensity of the object: on the other hand, it is essential to the act of the sensitive appetite; wherefore the material element in the definitions of the movements of the appetitive part, is the natural change of the organ; for instance, *anger* is said to be *a kindling of the blood about the heart*. Hence it is evident that the notion of passion is more consistent with the act of the sensitive appetite, than with that of the sensitive apprehension, although both are actions of a corporeal organ.

## THIRD ARTICLE.

### WHETHER PASSION IS IN THE SENSITIVE APPETITE RATHER THAN IN THE INTELLECTUAL APPETITE, WHICH IS CALLED THE WILL ?

*We proceed thus to the Third Article :—*

*Objection* 1. It would seem that passion is not more in the sensitive than in the intellectual appetite. For Dionysius declares (*Div. Nom.* ii.) Hierotheus *to be taught by a kind of yet more Godlike instruction ; not only by learning Divine things, but also by suffering (patiens) them.* But the sensitive appetite cannot *suffer* Divine things, since its object is the sensible good. Therefore passion is in the intellectual appetite, just as it is also in the sensitive appetite.

*Obj.* 2. Further, the more powerful the active force, the more intense the passion. But the object of the intellectual appetite, which is the universal good, is a more powerful active force than the object of the sensitive appetite, which is a particular good. Therefore passion is more consistent with intellectual than with the sensitive appetite.

*Obj.* 3. Further, joy and love are said to be passions. But these are to be found in the intellectual and not only in the sensitive appetite: else they would not be ascribed by the Scriptures to God and the angels. Therefore the passions are not more in the sensitive than in the intellectual appetite.

*On the contrary,* Damascene says (*De Fide Orthod.* ii. 22), while describing the animal passions: *Passion is a movement of the sensitive appetite when we imagine good or evil : in other words, passion is a movement of the irrational soul, when we think of good or evil.*

*I answer that,* As stated above (A. 1) passion is properly to be found where there is corporeal transmutation. This corporeal transmutation is found in the act of the sensitive appetite, and is not only spiritual, as in the sensitive apprehension, but also natural. Now there is no need for corporeal transmutation in the act of the intellectual appetite: because this appetite is not exercised by means of a corporeal organ. It is therefore evident that passion is more properly in the act of the sensitive appetite, than in that of the intellectual appetite; and this is again evident from the definitions of Damascene quoted above.

*Reply Obj.* 1. By *suffering* Divine things is meant being well affected towards them, and united to them by love: and this takes place without any alteration in the body.

*Reply Obj.* 2. Intensity of passion depends not only on the power of the agent, but also on the passibility of the patient: because things that are disposed to passion, suffer much even from petty agents. Therefore although the object of the intellectual appetite has greater activity than the object of the sensitive appetite, yet the sensitive appetite is more passive.

*Reply Obj.* 3. When love and joy and the like are ascribed to God or the angels, or to man in respect of his intellectual appetite, they signify simple acts of the will having like effects, but without passion. Hence Augustine says (*De Civ. Dei* ix. 5): *The holy angels feel no anger while they punish . . ., no fellow-feeling with misery while they relieve the unhappy : and yet ordinary human speech is wont to ascribe to them also these passions by name, because, although they have none of our weakness, their acts bear a certain resemblance to ours.*

# QUESTION XXIII.

## HOW THE PASSIONS DIFFER FROM ONE ANOTHER.

### (*In Four Articles.*)

We must now consider how the passions differ from one another: and under this head there are four points of inquiry: (1) Whether the passions of the concupiscible part are different from those of the irascible part ? (2) Whether the contrariety of passions in the irascible part is based on the contrariety of good and evil ? (3) Whether there is any passion that has no contrary ? (4) Whether, in the same power, there are any passions, differing in species, but not contrary to one another ?

## FIRST ARTICLE.

### WHETHER THE PASSIONS OF THE CONCUPISCIBLE PART ARE DIFFERENT FROM THOSE OF THE IRASCIBLE PART ?

*We proceed thus to the First Article :—*

*Objection* 1. It would seem that the same passions are in the irascible and concupiscible parts. For the Philosopher says (*Ethic.* ii. 5) that the passions of the soul are those emotions *which are followed by joy or sorrow*. But joy and sorrow are in the concupiscible part. Therefore all the passions are in the concupiscible part, and not some in the irascible, others in the concupiscible part.

*Obj.* 2. Further, on the words of Matth. xiii. 33, *The kingdom of heaven is like to leaven*, etc., Jerome's gloss says: *We should have prudence in the reason ; hatred of vice, in the irascible faculty ; desire of virtue, in the concupiscible part.* But hatred is in the concupiscible faculty, as also is love, of which it is the contrary, as is stated in *Topic*. ii. 7. Therefore the same passion is in the concupiscible and irascible faculties.

*Obj.* 3. Further, passions and actions differ specifically according to their objects. But the objects of the irascible and concupiscible passions are the same, viz., good and evil. Therefore the same passions are in the irascible and concupiscible faculties.

*On the contrary*, The acts of different powers differ in species; for instance, to see, and to hear. But the irascible and the concupiscible are two powers into which the sensitive appetite is divided, as stated in the First Part (Q. LXXXI., A. 2). Therefore, since the passions are movements of the sensitive appetite, as stated above (Q. XXII., A. 3), the passions of the irascible faculty are specifically distinct from those of the concupiscible part.

*I answer that,* The passions of the irascible part differ in species from those of the concupiscible faculty. For since different powers have different objects, as stated in the First Part (Q. LXXVII., A. 3), the passions of different powers must of necessity be referred to different objects. Much more, therefore, do the passions of different faculties differ in species; since a greater difference in the object is required to diversify the species of the powers, than to diversify the species of passions or actions. For just as in the physical order, diversity of genus arises from diversity in the potentiality of matter, while diversity of species arises from diversity of form in the same matter; so in the acts of the soul, those that belong to different powers, differ not only in species but also in genus, while acts and passions regarding different specific objects, included under the one common object of a single power, differ as the species of that genus.

In order, therefore, to discern which passions are in the irascible, and which in the concupiscible, we must take the object of each of these powers. For we have stated in the First Part (Q. LXXXI., A. 2) that the object of the concupiscible power is sensible good or evil, simply apprehended as such, which causes pleasure or pain. But, since the soul must, of necessity, experience difficulty or struggle at times, in acquiring some such good, or in avoiding some such evil, in so far as such good or evil is more than our animal nature can easily acquire or avoid; therefore this very good or evil, inasmuch as it is of an arduous or difficult nature, is the object of the irascible faculty. (Therefore whatever passions regard good or evil absolutely, belong to the concupiscible power; for instance, joy, sorrow, love, hatred and suchlike: whereas those passions which regard good or bad as arduous, through being difficult to obtain or avoid, belong to the irascible faculty; such are daring, fear, hope and the like.

*Reply Obj*. 1. As stated in the First Part (*loc. cit.*), the irascible faculty is bestowed on animals, in order to remove the obstacles that hinder the concupiscible power from tending towards its object, either by making some good difficult to obtain, or by making some evil hard to avoid. The result is that all the irascible passions terminate in the concupiscible passions: and thus it is that even the passions which are in the irascible faculty are followed by joy and sadness which are in the concupiscible faculty.

*Reply Obj*. 2. Jerome ascribes hatred of vice to the irascible faculty, not by reason of hatred, which is properly a concupiscible passion; but on account of the struggle, which belongs to the irascible power.

*Reply Obj*. 3. Good, inasmuch as it is delightful, moves the concupiscible power. But if it prove difficult to obtain, from this very fact it has a certain contrariety to the concupiscible power: and hence the need of another power tending to that good. The same applies to evil. And this power is the irascible faculty. Consequently the concupiscible passions are specifically different from the irascible passions.

## SECOND ARTICLE.

### WHETHER THE CONTRARIETY OF THE IRASCIBLE PASSIONS IS BASED ON THE CONTRARIETY OF GOOD AND EVIL ?

*We proceed thus to the Second Article :—*

*Objection* 1. It would seem that the contrariety of the irascible passions is based on no other contrariety than that of good and evil. For the irascible passions are ordained to the concupiscible passions, as stated above (A. 1 *ad* 1). But the contrariety of the concupiscible passions is no other than that of good and evil; take, for instance, love and hatred, joy and sorrow. Therefore the same applies to the irascible passions.

*Obj.* 2. Further, passions differ according to their objects; just as movements differ according to their termini. But there is no other contrariety of movements, except that of the termini, as is stated in *Phys.* v. 3. Therefore there is no other contrariety of passions, save that of the objects. Now the object of the appetite is good or evil. Therefore in no appetitive power can there be contrariety of passions other than that of good and evil.

*Obj.* 3. Further, *every passion of the soul is by way of approach and withdrawal*, as Avicenna declares in his sixth book of *Physics*. Now approach results from the apprehension of good; withdrawal, from the apprehension of evil: since just as *good is what all desire* (*Ethic.* i. 1), so evil is what all shun. Therefore, in the passions of the soul, there can be no other contrariety than that of good and evil.

*On the contrary*, Fear and daring are contrary to one another, as stated in *Ethic.* iii. 7. But fear and daring do not differ in respect of good and evil: because each regards some kind of evil. Therefore not every contrariety of the irascible passions is that of good and evil.

*I answer that*, Passion is a kind of movement, as stated in *Phys.* iii. 3. Therefore contrariety of passions is based on contrariety of movements or changes. Now there is a twofold contrariety in changes and movements, as stated in *Phys.* v. 5. One is according to approach and withdrawal in respect of the same term: and this contrariety belongs properly to changes, *i.e.*, to generation, which is a change *to being*, and to corruption, which is change *from being*. The other contrariety is according to opposition of termini, and belongs properly to movements: thus whitening, which is movement from black to white, is contrary to blackening, which is movement from white to black.

Accordingly there is a twofold contrariety in the passions

of the soul: one, according to contrariety of objects, *i.e.*, of good and evil; the other, according to approach and withdrawal in respect of the same term. In the concupiscible passions the former contrariety alone is to be found; viz., that which is based on the objects: whereas in the irascible passions, we find both forms of contrariety. The reason of this is that the object of the concupiscible faculty, as stated above (A. 1), is sensible good or evil considered absolutely. Now good, as such, cannot be a term wherefrom, but only a term whereto, since nothing shuns good as such; on the contrary, all things desire it. In like manner, nothing desires evil, as such; but all things shun it: wherefore evil cannot have the aspect of a term whereto, but only of a term wherefrom. Accordingly every concupiscible passion in respect of good, tends to it, as love, desire and joy; while every concupiscible passion in respect of evil, tends from it, as hatred, avoidance or dislike, and sorrow. Wherefore, in the concupiscible passions, there can be no contrariety of approach and withdrawal in respect of the same object.

On the other hand, the object of the irascible faculty is sensible good or evil, considered not absolutely, but under the aspect of difficulty or arduousness. Now the good which is difficult or arduous, considered as good, is of such a nature as to produce in us a tendency to it, which tendency pertains to the passion of *hope* ; whereas, considered as arduous or difficult, it makes us turn from it; and this pertains to the passion of *despair*. In like manner the arduous evil, considered as an evil, has the aspect of something to be shunned; and this belongs to the passion of *fear* : but it also contains a reason for tending to it, as attempting something arduous, whereby to escape being subject to evil; and this tendency is called *daring*. Consequently, in the irascible passions we find contrariety in respect of good and evil (as between hope and fear); and also contrariety according to approach and withdrawal in respect of the same term (as between daring and fear).

From what has been said the replies to the objections are evident.

## THIRD ARTICLE.

### WHETHER ANY PASSION OF THE SOUL HAS NO CONTRARY?

*We proceed thus to the Third Article :—*

*Objection* 1. It would seem that every passion of the soul has a contrary. For every passion of the soul is either in the irascible or in the concupiscible faculty, as stated above (A. 1). But both kinds of passions have their respective modes of contrariety. Therefore every passion of the soul has its contrary.

*Obj.* 2. Further, every passion of the soul has either good or evil for its object; for these are the common objects of the appetitive part. But a passion having good for its object, is contrary to a passion having evil for its object. Therefore every passion has a contrary.

*Obj.* 3. Further, every passion of the soul is in respect of approach or withdrawal, as stated above (A. 2). But every approach has a corresponding contrary withdrawal, and vice versa. Therefore every passion of the soul has a contrary.

*On the contrary,* Anger is a passion of the soul. But no passion is set down as being contrary to anger, as stated in *Ethic.* iv. 5. Therefore not every passion has a contrary.

*I answer that,* The passion of anger is peculiar in this, that it cannot have a contrary, either according to approach and withdrawal, or according to the contrariety of good and evil. For anger is caused by a difficult evil already present: and when such an evil is present, the appetite must needs either succumb, so that it does not go beyond the limits of *sadness,* which is a concupiscible passion; or else it has a movement of attack on the hurtful evil, which movement is that of *anger.* But it cannot have a movement of withdrawal: because the evil is supposed to be already present or past. Thus no passion is contrary to anger according to contrariety of approach and withdrawal.

In like manner neither can there be according to contrariety of good and evil. Because the opposite of present evil is good obtained, which can no longer have the aspect

II. i. 19

of arduousness or difficulty. Nor, when once good is obtained, does there remain any other movement, except the appetite's repose in the good obtained; which repose belongs to joy, which is a passion of the concupiscible faculty.

Accordingly no movement of the soul can be contrary to the movement of anger, and nothing else than cessation from its movement is contrary thereto; thus the Philosopher says (*Rhetor.* ii. 3) that *calm is contrary to anger*, by opposition not of contrariety but of negation or privation.

From what has been said the replies to the objections are evident.

### Fourth Article.

#### WHETHER IN THE SAME POWER, THERE ARE ANY PASSIONS, SPECIFICALLY DIFFERENT, BUT NOT CONTRARY TO ONE ANOTHER ?

*We proceed thus to the Fourth Article :—*

*Objection* 1. It would seem that there cannot be, in the same power, specifically different passions that are not contrary to one another. For the passions of the soul differ according to their objects. Now the objects of the soul's passions are good and evil; and on this distinction is based the contrariety of the passions. Therefore no passions of the same power, that are not contrary to one another, differ specifically.

*Obj.* 2. Further, difference of species implies a difference of form. But every difference of form is in respect of some contrariety, as stated in *Metaph.* x. 8. Therefore passions of the same power, that are not contrary to one another, do not differ specifically.

*Obj.* 3. Further, since every passion of the soul consists in approach or withdrawal in respect of good or evil, it seems that every difference in the passions of the soul must needs arise from the difference of good and evil; or from the difference of approach and withdrawal; or from degrees in approach or withdrawal. Now the first two differences cause contrariety in the passions of the soul, as stated above (A. 2): whereas the third difference does not diversify the species; else the species of the soul's passions would be infinite. Therefore it is not possible for passions of the same power to differ in species, without being contrary to one another.

*On the contrary*, Love and joy differ in species, and are in the concupiscible power; and yet they are not contrary to one another; rather, in fact, one causes the other. Therefore in the same power there are passions that differ in species without being contrary to one another.

*I answer that*, Passions differ in accordance with their active causes, which, in the case of the passions of the soul, are their objects. Now the difference in active causes may be considered in two ways: first, from the point of view of their species or nature, as fire differs from water; secondly, from the point of view of the difference in their active power. In the passions of the soul we can treat the difference of their active or motive causes in respect of their motive power, as if they were natural agents. For every mover, in a fashion, either draws the patient to itself, or repels it from itself. Now in drawing it to itself, it does three things in the patient. Because, in the first place, it gives the patient an inclination or aptitude to tend to the mover: thus a light body, which is above, bestows lightness on the body generated, so that it has an inclination or aptitude to be above. Secondly, if the generated body be outside its proper place, the mover gives it movement towards that place.—Thirdly, it makes it to rest, when it shall have come to its proper place: since to the same cause are due, both rest in a place, and the movement to that place. The same applies to the cause of repulsion.

Now, in the movements of the appetitive faculty, good has, as it were, a force of attraction, while evil has a force of repulsion. In the first place, therefore, good causes, in the appetitive power, a certain inclination, aptitude or connaturalness in respect of good: and this belongs to the passion of *love :* the corresponding contrary of which is *hatred* in respect of evil.—Secondly, if the good be not yet possessed, it causes in the appetite a movement towards the attainment of the good beloved: and this belongs to the passion of *desire* or *concupiscence* : and contrary to it, in respect of evil, is the passion of *aversion* or *dislike*.— Thirdly, when the good is obtained, it causes the appetite to rest, as it were, in the good obtained: and this belongs to the passion of *delight* or *joy*: the contrary of which, in respect of evil, is *sorrow* or *sadness*.

On the other hand, in the irascible passions, the aptitude, or inclination to seek good, or to shun evil, is presupposed as arising from the concupiscible faculty, which regards good or evil absolutely.   And in respect of good not yet obtained, we have *hope* and *despair*.   In respect of evil not yet present we have *fear* and *daring*.   But in respect of good obtained there is no irascible passion: because it is no longer considered in the light of something arduous, as stated above (A. 3).   But evil already present gives rise to the passion of *anger*.

Accordingly it is clear that in the concupiscible faculty there are three couples of passions; viz., love and hatred, desire and aversion, joy and sadness.   In like manner there are three groups in the irascible faculty; viz., hope and despair, fear and daring, and anger which has no contrary passion.

Consequently there are altogether eleven passions differing specifically; six in the concupiscible faculty, and five in the irascible; and under these all the passions of the soul are contained.

From this the replies to the objections are evident.

# QUESTION XXIV.

## OF GOOD AND EVIL IN THE PASSIONS OF THE SOUL.

### (*In Four Articles.*)

WE must now consider good and evil in the passions of the soul: and under this head there are four points of inquiry: (1) Whether moral good and evil can be found in the passions of the soul? (2) Whether every passion of the soul is morally evil? (3) Whether every passion increases or decreases the goodness or malice of an act? (4) Whether any passion is good or evil specifically?

## FIRST ARTICLE.

### WHETHER MORAL GOOD AND EVIL CAN BE FOUND IN THE PASSIONS OF THE SOUL?

*We proceed thus to the First Article :—*

*Objection* 1. It would seem that no passion of the soul is morally good or evil. For moral good and evil are proper to man: since *morals are properly predicated of man,* as Ambrose says (*Super Luc., Prolog.*). But passions are not proper to man, for he has them in common with other animals. Therefore no passion of the soul is morally good or evil.

*Obj.* 2. Further, the good or evil of man consists in *being in accord, or in disaccord with reason,* as Dionysius says (*Div. Nom.* iv.). Now the passions of the soul are not in the reason, but in the sensitive appetite, as stated above (Q. XXII., A. 3). Therefore they have no connection with human, *i.e.,* moral, good or evil.

*Obj.* 3. Further, the Philosopher says (*Ethic.* ii. 5) that *we are neither praised nor blamed for our passions.* But we are

293

praised and blamed for moral good and evil. Therefore the passions are not morally good or evil.

*On the contrary*, Augustine says (*De Civ. Dei* xiv. 7) while speaking of the passions of the soul: *They are evil if our love is evil ; good if our love is good.*

*I answer that*, We may consider the passions of the soul in two ways: first, in themselves; secondly, as being subject to the command of the reason and will.—If then the passions be considered in themselves, to wit, as movements of the irrational appetite, thus there is no moral good or evil in them, since this depends on the reason, as stated above (Q. XVIII., A. 5). If, however, they be considered as subject to the command of the reason and will, then moral good and evil are in them. Because the sensitive appetite is nearer than the outward members to the reason and will; and yet the movements and actions of the outward members are morally good or evil, inasmuch as they are voluntary. Much more, therefore, may the passions, in so far as they are voluntary, be called morally good or evil. And they are said to be voluntary, either from being commanded by the will, or from not being checked by the will.

*Reply Obj.* 1. These passions, considered in themselves, are common to man and other animals: but, as commanded by the reason, they are proper to man.

*Reply Obj.* 2. Even the lower appetitive powers are called rational, in so far as *they partake of reason in some sort* (*Ethic.* i. 13).

*Reply Obj.* 3. The Philosopher says that we are neither praised nor blamed for our passions considered absolutely; but he does not exclude their becoming worthy of praise or blame, in so far as they are subordinate to reason. Hence he continues: *For the man who fears or is angry, is not praised . . . or blamed, but the man who is angry in a certain way, i.e., according to, or against reason.*

## SECOND ARTICLE.

### WHETHER EVERY PASSION OF THE SOUL IS EVIL MORALLY?

*We proceed thus to the Second Article :—*

*Objection* 1. It would seem that all the passions of the soul are morally evil. For Augustine says (*De Civ. Dei* ix. 4) that *some call the soul's passions diseases or disturbances of the soul.*\* But every disease or disturbance of the soul is morally evil. Therefore every passion of the soul is evil morally.

*Obj.* 2. Further, Damascene says (*De Fide Orthod.* ii. 22) that *movement in accord with nature is an action, but movement contrary to nature is passion.* But in movements of the soul, what is against nature is sinful and morally evil: hence he says elsewhere (*ibid.* 4) that *the devil turned from that which is in accord with nature to that which is against nature.* Therefore these passions are morally evil.

*Obj.* 3. Further, whatever leads to sin, has an aspect of evil. But these passions lead to sin: wherefore they are called *the passions of sins* (Rom. vii. 5). Therefore it seems that they are morally evil.

*On the contrary*, Augustine says (*De Civ. Dei* xiv. 9) that *all these emotions are right in those whose love is rightly placed. . . . For they fear to sin, they desire to persevere ; they grieve for sin, they rejoice in good works.*

*I answer that,* On this question the opinion of the Stoics differed from that of the Peripatetics: for the Stoics held that all passions are evil, while the Peripatetics maintained that moderate passions are good. This difference, although it appears great in words, is nevertheless, in reality, none at all, or but little, if we consider the intent of either school. For the Stoics did not discern between sense and intellect; and consequently neither between the intellectual and sensitive appetite. Hence they did not discriminate the passions of the soul from the movements of the will, in so far as the passions of the soul are in the sensitive appetite, while the simple movements of the will are in the intellectual

\* *Cf.* Q. XXII., A. 2, footnote.

appetite: but every rational movement of the appetitive part they called will, while they called passion, a movement that exceeds the limits of reason.   Wherefore Cicero, following their opinion (*De Tusc. Quæst.* iii. 4) calls all passions *diseases of the soul :* whence he argues that *those who are diseased are unsound ; and those who are unsound are wanting in sense.* Hence we speak of those who are wanting in sense as being *unsound.*

On the other hand, the Peripatetics give the name of *passions* to all the movements of the sensitive appetite. Wherefore they esteem them good, when they are controlled by reason; and evil when they are not controlled by reason. Hence it is evident that Cicero was wrong in disapproving (*ibid.*) of the Peripatetic theory of a mean in the passions, when he says that *every evil, though moderate, should be shunned ; for, just as a body, though it be moderately ailing, is not sound ; so, this mean in the diseases or passions of the soul, is not sound.*   For passions are not called *diseases* or *disturbances* of the soul, save when they are not controlled by reason.

Hence the reply to the First Objection is evident.

*Reply Obj.* 2. In every passion there is an increase or decrease in the natural movement of the heart, according as the heart is moved more or less intensely by contraction and dilatation; and hence it derives the character of passion. But there is no need for passion to deviate always from the order of natural reason.

*Reply Obj.* 3. The passions of the soul, in so far as they are contrary to the order of reason, incline us to sin: but in so far as they are controlled by reason, they pertain to virtue.

### THIRD ARTICLE.

#### WHETHER PASSION INCREASES OR DECREASES THE GOODNESS OR MALICE OF AN ACT ?

*We proceed thus to the Third Article :—*

*Objection* 1. It would seem that every passion decreases the goodness of a moral action.   For anything that hinders the judgment of reason, on which depends the goodness of a moral act, consequently decreases the goodness of the moral act. But every passion hinders the judgment of reason: for Sallust says (*Catilin.*): *All those that take counsel about matters of doubt, should be free from hatred, anger, friendship and pity.* Therefore passion decreases the goodness of a moral act.

*Obj.* 2. Further, the more a man's action is like to God, the better it is: hence the Apostle says (Eph. v. 1): *Be ye followers of God, as most dear children.* But *God and the holy angels feel no anger when they punish . . . no fellow-feeling with misery when they relieve the unhappy*, as Augustine says (*De Civ. Dei* ix. 5). Therefore it is better to do suchlike deeds without than with a passion of the soul.

*Obj.* 3. Further, just as moral evil depends on its relation to reason, so also does moral good. But moral evil is lessened by passion: for he sins less, who sins from passion, than he who sins deliberately. Therefore he does a better deed, who does well without passion, than he who does with passion.

*On the contrary*, Augustine says (*De Civ. Dei* ix. 5) that *the passion of pity is obedient to reason, when pity is bestowed without violating right, as when the poor are relieved, or the penitent forgiven.* But nothing that is obedient to reason lessens the moral good. Therefore a passion of the soul does not lessen moral good.

*I answer that*, As the Stoics held that every passion of the soul is evil, they consequently held that every passion of the soul lessens the goodness of an act; since the admixture of evil either destroys good altogether, or makes it to be less good. And this is true indeed, if by passions we understand none but the inordinate movements of the sensitive appetite, considered as disturbances or ailments. But if we give the name of passions to all the movements of the sensitive appetite, then it belongs to the perfection of man's good that his passions be moderated by reason. For since man's good is founded on reason as its root, that good will be all the more perfect, according as it extends to more things pertaining to man. Wherefore no one questions the fact that it belongs to the perfection of moral good, that the actions of the outward members be controlled by the law of reason. Hence, since the sensitive appetite can obey reason, as stated above (Q. XVII., A. 7), it belongs to the perfection of moral or human good, that the passions themselves also should be controlled by reason.

Accordingly just as it is better that man should both will good and do it in his external act; so also does it belong to the perfection of moral good, that man should be moved unto good, not only in respect of his will, but also in respect of his sensitive appetite; according to Ps. lxxxiii. 3: *My heart and my flesh have rejoiced in the living God :* where by *heart* we are to understand the intellectual appetite, and by *flesh* the sensitive appetite.

*Reply Obj.* 1. The passions of the soul may stand in a two-fold relation to the judgment of reason. First, antecedently: and thus, since they obscure the judgment of reason, on which the goodness of the moral act depends, they diminish the goodness of the act; for it is more praiseworthy to do a work of charity from the judgment of reason than from the mere passion of pity.—In the second place, consequently: and this in two ways. First, by way of redundance: because, to wit, when the higher part of the soul is intensely moved to anything, the lower part also follows that movement; and thus the passion that results in consequence, in the sensitive appetite, is a sign of the intensity of the will, and so indicates greater moral goodness.—Secondly, by way of choice; when, to wit, a man, by the judgment of his reason, chooses to be affected by a passion in order to work more promptly with the co-operation of the sensitive appetite. And thus a passion of the soul increases the goodness of an action.

*Reply Obj.* 2. In God and the angels there is no sensitive appetite, nor again bodily members: and so in them good does not depend on the right ordering of passions or of bodily actions, as it does in us.

*Reply Obj.* 3. A passion that tends to evil, and precedes the judgment of reason, diminishes sin; but if it be consequent in either of the ways mentioned above (*Reply Obj.* 1), it aggravates the sin, or else it is a sign of its being more grievous.

## Fourth Article.

### WHETHER ANY PASSION IS GOOD OR EVIL IN ITS SPECIES ?

*We proceed thus to the Fourth Article :—*

*Objection* 1. It would seem that no passion of the soul is good or evil morally according to its species.  Because moral good and evil depend on reason.  But the passions are in the sensitive appetite; so that accordance with reason is accidental to them.  Since, therefore, nothing accidental belongs to a thing's species, it seems that no passion is good or evil according to its species.

*Obj.* 2. Further, acts and passions take their species from their object.  If, therefore, any passion were good or evil, according to its species, it would follow that those passions the object of which is good, are specifically good, such as love, desire and joy: and that those passions, the object of which is evil, are specifically evil, as hatred, fear and sadness.  But this is clearly false.  Therefore no passion is good or evil according to its species.

*Obj.* 3. Further, there is no species of passion that is not to be found in other animals.  But moral good is in man alone.  Therefore no passion of the soul is good or evil according to its species.

*On the contrary*, Augustine says (*De Civ. Dei* ix. 5) that *pity is a kind of virtue*.  Moreover, the Philosopher says (*Ethic.* ii. 7) that modesty is a praiseworthy passion.  Therefore some passions are good or evil according to their species.

*I answer that*, We ought, seemingly, to apply to passions what has been said in regard to acts (Q. XVIII., AA. 5, 6; Q. XX., A. 1)—viz., that the species of a passion, as the species of an act, can be considered from two points of view. First, according to its natural genus; and thus moral good and evil have no connection with the species of an act or passion. Secondly, according to its moral genus, inasmuch as it is voluntary and controlled by reason. In this way moral good and evil can belong to the species of a passion, in so far as the object to which a passion tends, is, of itself, in harmony or in discord with reason: as is clear in the case of *shame* which is base fear; and of *envy* which is sorrow for another's good: for thus passions belong to the same species as the external act.

*Reply Obj.* 1. This argument considers the passions in their natural species, in so far as the sensitive appetite is considered in itself. But in so far as the sensitive appetite obeys reason, good and evil of reason are no longer accidentally in the passions of the appetite, but essentially.

*Reply Obj.* 2. Passions having a tendency to good, are themselves good, if they tend to that which is truly good, and in like manner, if they turn away from that which is truly evil. On the other hand, those passions which consist in aversion from good, and a tendency to evil, are themselves evil.

*Reply Obj.* 3. In irrational animals the sensitive appetite does not obey reason. Nevertheless, in so far as they are led by a kind of estimative power, which is subject to a higher, *i.e.*, the Divine, reason, there is a certain likeness of moral good in them, in regard to the soul's passions.

# QUESTION XXV.

## OF THE ORDER OF THE PASSIONS TO ONE ANOTHER.

### (*In Four Articles.*)

WE must now consider the order of the passions to one another: and under this head there are four points of inquiry: (1) The relation of the irascible passions to the concupiscible passions. (2) The relation of the concupiscible passions to one another. (3) The relation of the irascible passions to one another. (4) The four principal passions.

## FIRST ARTICLE.

### WHETHER THE IRASCIBLE PASSIONS PRECEDE THE CONCUPISCIBLE PASSIONS, OR VICE VERSA?

*We proceed thus to the First Article :—*

*Objection* 1. It would seem that the irascible passions precede the concupiscible passions. For the order of the passions is that of their objects. But the object of the irascible faculty is the difficult good, which seems to be the highest good. Therefore the irascible passions seem to precede the concupiscible passions.

*Obj.* 2. Further, the mover precedes that which is moved. But the irascible faculty is compared to the concupiscible, as mover to that which is moved: since it is given to animals, for the purpose of removing the obstacles that hinder the concupiscible faculty from enjoying its object, as stated above (Q. XXIII., A. 1 *ad* 1; P. 1, Q. LXXXI., A. 2). Now *that which removes an obstacle, is a kind of mover* (*Phys.* viii. 4). Therefore the irascible passions precede the concupiscible passions.

*Obj.* 3. Further, joy and sadness are concupiscible passions. But joy and sadness succeed to the irascible passions: for the Philosopher says (*Ethic.* iv. 5) that *retaliation causes anger to cease, because it produces pleasure instead of the previous pain.* Therefore the concupiscible passions follow the irascible passions.

*On the contrary,* The concupiscible passions regard the absolute good, while the irascible passions regard a restricted, viz., the difficult, good. Since, therefore, the absolute good precedes the restricted good, it seems that the concupiscible passions precede the irascible.

*I answer that,* In the concupiscible passions there is more diversity than in the passions of the irascible faculty. For in the former we find something relating to movement— *e.g.,* desire; and something belonging to repose, *e.g.,* joy and sadness. But in the irascible passions there is nothing pertaining to repose, and only that which belongs to movement. The reason of this is that when we find rest in a thing, we no longer look upon it as something difficult or arduous; whereas such is the object of the irascible faculty.

Now since rest is the end of movement, it is first in the order of intention, but last in the order of execution. If, therefore, we compare the passions of the irascible faculty with those concupiscible passions that denote rest in good, it is evident that in the order of execution, the irascible passions take precedence of suchlike passions of the concupiscible faculty: thus hope precedes joy, and hence causes it, according to the Apostle (Rom. xii. 12): *Rejoicing in hope.* But the concupiscible passion which denotes rest in evil, viz., sadness, comes between two irascible passions: because it follows fear; since we become sad when we are confronted by the evil that we feared: while it precedes the movement of anger; since the movement of self-vindication, that results from sadness, is the movement of anger. And because it is looked upon as a good thing to pay back the evil done to us; when the angry man has achieved this he rejoices. Thus it is evident that every passion of the irascible faculty terminates in a concupiscible passion denoting rest, viz., either in joy or in sadness.

But if we compare the irascible passions to those concupiscible passions that denote movement, then it is clear that the latter take precedence: because the passions of the irascible faculty add something to those of the concupiscible faculty; just as the object of the irascible adds the aspect of arduousness or difficulty to the object of the concupiscible faculty. Thus hope adds to desire a certain effort, and a certain raising of the spirits to the realization of the arduous good. In like manner fear adds to aversion or detestation a certain lowness of spirits, on account of difficulty in shunning the evil.

Accordingly the passions of the irascible faculty stand between those concupiscible passions that denote movement towards good or evil, and those concupiscible passions that denote rest in good or evil. And it is therefore evident that the irascible passions both arise from and terminate in the passions of the concupiscible faculty.

*Reply Obj.* 1. This argument would prove, if the formal object of the concupiscible faculty were something contrary to the arduous, just as the formal object of the irascible faculty is that which is arduous. But because the object of the concupiscible faculty is good absolutely, it naturally precedes the object of the irascible, as the common precedes the proper.

*Reply Obj.* 2. The remover of an obstacle is not a direct but an accidental mover: and here we are speaking of passions as directly related to one another.—Moreover, the irascible passion removes the obstacle that hinders the concupiscible from resting in its object. Wherefore it only follows that the irascible passions precede those concupiscible passions that connote rest.—The third objection leads to the same conclusion.

## Second Article.

### WHETHER LOVE IS THE FIRST OF THE CONCUPISCIBLE PASSIONS?

*We proceed thus to the Second Article :—*

*Objection* 1. It would seem that love is not the first of the concupiscible passions. For the concupiscible faculty is so called from concupiscence, which is the same passion as desire. But *things are named from their chief characteristic* (*De Anima* ii. 4). Therefore desire takes precedence of love.

*Obj.* 2. Further, love implies a certain union; since it is a *uniting and binding force*, as Dionysius states (*Div. Nom.* iv.). But concupiscence or desire is a movement towards union with the thing coveted or desired. Therefore desire precedes love.

*Obj.* 3. Further, the cause precedes its effect. But pleasure is sometimes the cause of love: since some love on account of pleasure (*Ethic.* viii. 3, 4). Therefore pleasure precedes love; and consequently love is not the first of the concupiscible passions.

*On the contrary*, Augustine says (*De Civ. Dei* xiv. 7, 9) that all the passions are caused by love: since *love yearning for the beloved object, is desire ; and, having and enjoying it, is joy.* Therefore love is the first of the concupiscible passions.

*I answer that*, Good and evil are the object of the concupiscible faculty. Now good naturally precedes evil; since evil is the privation of good. Wherefore all the passions, the object of which is good, are naturally before those, the object of which is evil,—that is to say, each precedes its contrary passion: because the quest of a good is the reason for shunning the opposite evil.

Now good has the aspect of an end, and the end is indeed first in the order of intention, but last in the order of execution. Consequently the order of the concupiscible passions can be considered either in the order of intention or in the order of execution. In the order of execution, the first place belongs to that which takes place first in the thing that tends to the end. Now it is evident that whatever tends to an end, has, in the first place, an aptitude or proportion to that end, for nothing tends to a disproportionate end; secondly, it is moved to that end; thirdly, it rests in the end, after having attained it. And this very aptitude or proportion of the appetite to good is love, which is complacency in good; while movement towards good is desire or concupiscence; and rest in good is joy or pleasure. Accordingly in this order, love precedes desire, and desire precedes pleasure.—But in the order of intention, it is the reverse: because the pleasure intended causes desire and love. For pleasure is the enjoyment of the good, which enjoyment is, in a way, the end, just as the good itself is, as stated above (Q. XI., A. 3 *ad* 3).

*Reply Obj*. 1. We name a thing as we understand it, for *words are signs of thoughts*, as the Philosopher states (*Peri Herm*. i. 1). Now in most cases we know a cause by its effect. But the effect of love, when the beloved object is possessed, is pleasure: when it is not possessed, it is desire or concupiscence: and, as Augustine says (*De Trin*. x. 12), *we are more sensible to love, when we lack that which we love.* Consequently of all the concupiscible passions, concupiscence is felt most; and for this reason the power is named after it.

*Reply Obj*. 2. The union of lover and beloved is twofold. There is real union, consisting in the conjunction of one with the other. This union belongs to joy or pleasure, which follows desire. There is also an affective union, consisting in an aptitude or proportion, in so far as one thing, from the very fact of its having an aptitude for and an inclination to another, partakes of it: and love betokens such a union. This union precedes the movement of desire.

*Reply Obj*. 3. Pleasure causes love, in so far as it precedes love in the order of intention.

## Third Article.

### WHETHER HOPE IS THE FIRST OF THE IRASCIBLE PASSIONS ?

*We proceed thus to the Third Article :—*

*Objection* 1. It would seem that hope is not the first of the irascible passions. Because the irascible faculty is denominated from anger. Since, therefore, *things are named from their chief characteristic* (*cf.* A. 2, *Obj.* 1), it seems that anger precedes and surpasses hope.

*Obj.* 2. Further, the object of the irascible faculty is something arduous. Now it seems more arduous to strive to overcome a contrary evil that threatens soon to overtake us, which pertains to daring; or an evil actually present, which pertains to anger; than to strive simply to obtain some good. Again, it seems more arduous to strive to overcome a present evil, than a future evil. Therefore anger seems to be a stronger passion than daring, and daring, than hope. And consequently it seems that hope does not precede them.

*Obj.* 3. Further, when a thing is moved towards an end, the movement of withdrawal precedes the movement of approach. But fear and despair imply withdrawal from something; while daring and hope imply approach towards something. Therefore fear and despair precede hope and daring.

*On the contrary,* The nearer a thing is to the first, the more it precedes others. But hope is nearer to love, which is the first of the passions. Therefore hope is the first of the passions in the irascible faculty.

*I answer that,* As stated above (A. 1) all the irascible passions imply movement towards something. Now this movement of the irascible faculty towards something may be due to two causes: one is the mere aptitude or proportion to the end; and this pertains to love or hatred; the other is the presence of good or evil; and this belongs to sadness or joy. As a matter of fact, the presence of good produces no passion in the irascible, as stated above (Q. XXIII., AA. 3, 4); but the presence of evil gives rise to the passion of anger.

Since then in the order of generation or execution, proportion or aptitude to the end precedes the achievement of the end; it follows that, of all the irascible passions, anger is the last in the order of generation. And among the other passions of the irascible faculty, which imply a movement arising from love of good or hatred of evil, those whose object is good, viz., hope and despair, must naturally precede those whose object is evil, viz., daring and fear: yet so that hope precedes despair; since hope is a movement towards good as such, which is essentially attractive, so that hope tends to good directly; whereas despair is a movement away from good, a movement which is consistent with good, not as such, but in respect of something else, wherefore its tendency from good is accidental, as it were. In like manner fear, through being a movement from evil, precedes daring.—And that hope and despair naturally precede fear and daring is evident from this,— that as the desire of good is the reason for avoiding evil, so hope and despair are the reason for fear and daring: because daring arises from the hope of victory, and fear arises from the despair of overcoming. Lastly, anger arises from daring: for no one is angry while seeking vengeance, unless he dare to avenge himself, as Avicenna observes in the sixth book of his *Physics*. Accordingly, it is evident that hope is the first of all the irascible passions.

And if we wish to know the order of all the passions in the way of generation, love and hatred are first; desire and aversion, second; hope and despair, third; fear and daring, fourth; anger, fifth; sixth and last, joy and sadness, which follow from all the passions, as stated in *Ethic.* ii. 5: yet so that love precedes hatred; desire precedes aversion; hope precedes despair; fear precedes daring; and joy precedes sadness, as may be gathered from what has been stated above.

*Reply Obj.* 1. Because anger arises from the other passions, as an effect from the causes that precede it, it is from anger, as being more manifest than the other passions, that the power takes its name.

*Reply Obj.* 2. It is not the arduousness but the good that is the reason for approach or desire. Consequently hope, which regards good more directly, takes precedence: although at times daring or even anger regards something more arduous.

*Reply Obj.* 3. The movement of the appetite is essentially and directly towards the good as towards its proper object; its movement from evil results from this. For the movement of the appetitive part is in proportion, not to natural movement, but to the intention of nature, which intends the end before intending the removal of a contrary, which removal is desired only for the sake of obtaining the end.

## FOURTH ARTICLE.

### WHETHER THESE ARE THE FOUR PRINCIPAL PASSIONS,—JOY, SADNESS, HOPE, AND FEAR ?

*We proceed thus to the Fourth Article :—*

*Objection* 1. It would seem that joy, sadness, hope and fear are not the four principal passions. For Augustine (*De Civ. Dei* xiv. 3, 7 *sqq.*) omits hope and puts desire in its place.

*Obj.* 2. Further, there is a twofold order in the passions of the soul: the order of intention, and the order of execution or generation. The principal passions should therefore be taken, either in the order of intention; and thus joy and sadness, which are the final passions, will be the principal passions; or in the order of execution or generation, and thus love will be the principal passion. Therefore joy and sadness, hope and fear should in no way be called the four principal passions.

*Obj.* 3. Further, just as daring is caused by hope, so fear is caused by despair. Either, therefore, hope and despair should be reckoned as principal passions, since they cause others: or hope and daring, from being akin to one another.

*Ont he contrary*, Boethius (*De Consol.* i.) in enumerating the four principal passions, says:

> Banish joys: banish fears:
> Away with hope: away with tears.

*I answer that*, These four are commonly called the principal passions. Two of them, viz., joy and sadness, are said to be principal, because in them all the other passions have their completion and end; wherefore they arise from all the other passions, as is stated in *Ethic.* ii. 5.—Fear and hope are principal passions, not because they complete the others simply, but because they complete them as regards the movement of the appetite towards something: for in respect of good, movement begins in love, goes forward to desire, and ends in hope; while in respect of evil, it begins in hatred, goes on to aversion, and ends in fear.—Hence it is customary to distinguish these four passions in relation to the present and the future: for movement regards the future, while rest is in something present: so that joy relates to present good, sadness relates to present evil; hope regards future good, and fear, future evil.

As to the other passions that regard good or evil, present or future, they all culminate in these four. For this reason some have said that these four are the principal passions, because they are general passions; and this is true, provided that by hope and fear we understand the appetite's common tendency to desire or shun something.

*Reply Obj*. 1. Augustine puts desire or covetousness in place of hope, in so far as they seem to regard the same object, viz., some future good.

*Reply Obj*. 2. These are called principal passions, in the order of intention and completion. And though fear and hope are not the last passions simply, yet they are the last of those passions that tend towards something as future. Nor can the argument be pressed any further except in the case of anger: yet neither can anger be reckoned a principal passion, because it is an effect of daring, which cannot be a principal passion, as we shall state further on (*Reply Obj.* 3).

*Reply Obj.* 3. Despair implies movement away from good; and this is, as it were, accidental: and daring implies movement towards evil; and this too is accidental. Consequently these cannot be principal passions; because that which is accidental cannot be said to be principal. And so neither can anger be called a principal passion, because it arises from daring.

# QUESTION XXVI.

## OF THE PASSIONS OF THE SOUL IN PARTICULAR: AND FIRST, OF LOVE.

### (*In Four Articles.*)

WE have now to consider the soul's passions in particular, and (1) the passions of the concupiscible faculty; (2) the passions of the irascible faculty.

The first of these considerations will be threefold: since we shall consider (1) Love and hatred; (2) Desire and aversion; (3) Pleasure and sadness.

Concerning love, three points must be considered: (1) Love itself; (2) The cause of love; (3) The effects of love. Under the first head there are four points of inquiry: (1) Whether love is in the concupiscible power? (2) Whether love is a passion? (3) Whether love is the same as dilection? (4) Whether love is properly divided into love of friendship, and love of concupiscence?

## FIRST ARTICLE.

### WHETHER LOVE IS IN THE CONCUPISCIBLE POWER?

*We proceed thus to the First Article :—*

*Objection* 1. It would seem that love is not in the concupiscible power. For it is written (Wis. viii. 2): *Her,* namely, wisdom, *have I loved, and have sought her out from my youth.* But the concupiscible power, being a part of the sensitive appetite, cannot tend to wisdom, which is not apprehended by the senses. Therefore love is not in the concupiscible power.

*Obj.* 2. Further, love seems to be identified with every passion: for Augustine says (*De Civ. Dei* xiv. 7): *Love, yearn-*

*ing for the object beloved, is desire ; having and enjoying it, is joy ; fleeing what is contrary to it, is fear ; and feeling what is contrary to it, is sadness.* But not every passion is in the concupiscible power; indeed, fear, which is mentioned in this passage, is in the irascible power. Therefore we must not say absolutely that love is in the concupiscible power.

*Obj.* 3. Further, Dionysius (*Div. Nom.* iv.) mentions a *natural love.* But natural love seems to pertain rather to the natural powers, which belong to the vegetal soul. Therefore love is not simply in the concupiscible power.

*On the contrary,* The Philosopher says (*Topic.* ii. 7) that *love is in the concupiscible power.*

*I answer that,* Love is something pertaining to the appetite; since good is the object of both. Wherefore love differs according to the difference of appetites. For there is an appetite which arises from an apprehension existing, not in the subject of the appetite, but in some other: and this is called the *natural appetite.* Because natural things seek what is suitable to them according to their nature, by reason of an apprehension which is not in them, but in the Author of their nature, as stated in the First Part (Q. VI., A. 1 *ad* 2; Q. CIII., A. 1 *ad* 1, 3).—And there is another appetite arising from an apprehension in the subject of the appetite, but from necessity and not from free-will. Such is, in irrational animals, the *sensitive appetite,* which, however, in man, has a certain share of liberty, in so far as it obeys reason.—Again, there is another appetite following freely from an apprehension in the subject of the appetite. And this is the rational or intellectual appetite, which is called the *will.*

Now in each of these appetites, the name *love* is given to the principle of movement towards the end loved. In the natural appetite the principle of this movement is the appetitive subject's connaturalness with the thing to which it tends, and may be called *natural love :* thus the connaturalness of a heavy body for the centre, is by reason of its weight and may be called *natural love.* In like manner the aptitude of the sensitive appetite or of the will to some good, that is to say, its very complacency in good, is called *sensitive love*, or *intellectual* or *rational love*. So that sensitive love is in the sensitive appetite, just as intellectual love is in the intellectual appetite. And it belongs to the concupiscible power, because it regards good absolutely, and not under the aspect of difficulty, which is the object of the irascible faculty.

*Reply Obj*. 1. The words quoted refer to intellectual or rational love.

*Reply Obj*. 2. Love is spoken of as being fear, joy, desire and sadness, not essentially but causally.

*Reply Obj*. 3. Natural love is not only in the powers of the vegetal soul, but in all the soul's powers, and also in all the parts of the body, and universally in all things: because, as Dionysius says (*Div. Nom.* iv.), *Beauty and goodness are beloved by all things ;* since each single thing has a connaturalness with that which is naturally suitable to it.

## Second Article.

### whether love is a passion ?

*We proceed thus to the Second Article :—*

*Objection* 1. It would seem that love is not a passion. For no power is a passion. But every love is a power, as Dionysius says (*Div. Nom.* iv.). Therefore love is not a passion.

*Obj*. 2. Further, love is a kind of union or bond, as Augustine says (*De Trin.* viii. 10). But a union or bond is not a passion, but rather a relation. Therefore love is not a passion.

*Obj*. 3. Further, Damascene says (*De Fide Orthod*. ii. 22) that passion is a movement. But love does not imply the movement of the appetite; for this is desire, of which movement love is the principle. Therefore love is not a passion.

*On the contrary*, The Philosopher says (*Ethic*. viii. 5) that *love is a passion*.

*I answer that*, Passion is the effect of the agent on the patient. Now a natural agent produces a twofold effect on the patient: for in the first place it gives it the form; and secondly it gives it the movement that results from the form. Thus the generator gives the generated body both weight and the movement resulting from weight: so that weight, from being the principle of movement to the place, which is connatural to that body by reason of its weight, can, in a way, be called *natural love*. In the same way the appetible object gives the appetite, first, a certain adaptation to itself, which consists in complacency in that object; and from this follows movement towards the appetible object. For *the appetitive movement is circular*, as stated in *De Anima* iii. 10; because the appetible object moves the appetite, introducing itself, as it were, into its intention; while the appetite moves towards the realization of the appetible object, so that the movement ends where it began. Accordingly, the first change wrought in the appetite by the appetible object is called *love*, and is nothing else than complacency in that object; and from this complacency results a movement towards that same object, and this movement is *desire ;* and lastly, there is rest which is *joy*. Since, therefore, love consists in a change wrought in the appetite by the appetible object, it is evident that love is a passion: properly so called, according as it is in the concupiscible faculty; in a wider and extended sense, according as it is in the will.

*Reply Obj.* 1. Since power denotes a principle of movement or action, Dionysius calls love a power, in so far as it is a principle of movement in the appetite.

*Reply Obj.* 2. Union belongs to love in so far as by reason of the complacency of the appetite, the lover stands in relation to that which he loves, as though it were himself or part of himself. Hence it is clear that love is not the very relation of union, but that union is a result of love. Hence, too, Dionysius says that *love is a unitive force* (*Div. Nom.* iv.), and the Philosopher says (*Polit.* ii. 1) that union is the work of love.

*Reply Obj.* 3. Although love does not denote the movement of the appetite in tending towards the appetible object, yet it denotes that movement whereby the appetite is changed by the appetible object, so as to have complacency therein.

## THIRD ARTICLE.

### WHETHER LOVE IS THE SAME AS DILECTION?

*We proceed thus to the Third Article :—*

*Objection* 1. It would seem that love is the same as dilection. For Dionysius says (*Div. Nom.* iv.) that love is to dilection, *as four is to twice two, and as a rectilinear figure is to one composed of straight lines.* But these have the same meaning. Therefore love and dilection denote the same thing.

*Obj.* 2. Further, the movements of the appetite differ by reason of their objects. But the objects of dilection and love are the same. Therefore these are the same.

*Obj.* 3. Further, if dilection and love differ, it seems that it is chiefly in the fact that *dilection refers to good things, love to evil things, as some have maintained,* according to Augustine (*De Civ. Dei* xiv. 7). But they do not differ thus; because as Augustine says (*ibid.*) the holy Scripture uses both words in reference to either good or bad things. Therefore love and dilection do not differ: thus indeed Augustine concludes (*ibid.*) that *it is not one thing to speak of love, and another to speak of dilection.*

*On the contrary,* Dionysius says (*Div. Nom.* iv.) that *some holy men have held that love means something more Godlike than dilection does.*

*I answer that,* We find four words referring, in a way, to the same thing: viz., love, dilection, charity and friendship. They differ, however, in this, that *friendship,* according to the Philosopher (*Ethic.* viii. 5), *is like a habit,* whereas *love* and *dilection* are expressed by way of act or passion; and *charity* can be taken either way.

Moreover these three express act in different ways. For love has a wider signification than the others, since every dilection or charity is love, but not vice versa. Because dilection implies, in addition to love, a choice (*electionem*) made beforehand, as the very word denotes: and therefore dilection is not in the concupiscible power, but only in the will, and only in the rational nature.—Charity denotes, in addition to love, a certain perfection of love, in so far as that which is loved is held to be of great price, as the word itself implies.*

*Reply Obj.* 1. Dionysius is speaking of love and dilection, in so far as they are in the intellectual appetite; for thus love is the same as dilection.

*Reply Obj.* 2. The object of love is more general than the object of dilection: because love extends to more than dilection does, as stated above.

*Reply Obj.* 3. Love and dilection differ, not in respect of good and evil, but as stated.   Yet in the intellectual faculty love is the same as dilection.   And it is in this sense that Augustine speaks of love in the passage quoted: hence a little further on he adds that *a right will is well-directed love, and a wrong will is ill-directed love*.   However, the fact that love, which is a concupiscible passion, inclines many to evil, is the reason why some assigned the difference spoken of.

*Reply Obj.* 4. The reason why some held that, even when applied to the will itself, the word *love* signifies something more Godlike than *dilection*, was because love denotes a passion, especially in so far as it is in the sensitive appetite; whereas dilection presupposes the judgment of reason.   But it is possible for man to tend to God by love, being as it were passively drawn by Him, more than he can possibly be drawn thereto by his reason, which pertains to the nature of dilection, as stated above.   And consequently love is more Godlike than dilection.

## FOURTH ARTICLE.

### WHETHER LOVE IS PROPERLY DIVIDED INTO LOVE OF FRIENDSHIP AND LOVE OF CONCUPISCENCE ?

*We proceed thus to the Fourth Article :—*

*Objection* 1. It would seem that love is not properly divided into love of friendship and love of concupiscence.

* Referring to the Latin *carus* (*dear*).

For *love is a passion, while friendship is a habit,* according to the Philosopher (*Ethic.* viii. 5). But habit cannot be the member of a division of passions. Therefore love is not properly divided into love of concupiscence and love of friendship.

*Obj.* 2. Further, a thing cannot be divided by another member of the same division; for *man* is not a member of the same division as *animal.* But concupiscence is a member of the same division as love, as a passion distinct from love. Therefore concupiscence is not a division of love.

*Obj.* 3. Further, according to the Philosopher (*Ethic.* viii. 3) friendship is threefold, that which is founded on *usefulness,* that which is founded on *pleasure,* and that which is founded on *goodness.* But useful and pleasant friendship are not without concupiscence. Therefore concupiscence should not be contrasted with friendship.

*On the contrary,* We are said to love certain things, because we desire them: thus *a man is said to love wine, on account of its sweetness which he desires;* as stated in *Topic.* ii. 3. But we have no friendship for wine and suchlike things, as stated in *Ethic.* viii. 2. Therefore love of concupiscence is distinct from love of friendship.

*I answer that,* As the Philosopher says (*Rhet.* ii. 4), *to love is to wish good to someone.* Hence the movement of love has a twofold tendency: towards the good which a man wishes to someone,—to himself or to another, and towards that to which he wishes some good. Accordingly, man has love of concupiscence towards the good that he wishes to another, and love of friendship, towards him to whom he wishes good.

Now the members of this division are related as primary and secondary: since that which is loved with the love of friendship is loved simply and for itself; whereas that which is loved with the love of concupiscence, is loved, not simply and for itself, but for something else. For just as that which has existence, is a being simply, while that which exists in another is a relative being; so, because good is convertible with being, the good, which itself has goodness, is good simply; but that which is another's good, is a relative good. Consequently the love with which a thing is loved, that it may have some good, is love simply; while the love, with which a thing is loved, that it may be another's good, is relative love.

*Reply Obj.* 1. Love is not divided into friendship and concupiscence, but into love of friendship, and love of concupiscence. For a friend is, properly speaking, one to whom we wish good: while we are said to desire, what we wish for ourselves.

Hence the Reply to the Second Objection is evident.

*Reply Obj.* 3. When friendship is based on usefulness or pleasure, a man does indeed wish his friend some good: and in this respect the character of friendship is preserved. But since he refers this good further to his own pleasure or use, the result is that friendship of the useful or pleasant, in so far as it is connected with love of concupiscence, loses the character of true friendship.

# QUESTION XXVII.

## OF THE CAUSE OF LOVE.

### (*In Four Articles.*)

WE must now consider the cause of love: and under this head there are four points of inquiry: (1) Whether good is the only cause of love? (2) Whether knowledge is a cause of love? (3) Whether likeness is a cause of love? (4) Whether any other passion of the soul is a cause of love?

### FIRST ARTICLE.

#### WHETHER GOOD IS THE ONLY CAUSE OF LOVE?

*We proceed thus to the First Article :—*

*Objection* 1. It would seem that good is not the only cause of love. For good does not cause love, except because it is loved. But it happens that evil also is loved, according to Ps. x. 6: *He that loveth iniquity, hateth his own soul* : else, every love would be good. Therefore good is not the only cause of love.

*Obj.* 2. Further, the Philosopher says (*Rhet.* ii. 4) that *we love those who acknowledge their evils*. Therefore it seems that evil is the cause of love.

*Obj.* 3. Further, Dionysius says (*Div. Nom.* iv.) that not *the good* only but also *the beautiful is beloved by all*.

*On the contrary*, Augustine says (*De Trin.* viii. 3): *Assuredly, the good alone is beloved*. Therefore good alone is the cause of love.

*I answer that*, As stated above (Q. XXVI., A. 1), Love belongs to the appetitive power which is a passive faculty. Wherefore its object stands in relation to it as the cause of its movement or act. Therefore the cause of love must needs be love's object. Now the proper object of love is the good; because, as stated above (Q. XXVI., AA. 1, 2), love implies a certain connaturalness or complacency of the lover for the thing beloved, and to everything, that thing is a good, which is akin and proportionate to it. It follows, therefore, that good is the proper cause of love.

*Reply Obj.* 1. Evil is never loved except under the aspect of good, that is to say, in so far as it is good in some respect, and is considered as being good simply. And thus a certain love is evil, in so far as it tends to that which is not simply a true good. It is in this way that man *loves iniquity*, inasmuch as, by means of iniquity, some good is gained; pleasure, for instance, or money, or suchlike.

*Reply Obj.* 2. Those who acknowledge their evils, are beloved, not for their evils, but because they acknowledge them, for it is a good thing to acknowledge one's faults, in so far as it excludes insincerity or hypocrisy.

*Reply Obj.* 3. The beautiful is the same as the good, and they differ in aspect only. For since good is what all seek, the notion of good is that which calms the desire; while the notion of the beautiful is that which calms the desire, by being seen or known. Consequently those senses chiefly regard the beautiful, which are the most cognitive, viz., sight and hearing, as ministering to reason; for we speak of beautiful sights and beautiful sounds. But in reference to the other objects of the other senses, we do not use the expression *beautiful*, for we do not speak of beautiful tastes, and beautiful odours. Thus it is evident that beauty adds to goodness a relation to the cognitive faculty: so that *good* means that which simply pleases the appetite; while the *beautiful* is something pleasant to apprehend.

## SECOND ARTICLE.

### WHETHER KNOWLEDGE IS A CAUSE OF LOVE ?

*We proceed thus to the Second Article :—*

*Objection* 1. It would seem that knowledge is not a cause of love. For it is due to love that a thing is sought. But some things are sought without being known, for instance, the sciences; for since *to have them is the same as to know them*, as Augustine says (QQ. LXXXIII., qu. 35), if we knew them we should have them, and should not seek them. Therefore knowledge is not the cause of love.

*Obj.* 2. Further, to love what we know not seems like loving something more than we know it. But some things are loved more than they are known: thus in this life God can be loved in Himself, but cannot be known in Himself. Therefore knowledge is not the cause of love.

*Obj.* 3. Further, if knowledge were the cause of love, there would be no love, where there is no knowledge. But in all things there is love, as Dionysius says (*Div. Nom.* iv.); whereas there is not knowledge in all things. Therefore knowledge is not the cause of love.

*On the contrary*, Augustine proves (*De Trin.* x. 1, 2) that *none can love what he does not know*.

*I answer that*, As stated above (A. 1), good is the cause of love, as being its object. But good is not the object of the appetite, except as apprehended. And therefore love demands some apprehension of the good that is loved. For this reason the Philosopher (*Ethic.* ix. 5, 12) says that bodily sight is the beginning of sensitive love: and in like manner the contemplation of spiritual beauty or goodness is the beginning of spiritual love. Accordingly knowledge is the cause of love for the same reason as good is, which can be loved only if known.

*Reply Obj.* 1. He who seeks science, is not entirely without knowledge thereof: but knows something about it already in some respect, either in a general way, or in some one of its effects, or from having heard it commended, as Augustine says (*De Trin.* x. 1, 2). But to have it is not to know it thus, but to know it perfectly.

*Reply Obj.* 2. Something is required for the perfection of knowledge, that is not requisite for the perfection of love. For knowledge belongs to the reason, whose function it is to distinguish things which in reality are united, and to unite together, after a fashion, things that are distinct, by comparing one with another.  Consequently the perfection of knowledge requires that man should know distinctly all that is in a thing, such as its parts, powers, and properties.  On the other hand, love is in the appetitive power, which regards a thing as it is in itself: wherefore it suffices, for the perfection of love, that a thing be loved according as it is known in itself.  Hence it is, therefore, that a thing is loved more than it is known; since it can be loved perfectly, even without being perfectly known.  This is most evident in regard to the sciences, which some love through having a certain general knowledge of them: for instance, they know that rhetoric is a science that enables man to persuade others; and this is what they love in rhetoric.  The same applies to the love of God.

*Reply Obj.* 3.  Even natural love, which is in all things, is caused by a kind of knowledge, not indeed existing in natural things themselves, but in Him Who created their nature, as stated above (Q. XXVI., A. 1; *cf.* P. 1, Q. VI., A. 1 *ad* 2).

### THIRD ARTICLE.

#### WHETHER LIKENESS IS A CAUSE OF LOVE?

*We proceed thus to the Third Article :—*

*Objection* 1.  It would seem that likeness is not a cause of love.  For the same thing is not the cause of contraries. But likeness is the cause of hatred; for it is written (Prov. xiii. 10) that *among the proud there are always contentions*; and the Philosopher says (*Ethic.* viii. 1) that *potters quarrel with one another*.  Therefore likeness is not a cause of love.

*Obj.* 2.  Further, Augustine says (*Confess.* iv. 14) that *a man loves in another that which he would not be himself: thus he loves an actor, but would not himself be an actor*.  But it would not be so, if likeness were the proper cause of love; for in that case a man would love in another, that which he possesses himself, or would like to possess.  Therefore likeness is not a cause of love.

*Obj.* 3.  Further, Everyone loves that which he needs, even if he have it not: thus a sick man loves health, and a

poor man loves riches.   But in so far as he needs them and
lacks them, he is unlike them.   Therefore not only likeness
but also unlikeness is a cause of love.

*Obj.* 4. Further, the Philosopher says (*Rhet.* ii. 4) that *we
love those who bestow money and health on us ; and also those
who retain their friendship for the dead.*   But all are not such.
Therefore likeness is not a cause of love.

*On the contrary*, It is written (Ecclus. xiii. 19): *Every beast
loveth its like.*

*I answer that*, Likeness, properly speaking, is a cause of
love.   But it must be observed that likeness between things
is twofold.   One kind of likeness arises from each thing
having the same quality actually: for example, two things
possessing the quality of whiteness are said to be alike.
Another kind of likeness arises from one thing having
potentially and by way of inclination, a quality which the
other has actually: thus we may say that a heavy body
existing outside its proper place is like another heavy body
that exists in its proper place: or again, according as potentiality bears a resemblance to its act; since act is contained,
in a manner, in the potentiality itself.

Accordingly the first kind of likeness causes love of friendship or well-wishing.   For the very fact that two men are
alike, having, as it were, one form, makes them to be, in a
manner, one in that form: thus two men are one thing in the
species of humanity, and two white men are one thing in
whiteness.   Hence the affections of one tend to the other,
as being one with him; and he wishes good to him as to
himself.   But the second kind of likeness causes love of
concupiscence, or friendship founded on usefulness or
pleasure: because whatever is in potentiality, as such, has
the desire for its act; and it takes pleasure in its realization,
if it be a sentient and cognitive being.

Now it has been stated above (Q. XXVI., A. 4), that in
the love of concupiscence, the lover, properly speaking,
loves himself, in willing the good that he desires.   But a
man loves himself more than another: because he is one with
himself substantially, whereas with another he is one only

in the likeness of some form. Consequently, if this other's likeness to him arising from the participation of a form, hinders him from gaining the good that he loves, he becomes hateful to him, not for being like him, but for hindering him from gaining his own good. This is why *potters quarrel among themselves*, because they hinder one another's gain: and why *there are contentions among the proud*, because they hinder one another in attaining the position they covet.

Hence the Reply to the First Objection is evident.

*Reply Obj.* 2. Even when a man loves in another what he loves not in himself, there is a certain likeness of proportion: because as the latter is to that which is loved in him, so is the former to that which he loves in himself: for instance, if a good singer love a good writer, we can see a likeness of proportion, inasmuch as each one has that which is becoming to him in respect of his art.

*Reply Obj.* 3. He that loves what he needs, bears a likeness to what he loves, as potentiality bears a likeness to its act, as stated above.

*Reply Obj.* 4. According to the same likeness of potentiality to its act, the illiberal man loves the man who is liberal, in so far as he expects from him something which he desires. The same applies to the man who is constant in his friendship as compared to one who is inconstant. For in either case friendship seems to be based on usefulness. We might also say that although not all men have these virtues in the complete habit, yet they have them according to certain seminal principles in the reason, in force of which principles the man who is not virtuous loves the virtuous man, as being in conformity with his own natural reason.

## FOURTH ARTICLE.

### WHETHER ANY OTHER PASSION OF THE SOUL IS A CAUSE OF LOVE?

*We proceed thus to the Fourth Article :—*

*Objection* 1. It would seem that some other passion can be the cause of love. For the Philosopher (*Ethic.* viii. 3) says that some are loved for the sake of the pleasure they give. But pleasure is a passion. Therefore another passion is a cause of love.

*Obj.* 2. Further, desire is a passion. But we love some because we desire to receive something from them: as happens in every friendship based on usefulness. Therefore another passion is a cause of love.

*Obj.* 3. Further, Augustine says (*De Trin.* x. 1): *When we have no hope of getting a thing, we love it but half-heartedly or not at all, even if we see how beautiful it is.* Therefore hope too is a cause of love.

*On the contrary,* All the other emotions of the soul are caused by love, as Augustine says (*De Civ. Dei* xiv. 7, 9).

*I answer that,* There is no other passion of the soul that does not presuppose love of some kind. The reason is that every other passion of the soul implies either movement towards something, or rest in something. Now every movement towards something, or rest in something, arises from some kinship or aptness to that thing; and in this does love consist. Therefore it is not possible for any other passion of the soul to be universally the cause of every love. But it may happen that some other passion is the cause of some particular love: just as one good is the cause of another.

*Reply Obj.* 1. When a man loves a thing for the pleasure it affords, his love is indeed caused by pleasure; but that very pleasure is caused, in its turn, by another preceding love; for none takes pleasure save in that which is loved in some way.

*Reply Obj.* 2. Desire for a thing always presupposes love for that thing. But desire of one thing can be the cause of another thing's being loved; thus he that desires money, for this reason loves him from whom he receives it.

*Reply Obj.* 3. Hope causes or increases love; both by reason of pleasure, because it causes pleasure; and by reason of desire, because hope strengthens desire, since we do not desire so intensely that which we have no hope of receiving. Nevertheless hope itself is of a good that is loved.

# QUESTION XXVIII.

## OF THE EFFECTS OF LOVE.
### (*In Six Articles.*)

WE now have to consider the effects of love: under which head there are six points of inquiry: (1) Whether union is an effect of love ?  (2) Whether mutual indwelling is an effect of love ?  (3) Whether extasy is an effect of love ? (4) Whether zeal is an effect of love ?  (5) Whether love is a passion that is hurtful to the lover ?  (6) Whether love is cause of all that the lover does ?

## FIRST ARTICLE.
### WHETHER UNION IS AN EFFECT OF LOVE ?

*We proceed thus to the First Article :—*

*Objection* 1. It would seem that union is not an effect of love.  For absence is incompatible with union.  But love is compatible with absence; for the Apostle says (Gal. iv. 18): *Be zealous for that which is good in a good thing always* (speaking of himself, according to a gloss), *and not only when I am present with you.*  Therefore union is not an effect of love.

*Obj.* 2. Further, every union is either according to essence, —thus form is united to matter, accident to subject, and a part to the whole, or to another part in order to make up the whole: or according to likeness, in genus, species, or accident. But love does not cause union of essence; else love could not be between things essentially distinct.  On the other hand, love does not cause union of likeness, but rather is caused by it, as stated above (Q. XXVII., A. 3).  Therefore union is not an effect of love.

*Obj.* 3. Further, the sense in act is the sensible in act, and the intellect in act is the thing actually understood. But the lover in act is not the beloved in act. Therefore union is the effect of knowledge rather than of love.

*On the contrary*, Dionysius says (*Div. Nom.* iv.) that every love is a *unitive force*.

*I answer that*, The union of lover and beloved is twofold. The first is real union; for instance, when the beloved is present with the lover.—The second is union of affection: and this union must be considered in relation to the preceding apprehension; since movement of the appetite follows apprehension. Now love being twofold, viz., love of concupiscence, and love of friendship; each of these arises from a kind of apprehension of the oneness of the thing loved with the lover. For when we love a thing, by desiring it, we apprehend it as belonging to our well-being. In like manner when a man loves another with the love of friendship, he wills good to him, just as he wills good to himself: wherefore he apprehends him as his other self, in so far, to wit, as he wills good to him as to himself. Hence a friend is called a man's *other self* (*Ethic.* ix. 4), and Augustine says (*Confess.* iv. 6), *Well did one say to his friend: Thou half of my soul.*

The first of these unions is caused *effectively* by love; because love moves man to desire and seek the presence of the beloved, as of something suitable and belonging to him. The second union is caused *formally* by love; because love itself is this union or bond. In this sense Augustine says (*De Trin.* viii. 10) that *love is a vital principle uniting, or seeking to unite two together, the lover, to wit, and the beloved.* For in describing it as *uniting* he refers to the union of affection, without which there is no love: and in saying that *it seeks to unite*, he refers to real union.

*Reply Obj.* 1. This argument is true of real union. That is necessary to pleasure as being its cause; desire implies the real absence of the beloved: but love remains whether the beloved be absent or present.

*Reply Obj.* 2. Union has a threefold relation to love. There is a union which causes love; and this is substantial union, as regards the love with which one loves oneself; while as regards the love wherewith one loves other things, it is the union of likeness, as stated above (Q. XXVII., A. 3). There is also a union which is essentially love itself. This union is according to a bond of affection, and is likened to substantial union, inasmuch as the lover stands to the object of his love, as to himself, if it be love of friendship; as to something belonging to himself, if it be love of concupiscence. Again there is a union, which is the effect of love. This is real union, which the lover seeks with the object of his love. Moreover this union is in keeping with the demands of love: for as the Philosopher relates (*Polit*. ii. 1), *Aristophanes stated that lovers would wish to be united both into one*, but since *this would result in either one or both being destroyed*, they seek a suitable and becoming union;—to live together, speak together, and be united in other like things.

*Reply Obj*. 3. Knowledge is perfected by the thing known being united, through its likeness, to the knower. But the effect of love is that the thing itself which is loved, is, in a way, united to the lover, as stated above. Consequently the union caused by love is closer than that which is caused by knowledge.

## SECOND ARTICLE.

### WHETHER MUTUAL INDWELLING IS AN EFFECT OF LOVE ?

*We proceed thus to the Second Article :—*

*Objection* 1. It would seem that love does not cause mutual indwelling, so that the lover be in the beloved and vice versa. For that which is in another is contained in it. But the same cannot be container and contents. Therefore love cannot cause mutual indwelling, so that the lover be in the beloved and vice versa.

*Obj*. 2. Further, nothing can penetrate within a whole, except by means of a division of the whole. But it is the function of the reason, not of the appetite where love resides, to divide things that are really united. Therefore mutual indwelling is not an effect of love.

*Obj.* 3. Further, if love involves the lover being in the beloved and vice versa, it follows that the beloved is united to the lover, in the same way as the lover is united to the beloved. But the union itself is love, as stated above (A. 1). Therefore it follows that the lover is always loved by the object of his love; which is evidently false. Therefore mutual indwelling is not an effect of love.

*On the contrary,* It is written (1 Jo. iv. 16): *He that abideth in charity abideth in God, and God in him.* Now charity is the love of God. Therefore, for the same reason, every love makes the beloved to be in the lover, and vice versa.

*I answer that,* This effect of mutual indwelling may be understood as referring both to the apprehensive and to the appetitive power. Because, as to the apprehensive power, the beloved is said to be in the lover, inasmuch as the beloved abides in the apprehension of the lover, according to Phil. i. 7, *For that I have you in my heart* : while the lover is said to be in the beloved, according to apprehension, inasmuch as the lover is not satisfied with a superficial apprehension of the beloved, but strives to gain an intimate knowledge of everything pertaining to the beloved, so as to penetrate into his very soul. Thus it is written concerning the Holy Ghost, Who is God's Love, that He *searcheth all things, yea the deep things of God* (1 Cor. ii. 10).

As to the appetitive power, the object loved is said to be in the lover, inasmuch as it is in his affections, by a kind of complacency: causing him either to take pleasure in it, or in its good, when present; or, in the absence of the object loved, by his longing, to tend towards it with the love of concupiscence, or towards the good that he wills to the beloved, with the love of friendship: not indeed from any extrinsic cause (as when we desire one thing on account of another, or wish good to another on account of something else), but because the complacency in the beloved is rooted in the lover's heart. For this reason we speak of love as being *intimate* ; and of *the bowels of charity.* On the other hand, the lover is in the beloved, by the love of concupiscence and by the love of friendship, but not in the same way. For the love of concupiscence is not satisfied with any external or superficial possession or enjoyment of the beloved; but seeks to possess the beloved perfectly, by penetrating into his heart, as it were.　Whereas, in the love of friendship, the lover is in the beloved, inasmuch as he reckons what is good or evil to his friend, as being so to himself; and his friend's will as his own, so that it seems as though he felt the good or suffered the evil in the person of his friend.　Hence it is proper to friends *to desire the same things, and to grieve and rejoice at the same*, as the Philosopher says (*Ethic.* ix. 3 and *Rhet.* ii. 4). Consequently in so far as he reckons what affects his friend as affecting himself, the lover seems to be in the beloved, as though he were become one with him: but in so far as, on the other hand, he wills and acts for his friend's sake as for his own sake, looking on his friend as identified with himself, thus the beloved is in the lover.

In yet a third way, mutual indwelling in the love of friendship can be understood in regard to reciprocal love: inasmuch as friends return love for love, and both desire and do good things for one another.

*Reply Obj.* 1. The beloved is contained in the lover, by being impressed on his heart and thus becoming the object of his complacency.　On the other hand, the lover is contained in the beloved, inasmuch as the lover penetrates, so to speak, into the beloved.　For nothing hinders a thing from being both container and contents in different ways: just as a genus is contained in its species, and vice versa.

*Reply Obj.* 2. The apprehension of the reason precedes the movement of love.　Consequently, just as the reason divides, so does the movement of love penetrate into the beloved, as was explained above.

*Reply Obj.* 3. This argument is true of the third kind of mutual indwelling, which is not to be found in every kind of love.

## Third Article.

### whether extasy is an effect of love?

*We proceed thus to the Third Article :—*

*Objection* 1. It would seem that extasy is not an effect of love. For extasy seems to imply loss of reason. But love does not always result in loss of reason: for lovers are masters of themselves at times. Therefore love does not cause extasy.

*Obj.* 2. Further, the lover desires the beloved to be united to him. Therefore he draws the beloved to himself, rather than betakes himself into the beloved, going forth out from himself as it were.

*Obj.* 3. Further, love unites the beloved to the lover, as stated above (A. 1). If, therefore, the lover goes out from himself, in order to betake himself into the beloved, it follows that the lover always loves the beloved more than himself: which is evidently false. Therefore extasy is not an effect of love.

*On the contrary*, Dionysius says (*Div. Nom.* iv.) that *the Divine love produces extasy*, and that *God Himself suffered extasy through love*. Since therefore according to the same author (*ibid.*), every love is a participated likeness of the Divine Love, it seems that every love causes extasy.

*I answer that*, To suffer extasy means to be placed outside oneself. This happens as to the apprehensive power and as to the appetitive power. As to the apprehensive power, a man is said to be placed outside himself, when he is placed outside the knowledge proper to him. This may be due to his being raised to a higher knowledge; thus, a man is said to suffer extasy, inasmuch as he is placed outside the connatural apprehension of his sense and reason, when he is raised up so as to comprehend things that surpass sense and reason: or it may be due to his being cast down into a state of debasement; thus a man may be said to suffer extasy, when he is overcome by violent passion or madness.—As to the appetitive power, a man is said to suffer extasy, when that power is borne towards something else, so that it goes forth out from itself, as it were.

The first of these extasies is caused by love dispositively, in so far, namely, as love makes the lover dwell on the beloved, as stated above (A. 2), and to dwell intently on one thing draws the mind from other things.—The second extasy is caused by love directly; by love of friendship, simply; by love of concupiscence, not simply but in a restricted sense. Because in love of concupiscence, the lover is carried out of himself, in a certain sense; in so far, namely, as not being satisfied with enjoying the good that he has, he seeks to enjoy something outside himself. But since he seeks to have this extrinsic good for himself, he does not go out from himself simply, and this movement remains finally within him. On the other hand, in the love of friendship, a man's affection goes out from itself simply; because he wishes and does good to his friend, by caring and providing for him, for his sake.

*Reply Obj.* 1. This argument is true of the first kind of extasy.

*Reply Obj.* 2. This argument applies to love of concupiscence, which, as stated above, does not cause extasy simply.

*Reply Obj.* 3. He who loves, goes out from himself, in so far as he wills the good of his friend and works for it. Yet he does not will the good of his friend more than his own good: and so it does not follow that he loves another more than himself.

### FOURTH ARTICLE.

#### WHETHER ZEAL IS AN EFFECT OF LOVE ?

*We proceed thus to the Fourth Article :—*

*Objection* 1. It would seem that zeal is not an effect of love. For zeal is a beginning of contention; wherefore it is written (1 Cor. iii. 3): *Whereas there is among you zeal* (Douay,—*envying*) *and contention*, etc. But contention is incompatible with love. Therefore zeal is not an effect of love.

*Obj.* 2. Further, the object of love is the good, which communicates itself to others. But zeal is opposed to communication; since it seems an effect of zeal, that a man refuses to share the object of his love with another: thus husbands are said to be jealous of (*zelare*) their wives, because they will not share them with others. Therefore zeal is not an effect of love.

*Obj.* 3. Further, there is no zeal without hatred, as neither is there without love: for it is written (Ps. lxxii. 3): *I had a zeal on occasion of the wicked*. Therefore it should not be set down as an effect of love any more than of hatred.

*On the contrary*, Dionysius says (*Div. Nom.* iv.): *God is said to be a zealot, on account of his great love for all things*.

*I answer that*, Zeal, whatever way we take it, arises from the intensity of love. For it is evident that the more intensely a power tends to anything, the more vigorously it withstands opposition or resistance. Since therefore love is *a movement towards the object loved*, as Augustine says (QQ. LXXXIII., qu. 35), an intense love seeks to remove everything that opposes it.

But this happens in different ways according to love of concupiscence, and love of friendship. For in love of concupiscence he who desires something intensely, is moved against all that hinders his gaining or quietly enjoying the object of his love. It is thus that husbands are said to be jealous of their wives, lest association with others prove a hindrance to their exclusive individual rights. In like manner those who seek to excel, are moved against those who seem to excel, as though these were a hindrance to their excelling. And this is the zeal of envy, of which it is written (Ps. xxxvi. 1): *Be not emulous of evil doers, nor envy (zelaveris) them that work iniquity*.

On the other hand, love of friendship seeks the friend's good: wherefore, when it is intense, it causes a man to be moved against everything that opposes the friend's good. In this respect, a man is said to be zealous on behalf of his friend, when he makes a point of repelling whatever may be said or done against his friend's good. In this way, too, a man is said to be zealous on God's behalf, when he endeavours, to the best of his means, to repel whatever is contrary to the honour or will of God; according to 3 Kings xix. 14: *With zeal have I been zealous for the Lord of hosts.* Again on the words of Jo. ii. 17: *The zeal of Thy house hath eaten me up*, a gloss says that *a man is eaten up with a good zeal, who strives to remedy whatever evil he perceives ; and if he cannot, bears with it and laments it.*

*Reply Obj.* 1. The Apostle is speaking in this passage of the zeal of envy; which is indeed the cause of contention, not against the object of love, but for it, and against that which is opposed to it.

*Reply Obj.* 2. Good is loved inasmuch as it can be communicated to the lover. Consequently whatever hinders the perfection of this communication, becomes hateful. Thus zeal arises from love of good.—But through defect of goodness, it happens that certain small goods cannot, in their entirety, be possessed by many at the same time: and from the love of such things arises the zeal of envy. But it does not arise, properly speaking, in the case of those things which, in their entirety, can be possessed by many: for no one envies another the knowledge of truth, which can be known entirely by many; except perhaps one may envy another his superiority in the knowledge of it.

*Reply Obj.* 3. The very fact that a man hates whatever is opposed to the object of his love, is the effect of love. Hence zeal is set down as an effect of love rather than of hatred.

### FIFTH ARTICLE.

#### WHETHER LOVE IS A PASSION THAT WOUNDS THE LOVER ?

*We proceed thus to the Fifth Article :—*

*Objection* 1. It would seem that love wounds the lover. For languor denotes a hurt in the one that languishes. But love causes languor: for it is written (Cant. ii. 5): *Stay me up with flowers, compass me about with apples ; because I languish with love.* Therefore love is a wounding passion.

*Obj.* 2. Further, melting is a kind of dissolution. But love melts that in which it is: for it is written (Cant. v. 6): *My soul melted when my beloved spoke.* Therefore love is a dissolvent: therefore it is a corruptive and a wounding passion.

*Obj.* 3. Further, fervour denotes a certain excess of heat; which excess has a corruptive effect. But love causes fervour: for Dionysius (*Cœl. Hier.* vii.) in reckoning the properties belonging to the Seraphim's love, includes *hot* and *piercing* and *most fervent*. Moreover it is said of love (Cant. viii. 6) that *its lamps are fire and flames*. Therefore love is a wounding and corruptive passion.

*On the contrary*, Dionysius says (*Div. Nom.* iv.) that *everything loves itself with a love that holds it together*, *i.e.*, that preserves it. Therefore love is not a wounding passion, but rather one that preserves and perfects.

*I answer that*, As stated above (Q. XXVI., AA. 1, 2; Q. XXVII., A. 1), love denotes a certain adapting of the appetitive power to some good. Now nothing is hurt by being adapted to that which is suitable to it; rather, if possible, it is perfected and bettered. But if a thing be adapted to that which is not suitable to it, it is hurt and made worse thereby. Consequently love of a suitable good perfects and betters the lover; but love of a good which is unsuitable to the lover, wounds and worsens him. Wherefore man is perfected and bettered chiefly by the love of God: but is wounded and worsened by the love of sin, according to Osee ix. 10: *They became abominable, as those things which they loved*.

And let this be understood as applying to love in respect of its formal element, *i.e.*, in regard to the appetite. But in respect of the material element in the passion of love, *i.e.*, a certain bodily change, it happens that love is hurtful, by reason of this change being excessive: just as it happens in the senses, and in every act of a power of the soul that is exercised through the change of some bodily organ.

In reply to the objections, it is to be observed that four proximate effects may be ascribed to love: viz., melting, enjoyment, languor, and fervour. Of these the first is *melting*, which is opposed to freezing. For things that are frozen, are closely bound together, so as to be hard to pierce.

But it belongs to love that the appetite is fitted to receive the good which is loved, inasmuch as the object loved is in the lover, as stated above (A. 2).   Consequently the freezing or hardening of the heart is a disposition incompatible with love: while melting denotes a softening of the heart, whereby the heart shows itself to be ready for the entrance of the beloved.—If, then, the beloved is present and possessed, pleasure or enjoyment ensues.   But if the beloved be absent, two passions arise; viz., sadness at its absence, which is denoted by *languor* (hence Cicero in *De Tuscul. Quæst*. iii. 11 applies the term *ailment* chiefly to sadness); and an intense desire to possess the beloved, which is signified by *fervour*. —And these are the effects of love considered formally, according to the relation of the appetitive power to its object. But in the passion of love, other effects ensue, proportionate to the above, in respect of a change in the organ.

### SIXTH ARTICLE.

#### WHETHER LOVE IS CAUSE OF ALL THAT THE LOVER DOES ?

*We proceed thus to the Sixth Article :*—

*Objection* 1. It would seem that the lover does not do everything from love.   For love is a passion, as stated above (Q. XXVI., A. 2).   But man does not do everything from passion: but some things he does from choice, and some things from ignorance, as stated in *Ethic*. v. 8.   Therefore not everything that a man does, is done from love.

*Obj*. 2. Further, the appetite is a principle of movement and action in all animals, as stated in *De Anima* iii. 10. If, therefore, whatever a man does is done from love, the other passions of the appetitive faculty are superfluous.

*Obj*. 3. Further, nothing is produced at one and the same time by contrary causes.   But some things are done from hatred.   Therefore all things are not done from love.

*On the contrary*, Dionysius says (*Div. Nom*. iv.) that *all things, whatever they do, they do for the love of good.*

*I answer that*, Every agent acts for an end, as stated above

(Q. I., A. 2).   Now the end is the good desired and loved by each one.   Wherefore it is evident that every agent, whatever it be, does every action from love of some kind.

*Reply Obj*. 1. This objection takes love as a passion existing in the sensitive appetite.   But here we are speaking of love in a general sense, inasmuch as it includes intellectual, rational, animal, and natural love: for it is in this sense that Dionysius speaks of love in chap. iv. of *De Divinis Nominibus*.

*Reply Obj*. 2. As stated above (A. 5; Q. XXVII., A. 4) desire, sadness and pleasure, and consequently all the other passions of the soul, result from love.   Wherefore every act that proceeds from any passion, proceeds also from love as from a first cause: and so the other passions, which are proximate causes, are not superfluous.

*Reply Obj*. 3. Hatred also is a result of love, as we shall state further on (Q. XXIX., A. 2).

# QUESTION XXIX.

## OF HATRED.

### (*In Six Articles.*)

WE must now consider hatred: concerning which there are six points of inquiry: (1) Whether evil is the cause and the object of hatred? (2) Whether love is the cause of hatred? (3) Whether hatred is stronger than love? (4) Whether a man can hate himself? (5) Whether a man can hate the truth? (6) Whether a thing can be the object of universal hatred?

## FIRST ARTICLE.

### WHETHER EVIL IS THE CAUSE AND OBJECT OF HATRED?

*We proceed thus to the First Article :—*

*Objection* 1. It would seem that evil is not the object and cause of hatred. For everything that exists, as such, is good. If therefore evil be the object of hatred, it follows that nothing but the lack of something can be the object of hatred: which is clearly untrue.

*Obj.* 2. Further, hatred of evil is praiseworthy; hence (2 Machab. iii. 1) some are praised for that *the laws were very well kept, because of the godliness of Onias the high-priest, and the hatred their souls* (Douay, *his soul*) *had of evil*. If, therefore, nothing but evil be the object of hatred, it would follow that all hatred is commendable: and this is clearly false.

*Obj.* 3. Further, the same thing is not at the same time both good and evil. But the same thing is lovable and hateful to different subjects. Therefore hatred is not only of evil, but also of good.

*On the contrary*, Hatred is the opposite of love. But the object of love is good, as stated above (Q. XXVI., A. 1; Q. XXVII., A. 1). Therefore the object of hatred is evil.

*I answer that*, Since the natural appetite is the result of apprehension (though this apprehension is not in the same subject as the natural appetite), it seems that what applies to the inclination of the natural appetite, applies also to the animal appetite, which does result from an apprehension in the same subject, as stated above (Q. XXVI., A. 1). Now, with regard to the natural appetite, it is evident, that just as each thing is naturally attuned and adapted to that which is suitable to it, wherein consists natural love; so has it a natural dissonance from that which opposes and destroys it; and this is natural hatred. So, therefore, in the animal appetite, or in the intellectual appetite, love is a certain harmony of the appetite with that which is apprehended as suitable; while hatred is dissonance of the appetite from that which is apprehended as repugnant and hurtful. Now, just as whatever is suitable, as such, bears the aspect of good; so whatever is repugnant, as such, bears the aspect of evil. And therefore, just as good is the object of love, so evil is the object of hatred.

*Reply Obj.* 1. Being, as such, has not the aspect of repugnance but only of fittingness; because being is common to all things. But being, inasmuch as it is this determinate being, has an aspect of repugnance to some determinate being. And in this way, one being is hateful to another, and is evil; though not in itself, but by comparison with something else.

*Reply Obj.* 2. Just as a thing may be apprehended as good, when it is not truly good; so a thing may be apprehended as evil, whereas it is not truly evil. Hence it happens sometimes that neither hatred of evil nor love of good is good.

*Reply Obj.* 3. To different things the same thing may be lovable or hateful: in respect of the natural appetite, owing to one and the same thing being naturally suitable to one thing, and naturally unsuitable to another: thus heat is becoming to fire and unbecoming to water: and in respect of the animal appetite, owing to one and the same thing being apprehended by one as good, by another as bad.

## SECOND ARTICLE.
### WHETHER LOVE IS A CAUSE OF HATRED ?

*We proceed thus to the Second Article :—*

*Objection* 1. It would seem that love is not a cause of hatred. For *the opposite members of a division are naturally simultaneous* (*Prædic.* x.). But love and hatred are opposite members of a division, since they are contrary to one another. Therefore they are naturally simultaneous. Therefore love is not the cause of hatred.

*Obj.* 2. Further, of two contraries, one is not the cause of the other. But love and hatred are contraries. Therefore love is not the cause of hatred.

*Obj.* 3. Further, that which follows is not the cause of that which precedes. But hatred precedes love, seemingly: since hatred implies a turning away from evil, whereas love implies a turning towards good. Therefore love is not the cause of hatred.

*On the contrary*, Augustine says (*De Civ. Dei* xiv. 7, 9) that all emotions are caused by love. Therefore hatred also, since it is an emotion of the soul, is caused by love.

*I answer that*, As stated above (A. 1), love consists in a certain agreement of the lover with the object loved, while hatred consists in a certain disagreement or dissonance. Now we should consider in each thing, what agrees with it, before that which disagrees: since a thing disagrees with another, through destroying or hindering that which agrees with it. Consequently love must needs precede hatred; and nothing is hated, save through being contrary to a suitable thing which is loved. And hence it is that every hatred is caused by love.

*Reply Obj.* 1. The opposite members of a division are sometimes naturally simultaneous, both really and logically *e.g.*, two species of animal, or two species of colour. Sometimes they are simultaneous logically, while, in reality, one precedes, and causes the other; *e.g.*, the species of numbers, figures and movements. Sometimes they are not simultaneous either really or logically; *e.g.*, substance and accident; for substance is in reality the cause of accident; and being is predicated of substance before it is predicated of accident, by a priority of reason, because it is not predicated of accident except inasmuch as the latter is in substance.— Now love and hatred are naturally simultaneous, logically but not really. Wherefore nothing hinders love from being the cause of hatred.

*Reply Obj.* 2. Love and hatred are contraries if considered in respect of the same thing. But if taken in respect of contraries, they are not themselves contrary, but consequent to one another: for it amounts to the same that one love a certain thing, or that one hate its contrary. Thus love of one thing is the cause of one's hating its contrary.

*Reply Obj.* 3. In the order of execution, the turning away from one term precedes the turning towards the other. But the reverse is the case in the order of intention: since approach to one term is the reason for turning away from the other. Now the appetitive movement belongs rather to the order of intention than to that of execution. Wherefore love precedes hatred: because each is an appetitive movement.

## THIRD ARTICLE.

### WHETHER HATRED IS STRONGER THAN LOVE?

*We proceed thus to the Third Article :—*

*Objection* 1. It would seem that hatred is stronger than love. For Augustine says (QQ. LXXXIII, qu. 36): *There is no one who does not flee from pain, more than he desires pleasure.* But flight from pain pertains to hatred; while desire for pleasure belongs to love. Therefore hatred is stronger than love.

*Obj.* 2. Further, the weaker is overcome by the stronger. But love is overcome by hatred: when, that is to say, love is turned into hatred. Therefore hatred is stronger than love.

*Obj.* 3. Further, the emotions of the soul are shown by

their effects. But man insists more on repelling what is hateful, than on seeking what is pleasant: thus also irrational animals refrain from pleasure for fear of the whip, as Augustine instances (*loc. cit.*). Therefore hatred is stronger than love.

*On the contrary*, Good is stronger than evil; because *evil does nothing except in virtue of good*, as Dionysius says (*Div. Nom.* iv.). But hatred and love differ according to the difference of good and evil. Therefore love is stronger than hatred.

*I answer that*, It is impossible for an effect to be stronger than its cause. Now every hatred arises from some love as its cause, as above stated (A. 2). Therefore it is impossible for hatred to be stronger than love absolutely.

But furthermore, love must needs be, absolutely speaking, stronger than hatred. Because a thing is moved to the end more strongly than to the means. Now turning away from evil is directed as a means to the gaining of good. Wherefore, absolutely speaking, the soul's movement in respect of good is stronger than its movement in respect of evil.

Nevertheless hatred sometimes seems to be stronger than love, for two reasons. First, because hatred is more keenly felt than love. For, since the sensitive perception is accompanied by a certain impression; when once the impression has been received it is not felt so keenly as in the moment of receiving it. Hence the heat of a hectic fever, though greater, is nevertheless not felt so much as the heat of a tertian fever; because the heat of the hectic fever is habitual and like a second nature. For this reason, love is felt more keenly in the absence of the object loved; thus Augustine says (*De Trin.* x. 12) that *love is felt more keenly, when we lack what we love*. And for the same reason, the unbecomingness of that which is hated is felt more keenly than the becomingness of that which is loved.—Secondly, because comparison is made between a hatred and a love which are not mutually corresponding. Because, according to different degrees of good there are different degrees of love to which correspond different degrees of hatred. Wherefore a hatred that corresponds to a greater love, moves us more than a lesser love.

Hence it is clear how to reply to the First Objection. For the love of pleasure is less than the love of self-preservation, to which corresponds flight from pain. Wherefore we flee from pain more than we love pleasure.

*Reply Obj.* 2. Hatred would never overcome love, were it not for the greater love to which that hatred corresponds. Thus man loves himself, more than he loves his friend: and because he loves himself, his friend is hateful to him, if he oppose him.

*Reply Obj.* 3. The reason why we act with greater insistence in repelling what is hateful, is because we feel hatred more keenly.

## FOURTH ARTICLE.

### WHETHER A MAN CAN HATE HIMSELF?

*We proceed thus to the Fourth Article :—*

*Objection* 1. It would seem that a man can hate himself. For it is written (Ps. x. 6): *He that loveth iniquity, hateth his own soul.* But many love iniquity. Therefore many hate themselves.

*Obj.* 2. Further, him we hate, to whom we wish and work evil. But sometimes a man wishes and works evil to himself; *e.g.*, a man who kills himself. Therefore some men hate themselves.

*Obj.* 3. Further, Boethius says (*De Consol.* ii.) that *avarice makes a man hateful ;* whence we may conclude that everyone hates a miser. But some men are misers. Therefore they hate themselves.

*On the contrary,* The Apostle says (Eph. v. 29) that *no man ever hated his own flesh.*

*I answer that,* Properly speaking, it is impossible for a man to hate himself. For everything naturally desires good, nor can anyone desire anything for himself, save under the aspect of good: for *evil is outside the scope of the will,* as Dionysius says (*Div. Nom.* iv.). Now to love a man is to will good to him, as stated above (Q. XXVI., A. 4). Consequently, a

man must, of necessity, love himself; and it is impossible
for a man to hate himself, properly speaking.

But accidentally it happens that a man hates himself:
and this in two ways.  First, on the part of the good which
a man wills to himself.  For it happens sometimes that what
is desired as good in some particular respect, is simply evil;
and in this way, a man accidentally wills evil to himself;
and thus hates himself.—Secondly, in regard to himself, to
whom he wills good.  For each thing is that which is predominant in it; wherefore the state is said to do what the
king does, as if the king were the whole state.  Now it is
clear that man is principally the mind of man.  And it
happens that some men account themselves as being
principally that which they are in their material and sensitive nature.  Wherefore they love themselves according to
what they take themselves to be, while they hate that
which they really are, by desiring what is contrary to
reason.—And in both these ways, *he that loveth iniquity
hateth* not only *his own soul*, but also himself.

Wherefore the reply to the First Objection is evident.

*Reply Obj*. 2. No man wills and works evil to himself,
except he apprehend it under the aspect of good.  For even
they who kill themselves, apprehend death itself as a good,
considered as putting an end to some unhappiness or pain.

*Reply Obj*. 3. The miser hates something accidental to
himself, but not for that reason does he hate himself: thus
a sick man hates his sickness for the very reason that he
loves himself.—Or we may say that avarice makes man
hateful to others, but not to himself.  In fact, it is caused
by inordinate self-love, in respect of which, man desires
temporal goods for himself more than he should.

## Fifth Article.

### WHETHER A MAN CAN HATE THE TRUTH?

*We proceed thus to the Fifth Article :—*

*Objection* 1. It would seem that a man cannot hate the
truth.  For good, true, and being are convertible.  But a

man cannot hate good. Neither, therefore, can he hate the truth.

*Obj.* 2. Further, *All men have a natural desire for knowledge*, as stated in the beginning of the *Metaphysics* (i. 1). But knowledge is only of truth. Therefore truth is naturally desired and loved. But that which is in a thing naturally, is always in it. Therefore no man can hate the truth.

*Obj.* 3. Further, the Philosopher says (*Rhetor.* ii. 4) that *men love those who are straightforward.* But there can be no other motive for this save truth. Therefore man loves the truth naturally. Therefore he cannot hate it.

*On the contrary*, The Apostle says (Gal. iv. 16): *Am I become your enemy because I tell you the truth?** 

*I answer that*, Good, true and being are the same in reality, but differ as considered by reason. For good is considered in the light of something desirable, while being and true are not so considered: because good is *what all things seek.* Wherefore good, as such, cannot be the object of hatred, neither in general nor in particular.—Being and truth in general cannot be the object of hatred: because disagreement is the cause of hatred, and agreement is the cause of love; while being and truth are common to all things. But nothing hinders some particular being or some particular truth being an object of hatred, in so far as it is considered as hurtful and repugnant; since hurtfulness and repugnance are not incompatible with the notion of being and truth, as they are with the notion of good.

Now it may happen in three ways that some particular truth is repugnant or hurtful to the good we love. First, according as truth is in things as in its cause and origin. And thus man sometimes hates a particular truth, when he wishes that what is true were not true.—Secondly, according as truth is in man's knowledge, which hinders him from gaining the object loved: such is the case of those who wish not to know the truth of faith, that they may sin freely; in whose person it is said (Job xxi. 14): *We desire not the*

---

* St. Thomas quotes the passage, probably from memory, as though it were an assertion: *I am become, etc.*

*knowledge of Thy ways.*—Thirdly, a particular truth is hated, as being repugnant, inasmuch as it is in the intellect of another man: as, for instance, when a man wishes to remain hidden in his sin, he hates that anyone should know the truth about his sin.   In this respect, Augustine says (*Confess.* x. 23) that men *love truth when it enlightens, they hate it when it reproves.*   This suffices for the Reply to the First Objection.

*Reply Obj.* 2. The knowledge of truth is lovable in itself: hence Augustine says that men love it when it enlightens. But accidentally, the knowledge of truth may become hateful, in so far as it hinders one from accomplishing one's desire.

*Reply Obj.* 3. The reason why we love those who are straightforward is that they make known the truth, and the knowledge of the truth, considered in itself, is a desirable thing.

### Sixth Article.

#### WHETHER ANYTHING CAN BE AN OBJECT OF UNIVERSAL HATRED ?

*We proceed thus to the Sixth Article :—*

*Objection* 1. It would seem that a thing cannot be an object of universal hatred.   Because hatred is a passion of the sensitive appetite, which is moved by an apprehension in the senses.   But the senses cannot apprehend the universal. Therefore a thing cannot be an object of universal hatred.

*Obj.* 2. Further, hatred is caused by disagreement; and where there is disagreement, there is nothing in common. But the notion of universality implies something in common. Therefore nothing can be the object of universal hatred.

*Obj.* 3. Further, the object of hatred is evil.   But *evil is in things, and not in the mind* (*Metaph.* vi. 4).   Since therefore the universal is in the mind only, which abstracts the universal from the particular, it would seem that hatred cannot have a universal object.

*On the contrary*, The Philosopher says (*Rhetor.* ii. 4) that *anger is directed to something singular, whereas hatred is also directed to a thing in general ; for everybody hates the thief and the backbiter.*

*I answer that*, There are two ways of speaking of the universal: first, as considered under the aspect of universality; secondly, as considered in the nature to which it is ascribed: for it is one thing to consider the universal man, and another to consider a man as man. If, therefore, we take the universal, in the first way, no sensitive power, whether of apprehension or of appetite, can attain the universal: because the universal is obtained by abstraction from individual matter, on which every sensitive power is based.

Nevertheless the sensitive powers, both of apprehension and of appetite, can tend to something universally. Thus we say that the object of sight is colour considered generically; not that the sight is cognizant of universal colour, but because the fact that colour is cognizable by the sight, is attributed to colour, not as being this particular colour, but simply because it is colour. Accordingly hatred in the sensitive faculty can regard something universally: because this thing, by reason of its common nature, and not merely as an individual, is hostile to the animal—for instance, a wolf in regard to a sheep. Hence a sheep hates the wolf universally.—On the other hand, anger is always caused by something in particular: because it is caused by some action of the one that hurts us; and actions proceed from individuals. For this reason the Philosopher says (*ibid.*) that *anger is always directed to something singular, whereas hatred can be directed to a thing in general.*

But according as hatred is in the intellectual part, since it arises from the universal apprehension of the intellect, it can regard the universal in both ways.

*Reply Obj.* 1. The senses do not apprehend the universal, as such: but they apprehend something to which the character of universality is given by abstraction.

*Reply Obj.* 2. That which is common to all cannot be a reason of hatred. But nothing hinders a thing from being common to many, and at variance with others, so as to be hateful to them.

*Reply Obj.* 3. This argument considers the universal under the aspect of universality: and thus it does not come under the sensitive apprehension or appetite.

# QUESTION XXX.

## OF CONCUPISCENCE.

### (*In Four Articles.*)

WE have now to consider concupiscence: under which head there are four points of inquiry: (1) Whether concupiscence is in the sensitive appetite only? (2) Whether concupiscence is a specific passion? (3) Whether some concupiscences are natural, and some not natural? (4) Whether concupiscence is infinite?

## FIRST ARTICLE.

### WHETHER CONCUPISCENCE IS IN THE SENSITIVE APPETITE ONLY?

*We proceed thus to the First Article :—*

*Objection* 1. It would seem that concupiscence is not only in the sensitive appetite. For there is a concupiscence of wisdom, according to Wis. vi. 21: *The concupiscence* (Douay, *desire*) *of wisdom bringeth to the everlasting kingdom.* But the sensitive appetite can have no tendency to wisdom. Therefore concupiscence is not only in the sensitive appetite.

*Obj.* 2. Further, the desire for the commandments of God is not in the sensitive appetite: in fact the Apostle says (Rom. vii. 18): *There dwelleth not in me, that is to say, in my flesh, that which is good.* But desire for God's commandments is an act of concupiscence, according to Ps. cxviii. 20: *My soul hath coveted* (*concupivit*) *to long for thy justifications.* Therefore concupiscence is not only in the sensitive appetite.

*Obj.* 3. Further, to each power, its proper good is a matter

348

of concupiscence. Therefore concupiscence is in each power of the soul, and not only in the sensitive appetite.

*On the contrary*, Damascene says (*De Fide Orthod.* ii. 12) that *the irrational part which is subject and amenable to reason, is divided into the faculties of concupiscence and anger. This is the irrational part of the soul, passive and appetitive.* Therefore concupiscence is in the sensitive appetite.

*I answer that*, As the Philosopher says (*Rhetor.* i. 11), *concupiscence is a craving for that which is pleasant.* Now pleasure is twofold, as we shall state later on (Q. XXXI., AA. 3, 4): one is in the intelligible good, which is the good of reason; the other is in good perceptible to the senses. The former pleasure seems to belong to the soul alone: whereas the latter belongs to both soul and body: because the sense is a power seated in a bodily organ: wherefore sensible good is the good of the whole composite. Now concupiscence seems to be the craving for this latter pleasure, since it belongs to the united soul and body, as is implied by the Latin word *concupiscentia*. Therefore, properly speaking, concupiscence is in the sensitive appetite, and in the concupiscible faculty, which takes its name from it.

*Reply Obj.* 1. The craving for wisdom, or other spiritual goods, is sometimes called concupiscence; either by reason of a certain likeness; or on account of the craving in the higher part of the soul being so vehement that it overflows into the lower appetite, so that the latter also, in its own way, tends to the spiritual good, following the lead of the higher appetite, the result being that the body itself renders its service in spiritual matters, according to Ps. lxxxiii. 3: *My heart and my flesh have rejoiced in the living God.*

*Reply Obj.* 2. Properly speaking, desire may be not only in the lower, but also in the higher appetite. For it does not imply fellowship in craving, as concupiscence does; but simply movement towards the thing desired.

*Reply Obj.* 3. It belongs to each power of the soul to seek its proper good by the natural appetite, which does not arise from apprehension. But the craving for good, by the animal appetite, which arises from apprehension, belongs to

the appetitive power alone.   And to crave for a thing under
the aspect of something delightful to the senses, wherein
concupiscence properly consists, belongs to the concupiscible
power.

## Second Article.

### WHETHER CONCUPISCENCE IS A SPECIFIC PASSION ?

*We proceed thus to the Second Article :—*

*Objection* 1. It would seem that concupiscence is not a
specific passion of the concupiscible power.   For passions
are distinguished by their objects.   But the object of the
concupiscible power is something delightful to the senses;
and this is also the object of concupiscence, as the Philosopher
declares (*Rhetor.* i. 11).   Therefore concupiscence is not a
specific passion of the concupiscible faculty.

*Obj.* 2. Further, Augustine says (QQ. LXXXIII., qu. 33)
that *covetousness is the love of transitory things :* so that it is
not distinct from love.   But all specific passions are distinct
from one another.   Therefore concupiscence is not a specific
passion in the concupiscible faculty.

*Obj.* 3. Further, to each passion of the concupiscible
faculty there is a specific contrary passion in that faculty,
as stated above (Q. XXIII., A. 4).   But no specific passion
of the concupiscible faculty is contrary to concupiscence.
For Damascene says (*De Fide Orthod.* ii. 12) that *good when
desired gives rise to concupiscence ; when present, it gives joy :
in like manner, the evil we apprehend makes us fear, the evil
that is present makes us sad :* from which we gather that as
sadness is contrary to joy, so is fear contrary to concupiscence.   But fear is not in the concupiscible, but in the
irascible part.   Therefore concupiscence is not a specific
passion of the concupiscible faculty.

*On the contrary*, Concupiscence is caused by love, and
tends to pleasure, both of which are passions of the concupiscible faculty.   Hence it is distinguished from the other
concupiscible passions, as a specific passion.

*I answer that*, As stated above (A. 1; Q. XXIII., A. 1),
the good which gives pleasure to the senses is the common

object of the concupiscible faculty. Hence the various concupiscible passions are distinguished according to the differences of that good. Now the diversity of this object can arise from the very nature of the object, or from a diversity in its active power. The diversity, derived from the nature of the active object, causes a material difference of passions: while the difference in regard to its active power causes a formal diversity of passions, in respect of which the passions differ specifically.

Now the nature of the motive power of the end or of the good, differs according as it is really present, or absent: because, according as it is present, it causes the faculty to find rest in it; whereas, according as it is absent, it causes the faculty to be moved towards it. Wherefore the object of sensible pleasure causes love, inasmuch as, so to speak, it attunes and conforms the appetite to itself; it causes concupiscence, inasmuch as, when absent, it draws the faculty to itself; and it causes pleasure, inasmuch as, when present, it makes the faculty to find rest in itself. Accordingly, concupiscence is a passion differing *in species* from both love and pleasure.—But concupiscences of this or that pleasurable object differ *in number*.

*Reply Obj.* 1. Pleasurable good is the object of concupiscence, not absolutely, but considered as absent: just as the sensible, considered as past, is the object of memory. For these particular conditions diversify the species of passions, and even of the powers of the sensitive part, which regards particular things.

*Reply Obj.* 2. In the passage quoted we have causal, not essential, predication: for covetousness is not essentially love, but an effect of love.—We may also say that Augustine is taking covetousness in a wide sense, for any movement of the appetite in respect of good to come: so that it includes both love and hope.

*Reply Obj.* 3. The passion which is directly contrary to concupiscence has no name, and stands in relation to evil, as concupiscence in regard to good. But since, like fear, it regards the absent evil; sometimes it goes by the name of fear, just as hope is sometimes called covetousness. For a small good or evil is reckoned as though it were nothing: and consequently every movement of the appetite in future good or evil is called hope or fear, which regard good and evil as arduous.

### THIRD ARTICLE.

#### WHETHER SOME CONCUPISCENCES ARE NATURAL, AND SOME NOT NATURAL?

*We proceed thus to the Third Article :—*

*Objection* 1. It would seem that concupiscences are not divided into those which are natural and those which are not. For concupiscence belongs to the animal appetite, as stated above (A. 1 *ad* 3). But the natural appetite is contrasted with the animal appetite. Therefore no concupiscence is natural.

*Obj.* 2. Further, material difference makes no difference of species, but only numerical difference;—a difference which is outside the purview of science. But if some concupiscences are natural, and some not, they differ only in respect of their objects; which amounts to a material difference, which is one of number only. Therefore concupiscences should not be divided into those that are natural and those that are not.

*Obj.* 3. Further, reason is contrasted with nature, as stated in *Phys.* ii. 5. If therefore in man there is a concupiscence which is not natural, it must needs be rational. But this is impossible: because, since concupiscence is a passion, it belongs to the sensitive appetite, and not to the will, which is the rational appetite. Therefore there are no concupiscences which are not natural.

*On the contrary,* The Philosopher (*Ethic.* iii. 11 and *Rhetor.* i. 11) distinguishes natural concupiscences from those that are not natural.

*I answer that,* As stated above (A. 1), concupiscence is the craving for pleasurable good. Now a thing is pleasurable in two ways. First, because it is suitable to the nature of the animal; for example, food, drink, and the like: and concupiscence of such pleasurable things is said to be natural.—

Secondly, a thing is pleasurable because it is apprehended as suitable to the animal: as when one apprehends something as good and suitable, and consequently takes pleasure in it: and concupiscence of such pleasurable things is said to be not natural, and is more wont to be called *cupidity*.

Accordingly concupiscences of the first kind, or natural concupiscences, are common to men and other animals: because to both is there something suitable and pleasurable according to nature: and in these all men agree; wherefore the Philosopher (*Ethic.* iii. 11) calls them *common* and *necessary*. —But concupiscences of the second kind are proper to men, to whom it is proper to devise something as good and suitable, beyond that which nature requires. Hence the Philosopher says (*Rhetor.* i. 11) that the former concupiscences are *irrational*, but the latter, *rational*. And because different men reason differently, therefore the latter are also called (*Ethic.* iii. 11) *peculiar and acquired, i.e.,* in addition to those that are natural.

*Reply Obj.* 1. The same thing that is the object of the natural appetite, may be the object of the animal appetite, once it is apprehended. And in this way there may be an animal concupiscence for food, drink and the like, which are objects of the natural appetite.

*Reply Obj.* 2. The difference between those concupiscences that are natural and those that are not, is not merely a material difference; it is also, in a way, formal, in so far as it arises from a difference in the active object. Now the object of the appetite is the apprehended good. Hence diversity of the active object follows from diversity of apprehension: according as a thing is apprehended as suitable, either by absolute apprehension, whence arise natural concupiscences, which the Philosopher calls *irrational* (*Rhetor.* i. 11); or by apprehension together with deliberation, whence arise those concupiscences that are not natural, and which for this very reason the Philosopher calls *rational* (*ibid.*).

*Reply Obj.* 3. Man has not only universal reason, pertaining to the intellectual faculty; but also particular reason

II. i.

23

pertaining to the sensitive faculty, as stated in the First Part (Q. LXXVIII., A. 4; Q. LXXXI., A. 3): so that even rational concupiscence may pertain to the sensitive appetite.—Moreover the sensitive appetite can be moved by the universal reason also, through the medium of the particular imagination.

## FOURTH ARTICLE.

### WHETHER CONCUPISCENCE IS INFINITE ?

*We proceed thus to the Fourth Article :—*

*Objection* 1. It would seem that concupiscence is not infinite. For the object of concupiscence is good, which has the aspect of an end. But where there is infinity there is no end (*Metaph.* ii. 2). Therefore concupiscence cannot be infinite.

*Obj.* 2. Further, concupiscence is of the fitting good, since it proceeds from love. But the infinite is without proportion, and therefore unfitting. Therefore concupiscence cannot be infinite.

*Obj.* 3. Further, there is no passing through infinite things: and thus there is no reaching an ultimate term in them. But the subject of concupiscence is not delighted until he attain the ultimate term. Therefore, if concupiscence were infinite, no delight would ever ensue.

*On the contrary*, The Philosopher says (*Polit.* i. 3) that *since concupiscence is infinite, men desire an infinite number of things*

*I answer that*, As stated above (A. 3), concupiscence is twofold; one is natural, the other is not natural. Natural concupiscence cannot be actually infinite: because it is of that which nature requires; and nature ever tends to something finite and fixed. Hence man never desires infinite meat, or infinite drink.—But just as in nature there is potential successive infinity, so can this kind of concupiscence be infinite successively; so that, for instance after getting food, a man may desire food yet again; and so of anything else that nature requires: because these bodily goods, when obtained, do not last for ever, but fail. Hence

Our Lord said to the woman of Samaria (Jo. iv. 13): *Whosoever drinketh of this water, shall thirst again.*

But non-natural concupiscence is altogether infinite. Because, as stated above (A. 3) it follows from the reason, and it belongs to the reason to proceed to infinity. Hence he that desires riches, may desire to be rich, not up to a certain limit, but to be simply as rich as possible.

Another reason may be assigned, according to the Philosopher (*Polit.* i. 3), why a certain concupiscence is finite, and another infinite. Because concupiscence of the end is always infinite: since the end is desired for its own sake, *e.g.*, health: and thus greater health is more desired, and so on to infinity; just as, if a white thing of itself dilates the sight, that which is more white dilates yet more. On the other hand, concupiscence of the means is not infinite, because the concupiscence of the means is in suitable proportion to the end. Consequently those who place their end in riches have an infinite concupiscence of riches; whereas those who desire riches, on account of the necessities of life, desire a finite measure of riches, sufficient for the necessities of life, as the Philosopher says (*ibid.*). The same applies to the concupiscence of any other things.

*Reply Obj.* 1. Every object of concupiscence is taken as something finite: either because it is finite in reality, as being once actually desired; or because it is finite as apprehended. For it cannot be apprehended as infinite, since the infinite is that *from which, however much we may take, there always remains something to be taken* (*Phys.* iii. 6).

*Reply Obj.* 2. The reason is possessed of infinite power, in a certain sense, in so far as it can consider a thing infinitely, as appears in the addition of numbers and lines. Consequently, the infinite, taken in a certain way, is proportionate to reason. In fact the universal which the reason apprehends, is infinite in a sense, inasmuch as it contains potentially an infinite number of singulars.

*Reply Obj.* 3. In order that a man be delighted, there is no need for him to realize all that he desires: for he delights in the realization of each object of his concupiscence.

# QUESTION XXXI.

## OF DELIGHT* CONSIDERED IN ITSELF.

### (*In Eight Articles.*)

WE must now consider delight and sadness. Concerning delight four things must be considered : (1) Delight in itself: (2) The causes of delight: (3) Its effects: (4) Its goodness and malice.

Under the first head there are eight points of inquiry: (1) Whether delight is a passion? (2) Whether delight is subject to time? (3) Whether it differs from joy? (4) Whether it is in the intellectual appetite? (5) Of the delights of the higher appetite compared with the delight of the lower. (6) Of sensible delights compared with one another. (7) Whether any delight is non-natural? (8) Whether one delight can be contrary to another?

### FIRST ARTICLE.

#### WHETHER DELIGHT IS A PASSION?

*We proceed thus to the First Article :—*

*Objection* 1. It would seem that delight is not a passion. For Damascene (*De Fide Orthod.* ii. 22) distinguishes operation from passion, and says that *operation is a movement in accord with nature, while passion is a movement contrary to nature.* But delight is an operation, according to the Philosopher (*Ethic.* vii. 12, x. 5). Therefore delight is not a passion.

*Obj.* 2. Further, *To be passive is to be moved,* as stated in *Phys.* iii. 3. But delight does not consist in being moved, but in having been moved; for it arises from good already gained. Therefore delight is not a passion.

* Or, Pleasure.

356

*Obj.* 3. Further, delight is a kind of a perfection of the one who is delighted; since it *perfects operation*, as stated in *Ethic.* x. 4, 5. But to be perfected does not consist in being passive or in being altered, as stated in *Phys.* vii. 3 and *De Anima* ii. 5. Therefore delight is not a passion.

*On the contrary*, Augustine (*De Civ. Dei* ix. 2, xiv. 5 sqq.) reckons delight, joy or gladness among the other passions of the soul.

*I answer that*, The movements of the sensitive appetite, are properly called passions, as stated above (Q. XXII., A. 3). Now every emotion arising from a sensitive apprehension, is a movement of the sensitive appetite: and this must needs be said of delight, since, according to the Philosopher (*Rhetor.* i. 11) *delight is a certain movement of the soul and a sensible establishing thereof all at once, in keeping with the nature of the thing.*

In order to understand this, we must observe that just as in natural things some happen to attain to their natural perfections, so does this happen in animals. And though movement towards perfection does not occur all at once, yet the attainment of natural perfection does occur all at once. Now there is this difference between animals and other natural things, that when these latter are established in the state becoming their nature, they do not perceive it, whereas animals do. And from this perception there arises a certain movement of the soul in the sensitive appetite; which movement is called delight. Accordingly by saying that delight is *a movement of the soul*, we designate its genus. By saying that it is *an establishing in keeping with the thing's nature, i.e.*, with that which exists in the thing, we assign the cause of delight, viz., the presence of a becoming good. By saying that this establishing is *all at once*, we mean that this establishing is to be understood not as in the process of establishment, but as in the fact of complete establishment, in the term of the movement, as it were: for delight is not a *becoming* as Plato* maintained, but a *complete fact*, as stated in *Ethic.* vii. 12. Lastly, by saying that this establishing is

* *Phileb.* 32, 33.

*sensible*, we exclude the perfections of insensible things wherein there is no delight.—It is therefore evident that, since delight is a movement of the animal appetite arising from an apprehension of sense, it is a passion of the soul.

*Reply Obj.* 1. Connatural operation, which is unhindered, is a second perfection, as stated in *De Anima* ii. 1: and therefore when a thing is established in its proper connatural and unhindered operation, delight follows, which consists in a state of completion, as observed above. Accordingly when we say that delight is an operation, we designate, not its essence, but its cause.

*Reply Obj.* 2. A twofold movement is to be observed in an animal: one, according to the intention of the end, and this belongs to the appetite; the other, according to the execution, and this belongs to the external operation. And so, although in him who has already gained the good in which he delights, the movement of execution ceases, by which he tends to the end; yet the movement of the appetitive faculty does not cease, since, just as before it desired that which it had not, so afterwards does it delight in that which it possesses. For though delight is a certain repose of the appetite, if we consider the presence of the pleasurable good that satisfies the appetite, nevertheless there remains the impression made on the appetite by its object, by reason of which delight is a kind of movement.

*Reply Obj.* 3. Although the name of passion is more appropriate to those passions which have a corruptive and evil tendency, such as bodily ailments, as also sadness and fear in the soul; yet some passions have a tendency to something good, as stated above (Q. XXIII., AA. 1, 4): and in this sense delight is called a passion.

## SECOND ARTICLE.

### WHETHER DELIGHT IS IN TIME ?

*We proceed thus to the Second Article :—*

*Objection* 1. It would seem that delight is in time. For *delight is a kind of movement*, as the Philosopher says (*Rhetor.*

i. 11). But all movement is in time. Therefore delight is in time.

*Obj.* 2. Further, a thing is said to last long and to be morose in respect of time. But some pleasures are called morose. Therefore pleasure is in time.

*Obj.* 2. Further, the passions of the soul are of one same genus. But some passions of the soul are in time. Therefore delight is too.

*On the contrary*, The Philosopher says (*Ethic.* x. 4) that *no one takes pleasure according to time*.

*I answer that*, A thing may be in time in two ways: first, by itself; secondly, by reason of something else, and accidentally as it were. For since time is the measure of successive things, those things are of themselves said to be in time, to which succession or something pertaining to succession is essential: such are movement, repose, speech and suchlike. On the other hand, those things are said to be in time, by reason of something else and not of themselves, to which succession is not essential, but which are subject to something successive. Thus the fact of being a man is not essentially something successive; since it is not a movement, but the term of a movement or change, viz., of his being begotten: yet, because human being is subject to changeable causes, in this respect, to be a man is in time.

Accordingly, we must say that delight, of itself indeed, is not in time: for it regards good already gained, which is, as it were, the term of the movement. But if this good gained be subject to change, the delight therein will be in time accidentally: whereas if it be altogether unchangeable, the delight therein will not be in time, either by reason of itself or accidentally.

*Reply Obj.* 1. As stated in *De Anima* iii. 7, movement is twofold. One is *the act of something imperfect, i.e., of something existing in potentiality, as such*: this movement is successive and is in time. Another movement is *the act of something perfect, i.e., of something existing in act*, *e.g.*, to understand, to feel, and to will and suchlike, also to have delight. This movement is not successive, nor is it of itself in time.

*Reply Obj.* 2. Delight is said to be long lasting or morose, according as it is accidentally in time.

*Reply Obj.* 3. Other passions have not for their object a good obtained, as delight has. Wherefore there is more of the movement of the imperfect in them than in delight. And consequently it belongs more to delight not to be in time.

### THIRD ARTICLE.

#### WHETHER DELIGHT DIFFERS FROM JOY ?

*We proceed thus to the Third Article :—*

*Objection* 1. It would seem that delight is altogether the same as joy. Because the passions of the soul differ according to their objects. But delight and joy have the same object, namely, a good obtained. Therefore joy is altogether the same as delight.

*Obj.* 2. Further, one movement does not end in two terms. But one and the same movement, that of desire, ends in joy and delight. Therefore delight and joy are altogether the same.

*Obj.* 3. Further, if joy differs from delight, it seems that there is equal reason for distinguishing gladness, exultation, and cheerfulness from delight, so that they would all be various passions of the soul. But this seems to be untrue. Therefore joy does not differ from delight.

*On the contrary*, We do not speak of joy in irrational animals; whereas we do speak of delight in them. Therefore joy is not the same as delight.

*I answer that*, Joy, as Avicenna states (*De Anima* iv.), is a kind of delight. For we must observe that, just as some concupiscences are natural, and some not natural, but consequent to reason, as stated above (Q. XXX., A. 3), so also some delights are natural, and some are not natural but rational. Or, as Damascene (*De Fide Orthod.* ii. 13) and Gregory of Nyssa* put it, *some delights are of the body,*

* Nemesius, *De Nat. Hom.* xviii.

*some are of the soul ;* which amounts to the same. For we take delight both in those things which we desire naturally, when we get them, and in those things which we desire as a result of reason. But we do not speak of joy except when delight follows reason; and so we do not ascribe joy to irrational animals, but only delight.

Now whatever we desire naturally, can also be the object of reasoned desire and delight, but not vice versa. Consequently whatever can be the object of delight, can also be the object of joy in rational beings. And yet everything is not always the object of joy; since sometimes one feels a certain delight in the body, without rejoicing thereat according to reason. And accordingly delight extends to more things than does joy.

*Reply Obj.* 1. Since the object of the appetite of the soul is an apprehended good, diversity of apprehension pertains, in a way, to diversity of the object. And so delights of the soul, which are also called joys, are distinct from bodily delights, which are not called otherwise than delights: as we have observed above in regard to concupiscences (Q. XXX., A. 3 *ad* 2).

*Reply Obj.* 2. A like difference is to be observed in concupiscences also: so that delight corresponds to concupiscence, while joy corresponds to desire, which seems to pertain more to concupiscence of the soul. Hence there is a difference of repose corresponding to the difference of movement.

*Reply Obj.* 3. These other names pertaining to delight are derived from the effects of delight; for *lætitia* (gladness) is derived from the *dilatation* of the heart, as if one were to say *latitia*; *exultation* is derived from the exterior signs of inward delight, which appear outwardly in so far as the inward joy breaks forth from its bounds; and *cheerfulness* is so called from certain special signs and effects of gladness. Yet all these names seem to belong to joy; for we do not employ them save in speaking of rational beings.

## FOURTH ARTICLE.

### WHETHER DELIGHT IS IN THE INTELLECTUAL APPETITE ?

*We proceed thus to the Fourth Article :*—

*Objection* 1. It would seem that delight is not in the intellectual appetite.   Because the Philosopher says (*Rhet.* i. 11) that *delight is a sensible movement.*   But sensible movement is not in an intellectual power.   Therefore delight is not in the intellectual appetite.

*Obj.* 2. Further, delight is a passion.   But every passion is in the sensitive appetite.   Therefore delight is only in the sensitive appetite.

*Obj.* 3. Further, delight is common to us and to the irrational animals.   Therefore it is not elsewhere than in that power which we have in common with irrational animals.

*On the contrary,* It is written (Ps. xxxvi. 4): *Delight in the Lord.*   But the sensitive appetite cannot reach to God; only the intellectual appetite can.   Therefore delight can be in the intellectual appetite.

*I answer that,* As stated above (A. 3), a certain delight arises from the apprehension of the reason.   Now on the reason apprehending something, not only the sensitive appetite is moved, as regards its application to some particular thing, but also the intellectual appetite, which is called the will.   And accordingly, in the intellectual appetite or will there is that delight which is called joy, but not bodily delight.

However, there is this difference of delight in either power, that delight of the sensitive appetite is accompanied by a bodily transmutation, whereas delight of the intellectual appetite is nothing but the mere movement of the will.   Hence Augustine says (*De Civ. Dei* xiv. 6) that *desire and joy are nothing else but a volition of consent to the things we wish.*

*Reply Obj.* 1. In this definition of the Philosopher, he uses the word *sensible* in its wide acceptation for any kind of perception.   For he says (*Ethic.* x. 4) that *delight is attendant upon every sense, as it is also upon every act of the intellect and contemplation.*—Or we may say that he is defining delight of the sensitive appetite.

*Reply Obj.* 2. Delight has the character of passion, properly speaking, when accompanied by bodily transmutation. It is not thus in the intellectual appetite, but according to simple movement: for thus it is also in God and the angels. Hence the Philosopher says (*Ethic.* vii. 14) that *God rejoices by one simple act :* and Dionysius says at the end of *De Cœl. Hier.*, that *the angels are not susceptible to our passible delight, but rejoice together with God with the gladness of incorruption.*

*Reply Obj.* 3. In us there is delight, not only in common with dumb animals, but also in common with angels. Wherefore Dionysius says (*ibid.*) that *holy men often take part in the angelic delights.* Accordingly we have delight, not only in the sensitive appetite, which we have in common with dumb animals, but also in the intellectual appetite, which we have in common with the angels.

## FIFTH ARTICLE.

### WHETHER BODILY AND SENSIBLE PLEASURES ARE GREATER THAN SPIRITUAL AND INTELLECTUAL PLEASURES ?

*We proceed thus to the Fifth Article :—*

*Objection* 1. It would seem that bodily and sensible pleasures are greater than spiritual and intelligible pleasures. For all men seek some pleasure, according to the Philosopher (*Ethic.* x. 2, 4). But more seek sensible pleasures, than intelligible spiritual pleasures. Therefore bodily pleasures are greater.

*Obj.* 2. Further, the greatness of a cause is known by its effect. But bodily pleasures have greater effects; since *they alter the state of the body, and in some they cause madness* (*Ethic.* vii. 3). Therefore bodily pleasures are greater.

*Obj.* 3. Further, bodily pleasures need to be tempered and checked, by reason of their vehemence: whereas there is no need to check spiritual pleasures. Therefore bodily pleasures are greater.

*On the contrary*, It is written (Ps. cxviii. 103): *How sweet are Thy words to my palate ; more than honey to my mouth !* And the Philosopher says (*Ethic.* x. 7) that *the greatest pleasure is derived from the operation of wisdom.*

*I answer that*, As stated above (A. 1), pleasure arises from union with a suitable object perceived or known. Now, in the operations of the soul, especially of the sensitive and intellectual soul, it must be noted that, since they do not pass into outward matter, they are acts or perfections of the agent, *e.g.*, to understand, to feel, to will, and the like: because actions which pass into outward matter, are actions and perfections rather of the matter transformed; for *movement is the act produced by the mover in the thing moved* (*Phys.* iii. 3). Accordingly the aforesaid actions of the sensitive and intellectual soul, are themselves a certain good of the agent, and are known by sense and intellect. Wherefore from them also does pleasure arise, and not only from their objects.

If therefore we compare intellectual pleasures with sensible pleasures, according as we delight in the very actions, for instance in sensitive and in intellectual knowledge; without doubt intellectual pleasures are much greater than sensible pleasures. For man takes much more delight in knowing something, by understanding it, than in knowing something by perceiving it with his sense. Because intellectual knowledge is more perfect; and because it is better known, since the intellect reflects on its own act more than sense does. Moreover intellectual knowledge is more beloved: for there is no one who would not forfeit his bodily sight rather than his intellectual vision, as beasts or fools are deprived thereof, as Augustine says in *De Civ. Dei* (*De Trin.* xiv. 14).

If, however, intellectual spiritual pleasures be compared with sensible bodily pleasures, then, in themselves and absolutely speaking, spiritual pleasures are greater. And this appears from the consideration of the three things needed for pleasure, viz., the good which is brought into conjunction, that to which it is conjoined, and the conjunction itself. For spiritual good is both greater and more beloved than bodily good: a sign whereof is that men abstain from even the greatest bodily pleasures, rather than suffer loss of honour which is an intellectual good.—Likewise the intellectual faculty is much more noble and more knowing than the sensitive faculty.—Also the conjunction is more intimate, more perfect and more firm. More intimate, because the senses stop at the outward accidents of a thing, whereas the intellect penetrates to the essence; for the object of the intellect is *what a thing is*. More perfect, because the conjunction of the sensible to the sense implies movement, which is an imperfect act: wherefore sensible pleasures are not perceived all at once, but some part of them is passing away, while some other part is looked forward to as yet to be realized, as is manifest in pleasures of the table and in sexual pleasures: whereas intelligible things are without movement: hence pleasures of this kind are realized all at once. More firm; because the objects of bodily pleasure are corruptible, and soon pass away; whereas spiritual goods are incorruptible.

On the other hand, in relation to us, bodily pleasures are more vehement, for three reasons. First, because sensible things are more known to us, than intelligible things.— Secondly, because sensible pleasures, through being passions of the sensitive appetite, are accompanied by some alteration in the body: whereas this does not occur in spiritual pleasures, save by reason of a certain reaction of the superior appetite on the lower. Thirdly, because bodily pleasures are sought as remedies for bodily defects or troubles, whence various griefs arise. Wherefore bodily pleasures, by reason of their succeeding griefs of this kind, are felt the more, and consequently are welcomed more than spiritual pleasures, which have no contrary griefs, as we shall state farther on (Q. XXXV., A. 5).

*Reply Obj.* 1. The reason why more seek bodily pleasures is because sensible goods are known better and more generally: and, again, because men need pleasures as remedies for many kinds of sorrow and sadness: and since the majority cannot attain spiritual pleasures, which are proper to the virtuous, hence it is that they turn aside to seek those of the body.

*Reply Obj.* 2. Bodily transmutation arises more from bodily pleasures, inasmuch as they are passions of the sensitive appetite.

*Reply Obj.* 3. Bodily pleasures are realized in the sensitive faculty which is governed by reason: wherefore they need to be tempered and checked by reason. But spiritual pleasures are in the mind, which is itself the rule: wherefore they are in themselves both sober and moderate.

## Sixth Article.

### WHETHER THE PLEASURES OF TOUCH ARE GREATER THAN THE PLEASURES AFFORDED BY THE OTHER SENSES?

*We proceed thus to the Sixth Article :—*

*Objection* 1. It would seem that the pleasures of touch are not greater than the pleasures afforded by the other senses. Because the greatest pleasure seems to be that without which all joy is at an end. But such is the pleasure afforded by the sight, according to the words of Tobias v. 12: *What manner of joy shall be to me, who sit in darkness, and see not the light of heaven?* Therefore the pleasure afforded by the sight is the greatest of sensible pleasures.

*Obj.* 2. Further, *every one finds pleasure in what he loves*, as the Philosopher says (*Rhet.* i. 11). But *of all the senses the sight is loved most.** Therefore the greatest pleasure is that which is afforded by the sight.

*Obj.* 3. Further, the beginning of friendship which is for the sake of the pleasant is principally sight. But pleasure is the cause of such friendship. Therefore the greatest pleasure seems to be afforded by sight.

*On the contrary*, The Philosopher says (*Ethic.* iii. 10) that the greatest pleasures are those which are afforded by the touch.

*I answer that*, As stated above (Q. XXV., A. 2 *ad* 1;

* *Metaph.* i. 1.

Q. XXVII., A. 4 *ad* 1), everything gives pleasure according as it is loved. Now, as stated in *Metaph*. i. 1, the senses are loved for two reasons: for the purpose of knowledge, and on account of their usefulness. Wherefore the senses afford pleasure in both these ways. But because it is proper to man to apprehend knowledge itself as something good, it follows that the former pleasures of the senses, *i.e.*, those which arise from knowledge, are proper to man: whereas pleasures of the senses, as loved for their usefulness, are common to all animals.

If therefore we speak of that sensible pleasure which is by reason of knowledge, it is evident that the sight affords greater pleasure than any other sense.—On the other hand, if we speak of that sensible pleasure which is by reason of usefulness, then the greatest pleasure is afforded by the touch. For the usefulness of sensible things is gauged by their relation to the preservation of the animal's nature. Now the sensible objects of touch bear the closest relation to this usefulness: for the touch takes cognizance of those things which are vital to an animal—namely, of things hot and cold and the like. Wherefore in this respect, the pleasures of touch are greater as being more closely related to the end. For this reason, too, other animals which do not experience sensible pleasure save by reason of usefulness, derive no pleasure from the other senses except as subordinated to the sensible objects of the touch: *for dogs do not take delight in the smell of hares, but in eating them; . . . nor does the lion feel pleasure in the lowing of an ox, but in devouring it* (*Ethic*. iii. 10).

Since then the pleasure afforded by touch is the greatest in respect of usefulness, and the pleasure afforded by sight the greatest in respect of knowledge; if anyone wish to compare these two, he will find that the pleasure of touch is, absolutely speaking, greater than the pleasure of sight, so far as the latter remains within the limits of sensible pleasure. Because it is evident that in everything, that which is natural is most powerful: and it is to these pleasures of the touch that the natural concupiscences,

such as those of food, sexual union, and the like, are ordained.
—If, however, we consider the pleasures of sight, inasmuch
as sight is the handmaid of the mind, then the pleasures
of sight are greater, forasmuch as intellectual pleasures are
greater than sensible.

*Reply Obj.* 1. Joy, as stated above (A. 3), denotes pleasure
of the soul; and this belongs principally to the sight. But
natural pleasure belongs principally to the touch.

*Reply Obj.* 2. The sight is loved most, *on account of knowledge, because it helps us to distinguish many things* as is
stated in the same passage (*Metaph.* i. 1).

*Reply Obj.* 3. Pleasure causes carnal love in one way; the
sight, in another. For pleasure, especially that which is
afforded by the touch, is the final cause of the friendship
which is for the sake of the pleasant: whereas the sight is a
cause like that from which a movement has its beginning,
inasmuch as the beholder on seeing the lovable object receives an impression of its image, which entices him to love
it and to seek its delight.

## Seventh Article.

### WHETHER ANY PLEASURE IS NOT NATURAL ?

*We proceed thus to the Seventh Article :—*

*Objection* 1. It would seem that no pleasure is not natural.
For pleasure is to the emotions of the soul what repose is
to bodies. But the appetite of a natural body does not
repose save in a connatural place. Neither, therefore, can
the repose of the animal appetite, which is pleasure, be
elsewhere than in something connatural. Therefore no
pleasure is non-natural.

*Obj.* 2. Further, what is against nature is violent. But
*whatever is violent causes grief* (*Metaph.* v. 5). Therefore
nothing which is unnatural can give pleasure.

*Obj.* 3. Further, the fact of being established in one's
own nature, if perceived, gives rise to pleasure, as is evident
from the Philosopher's definition quoted above (A. 1).
But it is natural to every thing to be established in its nature;

because natural movement tends to a natural end. Therefore every pleasure is natural.

*On the contrary*, The Philosopher says (*Ethic.* vii. 5, 6) that some things are pleasant *not from nature but from disease*.

*I answer that*, We speak of that as being natural, which is in accord with nature, as stated in *Phys.* ii. 1. Now, in man, nature can be taken in two ways. First, inasmuch as intellect and reason is the principal part of man's nature, since in respect thereof he has his own specific nature. And in this sense, those pleasures may be called natural to man, which are derived from things pertaining to man in respect of his reason: for instance, it is natural to man to take pleasure in contemplating the truth and in doing works of virtue.—Secondly, nature in man may be taken as contrasted with reason, and as denoting that which is common to man and other animals, especially that part of man which does not obey reason. And in this sense, that which pertains to the preservation of the body, either as regards the individual, as food, drink, sleep, and the like, or as regards the species, as sexual intercourse, are said to afford man natural pleasure. Under each kind of pleasures, we find some that are *not natural* speaking absolutely, and yet *connatural* in some respect. For it happens in an individual that some one of the natural principles of the species is corrupted, so that something which is contrary to the specific nature, becomes accidentally natural to this individual: thus it is natural to this hot water to give heat. Consequently it happens that something which is not natural to man, either in regard to reason, or in regard to the preservation of the body, becomes connatural to this individual man, on account of there being some corruption of nature in him. And this corruption may be either on the part of the body,—from some ailment; thus to a man suffering from fever, sweet things seem bitter, and vice versa,—or from an evil temperament; thus some take pleasure in eating earth and coals and the like; or on the part of the soul; thus from custom some take pleasure in cannibalism or

in the unnatural intercourse of man and beast, or other
suchlike things, which are not in accord with human
nature.

This suffices for the answers to the objections.

### EIGHTH ARTICLE.

#### WHETHER ONE PLEASURE CAN BE CONTRARY TO ANOTHER ?

*We proceed thus to the Eighth Article :—*

*Objection* 1. It would seem that one pleasure cannot be
contrary to another. Because the passions of the soul derive
their species and contrariety from their objects. Now the
object of pleasure is the good. Since therefore good is not
contrary to good, but *good is contrary to evil, and evil to good*,
as stated in *Prædic.* viii.; it seems that one pleasure is not
contrary to another.

*Obj.* 2. Further, to one thing there is one contrary, as is
proved in *Metaph.* x. 4. But sadness is contrary to pleasure.
Therefore pleasure is not contrary to pleasure.

*Obj.* 3. Further, if one pleasure is contrary to another,
this is only on account of the contrariety of the things which
give pleasure. But this difference is material: whereas contrariety is a difference of form, as stated in *Metaph.* x. 4.
Therefore there is no contrariety between one pleasure and
another.

*On the contrary,* Things of the same genus that impede
one another are contraries, as the Philosopher states (*Phys.*
viii. 8). But some pleasures impede one another, as stated
in *Ethic.* x. 5. Therefore some pleasures are contrary to one
another.

*I answer that,* Pleasure, in the emotions of the soul, is
likened to repose in natural bodies, as stated above
(Q. XXIII., A. 4). Now one repose is said to be contrary
to another when they are in contrary *termini*; thus *repose
in a high place is contrary to repose in a low place* (*Phys.* v. 6).
Wherefore it happens in the emotions of the soul that one
pleasure is contrary to another.

work: and they are objects of pleasure (*Rhet.* i., *loc. cit.*).
Therefore operation is not the proper cause of pleasure.

*On the contrary*, The Philosopher says (*Ethic.* vii. 12, 13;
x. 4) that *pleasure is a connatural and uninterrupted operation.*

*I answer that*, As stated above (Q. XXXI., A. 1), two
things are requisite for pleasure: namely, the attainment
of the suitable good, and knowledge of this attainment.
Now each of these consists in a kind of operation: because
actual knowledge is an operation; and the attainment of
the suitable good is by means of an operation.    Moreover,
the proper operation itself is a suitable good.    Wherefore
every pleasure must needs be the result of some operation.

*Reply Obj*. 1. The objects of operations are not pleasurable save inasmuch as they are united to us; either by
knowledge alone, as when we take pleasure in thinking of
or looking at certain things; or in some other way in addition
to knowledge; as when a man takes pleasure in knowing
that he has something good,—riches, honour, or the like;
which would not be pleasurable unless they were apprehended as possessed.    For as the Philosopher observes
(*Polit.* ii. 2) *we take great pleasure in looking upon a thing as
our own, by reason of the natural love we have for ourselves.*
Now to have suchlike things is nothing else but to use
them or to be able to use them: and this is through some
operation.    Wherefore it is evident that every pleasure is
traced to some operation as its cause.

*Reply Obj*. 2. Even when it is not an operation, but the
effect of an operation, that is the end, this effect is pleasant
in so far as possessed or effected: and this implies use or
operation.

*Reply Obj*. 3. Operations are pleasant, in so far as they are
proportionate and connatural to the agent.    Now, since
human power is finite, operation is proportionate thereto
according to a certain measure.    Wherefore if it exceed that
measure, it will be no longer proportionate or pleasant, but, on
the contrary, painful and irksome.    And in this sense, leisure
and play and other things pertaining to repose, are pleasant,
inasmuch as they banish sadness which results from labour.

## Second Article.

### WHETHER MOVEMENT IS A CAUSE OF PLEASURE ?

*We proceed thus to the Second Article :—*

*Objection* 1. It would seem that movement is not a cause of pleasure.   Because, as stated above (Q. XXXI., A. 1), the good which is obtained and is actually possessed, is the cause of pleasure: wherefore the Philosopher says (*Ethic*. vii. 12) that pleasure is not compared with generation, but with the operation of a thing already in existence.   Now that which is being moved towards something has it not as yet; but, so to speak, is being generated in its regard, forasmuch as generation or corruption are united to every movement, as stated in *Phys*. viii. 3.   Therefore movement is not a cause of pleasure.

*Obj*. 2. Further, movement is the chief cause of toil and fatigue in our works.   But operations through being toilsome and fatiguing are not pleasant but disagreeable.   Therefore movement is not a cause of pleasure.

*Obj*. 3. Further, movement implies a certain innovation, which is the opposite of custom.   But things *which we are accustomed to, are pleasant,* as the Philosopher says (*Rhet*. i. 11).   Therefore movement is not a cause of pleasure.

*On the contrary*, Augustine says (*Conf*. viii. 3): *What means this, O Lord my God, whereas Thou art everlasting joy to Thyself, and some things around Thee evermore rejoice in Thee ?   What means this, that this portion of things ebbs and flows alternately displeased and reconciled ?*   From these words we gather that man rejoices and takes pleasure in some kind of alternations: and therefore movement seems to cause pleasure.

*I answer that*, Three things are requisite for pleasure; two, *i.e.*, the one that is pleased and the pleasurable object conjoined to him; and a third, which is knowledge of this conjunction: and in respect of these three, movement is pleasant, as the Philosopher says (*Ethic*. vii. 14 and *Rhet*. i. 11).   For as far as we who feel pleasure are concerned, change is pleasant to us because our nature is changeable; for which reason that which is suitable to us at one time is not suitable at another,—thus to warm himself at a fire is suitable to man in winter and not in summer.—Again, on the part of the pleasing good which is united to us, change is pleasant. Because the continued action of an agent increases its effect: thus the longer a person remains near the fire, the more he is warmed and dried. Now the natural mode of being consists in a certain measure; and therefore when the continued presence of a pleasant object exceeds the measure of one's natural mode of being, the removal of that object becomes pleasant.—On the part of the knowledge itself (change becomes pleasant), because man desires to know something whole and perfect: when therefore a thing cannot be apprehended all at once as a whole, change in such a thing is pleasant, so that one part may pass and another succeed, and thus the whole be perceived. Hence Augustine says (*Conf.* iv. 11): *Thou wouldst not have the syllables stay, but fly away, that others may come, and thou hear the whole. And so whenever any one thing is made up of many, all of which do not exist together, all would please collectively more than they do severally, if all could be perceived collectively.*

If therefore there be any thing, whose nature is unchangeable; the natural mode of whose being cannot be exceeded by the continuation of any pleasing object; and which can behold the whole object of its delight at once,—to such a one change will afford no delight. And the more any pleasures approach to this, the more are they capable of being continual.

*Reply Obj.* 1. Although the subject of movement has not yet perfectly that to which it is moved, nevertheless it is beginning to have something thereof: and in this respect movement itself has something of pleasure. But it falls short of the perfection of pleasure; because the more perfect pleasures regard things that are unchangeable.—Moreover movement becomes the cause of pleasure, in so far as thereby something which previously was unsuitable, becomes suitable or ceases to be, as stated above.

*Reply Obj.* 2. Movement causes toil and fatigue, when it exceeds our natural aptitude. It is not thus that it causes pleasure, but by removing the obstacles to our natural aptitude.

*Reply Obj.* 3. What is customary becomes pleasant, in so far as it becomes natural: because custom is like a second nature. But the movement which gives pleasure is not that which departs from custom, but rather that which prevents the corruption of the natural mode of being, that might result from continued operation. And thus from the same cause of connaturalness, both custom and movement become pleasant.

### Third Article.

#### WHETHER HOPE AND MEMORY CAUSE PLEASURE?

*We proceed thus to the Third Article :—*

*Objection* 1. It would seem that memory and hope do not cause pleasure. Because pleasure is caused by present good, as Damascene says (*De Fide Orthod*. ii. 12). But hope and memory regard what is absent: since memory is of the past, and hope of the future. Therefore memory and hope do not cause pleasure.

*Obj.* 2. Further, the same thing is not the cause of contraries. But hope causes affliction, according to Prov. xiii. 12: *Hope that is deferred afflicteth the soul.* Therefore hope does not cause pleasure.

*Obj.* 3. Further, just as hope agrees with pleasure in regarding good, so also do desire and love. Therefore hope should not be assigned as a cause of pleasure, any more than desire or love.

*On the contrary*, It is written (Rom. xii. 12): *Rejoicing in hope ;* and (Ps. lxxvi. 4): *I remembered God, and was delighted.*

*I answer that*, Pleasure is caused by the presence of suitable good, in so far as it is felt, or perceived in any way. Now a thing is present to us in two ways. First, in knowledge—*i.e.*, according as the thing known is in the knower by its likeness; secondly, in reality—*i.e.*, according as one thing is in real conjunction of any kind with another, either actually or potentially. And since real conjunction is greater than conjunction by likeness, which is the conjunction of knowledge; and again, since actual is greater than potential conjunction: therefore the greatest pleasure is that which arises from sensation which requires the presence of the sensible object. The second place belongs to the pleasure of hope, wherein there is pleasurable conjunction, not only in respect of apprehension, but also in respect of the faculty or power of obtaining the pleasurable object. The third place belongs to the pleasure of memory, which has only the conjunction of apprehension.

*Reply Obj.* 1. Hope and memory are indeed of things which, absolutely speaking, are absent: and yet these are, after a fashion, present, *i.e.*, either according to apprehension only; or according to apprehension and possibility, at least supposed, of attainment.

*Reply Obj.* 2. Nothing prevents the same thing, in different ways, being the cause of contraries. And so hope, inasmuch as it implies a present appraising of a future good, causes pleasure; whereas, inasmuch as it implies absence of that good, it causes affliction.

*Reply Obj.* 3. Love and concupiscence also cause pleasure. For everything that is loved becomes pleasing to the lover, since love is a kind of union or connaturalness of lover and beloved. In like manner every object of desire is pleasing to the one that desires, since desire is chiefly a craving for pleasure. However hope, as implying a certainty of the real presence of the pleasing good, that is not implied either by love or by concupiscence, is reckoned in preference to them as causing pleasure; and also in preference to memory, which is of that which has already passed away.

## Fourth Article.

### WHETHER SADNESS CAUSES PLEASURE?

*We proceed thus to the Fourth Article :—*

*Objection* 1. It would seem that sadness does not cause pleasure. For nothing causes its own contrary. But sadness is contrary to pleasure. Therefore it does not cause it.

*Obj.* 2. Further, contraries have contrary effects. But pleasures, when called to mind, cause pleasure. Therefore sad things, when remembered, cause sorrow and not pleasure.

*Obj.* 3. Further, as sadness is to pleasure, so is hatred to love. But hatred does not cause love, but rather the other way about, as stated above (Q. XXIX., A. 2). Therefore sadness does not cause pleasure.

*On the contrary*, It is written (Ps. xli. 4): *My tears have been my bread day and night :* where bread denotes the refreshment of pleasure. Therefore tears, which arise from sadness, can give pleasure.

*I answer that*, Sadness may be considered in two ways: as existing actually, and as existing in the memory: and in both ways sadness can cause pleasure. Because sadness, as actually existing, causes pleasure, inasmuch as it brings to mind that which is loved, the absence of which causes sadness; and yet the mere thought of it gives pleasure.— The recollection of sadness becomes a cause of pleasure, on account of the deliverance which ensued: because absence of evil is looked upon as something good; wherefore so far as a man thinks that he has been delivered from that which caused him sorrow and pain, so much reason has he to rejoice. Hence Augustine says in *De Civ. Dei* xxii. 31* that *oftentimes in joy we call to mind sad things . . . and in the season of health we recall past pains without feeling pain, . . . and in proportion are the more filled with joy and gladness :* and again (*Conf.* viii. 3) he says that *the more peril there was in the battle, so much the more joy will there be in the triumph.*

*Reply Obj.* 1. Sometimes accidentally a thing is the cause of its contrary: thus *that which is cold sometimes causes heat,*

* Gregory, *Moral.* iv.

as stated in *Phys.* viii. 1. In like manner sadness is the accidental cause of pleasure, in so far as it gives rise to the apprehension of something pleasant.

*Reply Obj.* 2. Sad things, called to mind, cause pleasure, not in so far as they are sad and contrary to pleasant things; but in so far as man is delivered from them. In like manner the recollection of pleasant things, by reason of these being lost, may cause sadness.

*Reply Obj.* 3. Hatred also can be the accidental cause of love: *i.e.*, so far as some love one another, inasmuch as they agree in hating one and the same thing.

## Fifth Article.

### WHETHER THE ACTIONS OF OTHERS ARE A CAUSE OF PLEASURE TO US ?

*We proceed thus to the Fifth Article :—*

*Objection* 1. It would seem that the actions of others are not a cause of pleasure to us. Because the cause of pleasure is our own good when conjoined to us. But the actions of others are not conjoined to us. Therefore they are not a cause of pleasure to us.

*Obj.* 2. Further, action is the agent's own good. If, therefore, the actions of others are a cause of pleasure to us, for the same reason all goods belonging to others will be pleasing to us: which is evidently untrue.

*Obj.* 3. Further, action is pleasant through proceeding from an innate habit; hence it is stated in *Ethic.* ii. 3 that *we must reckon the pleasure which follows after action, as being the sign of a habit existing in us.* But the actions of others do not proceed from habits existing in us, but, sometimes, from habits existing in the agents. Therefore the actions of others are not pleasing to us, but to the agents themselves.

*On the contrary*, It is written in the second canonical epistle of John (*verse* 4): *I was exceeding glad that I found thy children walking in truth.*

*I answer that*, As stated above (A. 1; Q. XXXI., A. 1),

two things are requisite for pleasure, namely, the attainment of one's proper good, and the knowledge of having obtained it.   Wherefore the action of another may cause pleasure to us in three ways.   First, from the fact that we obtain some good through the action of another.   And in this way, the actions of those who do some good to us, are pleasing to us: since it is pleasant to be benefited by another.— Secondly, from the fact that another's action makes us to know or appreciate our own good: and for this reason men take pleasure in being praised or honoured by others, because, to wit, they thus become aware of some good existing in themselves.   And since this appreciation receives greater weight from the testimony of good and wise men, hence men take greater pleasure in being praised and honoured by them.   And because a flatterer appears to praise, therefore flattery is pleasing to some.   And as love is for something good, while admiration is for something great, so it is pleasant to be loved and admired by others, inasmuch as a man thus becomes aware of his own goodness or greatness, through their giving pleasure to others.—Thirdly, from the fact that another's actions, if they be good, are reckoned as one's own good, by reason of the power of love, which makes a man to regard his friend as one with himself.   And on account of hatred, which makes one to reckon another's good as being in opposition to oneself, the evil action of an enemy becomes an object of pleasure: whence it is written (1 Cor. xiii. 6) that charity *rejoiceth not in iniquity, but rejoiceth with the truth.*

*Reply Obj.* 1. Another's action may be conjoined to me, either by its effect, as in the first way, or by knowledge, as in the second way; or by affection, as in the third way.

*Reply Obj.* 2. This argument avails for the third mode, but not for the first two.

*Reply Obj.* 3. Although the actions of another do not proceed from habits that are in me, yet they either produce in me something that gives pleasure; or they make me appreciate or know a habit of mine; or they proceed from the habit of one who is united to me by love.

## SIXTH ARTICLE.

### WHETHER DOING GOOD TO ANOTHER IS A CAUSE OF PLEASURE ?

*We proceed thus to the Sixth Article :—*

*Objection* 1. It would seem that doing good to another is not a cause of pleasure. Because pleasure is caused by one's obtaining one's proper good, as stated above (AA. 1, 5; Q. XXXI., A. 1). But doing good pertains not to the obtaining but to the spending of one's proper good. Therefore it seems to be the cause of sadness rather than of pleasure.

*Obj.* 2. Further, the Philosopher says (*Ethic.* iv. 1) that *illiberality is more connatural to man than prodigality.* Now it is a mark of prodigality to do good to others; while it is a mark of illiberality to desist from doing good. Since therefore everyone takes pleasure in a connatural operation, as stated in *Ethic.* vii. 14 and x. 4, it seems that doing good to others is not a cause of pleasure.

*Obj.* 3. Further, contrary effects proceed from contrary causes. But man takes a natural pleasure in certain kinds of ill-doing, such as overcoming, contradicting or scolding others, or, if he be angry, in punishing them, as the Philosopher says (*Rhet.* i. 11). Therefore doing good to others is a cause of sadness rather than of pleasure.

*On the contrary*, The Philosopher says (*Polit.* ii. 2) that *it is most pleasant to give presents or assistance to friends and strangers.*

*I answer that*, Doing good to another may give pleasure in three ways. First, in consideration of the effect, which is the good conferred on another. In this respect, inasmuch as through being united to others by love, we look upon their good as being our own, we take pleasure in the good we do to others, especially to our friends, as in our own good.— Secondly, in consideration of the end; as when a man, from doing good to another, hopes to get some good for himself, either from God or from man: for hope is a cause of pleasure.—Thirdly, in consideration of the principle: and thus, doing good to another, can give pleasure in respect of a threefold principle. One is the faculty of doing good: and in this regard, doing good to another becomes pleasant, in so far as it arouses in man an imagination of abundant good existing in him, whereof he is able to give others a share. Wherefore men take pleasure in their children, and in their own works, as being things on which they bestow a share of their own good. Another principle is a man's habitual inclination to do good, by reason of which doing good becomes connatural to him: for which reason the liberal man takes pleasure in giving to others. The third principle is the motive: for instance when a man is moved by one whom he loves, to do good to someone: for whatever we do or suffer for a friend is pleasant, because love is the principal cause of pleasure.

*Reply Obj.* 1. Spending gives pleasure as showing forth one's good. But in so far as it empties us of our own good it may be a cause of sadness; for instance when it is excessive.

*Reply Obj.* 2. Prodigality is an excessive spending, which is unnatural: wherefore prodigality is said to be contrary to nature.

*Reply Obj.* 3. To overcome, to contradict and to punish, give pleasure, not as tending to another's ill, but as pertaining to one's own good, which man loves more than he hates another's ill. For it is naturally pleasant to overcome, inasmuch as it makes a man to appreciate his own superiority. Wherefore all those games in which there is a striving for the mastery, and a possibility of winning it, afford the greatest pleasure: and speaking generally all contests, in so far as they admit hope of victory.—To contradict and to scold can give pleasure in two ways. First, as making man imagine himself to be wise and excellent; since it belongs to wise men and elders to reprove and to scold. Secondly, in so far as by scolding and reproving, one does good to another: for this gives one pleasure, as stated above.—It is pleasant to an angry man to punish, in so far as he thinks himself to be removing an apparent slight, which seems to be due to a previous hurt: for when a man is hurt by another, he seems to be slighted thereby; and therefore he wishes to be quit of this slight by paying back the hurt.—And thus it is clear that doing good to another may be of itself pleasant: whereas doing evil to another is not pleasant, except in so far as it seems to affect one's own good.

## SEVENTH ARTICLE.

### WHETHER LIKENESS IS A CAUSE OF PLEASURE ?

*We proceed thus to the Seventh Article :—*

*Objection* 1. It would seem that likeness is not a cause of pleasure. Because ruling and presiding seem to imply a certain unlikeness. But *it is natural to take pleasure in ruling and presiding,* as stated in *Rhet.* i. 11. Therefore unlikeness, rather than likeness, is a cause of pleasure.

*Obj.* 2. Further, nothing is more unlike pleasure than sorrow. But those who are burdened by sorrow are most inclined to seek pleasures, as the Philosopher says (*Ethic.* vii. 14). Therefore unlikeness, rather than likeness, is a cause of pleasure.

*Obj.* 3. Further, those who are satiated with certain delights, derive not pleasure but disgust from them; as when one is satiated with food. Therefore likeness is not a cause of pleasure.

*On the contrary,* Likeness is a cause of love, as above stated (Q. XXVII., A. 3): and love is the cause of pleasure. Therefore likeness is a cause of pleasure.

*I answer that,* Likeness is a kind of unity; hence that which is like us, as being one with us, causes pleasure; just as it causes love, as stated above (Q. XXVII., A. 3). And if that which is like us does not hurt our own good, but increase it, it is pleasurable simply; for instance one man in respect of another, one youth in relation to another.—But if it be hurtful to our own good, thus accidentally it causes disgust or sadness, not as being like and one with us, but as hurtful to that which is yet more one with us.

Now it happens in two ways that something like is hurtful to our own good. First, by destroying the measure of our own good, by a kind of excess; because good, especially bodily good, as health, is conditioned by a certain measure: wherefore superfluous food or any bodily pleasure, causes disgust.—Secondly, by being directly contrary to one's own good: thus a potter dislikes other potters, not because they are potters, but because they deprive him of his own excellence or profits, which he seeks as his own good.

*Reply Obj.* 1. Since ruler and subject are in communion with one another, there is a certain likeness between them: but this likeness is conditioned by a certain superiority, since ruling and presiding pertain to the excellence of a man's own good: because they belong to men who are wise and better than others; the result being that they give man an idea of his own excellence.—Another reason is that by ruling and presiding, a man does good to others, which is pleasant.

*Reply Obj.* 2. That which gives pleasure to the sorrowful man, though it be unlike sorrow, bears some likeness to the man that is sorrowful: because sorrows are contrary to his own good. Wherefore the sorrowful man seeks pleasure as making for his own good, in so far as it is a remedy for its contrary. And this is why bodily pleasures, which are contrary to certain sorrows, are more sought than intellectual pleasures, which have no contrary sorrow, as we shall state later on (Q. XXXV., A. 5). And this explains why all animals naturally desire pleasure: because animals ever work through sense and movement. For this reason also young people are most inclined to seek pleasures; on account of the many changes to which they are subject, while yet growing. Moreover this is why the melancholic has a strong desire for pleasures, in order to drive away sorrow: because his *body is corroded by a base humour*, as stated in *Ethic*. vii. 14.

*Reply Obj.* 3. Bodily goods are conditioned by a certain fixed measure: wherefore surfeit of such things destroys the proper good, and consequently gives rise to disgust and sorrow, through being contrary to the proper good of man.

## EIGHTH ARTICLE.

### WHETHER WONDER IS A CAUSE OF PLEASURE ?

*We proceed thus to the Eighth Article :—*

*Objection* 1. It would seem that wonder is not a cause of pleasure. Because wonder is the act of one who is ignorant of the nature of something, as Damascene says. But knowledge, rather than ignorance, is a cause of pleasure. Therefore wonder is not a cause of pleasure.

*Obj.* 2. Further, wonder is the beginning of wisdom, being as it were, the road to the search of truth, as stated in the beginning of *Metaph.* (i. 2). But *it is more pleasant to think of what we know, than to seek for what we know not,* as the Philosopher says (*Ethic.* x. 7): since in the latter case we encounter difficulties and hindrances, in the former not; while pleasure arises from an operation which is unhindered, as stated in *Ethic.* vii. 12, 13. Therefore wonder hinders rather than causes pleasure.

*Obj.* 3. Further, everyone takes pleasure in what he is accustomed to: wherefore the actions of habits acquired by custom, are pleasant. But *we wonder at what is unwonted,* as Augustine says (*Tract.* xxiv. *in Joan.*). Therefore wonder is contrary to the cause of pleasure.

*On the contrary,* The Philosopher says (*Rhet.* i. 11) that wonder is the cause of pleasure.

*I answer that,* It is pleasant to get what one desires, as stated above (Q. XXIII., A. 4): and therefore the greater the desire for the thing loved, the greater the pleasure when it is attained: indeed the very increase of desire brings with it an increase of pleasure, according as it gives rise to the hope of obtaining that which is loved, since it was stated above (A. 3 *ad* 3) that desire resulting from hope is a cause of pleasure.—Now wonder is a kind of desire for knowledge; a desire which comes to man when he sees an effect of which the cause either is unknown to him, or surpasses his knowledge or faculty of understanding. Consequently wonder is a cause of pleasure, in so far as it includes

II. i.

a hope of getting the knowledge which one desires to have. For this reason whatever is wonderful is pleasing, for instance things that are scarce. Also, representations of things, even of those which are not pleasant in themselves, give rise to pleasure; for the soul rejoices in comparing one thing with another, because comparison of one thing with another is the proper and connatural act of the reason, as the Philosopher says (*Poet.* iv.). This again is why *it is more delightful to be delivered from great danger, because it is something wonderful*, as stated in *Rhet.* i. 11.

*Reply Obj.* 1. Wonder gives pleasure, not because it implies ignorance, but in so far as it includes the desire of learning the cause, and in so far as the wonderer learns something new, *i.e.*, that the cause is other than he had thought it to be.*

*Reply Obj.* 2. Pleasure includes two things; rest in the good, and perception of this rest. As to the former therefore, since it is more perfect to contemplate the known truth, than to seek for the unknown, the contemplation of what we know, is in itself more pleasing than the research of what we do not know. Nevertheless, as to the second, it happens that research is sometimes more pleasing accidentally, in so far as it proceeds from a greater desire: for greater desire is awakened when we are conscious of our ignorance. This is why man takes the greatest pleasure in finding or learning things for the first time.

*Reply Obj.* 3. It is pleasant to do what we are wont to do, inasmuch as this is connatural to us, as it were. And yet things that are of rare occurrence can be pleasant, either as regards knowledge, from the fact that we desire to know something about them, in so far as they are wonderful; or as regards action, from the fact that *the mind is more inclined by desire to act intensely in things that are new*, as stated in *Ethic.* x. 4, since more perfect operation causes more perfect pleasure.

* According to another reading:—that he is other than he thought himself to be.

# QUESTION XXXIII.

## OF THE EFFECTS OF PLEASURE.

### (*In Four Articles.*)

WE must now consider the effects of pleasure; and under this head there are four points of inquiry: (1) Whether expansion is an effect of pleasure? (2) Whether pleasure causes thirst or desire for itself? (3) Whether pleasure hinders the use of reason? (4) Whether pleasure perfects operation?

## FIRST ARTICLE.

### WHETHER EXPANSION IS AN EFFECT OF PLEASURE?

*We proceed thus to the First Article :—*

*Objection* 1. It would seem that expansion is not an effect of pleasure. For expansion seems to pertain more to love, according to the Apostle (2 Cor. vi. 11): *Our heart is enlarged.* Wherefore it is written (Ps. cxviii. 96) concerning the precept of charity: *Thy commandment is exceeding broad.* But pleasure is a distinct passion from love. Therefore expansion is not an effect of pleasure.

*Obj.* 2. Further, when a thing expands it is enabled to receive more. But receiving pertains to desire, which is for something not yet possessed. Therefore expansion seems to belong to desire rather than to pleasure.

*Obj.* 3. Further, contraction is contrary to expansion. But contraction seems to belong to pleasure, for the hand closes on that which we wish to grasp firmly: and such is the affection of appetite in regard to that which pleases it. Therefore expansion does not pertain to pleasure.

*On the contrary,* In order to express joy, it is written (Isa. lx. 5): *Thou shalt see and abound, thy heart shall wonder*

*and be enlarged.* Moreover pleasure is called by the name of
*laetitia,* as being derived from *dilatatio* (expansion), as stated
above (Q. XXXI., A. 3, *ad* 3).

*I answer that,* Breadth (*latitudo*) is a dimension of bodily
magnitude: hence it is not applied to the emotions of the
soul, save metaphorically. Now expansion denotes a kind
of movement towards breadth; and it belongs to pleasure
in respect of the two things requisite for pleasure. One of
these is on the part of the apprehensive power, which is
cognizant of the conjunction with some suitable good. As
a result of this apprehension, man perceives that he has
attained a certain perfection, which is a magnitude of the
spiritual order: and in this respect man's mind is said to
be magnified or expanded by pleasure.—The other requisite
for pleasure is on the part of the appetitive power, which
acquiesces in the pleasurable object, and rests therein,
offering, as it were, to enfold it within itself. And thus
man's affection is expanded by pleasure, as though it sur-
rendered itself to hold within itself the object of its pleasure.

*Reply Obj.* 1. In metaphorical expressions nothing hinders
one and the same thing from being attributed to different
things according to different likenesses. And in this way
expansion pertains to love by reason of a certain spreading
out, in so far as the affection of the lover spreads out
to others, so as to care, not only for his own interests,
but also for what concerns others. On the other hand
expansion pertains to pleasure, in so far as a thing becomes
more ample in itself so as to become more capacious.

*Reply Obj.* 2. Desire includes a certain expansion arising
from the imagination of the thing desired; but this expansion
increases at the presence of the pleasurable object: because
the mind surrenders itself more to that object when it is
already taking pleasure in it, than when it desires it before
possessing it; since pleasure is the end of desire.

*Reply Obj.* 3. He that takes pleasure in a thing holds it
fast, by clinging to it with all his might: but he opens his
heart to it that he may enjoy it perfectly.

## Second Article.

### whether pleasure causes thirst or desire for itself ?

*We proceed thus to the Second Article :—*

*Objection* 1. It would seem that pleasure does not cause desire for itself. Because all movement ceases when repose is reached. But pleasure is, as it were, a certain repose of the movement of desire, as stated above (Q. XXIII., A. 4; Q. XXV., A. 2). Therefore the movement of desire ceases when pleasure is reached. Therefore pleasure does not cause desire.

*Obj.* 2. Further, a thing does not cause its contrary. But pleasure is, in a way, contrary to desire, on the part of the object: since desire regards a good which is not yet possessed, whereas pleasure regards the good that is possessed. Therefore pleasure does not cause desire for itself.

*Obj.* 3. Further, distaste is incompatible with desire. But pleasure often causes distaste. Therefore it does not cause desire.

*On the contrary*, Our Lord said (Jo. iv. 13): *Whosoever drinketh of this water, shall thirst again* : where, according to Augustine (*Tract.* xv. *in Joan.*), water denotes pleasures of the body.

*I answer that*, Pleasure can be considered in two ways; first, as existing in reality; secondly, as existing in the memory.—Again thirst, or desire, can be taken in two ways; first, properly, as denoting a craving for something not possessed; secondly, in general, as excluding distaste.

Considered as existing in reality, pleasure does not of itself cause thirst or desire for itself, but only accidentally; provided we take thirst or desire as denoting a craving for some thing not possessed: because pleasure is an emotion of the appetite in respect of something actually present.—But it may happen that what is actually present is not perfectly possessed: and this may be on the part of the thing possessed, or on the part of the possessor. On the part of the thing possessed, this happens through the thing possessed not being a simultaneous whole; wherefore one obtains possession of it successively, and while taking pleasure in what one has, one desires to possess the remainder: thus if a man is pleased with the first part of a verse, he desires to hear the second part, as Augustine says (*Conf.* iv. 11). In this way nearly all bodily pleasures cause thirst for themselves, until they are fully realized, because pleasures of this kind arise from some movement: as is evident in pleasures of the table.—On the part of the possessor, this happens when a man possesses a thing which is perfect in itself, yet does not possess it perfectly, but obtains possession of it little by little. Thus in this life, a faint perception of Divine knowledge affords us delight, and delight sets up a thirst or desire for perfect knowledge; in which sense we may understand the words of Ecclus. xxiv. 29: *They that drink me shall yet thirst.*

On the other hand if by thirst or desire we understand the mere intensity of the emotion, that excludes distaste, thus more than all others spiritual pleasures cause thirst or desire for themselves. Because bodily pleasures become distasteful by reason of their causing an excess in the natural mode of being, when they are increased or even when they are protracted; as is evident in the case of pleasures of the table. This is why, when a man arrives at the point of perfection in bodily pleasures, he wearies of them, and sometimes desires another kind.—Spiritual pleasures, on the contrary, do not exceed the natural mode of being, but perfect nature. Hence when their point of perfection is reached, then do they afford the greatest delight: except, perchance, accidentally, in so far as the work of contemplation is accompanied by some operation of the bodily powers, which tire from protracted activity. And in this sense also we may understand those words of Ecclus. xxiv. 29: *They that drink me shall yet thirst* : for, even of the angels, who know God perfectly, and delight in Him, it is written (1 Pet. i. 12) that they *desire to look at* Him.

Lastly, if we consider pleasure, not as existing in reality, but as existing in the memory, thus it has of itself a natural tendency to cause thirst and desire for itself: when, to wit, man returns to that disposition, in which he was when he experienced the pleasure that is past. But if he be changed from that disposition, the memory of that pleasure does not give him pleasure, but distaste: for instance, the memory of food in respect of a man who has eaten to repletion.

*Reply Obj.* 1. When pleasure is perfect, then it includes complete rest; and the movement of desire, tending to what was not possessed, ceases. But when it is imperfect, then the desire, tending to what was not possessed, does not cease altogether.

*Reply Obj.* 2. That which is possessed imperfectly, is possessed in one respect, and in another respect is not possessed. Consequently it may be the object of desire and pleasure at the same time.

*Reply Obj.* 3. Pleasures cause distaste in one way, desire in another, as stated above.

### Third Article.

#### WHETHER PLEASURE HINDERS THE USE OF REASON?

*We proceed thus to the Third Article :—*

*Objection* 1. It would seem that pleasure does not hinder the use of reason. Because repose facilitates very much the due use of reason: wherefore the Philosopher says (*Phys.* vii. 3) that *while we sit and rest the soul is inclined to knowledge and prudence ;* and it is written (Wisd. viii. 16): *When I go into my house, I shall repose myself with her, i.e.,* wisdom. But pleasure is a kind of repose. Therefore it helps rather than hinders the use of reason.

*Obj.* 2. Further, things which are not in the same subject though they be contraries, do not hinder one another. But pleasure is in the appetitive faculty, while the use of reason is in the apprehensive power. Therefore pleasure does not hinder the use of reason.

*Obj.* 3. Further, that which is hindered by another, seems to be moved, as it were, thereby. But the use of an apprehensive power moves pleasure rather than is moved by it: because it is the cause of pleasure. Therefore pleasure does not hinder the use of reason.

*On the contrary*, The Philosopher says (*Ethic.* vi. 5), that *pleasure destroys the estimate of prudence.*

*I answer that*, As is stated in *Ethic.* x. 5, *appropriate pleasures increase activity . . . whereas pleasures arising from other sources are impediments to activity.* Accordingly there is a certain pleasure that is taken in the very act of reason, as when one takes pleasure in contemplating or in reasoning: and such pleasure does not hinder the act of reason, but helps it; because we are more attentive in doing that which gives us pleasure, and attention fosters activity.

On the other hand bodily pleasures hinder the use of reason in three ways. First, by distracting the reason. Because, as we have just observed, we attend much to that which pleases us. Now when the attention is firmly fixed on one thing, it is either weakened in respect of other things, or it is entirely withdrawn from them; and thus if the bodily pleasure be great, either it entirely hinders the use of reason, by concentrating the mind's attention on itself; or else it hinders it considerably.—Secondly, by being contrary to reason. Because some pleasures, especially those that are in excess, are contrary to the order of reason: and in this sense the Philosopher says that *bodily pleasures destroy the estimate of prudence, but not the speculative estimate*, to which they are not opposed, *for instance that the three angles of a triangle are together equal to two right angles.* In the first sense, however, they hinder both estimates.— Thirdly, by fettering the reason: in so far as bodily pleasure is followed by a certain alteration in the body, greater even than in the other passions, in proportion as the appetite is more vehemently affected towards a present than towards an absent thing. Now such bodily disturbances hinder the use of reason; as may be seen in the case of drunkards, in whom the use of reason is fettered or hindered.

*Reply Obj.* 1. Bodily pleasure implies indeed repose of the appetite in the object of pleasure; which repose is sometimes contrary to reason; but on the part of the body it always implies alteration. And in respect of both points, it hinders the use of reason.

*Reply Obj.* 2. The powers of appetite and of apprehension are indeed distinct parts, but belonging to the one soul. Consequently when the soul is very intent on the action of one part, it is hindered from attending to a contrary act of the other part.

*Reply Obj.* 3. The use of reason requires the due use of the imagination and of the other sensitive powers, which are exercised through a bodily organ. Consequently alteration in the body hinders the use of reason, because it hinders the acts of the imagination and of the other sensitive powers.

## Fourth Article.

### WHETHER PLEASURE PERFECTS OPERATION ?

*We proceed thus to the Fourth Article :—*

*Objection* 1. It would seem that pleasure does not perfect operation. For every human operation depends on the use of reason. But pleasure hinders the use of reason, as stated above (A. 3). Therefore pleasure does not perfect, but weakens human operation.

*Obj.* 2. Further, nothing perfects itself or its cause. But pleasure is an operation (*Ethic.* vii. 12, x. 4), *i.e.*, either in its essence or in its cause. Therefore pleasure does not perfect operation.

*Obj.* 3. Further, if pleasure perfects operation, it does so either as end, or as form, or as agent. But not as end; because operation is not sought for the sake of pleasure, but rather the reverse, as stated above (Q. IV., A. 2): nor as agent, because rather is it the operation that causes pleasure: nor again as form, because, according to the Philosopher (*Ethic.* x. 4), *pleasure does not perfect operation, as a habit does.* Therefore pleasure does not perfect operation.

*On the contrary,* The Philosopher says (*ibid.*) that *pleasure perfects operation.*

*I answer that,* Pleasure perfects operation in two ways. First, as an end: not indeed according as an end is that on *account of which a thing is* ; but according as every good which is added to a thing and completes it, can be called its end.   And in this sense the Philosopher says (*Ethic.* x., *loc. cit.*) that *pleasure perfects operation . . . as some end added to it* : that is to say, inasmuch as to this good, which is operation, there is added another good, which is pleasure, denoting the repose of the appetite in a good that is presupposed.—Secondly, as agent; not indeed directly, for the Philosopher says (*ibid.*) that *pleasure perfects operation, not as a physician makes a man healthy, but as health does :* but it does so indirectly; inasmuch as the agent, through taking pleasure in his action, is more eagerly intent on it, and carries it out with greater care.   And in this sense it is said in *Ethic.* x. 5, that *pleasures increase their appropriate activities, and hinder those that are not appropriate.*

*Reply Obj.* 1. It is not every pleasure that hinders the act of reason, but only bodily pleasure; for this arises, not from the act of reason, but from the act of the concupiscible faculty, which act is intensified by pleasure.   On the contrary, pleasure that arises from the act of reason, strengthens the use of reason.

*Reply Obj.* 2. As stated in *Phys.* ii. 3, two things may be causes of one another, if one be the efficient, the other the final cause.   And in this way, operation is the efficient cause of pleasure, while pleasure perfects operation by way of final cause, as stated above.

The Reply to the Third Objection is evident from what has been said.

# QUESTION XXXIV.

## OF THE GOODNESS AND MALICE OF PLEASURES.

### (*In Four Articles.*)

WE must now consider the goodness and malice of pleasures: under which head there are four points of inquiry: (1) Whether every pleasure is evil? (2) If not, whether every pleasure is good? (3) Whether any pleasure is the greatest good? (4) Whether pleasure is the measure or rule by which to judge of moral good and evil?

## FIRST ARTICLE.

### WHETHER EVERY PLEASURE IS EVIL?

*We proceed thus to the First Article :—*

*Objection* 1. It would seem that every pleasure is evil. For that which destroys prudence and hinders the use of reason, seems to be evil in itself: since man's good is to be *in accord with reason*, as Dionysius says (*Div. Nom.* iv.). But pleasure destroys prudence and hinders the use of reason; and so much the more, as the pleasure is greater: wherefore *in sexual pleasures*, which are the greatest of all, *it is impossible to understand anything*, as stated in *Ethic.* vii. 11. Moreover, Jerome says in his commentary on Matthew* that *at the time of conjugal intercourse, the presence of the Holy Ghost is not vouchsafed, even if it be a prophet that fulfils the conjugal duty.* Therefore pleasure is evil in itself; and consequently every pleasure is evil.

*Obj.* 2. Further, that which the virtuous man shuns, and the man lacking in virtue seeks, seems to be evil in itself, and should be avoided; because, as stated in *Ethic.* x. 5, *the*

---

* Origen, *Hom.* vi. *in Num.*

395

*virtuous man is a kind of measure and rule of human actions* ; and the Apostle says (1 Cor. ii. 15): *The spiritual man judgeth all things.* But children and dumb animals, in whom there is no virtue, seek pleasure: whereas the man who is master of himself does not. Therefore pleasures are evil in themselves and should be avoided.

*Obj.* 3. Further, *virtue and art are concerned about the difficult and the good* (*Ethic.* ii. 3). But no art is ordained to pleasure. Therefore pleasure is not something good.

*On the contrary,* It is written (Ps. xxxvi. 4): *Delight in the Lord.* Since, therefore, Divine authority leads to no evil, it seems that not every pleasure is evil.

*I answer that,* As stated in *Ethic.* x. 2, 3, some have maintained that all pleasure is evil. The reason seems to have been that they took account only of sensible and bodily pleasures which are more manifest; since, also in other respects, the ancient philosophers did not discriminate between the intelligible and the sensible, nor between intellect and sense (*cf. De Anima* iii. 3). And they held that all bodily pleasures should be reckoned as bad, and thus that man, being prone to immoderate pleasures, arrives at the mean of virtue by abstaining from pleasure.—But they were wrong in holding this opinion. Because, since none can live without some sensible and bodily pleasure, if they who teach that all pleasures are evil, are found in the act of taking pleasure; men will be more inclined to pleasure by following the example of their works instead of listening to the doctrine of their words: since, in human actions and passions, wherein experience is of great weight, example moves more than words.

We must therefore say that some pleasures are good, and that some are evil. For pleasure is a repose of the appetitive power in some loved good, and resulting from some operation; wherefore we may assign a twofold reason for this assertion. The first is in respect of the good in which a man reposes with pleasure. For good and evil in the moral order depend on agreement or disagreement with reason, as stated above (Q. XVIII., A. 5): just as in the order of nature, a thing is said to be natural, if it agrees with nature, and unnatural, if it disagrees. Accordingly, just as in the natural order there is a certain natural repose, whereby a thing rests in that which agrees with its nature, for instance, when a heavy body rests down below; and again an unnatural repose, whereby a thing rests in that which disagrees with its nature, as when a heavy body rests up aloft: so, in the moral order, there is a good pleasure, whereby the higher or lower appetite rests in that which is in accord with reason; and an evil pleasure, whereby the appetite rests in that which is discordant from reason and the law of God.

The second reason can be found by considering the actions, some of which are good, some evil. Now pleasures which are conjoined to actions are more akin to those actions, than desires, which precede them in point of time. Wherefore, since the desires of good actions are good, and of evil actions, evil; much more are the pleasures of good actions good, and those of evil actions evil.

*Reply Obj.* 1. As stated above (Q. XXXIII., A. 3), it is not the pleasures which result from an act of reason, that hinder the reason or destroy prudence, but extraneous pleasures, such as the pleasures of the body. These indeed hinder the use of reason, as stated above (*ibid.*), either by contrariety of the appetite that rests in something repugnant to reason, which makes the pleasure morally bad; or by fettering the reason: thus in conjugal intercourse, though the pleasure be in accord with reason, yet it hinders the use of reason, on account of the accompanying bodily change. But in this case the pleasure is not morally evil; as neither is sleep, whereby the reason is fettered, morally evil, if it be taken according to reason: for reason itself demands that the use of reason be interrupted at times.—We must add, however, that although this fettering of the reason through the pleasure of conjugal intercourse has no moral malice, since it is neither a mortal nor a venial sin; yet it proceeds from a kind of moral malice, namely, from the sin of our first parent; because, as stated in the First Part (Q. XCVIII., A. 2) the case was different in the state of innocence.

*Reply Obj*. 2. The temperate man does not shun all pleasures, but those that are immoderate, and contrary to reason. The fact that children and dumb animals seek pleasures, does not prove that all pleasures are evil: because they have from God their natural appetite, which is moved to that which is naturally suitable to them.

*Reply Obj*. 3. Art is not concerned with all kinds of good, but with the making of external things, as we shall state further on (Q. LVII., A. 3). But actions and passions, which are within us, are more the concern of prudence and virtue than of art. Nevertheless there is an art of making pleasure, namely, *the art of cookery and the art of making unguents*, as stated in *Ethic*. vii. 12.

## SECOND ARTICLE.

### WHETHER EVERY PLEASURE IS GOOD ?

*We proceed thus to the Second Article :—*

*Objection* 1. It would seem that every pleasure is good. Because as stated in the First Part (Q. V., A. 6), there are three kinds of good, the virtuous, the useful, and the pleasant. But everything virtuous is good; and in like manner everything useful is good. Therefore also every pleasure is good.

*Obj*. 2. Further, that which is not sought for the sake of something else, is good in itself, as stated in *Ethic*. i. 6, 7. But pleasure is not sought for the sake of something else; for it seems absurd to ask anyone why he seeks to be pleased. Therefore pleasure is good in itself. Now that which is predicated of a thing considered in itself, is predicated thereof universally. Therefore every pleasure is good.

*Obj*. 3. Further, that which is desired by all, seems to be good of itself: because good is *what all things seek*, as stated in *Ethic*. i. 1. But everyone seeks some kind of pleasure, even children and dumb animals. Therefore pleasure is good in itself: and consequently all pleasure is good.

*On the contrary*, It is written (Prov. ii. 14): *Who are glad when they have done evil, and rejoice in most wicked things*.

*I answer that*, While some of the Stoics maintained that all pleasures are evil, the Epicureans held that pleasure is good in itself, and that consequently all pleasures are good. They seem to have thus erred through not discriminating between that which is good simply, and that which is good in respect of a particular individual. That which is good simply, is good in itself. Now that which is not good in itself, may be good in respect of some individual in two ways. In one way, because it is suitable to him by reason of a disposition in which he is now, which disposition, however, is not natural: thus it is sometimes good for a leper to eat things that are poisonous, which are not suitable simply to the human temperament. In another way, through something unsuitable being esteemed suitable. And since pleasure is the repose of the appetite in some good, if the appetite reposes in that which is good simply, the pleasure will be pleasure simply, and good simply. But if a man's appetite repose in that which is good, not simply, but in respect of that particular man, then his pleasure will not be pleasure simply, but a pleasure to him; neither will it be good simply, but in a certain respect, or an apparent good.

*Reply Obj.* 1. The virtuous and the useful depend on accordance with reason, and consequently nothing is virtuous or useful, without being good. But the pleasant depends on agreement with the appetite, which tends sometimes to that which is discordant from reason. Consequently not every object of pleasure is good in the moral order which depends on the order of reason.

*Reply Obj.* 2. The reason why pleasure is not sought for the sake of something else is because it is repose in the end. Now the end may be either good or evil; although nothing can be an end except in so far as it is good in respect of such and such a man: and so too with regard to pleasure.

*Reply Obj.* 3. All things seek pleasure in the same way as they seek good: since pleasure is the repose of the appetite in good. But, just as it happens that not every good which is desired, is of itself and verily good; so not every pleasure is of itself and verily good.

## Third Article.

### WHETHER ANY PLEASURE IS THE GREATEST GOOD?

*We proceed thus to the Third Article :—*

*Objection* 1. It would seem that no pleasure is the greatest good.   Because nothing generated is the greatest good : since generation cannot be the last end.   But pleasure is a consequence of generation : for the fact that a thing takes pleasure is due to its being established in its own nature, as stated above (Q. XXXI., A. 1).   Therefore no pleasure is the greatest good.

*Obj.* 2. Further, that which is the greatest good cannot be made better by addition.   But pleasure is made better by addition ; since pleasure together with virtue is better than pleasure without virtue.   Therefore pleasure is not the greatest good.

*Obj.* 3. Further, that which is the greatest good is universally good, as being good of itself : since that which is such of itself is prior to and greater than that which is such accidentally.   But pleasure is not universally good, as stated above (A. 2).   Therefore pleasure is not the greatest good.

*On the contrary,* Happiness is the greatest good : since it is the end of man's life.   But Happiness is not without pleasure : for it is written (Ps. xv. 11) : *Thou shalt fill me with joy with Thy countenance ; at Thy right hand are delights even to the end.*

*I answer that,* Plato held neither with the Stoics, who asserted that all pleasures are evil, nor with the Epicureans, who maintained that all pleasures are good ; but he said that some are good, and some evil ; yet, so that no pleasure be the sovereign or greatest good.   But, judging from his arguments, he fails in two points. First, because, from observing that sensible and bodily pleasure consists in a certain movement and *becoming*, as is evident in satiety from eating and the like ; he concluded that all pleasure arises from some *becoming* and movement : and from this, since *becoming* and movement are the acts of something imperfect, it would follow that pleasure is not of the nature of ultimate perfection.—But this is seen to be evidently false as regards intellectual pleasures: because one takes pleasure, not only in the *becoming* of knowledge, for instance, when one learns or wonders, as stated above (Q. XXXII., A. 8 *ad* 2); but also in the act of contemplation, by making use of knowledge already acquired.

Secondly, because by greatest good he understood that which is the supreme good simply, *i.e.*, the good as existing apart from, and unparticipated by, all else, in which sense God is the Supreme Good; whereas we are speaking of the greatest good in human things. Now the greatest good of everything is its last end. And the end, as stated above (Q. I., A. 8; Q. II., A. 7) is twofold; namely, the thing itself, and the use of that thing; thus the miser's end is either money, or the possession of money. Accordingly, man's last end may be said to be either God Who is the Supreme Good simply; or the enjoyment of God, which implies a certain pleasure in the last end. And in this sense a certain pleasure of man may be said to be the greatest among human goods.

*Reply Obj.* 1. Not every pleasure arises from a *becoming* ; for some pleasures result from perfect operations, as stated above. Accordingly nothing prevents some pleasure being the greatest good, although every pleasure is not such.

*Reply Obj.* 2. This argument is true of the greatest good simply, by participation of which all things are good; wherefore no addition can make it better: whereas in regard to other goods, it is universally true that any good becomes better by the addition of another good.—Moreover it might be said that pleasure is not something extraneous to the operation of virtue, but that it accompanies it, as stated in *Ethic*. i. 8.

*Reply Obj.* 3. That pleasure is the greatest good is due not to the mere fact that it is pleasure, but to the fact that it is perfect repose in the perfect good. Hence it does not

II. i.

follow that every pleasure is supremely good, or even good at all. Thus a certain science is supremely good, but not every science is.

## FOURTH ARTICLE.

### WHETHER PLEASURE IS THE MEASURE OR RULE BY WHICH TO JUDGE OF MORAL GOOD OR EVIL?

*We proceed thus to the Fourth Article :—*

*Objection* 1. It would seem that pleasure is not the measure or rule of moral good and evil. Because *that which is first in a genus is the measure of all the rest* (*Metaph*. x. 1). But pleasure is not the first thing in the moral genus, for it is preceded by love and desire. Therefore it is not the rule of goodness and malice in moral matters.

*Obj.* 2. Further, a measure or rule should be uniform; hence that movement which is the most uniform, is the measure and rule of all movements (*Metaph*. x. 1). But pleasures are various and multiform: since some of them are good, and some evil. Therefore pleasure is not the measure and rule of morals.

*Obj.* 3. Further, judgment of the effect from its cause is more certain than judgment of cause from effect. Now goodness or malice of operation is the cause of goodness or malice of pleasure: because *those pleasures are good which result from good operations, and those are evil which arise from evil operations*, as stated in *Ethic*. x. 5. Therefore pleasures are not the rule and measure of moral goodness and malice.

*On the contrary*, Augustine, commenting on Ps. vii. 10, *The searcher of hearts and reins is God*, says: *The end of care and thought is the pleasure which each one aims at achieving*. And the Philosopher says (*Ethic*. vii. 11) that *pleasure is the architect*, i.e., the principal, *end,*\* *in regard to which, we say absolutely that this is evil, and that, good*.

*I answer that*, Moral goodness or malice depends chiefly on the will, as stated above (Q. XX., A. 1); and it is chiefly

\* St. Thomas took *finis* as being the nominative, whereas it is the genitive—τοῦ τέλους; and the Greek reads *He* (i.e., the political philosopher), *is the architect of the end*.

from the end that we discern whether the will is good or evil. Now the end is taken to be that in which the will reposes: and the repose of the will and of every appetite in the good is pleasure. And therefore man is reckoned to be good or bad chiefly according to the pleasure of the human will; since that man is good and virtuous, who takes pleasure in the works of virtue; and that man evil, who takes pleasure in evil works.

On the other hand, pleasures of the sensitive appetite are not the rule of moral goodness and malice; since food is universally pleasurable to the sensitive appetite both of good and of evil men. But the will of the good man takes pleasure in them in accordance with reason, to which the will of the evil man gives no heed.

*Reply Obj.* 1. Love and desire precede pleasure in the order of generation. But pleasure precedes them in the order of the end, which serves as a principle in actions; and it is by the principle, which is the rule and measure of such matters, that we form our judgment.

*Reply Obj.* 2. All pleasures are uniform in the point of their being the repose of the appetite in something good: and in this respect pleasure can be a rule or measure. Because that man is good, whose will rests in the true good: and that man evil, whose will rests in evil.

*Reply Obj.* 3. Since pleasure perfects operation as its end, as stated above (Q. XXXIII., A. 4); an operation cannot be perfectly good, unless there be also pleasure in good: because the goodness of a thing depends on its end. And thus, in a way, the goodness of the pleasure is the cause of goodness in the operation.

# QUESTION XXXV.

## OF PAIN OR SORROW, IN ITSELF.

### (*In Eight Articles.*)

WE have now to consider pain and sorrow: concerning which we must consider (1) Sorrow or pain in itself: (2) Its cause: (3) Its effects: (4) Its remedies: (5) Its goodness or malice.

Under the first head there are eight points of inquiry: (1) Whether pain is a passion of the soul? (2) Whether sorrow is the same as pain? (3) Whether sorrow or pain is contrary to pleasure? (4) Whether all sorrow is contrary to all pleasure? (5) Whether there is a sorrow contrary to the pleasure of contemplation? (6) Whether sorrow is to be shunned more than pleasure is to be sought? (7) Whether exterior pain is greater than interior? (8) Of the species of sorrow.

### FIRST ARTICLE.

#### WHETHER PAIN IS A PASSION OF THE SOUL?

*We proceed thus to the First Article :—*

*Objection* 1. It would seem that pain is not a passion of the soul. Because no passion of the soul is in the body. But pain can be in the body, since Augustine says (*De Vera Relig.* xii.), that *bodily pain is a sudden corruption of the well-being of that thing which the soul, by making evil use of it, made subject to corruption.* Therefore pain is not a passion of the soul.

*Obj.* 2. Further, every passion of the soul belongs to the appetitive faculty. But pain does not belong to the appetitive, but rather to the apprehensive part: for Augustine says (*De Nat. Boni,* xx.) that *bodily pain is caused by the sense resisting a more powerful body.* Therefore pain is not a passion of the soul.

*Obj.* 3. Further, every passion of the soul belongs to the animal appetite. But pain does not belong to the animal appetite, but rather to the natural appetite; for Augustine says (*Gen. ad lit.* viii. 14): *Had not some good remained in nature, we should feel no pain in being punished by the loss of good.* Therefore pain is not a passion of the soul.

*On the contrary,* Augustine (*De Civ. Dei* xiv. 8) reckons pain among the passions of the soul; quoting Virgil (*Æneid,* vi. 733):

> " Hence wild desires and grovelling fears
> And human laughter, human tears."
>                    (*Trl.* CONINGTON.)

*I answer that,* Just as two things are requisite for pleasure; namely, conjunction with good and perception of this conjunction; so also two things are requisite for pain; namely, conjunction with some evil (which is in so far evil as it deprives one of some good), and perception of this conjunction. Now whatever is conjoined, if it have not the aspect of good or evil in regard to the being to which it is conjoined, cannot cause pleasure or pain. Whence it is evident that something under the aspect of good or evil is the object of pleasure or pain. But good and evil, as such, are objects of the appetite. Consequently it is clear that pleasure and pain belong to the appetite.

Now every appetitive movement or inclination consequent to apprehension, belongs to the intellective or sensitive appetite: since the inclination of the natural appetite is not consequent to an apprehension of the subject of that appetite, but to the apprehension of another, as stated in the First Part (Q. CIII., AA. 1, 3). Since then pleasure and pain presuppose some sense or apprehension in the same subject, it is evident that pain, like pleasure, is in the intellective or sensitive appetite.

Again every movement of the sensitive appetite is called a passion, as stated above (Q. XXII., AA. 1, 3): and especially those which tend to some defect.   Consequently pain, according as it is in the sensitive appetite, is most properly called a passion of the soul: just as bodily ailments are properly called passions of the body.   Hence Augustine (*De Civ. Dei* xiv. 7, 8*) reckons pain especially as being a kind of ailment.

*Reply Obj.* 1.   We speak of pain of the body, because the cause of pain is in the body: as when we suffer something hurtful to the body.   But the movement of pain is always in the soul; since *the body cannot feel pain unless the soul feel it*, as Augustine says (*Super Psalm.* lxxxvii. 4).

*Reply Obj.* 2.   We speak of pain of the senses, not as though it were an act of the sensitive power; but because the senses are required for bodily pain, in the same way as for bodily pleasure.

*Reply Obj.* 3.   Pain at the loss of good proves the goodness of the nature, not because pain is an act of the natural appetite, but because nature desires something as good, the removal of which being perceived, there results the passion of pain in the sensitive appetite.

## SECOND ARTICLE.

### WHETHER SORROW IS THE SAME AS PAIN ?

*We proceed thus to the Second Article :—*

*Objection* 1.   It would seem that sorrow is not pain.   For Augustine says (*De Civ. Dei* xiv. 7) that *pain is used to express bodily suffering*.   But sorrow is used more in reference to the soul.   Therefore sorrow is not pain.

*Obj.* 2.   Further, pain is only in respect of present evil. But sorrow can refer to both past and future evil: thus repentance is sorrow for the past, and anxiety is sorrow for the future.   Therefore sorrow is quite different from pain.

*Obj.* 3.   Further, pain seems not to follow save from the sense of touch.   But sorrow can arise from all the senses. Therefore sorrow is not pain, and extends to more objects.

*On the contrary*, The Apostle says (Rom. ix. 2): *I have*

* Quoting Cicero.

*great sorrow* (Douay,—*sadness*) *and continual pain* (Douay,— *sorrow*) *in my heart*, thus denoting the same thing by sorrow and pain.

*I answer that*, Pleasure and pain can arise from a twofold apprehension, namely, from the apprehension of an exterior sense; and from the interior apprehension of the intellect or of the imagination. Now the interior apprehension extends to more objects than the exterior apprehension: because whatever things come under the exterior apprehension, come under the interior, but not conversely. Consequently that pleasure alone which is caused by an interior apprehension is called joy, as stated above (Q. XXXI., A. 3): and in like manner that pain alone which is caused by an interior apprehension, is called sorrow. And just as that pleasure which is caused by an exterior apprehension, is called pleasure but not joy; so too that pain which is caused by an exterior apprehension, is called pain indeed but not sorrow. Accordingly sorrow is a species of pain, as joy is a species of pleasure.

*Reply Obj.* 1. Augustine is speaking there of the use of the word: because *pain* is more generally used in reference to bodily pains, which are better known, than in reference to spiritual pains.

*Reply Obj.* 2. External sense perceives only what is present; but the interior cognitive power can perceive the present, past and future. Consequently sorrow can regard present, past and future: whereas bodily pain, which follows the apprehension of the external sense, can only regard something present.

*Reply Obj.* 3. The sensibles of touch are painful, not only in so far as they are disproportionate to the apprehensive power, but also in so far as they are contrary to nature: whereas the objects of the other senses can indeed be disproportionate to the apprehensive power, but they are not contrary to nature, save as they are subordinate to the sensibles of touch. Consequently man alone, who is a perfectly cognizant animal, takes pleasure in the objects of the other senses for their own sake; whereas other animals take no pleasure in them save as referable to the sensibles of touch, as stated in *Ethic*. iii. 10.   Accordingly, in referring to the objects of the other senses, we do not speak of pain in so far as it is contrary to natural pleasure: but rather of sorrow, which is contrary to joy.—So then if pain be taken as denoting bodily pain, which is its more usual meaning, then it is contrasted with sorrow, according to the distinction of interior and exterior apprehension; although, on the part of the objects, pleasure extends further than does bodily pain.   But if pain be taken in a wide sense, then it is the genus of sorrow, as stated above.

### Third Article.

#### WHETHER SORROW OR PAIN IS CONTRARY TO PLEASURE ?

*We proceed thus to the Third Article :—*

*Objection* 1. It would seem that sorrow is not contrary to pleasure.   For one of two contraries is not the cause of the other.   But sorrow can be the cause of pleasure; for it is written (*Matth.* v. 5): *Blessed are they that mourn, for they shall be comforted*.   Therefore they are not contrary to one another.

*Obj.* 2. Further, one contrary does not denominate the other.   But to some, pain or sorrow gives pleasure: thus Augustine says (*Conf.* iii. 2) that in stage-plays sorrow itself gives pleasure: and (*ibid.* iv. 5) that *weeping is a bitter thing, and yet it sometimes pleases us*.   Therefore pain is not contrary to pleasure.

*Obj.* 3. Further, one contrary is not the matter of the other; because contraries cannot co-exist together.   But sorrow can be the matter of pleasure; for Augustine says (*De Pœnit.* xiii.): *The penitent should ever sorrow, and rejoice in his sorrow*.   The Philosopher too says (*Ethic.* ix. 4) that, on the other hand, *the evil man feels pain at having been pleased*.   Therefore pleasure and pain are not contrary to one another.

*On the contrary*, Augustine says (*De Civ. Dei* xiv. 6) that *joy is the volition of consent to the things we wish : and that sorrow is the volition of dissent from the things we do not wish.* But consent and dissent are contraries. Therefore pleasure and sorrow are contrary to one another.

*I answer that,* As the Philosopher says (*Metaph.* x. 4), contrariety is a difference in respect of a form. Now the form or species of a passion or movement is taken from the object or term. Consequently, since the objects of pleasure and sorrow or pain, viz., present good and present evil, are contrary to one another, it follows that pain and pleasure are contrary to one another.

*Reply Obj.* 1. Nothing hinders one contrary causing the other accidentally: and thus sorrow can be the cause of pleasure. In one way, in so far as from sorrow at the absence of something, or at the presence of its contrary, one seeks the more eagerly for something pleasant: thus a thirsty man seeks more eagerly the pleasure of a drink, as a remedy for the pain that he suffers. In another way, in so far as, from a strong desire for a certain pleasure, one does not shrink from undergoing pain, so as to obtain that pleasure. In each of these ways, the sorrows of the present life lead us to the comfort of the future life. Because by the mere fact that man mourns for his sins, or for the delay of glory, he merits the consolation of eternity. In like manner a man merits it when he shrinks not from hardships and straits in order to obtain it.

*Reply Obj.* 2. Pain itself can be pleasurable accidentally in so far as it is accompanied by wonder, as in stage-plays; or in so far as it recalls a beloved object to one's memory, and makes one feel one's love for the thing, whose absence gives us pain. Consequently, since love is pleasant, both pain and whatever else results from love, forasmuch as they remind us of our love, are pleasant. And, for this reason, we derive pleasure even from pains depicted on the stage: in so far as, in witnessing them, we perceive ourselves to conceive a certain love for those who are there represented.

*Reply Obj.* 3. The will and the reason reflect on their own acts, inasmuch as the acts themselves of the will and reason are considered under the aspect of good or evil. In this way sorrow can be the matter of pleasure, or vice versa, not essentially but accidentally: that is, in so far as either of them is considered under the aspect of good or evil.

## Fourth Article.

### WHETHER ALL SORROW IS CONTRARY TO ALL PLEASURE ?

*We proceed thus to the Fourth Article :—*

*Objection* 1. It would seem that all sorrow is contrary to all pleasure. Because, just as whiteness and blackness are contrary species of colour, so pleasure and sorrow are contrary species of the soul's passions. But whiteness and blackness are universally contrary to one another. Therefore pleasure and sorrow are so too.

*Obj.* 2. Further, remedies are made of things contrary (to the evil). But every pleasure is a remedy for all manner of sorrow, as the Philosopher declares (*Ethic*. vii. 14). Therefore every pleasure is contrary to every sorrow.

*Obj.* 3. Further, contraries are hindrances to one another. But every sorrow hinders any kind of pleasure: as is evident from *Ethic*. x. 5. Therefore every sorrow is contrary to every pleasure.

*On the contrary*, The same thing is not the cause of contraries. But joy for one thing, and sorrow for the opposite thing, proceed from the same habit: thus from charity it happens that we *rejoice with them that rejoice*, and *weep with them that weep* (Rom. xii. 15). Therefore not every sorrow is contrary to every pleasure.

*I answer that*, As stated in *Metaph*. x. 4, contrariety is a difference in respect of a form. Now a form may be generic or specific. Consequently things may be contraries in respect of a generic form, as virtue and vice; or in respect of a specific form, as justice and injustice.

Now we must observe that some things are specified by absolute forms, *e.g.*, substances and qualities; whereas other things are specified in relation to something extrinsic, *e.g.*, passions and movements, which derive their species from their terms or objects. Accordingly in those things that are specified by absolute forms, it happens that species contained under contrary genera are not contrary as to their specific nature: but it does not happen for them to have any affinity or fittingness to one another. For intemperance and justice, which are in the contrary genera of virtue and vice, are not contrary to one another in respect of their specific nature; and yet they have no affinity or fittingness to one another.—On the other hand, in those things that are specified in relation to something extrinsic, it happens that species belonging to contrary genera, are not only not contrary to one another, but also that they have a certain mutual affinity or fittingness. The reason of this is that where there is one same relation to two contraries, there is contrariety; e.g., to approach to a white thing, and to approach to a black thing, are contraries; whereas contrary relations to contrary things, implies a certain likeness, e.g., to recede from something white, and to approach to something black. This is most evident in the case of contradiction, which is the principle of opposition: because opposition consists in affirming and denying the same thing, e.g., white and not-white; while there is fittingness and likeness in the affirmation of one contrary and the denial of the other, as, if I were to say black and not white.

Now sorrow and pleasure, being passions, are specified by their objects. According to their respective genera, they are contrary to one another: since one is a kind of *pursuit*, the other a kind of *avoidance*, which *are to the appetite, what affirmation and denial are to the intellect* (*Ethic*. vi. 2). Consequently sorrow and pleasure in respect of the same object, are specifically contrary to one another: whereas sorrow and pleasure in respect of objects that are not contrary but disparate, are not specifically contrary to one another, but are also disparate; for instance, sorrow at the death of a friend, and pleasure in contemplation. If, however, those diverse objects be contrary to one another, then pleasure and sorrow are not only not specifically contrary, but they also have a certain mutual fittingness and affinity: for instance to rejoice in good and to sorrow for evil.

*Reply Obj.* 1. Whiteness and blackness do not take their species from their relationship to something extrinsic, as pleasure and sorrow do: wherefore the comparison does not hold.

*Reply Obj.* 2. Genus is taken from matter, as is stated in *Metaph.* viii. 2: and in accidents the subject takes the place of matter. Now it has been said above that pleasure and sorrow are generically contrary to one another. Consequently in every sorrow the subject has a disposition contrary to the disposition of the subject of pleasure: because in every pleasure the appetite is viewed as accepting what it possesses, and in every sorrow, as avoiding it. And therefore on the part of the subject every pleasure is a remedy for any kind of sorrow, and every sorrow is a hindrance of all manner of pleasure: but chiefly when pleasure is opposed to sorrow specifically.

Wherefore the Reply to the Third Objection is evident.— Or we may say that, although not every sorrow is specifically contrary to every pleasure, yet they are contrary to one another in regard to their effects: since one has the effect of strengthening the animal nature, while the other results in a kind of discomfort.

### FIFTH ARTICLE.

#### WHETHER THERE IS ANY SORROW CONTRARY TO THE PLEASURE OF CONTEMPLATION ?

*We proceed thus to the Fifth Article :—*

*Objection* 1. It would seem that there is a sorrow that is contrary to the pleasure of contemplation. For the Apostle says (2 Cor. vii. 10): *The sorrow that is according to God, worketh penance steadfast unto salvation.* Now to look at God belongs to the higher reason, whose act is to give itself to contemplation, according to Augustine (*De Trin.* xii. 3, 4). Therefore there is a sorrow contrary to the pleasure of contemplation.

*Obj.* 2. Further, contrary things have contrary effects. If therefore the contemplation of one contrary gives pleasure, the other contrary will give sorrow: and so there will be a sorrow contrary to the pleasure of contemplation.

*Obj.* 3. Further, as the object of pleasure is good, so the object of sorrow is evil. But contemplation can be an evil: since the Philosopher says (*Metaph.* xii. 9) that *it is unfitting to think of certain things.* Therefore sorrow can be contrary to the pleasure of contemplation.

*Obj.* 4. Further, any work, so far as it is unhindered, can be a cause of pleasure, as stated in *Ethic.* vii. 12, 13, x. 4. But the work of contemplation can be hindered in many ways, either so as to destroy it altogether, or so as to make it difficult. Therefore in contemplation there can be a sorrow contrary to the pleasure.

*Obj.* 5. Further, affliction of the flesh is a cause of sorrow. But, as it is written (Eccles. xii. 12) *much study is an affliction of the flesh.* Therefore contemplation admits of sorrow contrary to its pleasure.

*On the contrary,* It is written (Wis. viii. 16): *Her,* i.e., wisdom's, *conversation hath no bitterness, nor her company any tediousness; but joy and gladness.* Now the conversation and company of wisdom are found in contemplation. Therefore there is no sorrow contrary to the pleasure of contemplation.

*I answer that,* The pleasure of contemplation can be understood in two ways. In one way, so that contemplation is the cause, but not the object of pleasure: and then pleasure is taken not in contemplating but in the thing contemplated. Now it is possible to contemplate something harmful and sorrowful, just as to contemplate something suitable and pleasant. Consequently if the pleasure of contemplation be taken in this way, nothing hinders some sorrow being contrary to the pleasure of contemplation.

In another way, the pleasure of contemplation is understood, so that contemplation is its object and cause; as when one takes pleasure in the very act of contemplating. And thus, according to Gregory of Nyssa,* *no sorrow is con-*

* Nemesius,—*De Nat. Hom.* xviii.

*trary to that pleasure which is about contemplation :* and the
Philosopher says the same (*Topic.* i. 13, *Ethic.* x. 3). This,
however, is to be understood as being the case properly
speaking. The reason is because sorrow is of itself contrary
to pleasure in a contrary object: thus pleasure in heat is contrary to sorrow caused by cold. But there is no contrary
to the object of contemplation: because contraries, as apprehended by the mind, are not contrary, but one is the means
of knowing the other. Wherefore, properly speaking, there
cannot be a sorrow contrary to the pleasure of contemplation.—Nor has it any sorrow annexed to it, as bodily
pleasures have, which are like remedies against certain
annoyances; thus a man takes pleasure in drinking through
being troubled with thirst, but when the thirst is quite driven
out, the pleasure of drinking ceases also. Because the
pleasure of contemplation is not caused by one's being quit
of an annoyance, but by the fact that contemplation is
pleasant in itself: for pleasure is not a *becoming* but a perfect
operation, as stated above (Q. XXXI., A. 1).

Accidentally, however, sorrow is mingled with the pleasure
of apprehension; and this in two ways: first, on the part of
an organ, secondly, through some impediment in the apprehension. On the part of an organ, sorrow or pain is mingled
with apprehension, directly, as regards the apprehensive
powers of the sensitive part, which have a bodily organ;—
either from the sensible object disagreeing with the normal
condition of the organ, as the taste of something bitter,
and the smell of something foul;—or from the sensible
object, though agreeable, being so continuous in its action
on the sense, that it exceeds the normal condition of the
organ, as stated above (Q. XXXIII., A. 2), the result being
that an apprehension which at first was pleasant becomes
tedious.—But these two things cannot occur directly in the
contemplation of the mind; because the mind has no
corporeal organ: wherefore it was said in the authority
quoted above that intellectual contemplation has neither
*bitterness*, nor *tediousness*. Since, however, the human
mind, in contemplation, makes use of the sensitive powers

of apprehension, to whose acts weariness is incidental; therefore some affliction or pain is indirectly mingled with contemplation.

Nevertheless, in neither of these ways, is the pain thus accidentally mingled with contemplation, contrary to the pleasure thereof. Because pain caused by a hindrance to contemplation, is not contrary to the pleasure of contemplation, but rather is in affinity and in harmony with it, as is evident from what has been said above (A. 4): while pain or sorrow caused by bodily weariness, does not belong to the same genus, wherefore it is altogether disparate. Accordingly it is evident that no sorrow is contrary to pleasure taken in the very act of contemplation; nor is any sorrow connected with it save accidentally.

*Reply Obj.* 1. The *sorrow which is according to God*, is not caused by the very act of intellectual contemplation, but by something which the mind contemplates: viz., by sin, which the mind considers as contrary to the love of God.

*Reply Obj.* 2. Things which are contrary according to nature are not contrary according as they exist in the mind: for things that are contrary in reality are not contrary in the order of thought; indeed rather is one contrary the reason for knowing the other. Hence one and the same science considers contraries.

*Reply Obj.* 3. Contemplation, in itself, is never evil, since it is nothing else than the consideration of truth, which is the good of the intellect: it can, however, be evil accidentally, *i.e.*, in so far as the contemplation of a less noble object hinders the contemplation of a more noble object; or on the part of the object contemplated, to which the appetite is inordinately attached.

*Reply Obj.* 4. Sorrow caused by a hindrance to contemplation, is not contrary to the pleasure of contemplation, but is in harmony with it, as stated above.

*Reply Obj.* 5. Affliction of the flesh affects contemplation accidentally and indirectly, as stated above.

### Sixth Article.

#### WHETHER SORROW IS TO BE SHUNNED MORE THAN PLEASURE IS TO BE SOUGHT ?

*We proceed thus to the Sixth Article :—*

*Objection* 1. It would seem that sorrow is to be shunned more than pleasure is to be sought. For Augustine says (QQ. LXXXIII. qu. 36): *There is nobody that does not shun sorrow more than he seeks pleasure.* Now that which all agree in doing, seems to be natural. Therefore it is natural and right for sorrow to be shunned more than pleasure is sought.

*Obj.* 2. Further, the action of a contrary conduces to rapidity and intensity of movement: for *hot water freezes quicker and harder*, as the Philosopher says (*Meteor.* i. 12). But the shunning of sorrow is due to the contrariety of the cause of sorrow; whereas the desire for pleasure does not arise from any contrariety, but rather from the suitableness of the pleasant object. Therefore sorrow is shunned more eagerly than pleasure is sought.

*Obj.* 3. Further, the stronger the passion which a man resists according to reason, the more worthy is he of praise, and the more virtuous: since *virtue is concerned with the difficult and the good* (*Ethic.* ii. 3). But the brave man who resists the movement of shunning sorrow, is more virtuous than the temperate man, who resists the movement of desire for pleasure: since the Philosopher says (*Rhet.* ii. 4) that *the brave and the just are chiefly praised.* Therefore the movement of shunning sorrow is more eager than the movement of seeking pleasure.

*On the contrary*, Good is stronger than evil, as Dionysius declares (*Div. Nom.* iv.). But pleasure is desirable for the sake of the good which is its object; whereas the shunning of sorrow is on account of evil. Therefore the desire for pleasure is more eager than the shunning of sorrow.

*I answer that,* The desire for pleasure is of itself more eager than the shunning of sorrow. The reason of this is that the cause of pleasure is a suitable good; while the cause of pain or sorrow is an unsuitable evil. Now it happens that a certain good is suitable without any repugnance at all: but it is not possible for any evil to be so unsuitable as not to be suitable in some way. Wherefore pleasure can be entire and perfect: whereas sorrow is always partial. Therefore desire for pleasure is naturally greater than the shunning of sorrow.—Another reason is because the good, which is the object of pleasure, is sought for its own sake: whereas the evil, which is the object of sorrow, is to be shunned as being a privation of good: and that which is by reason of itself is stronger than that which is by reason of something else.—Moreover we find a confirmation of this in natural movements. For every natural movement is more intense in the end, when a thing approaches the term that is suitable to its nature, than at the beginning, when it leaves the term that is unsuitable to its nature: as though nature were more eager in tending to what is suitable to it, than in shunning what is unsuitable. Therefore the inclination of the appetitive power is, of itself, more eager in tending to pleasure than in shunning sorrow.

But it happens accidentally that a man shuns sorrow more eagerly than he seeks pleasure: and this for three reasons. First, on the part of the apprehension. Because as Augustine says (*De Trin.* x. 12), *love is felt more keenly, when we lack that which we love.* Now from the lack of what we love, sorrow results, which is caused either by the loss of some loved good, or by the presence of some contrary evil. But pleasure suffers no lack of the good loved, for it rests in possession of it. Since then love is the cause of pleasure and sorrow, the latter is the more shunned, according as love is the more keenly felt on account of that which is contrary to it.—Secondly, on the part of the cause of sorrow or pain, which cause is repugnant to a good that is more loved than the good in which we take pleasure. For we love the natural well-being of the body more than the pleasure of eating: and consequently we would leave the pleasure of eating and the like, from fear of the pain occasioned by blows or other such causes, which are contrary to the well-being of the body.—Thirdly, on the part of the effect: namely, in so far as sorrow hinders not only one pleasure, but all.

*Reply Obj.* 1. The saying of Augustine that *sorrow is shunned more than pleasure is sought* is true accidentally but not simply. And this is clear from what he says after: *Since we see that the most savage animals are deterred from the greatest pleasures by fear of pain*, which pain is contrary to life which is loved above all.

*Reply Obj.* 2. It is not the same with movement from within and movement from without. For movement from within tends to what is suitable more than it recedes from that which is unsuitable; as we remarked above in regard to natural movement. But movement from without is intensified by the very opposition: because each thing strives in its own way to resist anything contrary to it, as aiming at its own preservation. Hence violent movement is intense at first, and slackens towards the end.—Now the movement of the appetitive faculty is from within: since it tends from the soul to the object. Consequently pleasure is, of itself, more to be sought than sorrow is to be shunned. But the movement of the sensitive faculty is from without, as it were from the object to the soul. Consequently the more contrary a thing is the more it is felt. And then too, accidentally, in so far as the senses are requisite for pleasure and pain, pain is shunned more than pleasure is sought.

*Reply Obj.* 3. A brave man is not praised because, in accordance with reason, he is not overcome by any kind of sorrow or pain whatever, but because he is not overcome by that which is concerned with the dangers of death. And this kind of sorrow is more shunned, than pleasures of the table or of sexual intercourse are sought, which latter pleasures are the object of temperance: thus life is loved more than food and sexual pleasure. But the temperate man is praised for refraining from pleasures of touch, more than for not shunning the pains which are contrary to them, as is stated in *Ethic*. iii. 11.

## SEVENTH ARTICLE.

### WHETHER OUTWARD PAIN IS GREATER THAN INTERIOR SORROW?

*We proceed thus to the Seventh Article :—*

*Objection* 1. It would seem that outward pain is greater than interior sorrow of the heart. Because outward pain arises from a cause repugnant to the well-being of the body in which is life: whereas interior sorrow is caused by some evil in the imagination. Since, therefore, life is loved more than an imagined good, it seems that, according to what has been said above (A. 6), outward pain is greater than interior sorrow.

*Obj.* 2. Further, the reality moves more than its likeness does. But outward pain arises from the real conjunction of some contrary: whereas inward sorrow arises from the apprehended likeness of a contrary. Therefore outward pain is greater than inward sorrow.

*Obj.* 3. Further, a cause is known by its effect. But outward pain has more striking effects: since man dies sooner of outward pain than of interior sorrow. Therefore outward pain is greater and is shunned more than interior sorrow.

*On the contrary,* It is written (Ecclus. xxv. 17): *The sadness of the heart is every wound* (Douay,—*plague*), *and the wickedness of a woman is all evil.* Therefore, just as the wickedness of a woman surpasses all other wickedness, as the text implies; so sadness of the heart surpasses every outward wound.

*I answer that,* Interior and exterior pain agree in one point, and differ in two. They agree in this, that each is a movement of the appetitive power, as stated above (A. 1). But they differ in respect of those two things which are requisite for pain and pleasure; namely, in respect of the cause, which is a conjoined good or evil; and in respect of the apprehension. For the cause of outward pain is a conjoined evil repugnant to the body; while the cause of inward pain is a conjoined evil repugnant to the appetite. Again, outward pain arises from an apprehension of sense, chiefly of touch; while inward pain arises from an interior apprehension, of the imagination or of the reason.

If then we compare the cause of inward pain to the cause of outward pain, the former belongs, of itself, to the appetite to which both these pains belong: while the latter belongs to the appetite indirectly. Because inward pain arises from something being repugnant to the appetite itself, while outward pain arises from something being repugnant to the appetite, through being repugnant to the body. Now, that which is of itself is always prior to that which is by reason of another. Wherefore, from this point of view, inward pain surpasses outward pain.—In like manner also on the part of apprehension: because the apprehension of reason and imagination is of a higher order than the apprehension of the sense of touch.—Consequently inward pain is, simply and of itself, more keen than outward pain: a sign whereof is that one willingly undergoes outward pain in order to avoid inward pain: and in so far as outward pain is not repugnant to the interior appetite, it becomes in a manner pleasant and agreeable by way of inward joy. Sometimes, however, outward pain is accompanied by inward pain, and then the pain is increased. Because inward pain is not only greater than outward pain, it is also more universal: since whatever is repugnant to the body, can be repugnant to the interior appetite; and whatever is apprehended by sense may be apprehended by imagination and reason, but not conversely. Hence in the passage quoted above it is said expressively: *Sadness of the heart is every wound*, because even the pains of outward wounds are comprised in the interior sorrows of the heart.

*Reply Obj*. 1. Inward pain can also arise from things that are destructive of life. And then the comparison of inward to outward pain must not be taken in reference to the various evils that cause pain; but in regard to the various ways in which this cause of pain is compared to the appetite.

*Reply Obj*. 2. Inward pain is not caused by the apprehended likeness of a thing: for a man is not inwardly pained by the apprehended likeness itself, but by the thing which the likeness represents. And this thing is all the more perfectly apprehended by means of its likeness, as this likeness is more immaterial and abstract. Consequently inward pain is, of itself, greater, as being caused by a greater evil, forasmuch as evil is better known by an inward apprehension.

*Reply Obj.* 3. Bodily changes are more liable to be caused by outward pain, both from the fact that outward pain is caused by a corruptive conjoined corporally, which is a necessary condition of the sense of touch; and from the fact that the outward sense is more material than the inward sense, just as the sensitive appetite is more material than the intellective. For this reason, as stated above (Q. XXII., A. 3; Q. XXXI., A. 5), the body undergoes a greater change from the movement of the sensitive appetite: and, in like manner, from outward than from inward pain.

## Eighth Article.

### WHETHER THERE ARE ONLY FOUR SPECIES OF SORROW ?

*We proceed thus to the Eighth Article :—*

*Objection* 1. It would seem that Damascene's (*De Fide Orthod.* ii. 14) division of sorrow into four species is incorrect; viz., into *torpor*, *distress*, which Gregory of Nyssa* calls *anxiety,—pity*, and *envy*. For sorrow is contrary to pleasure. But there are not several species of pleasure. Therefore it is incorrect to assign different species of sorrow.

*Obj.* 2. Further, *Repentance* is a species of sorrow; and so are *indignation* and *jealousy*, as the Philosopher states (*Rhet.* ii. 9, 11). But these are not included in the above species. Therefore this division is insufficient.

*Obj.* 3. Further, the members of a division should be things that are opposed to one another. But these species are not opposed to one another. For according to Gregory† *torpor is sorrow depriving of speech : anxiety is the sorrow that weighs down ; envy is sorrow for another's good ; pity is sorrow for another's wrongs.* But it is possible for one to sorrow for

---

* Nemesius,—*De Nat. Hom.* xix.                    † *Ibid.*

another's wrongs, and for another's good, and at the same time to be weighed down inwardly, and outwardly to be speechless. Therefore this division is incorrect.

*On the contrary* stands the twofold authority of Gregory of Nyssa* and of Damascene.

*I answer that,* It belongs to the notion of a species that it is something added to the genus. But a thing can be added to a genus in two ways. First, as something belonging of itself to the genus, and virtually contained therein: thus *rational* is added to *animal.* Such an addition makes true species of a genus: as the Philosopher says (*Metaph.* vii. 12, viii. 2, 3). But, secondly, a thing may be added to a genus, that is, as it were, foreign to the notion conveyed by that genus: thus *white* or something of the kind may be added to *animal.* Such an addition does not make true species of the genus, according to the usual sense in which we speak of genera and species. But sometimes a thing is said to be a species of a certain genus, through having something foreign to that genus indeed, but to which the notion of that genus is applicable: thus a live coal or a flame is said to be a species of fire, because in each of them the nature of fire is applied to a foreign matter. In like manner we speak of astronomy and perspective as being species of mathematics, inasmuch as the principles of mathematics are applied to natural matter.

In accordance with this manner of speaking, the species of sorrow are reckoned by an application of the notion of sorrow to something foreign to it. This foreign matter may be taken on the part of the cause or the object, or of the effect. For the proper object of sorrow is *one's own evil.* Hence sorrow may be concerned for an object foreign to it either through one's being sorry for an evil that is not one's own; and thus we have *pity* which is sorrow for another's evil, considered, however, as one's own:—or through one's being sorry for something that is neither evil nor one's own, but another's good, considered, however, as one's own evil: and thus we have *envy.*—The proper effect of sorrow

* Nemesius.

consists in a certain *flight of the appetite*. Wherefore the foreign element in the effect of sorrow, may be taken so as to affect the first part only, by excluding flight: and thus we have *anxiety* which weighs on the mind, so as to make escape seem impossible: hence it is also called *perplexity*. If, however, the mind be weighed down so much, that even the limbs become motionless, which belongs to *torpor*, then we have the foreign element affecting both, since there is neither flight, nor is the effect in the appetite. And the reason why torpor especially is said to deprive one of speech is because of all the external movements the voice is the best expression of the inward thought and desire, not only in men, but also in other animals, as is stated in *Polit.* i. 1.

*Reply Obj.* 1. Pleasure is caused by good, which has only one meaning: and so pleasure is not divided into several species as sorrow is; for the latter is caused by evil, which *happens in many ways*, as Dionysius says (*Div. Nom.* iv.).

*Reply Obj.* 2. Repentance is for one's own evil, which is the proper object of sorrow: wherefore it does not belong to these species.—Jealousy and indignation are included in envy, as we shall explain later (II.-II., Q. XXXVI., A. 2).

*Reply Obj.* 3. This division is not according to opposite species; but according to the diversity of foreign matter to which the notion of sorrow is applied, as stated above.

# QUESTION XXXVI.

## OF THE CAUSES OF SORROW OR PAIN.

*(In Four Articles.)*

WE must now consider the causes of sorrow: under which head there are four points of inquiry: (1) Whether sorrow is caused by the loss of a good or rather by the presence of an evil? (2) Whether desire is a cause of sorrow? (3) Whether the craving for unity is a cause of sorrow? (4) Whether an irresistible power is a cause of sorrow?

### FIRST ARTICLE.

#### WHETHER SORROW IS CAUSED BY THE LOSS OF GOOD OR BY THE PRESENCE OF EVIL?

*We proceed thus to the First Article :—*

*Objection* 1. It would seem that sorrow is caused by the loss of a good rather than by the presence of an evil. For Augustine says (*De* viii. *Qq. Dulcit.*, qu. 1) that sorrow is caused by the loss of temporal goods. Therefore, in like manner, every sorrow is caused by the loss of some good.

*Obj.* 2. Further, it was said above (Q. XXXV., A. 4) that the sorrow, which is contrary to a pleasure, has the same object as that pleasure. But the object of pleasure is good, as stated above (Q. XXIII., A. 4; Q. XXXI., A. 1; Q. XXXV., A. 3). Therefore sorrow is caused chiefly by the loss of good.

*Obj.* 3. Further, according to Augustine (*De Civ. Dei* xiv., 7, 9), love is the cause of sorrow, as of the other emotions of the soul. But the object of love is good. Therefore pain or sorrow is felt for the loss of good rather than for an evil that is present.

*On the contrary*, Damascene says (*De Fide Orthod*. ii. 12) that *the dreaded evil gives rise to fear, the present evil is the cause of sorrow*.

*I answer that,* If privations, as considered by the mind, were what they are in reality, this question would seem to be of no importance. For, as stated in the First Part (Q. XIV., A. 10; Q. XLVIII., A. 3), evil is the privation of good: and privation is in reality nothing else than the lack of the contrary habit; so that, in this respect, to sorrow for the loss of good, would be the same as to sorrow for the presence of evil.—But sorrow is a movement of the appetite in consequence of an apprehension: and even a privation, as apprehended, has the aspect of a being, wherefore it is called *a being of reason.* And in this way evil, being a privation, is regarded as a *contrary.* Accordingly, so far as the movement of the appetite is concerned, it makes a difference which of the two it regards chiefly, the present evil or the good which is lost.

Again, since the movement of the animal appetite holds the same place in the actions of the soul, as natural movement in natural things; the truth of the matter is to be found by considering natural movements. For if, in natural movements, we observe those of approach and withdrawal, approach is of itself directed to something suitable to nature; while withdrawal is of itself directed to something contrary to nature; thus a heavy body, of itself, withdraws from a higher place, and approaches naturally to a lower place. But if we consider the cause of both these movements, viz., gravity, then gravity itself inclines towards the lower place more than it withdraws from the higher place, since withdrawal from the latter is the reason for its downward tendency.

Accordingly, since, in the movements of the appetite, sorrow is a kind of flight or withdrawal, while pleasure is a kind of pursuit or approach; just as pleasure regards first the good possessed, as its proper object, so sorrow regards the evil that is present. On the other hand love, which is the cause of pleasure and sorrow, regards good rather than evil: and therefore, forasmuch as the object is the cause of a passion, the present evil is more properly the cause of sorrow or pain, than the good which is lost.

*Reply Obj.* 1. The loss itself of good is apprehended as an evil, just as the loss of evil is apprehended as a good: and in this sense Augustine says that pain results from the loss of temporal goods.

*Reply Obj.* 2. Pleasure and its contrary pain have the same object, but under contrary aspects: because if the presence of a particular thing be the object of pleasure, the absence of that same thing is the object of sorrow. Now one contrary includes the privation of the other, as stated in *Metaph.* x. 4: and consequently sorrow in respect of one contrary is, in a way, directed to the same thing under a contrary aspect.

*Reply Obj.* 3. When many movements arise from one cause, it does not follow that they all regard chiefly that which the cause regards chiefly, but only the first of them. And each of the others regards chiefly that which is suitable to it according to its own nature.

## SECOND ARTICLE.

### WHETHER DESIRE IS A CAUSE OF SORROW ?

*We proceed thus to the Second Article :—*

*Objection* 1. It would seem that desire is not a cause of pain or sorrow. Because sorrow of itself regards evil, as stated above (A. 1): whereas desire is a movement of the appetite towards good. Now movement towards one contrary is not a cause of the movement towards the other contrary. Therefore desire is not a cause of pain.

*Obj.* 2. Further, pain, according to Damascene (*De Fide Orthod.* ii. 12), is caused by something present; whereas the object of desire is something future. Therefore desire is not a cause of pain.

*Obj.* 3. Further, that which is pleasant in itself is not a cause of pain. But desire is pleasant in itself, as the

Philosopher says (*Rhet*. i. 11). Therefore desire is not a cause of pain or sorrow.

*On the contrary*, Augustine says (*Enchirid*. xxiv.): *When ignorance of things necessary to be done, and desire of things hurtful, found their way in : error and pain stole an entrance in their company*. But ignorance is the cause of error. Therefore desire is a cause of sorrow.

*I answer that*, Sorrow is a movement of the animal appetite. Now, as stated above (A. 1) the appetitive movement is likened to the natural appetite; a likeness, that may be assigned to a twofold cause; one, on the part of the end, the other, on the part of the principle of movement. Thus, on the part of the end, the cause of a heavy body's downward movement is the lower place; while the principle of that movement is a natural inclination resulting from gravity.

Now the cause of the appetitive movement, on the part of the end, is the object of that movement. And thus, it has been said above (A. 1) that the cause of pain or sorrow is a present evil.—On the other hand, the cause, by way of principle, of that movement, is the inward inclination of the appetite; which inclination regards, first of all, the good, and in consequence, the rejection of a contrary evil. Hence the first principle of this appetitive movement is love, which is the first inclination of the appetite towards the possession of good: while the second principle is hatred, which is the first inclination of the appetite towards the avoidance of evil. But since concupiscence or desire is the first effect of love, which gives rise to the greatest pleasure, as stated above (Q. XXXII., A. 6); hence it is that Augustine often speaks of desire or concupiscence in the sense of love, as was also stated (Q. XXX., A. 2 *ad* 2): and in this sense he says that desire is the universal cause of sorrow. Sometimes, however, desire taken in its proper sense, is the cause of sorrow. Because whatever hinders a movement from reaching its end is contrary to that movement. Now that which is contrary to the movement of the appetite, is a cause of sorrow. Consequently, desire becomes a cause of sorrow, in so far as we sorrow for the delay of a desired good, or for its entire removal. But it cannot be a universal cause of sorrow: since we sorrow more for the loss of present good, in which we have already taken pleasure, than for the withdrawal of future good which we desire to have.

*Reply Obj.* 1. The inclination of the appetite to the possession of good causes the inclination of the appetite to fly from evil, as stated above. And hence it is that the appetitive movements that regard good, are reckoned as causing the appetitive movements that regard evil.

*Reply Obj.* 2. That which is desired, though really future, is, nevertheless, in a way, present, inasmuch as it is hoped for.—Or we may say that although the desired good itself is future, yet the hindrance is reckoned as present, and so gives rise to sorrow.

*Reply Obj.* 3. Desire gives pleasure, so long as there is a hope of obtaining that which is desired. But, when hope is removed through the presence of an obstacle, desire causes sorrow.

## THIRD ARTICLE.

### WHETHER THE CRAVING FOR UNITY IS A CAUSE OF SORROW ?

*We proceed thus to the Third Article :—*

*Objection* 1. It would seem that the craving for unity is not a cause of sorrow. For the Philosopher says (*Ethic.* x. 3) that *this opinion*, which held repletion to be the cause of pleasure, and division* the cause of sorrow, *seems to have originated in pains and pleasures connected with food*. But not every pleasure or sorrow is of this kind. Therefore the craving for unity is not the universal cause of sorrow; since repletion pertains to unity, and division is the cause of multitude.

*Obj.* 2. Further, every separation is opposed to unity. If therefore sorrow were caused by a craving for unity, no separation would be pleasant: and this is clearly untrue as regards the separation of whatever is superfluous.

*Obj.* 3. Further, for the same reason we desire the conjunction of good and the removal of evil. But as conjunc-

* Aristotle wrote ἔνδειαν, want; St. Thomas, in the Latin version, read *incisionem ;* should he have read *indigentiam ?*

tion regards unity, since it is a kind of union; so separation is contrary to unity. Therefore the craving for unity should not be reckoned, rather than the craving for separation, as causing sorrow.

*On the contrary,* Augustine says (*De Lib. Arb.* iii. 23), that *from the pain that dumb animals feel, it is quite evident how their souls desire unity, in ruling and quickening their bodies. For what else is pain but a feeling of impatience of division or corruption?*

*I answer that,* Forasmuch as the desire or craving for good is reckoned as a cause of sorrow, so must a craving for unity, and love, be accounted as causing sorrow. Because the good of each thing consists in a certain unity, inasmuch as each thing has, united in itself, the elements of which its perfection consists: wherefore the Platonists held that *one* is a principle, just as *good* is. Hence everything naturally desires unity, just as it desires goodness: and therefore, just as love or desire for good is a cause of sorrow, so also is the love or craving for unity.

*Reply Obj.* 1. Not every kind of union causes perfect goodness, but only that on which the perfect being of a thing depends. Hence neither does the desire of any kind of unity cause pain or sorrow, as some have maintained: whose opinion is refuted by the Philosopher from the fact that repletion is not always pleasant; for instance, when a man has eaten to repletion, he takes no further pleasure in eating; because repletion or union of this kind, is repugnant rather than conducive to perfect being. Consequently sorrow is caused by the craving, not for any kind of unity, but for that unity in which the perfection of nature consists.

*Reply Obj.* 2. Separation can be pleasant, either because it removes something contrary to a thing's perfection, or because it has some union connected with it, such as union of the sense to its object.

*Reply Obj.* 3. Separation from things hurtful and corruptive is desired, in so far as they destroy the unity which is due. Wherefore the desire for a suchlike separation is not the first cause of sorrow, whereas the craving for unity is.

## Fourth Article.

### WHETHER AN IRRESISTIBLE POWER IS A CAUSE OF SORROW ?

*We proceed thus to the Fourth Article :—*

*Objection* 1. It would seem that a greater power should not be reckoned a cause of sorrow.   For that which is in the power of the agent is not present but future.   But sorrow is for present evil.   Therefore a greater power is not a cause of sorrow.

*Obj.* 2. Further, hurt inflicted is the cause of sorrow. But hurt can be inflicted even by a lesser power.   Therefore a greater power should not be reckoned as a cause of sorrow.

*Obj.* 3. Further, the interior inclinations of the soul are the causes of the movements of appetite.   But a greater power is something external.   Therefore it should not be reckoned as a cause of sorrow.

*On the contrary*, Augustine says (*De Nat. Boni* xx.): *Sorrow in the soul is caused by the will resisting a stronger power : while pain in the body is caused by sense resisting a stronger body.*

*I answer that*, As stated above (A. 1), a present evil, is cause of sorrow or pain, by way of object.   Therefore that which is the cause of the evil being present, should be reckoned as causing pain or sorrow.   Now it is evident that it is contrary to the inclination of the appetite to be united with a present evil: and whatever is contrary to a thing's inclination does not happen to it save by the action of something stronger.   Wherefore Augustine reckons a greater power as being the cause of sorrow.

But it must be noted that if the stronger power goes so far as to transform the contrary inclination into its own inclination, there will be no longer repugnance or violence: thus if a stronger agent, by its action on a heavy body, deprives it of its downward tendency, its consequent upward tendency is not violent but natural to it.

Accordingly if some greater power prevail so far as to take away from the will or the sensitive appetite, their respective inclinations, pain or sorrow will not result there-from; such is the result only when the contrary inclination of the appetite remains. And hence Augustine says (*loc. cit.*) that sorrow is caused by the will *resisting a stronger power*: for were it not to resist, but to yield by consenting, the result would be not sorrow but pleasure.

*Reply Obj.* 1. A greater power causes sorrow, as acting not potentially but actually, *i.e.*, by causing the actual presence of the corruptive evil.

*Reply Obj.* 2. Nothing hinders a power which is not simply greater, from being greater in some respect: and accordingly it is able to inflict some harm. But if it be nowise stronger, it can do no harm at all: wherefore it cannot bring about that which causes sorrow.

*Reply Obj.* 3. External agents can be the causes of appetitive movements, in so far as they cause the presence of the object: and it is thus that a greater power is reckoned to be the cause of sorrow.

# QUESTION XXXVII.

## OF THE EFFECTS OF PAIN OR SORROW.

### (*In Four Articles.*)

WE must now consider the effects of pain or sorrow: under which head there are four points of inquiry: (1) Whether pain deprives one of the power to learn ? (2) Whether the effect of sorrow or pain is to burden the soul ? (3) Whether sorrow or pain weakens all activity ? (4) Whether sorrow is more harmful to the body than all the other passions of the soul ?

## FIRST ARTICLE.

### WHETHER PAIN DEPRIVES ONE OF THE POWER TO LEARN ?

*We proceed thus to the First Article :—*

*Objection* 1. It would seem that pain does not deprive one of the power to learn. For it is written (Isa. xxvi. 9): *When Thou shalt do Thy judgments on the earth, the inhabitants of the world shall learn justice*: and further on (*verse* 16): *In the tribulation of murmuring Thy instruction was with them.* But the judgments of God and tribulation cause sorrow in men's hearts. Therefore pain or sorrow, far from destroying, increases the power of learning.

*Obj.* 2. Further, it is written (Isa. xxviii. 9): *Whom shall He teach knowledge ? And whom shall He make to understand the hearing ? Them that are weaned from the milk, that are drawn away from the breasts, i.e.*, from pleasures. But pain and sorrow are most destructive of pleasure; since sorrow hinders all pleasure, as stated in *Ethic.* vii. 14: and (Ecclus. xi. 29) it is stated that *the affliction of an hour maketh one forget great delights*. Therefore pain, instead of taking away, increases the faculty of learning.

*Obj.* 3. Further, inward sorrow surpasses outward pain, as stated above (Q. XXXV., A. 7). But man can learn while sorrowful. Much more, therefore, can he learn while in bodily pain.

*On the contrary,* Augustine says (*Soliloq.* i. 12): *Although during those days I was tormented with a violent tooth-ache,— I was not able to turn over in my mind other things than those I had already learnt; and as to learning anything, I was quite unequal to it, because it required undivided attention.*

*I answer that,* Since all the powers of the soul are rooted in the one essence of the soul, it must needs happen, when the intention of the soul is strongly drawn towards the action of one power, that it is withdrawn from the action of another power: because the soul, being one, can only have one intention. The result is that if one thing draws upon itself the entire intention of the soul, or a great portion thereof, anything else requiring considerable attention is incompatible therewith.

Now it is evident that sensible pain above all draws the soul's attention to itself; because it is natural for each thing to tend wholly to repel whatever is contrary to it, as may be observed even in natural things. It is likewise evident that in order to learn anything new, we require study and effort with a strong intention, as is clearly stated in Prov. ii. 4, 5: *If thou shalt seek* wisdom *as money, and shall dig for her as for a treasure, then shalt thou understand learning* (Vulg.,—*the fear of the Lord*). Consequently if the pain be acute, man is prevented at the time from learning anything: indeed it can be so acute, that, as long as it lasts, a man is unable to give his attention even to that which he knew already.—However a difference is to be observed according to the difference of love that a man has for learning or for considering: because the greater his love, the more will he retain the intention of his mind so as to prevent it from turning entirely to the pain.

*Reply Obj.* 1. Moderate sorrow, that does not cause the mind to wander, can conduce to the acquisition of learning especially in regard to those things by which a man hopes to be freed from sorrow. And thus, *in the tribulation of murmuring*, men are more apt to be taught of God.

*Reply Obj.* 2. Both pleasure and pain, in so far as they draw upon themselves the soul's intention, hinder the reason from the act of consideration, wherefore it is stated in *Ethic.* vii. 11 that *in the moment of sexual pleasure, a man cannot understand anything.* Nevertheless pain attracts the soul's intention more than pleasure does: thus we observe in natural things that the action of a natural body is more intense in regard to its contrary; for instance, hot water is more accessible to the action of cold, and in consequence freezes harder. If therefore pain or sorrow be moderate, it can conduce accidentally to the facility of learning, in so far as it takes away an excess of pleasure. But, of itself, it is a hindrance; and if it be intense, it prevents it altogether.

*Reply Obj.* 3. External pain arises from hurt done to the body, so that it involves bodily transmutation more than inward sorrow does: and yet the latter is greater in regard to the formal element of pain, which belongs to the soul. Consequently bodily pain is a greater hindrance to contemplation which requires complete repose, than inward sorrow is. Nevertheless if inward sorrow be very intense, it attracts the intention, so that man is unable to learn anything for the first time: wherefore on account of sorrow Gregory interrupted his commentary on Ezechiel (*Hom.* xxii *in Ezechiel*).

### SECOND ARTICLE.

#### WHETHER THE EFFECT OF SORROW OR PAIN IS TO BURDEN THE SOUL ?

*We proceed thus to the Second Article :—*

*Objection* 1. It would seem that it is not an effect of sorrow to burden the soul. For the Apostle says (2 Cor. vii. 11): *Behold this self-same thing, that you were made sorrowful according to God, how great carefulness it worketh in you : yea defence, yea indignation,* etc. Now carefulness and indignation imply that the soul is uplifted, which is contrary to being depressed. Therefore depression is not an effect of sorrow.

*Obj.* 2. Further, sorrow is contrary to pleasure. But the effect of pleasure is expansion: the opposite of which is not depression but contraction. Therefore depression should not be reckoned as an effect of sorrow.

*Obj.* 3. Further, sorrow consumes those who are afflicted therewith, as may be gathered from the words of the Apostle (2 Cor. ii. 7): *Lest perhaps such an one be swallowed up with overmuch sorrow.* But that which is depressed is not consumed; nay, it is weighed down by something heavy, whereas that which is consumed enters within the consumer. Therefore depression should not be reckoned an effect of sorrow.

*On the contrary,* Gregory of Nyssa\* and Damascene (*De Fide Orthod.* ii, 14) speak of *depressing sorrow.*

*I answer that,* The effects of the soul's passions are sometimes named metaphorically, from a likeness to sensible bodies: for the reason that the movements of the animal appetite are like the inclinations of the natural appetite. And in this way fervour is ascribed to love, expansion to pleasure, and depression to sorrow. For a man is said to be depressed, through being hindered in his own movement by some weight. Now it is evident from what has been said above (Q. XXIII., A. 4; Q. XXV., A. 4; Q. XXXVI., A. 1) that sorrow is caused by a present evil: and this evil, from the very fact that it is repugnant to the movement of the will, depresses the soul, inasmuch as it hinders it from enjoying that which it wishes to enjoy. And if the evil which is the cause of sorrow be not so strong as to deprive one of the hope of avoiding it, although the soul be depressed in so far as, for the present, it fails to grasp that which it craves for; yet it retains the movement whereby to repulse that evil. If, on the other hand, the strength of the evil be such as to exclude the hope of evasion, then even the interior movement of the afflicted soul is absolutely hindered, so that it cannot turn aside either this way or

---

\* Nemesius,—*De Nat. Hom.* xix.

that. Sometimes even the external movement of the body is paralyzed, so that a man becomes completely stupefied.

*Reply Obj.* 1. That uplifting of the soul ensues from the sorrow which is according to God, because it brings with it the hope of the forgiveness of sin.

*Reply Obj.* 2. As far as the movement of the appetite is concerned, contraction and depression amount to the same: because the soul, through being depressed so as to be unable to attend freely to outward things, withdraws to itself, closing itself up as it were.

*Reply Obj.* 3. Sorrow is said to consume man, when the force of the afflicting evil is such as to shut out all hope of evasion: and thus also it both depresses and consumes at the same time. For certain things, taken metaphorically, imply one another, which taken literally, appear to exclude one another.

### Third Article.

#### WHETHER SORROW OR PAIN WEAKENS ALL ACTIVITY ?

*We proceed thus to the Third Article :—*

*Objection* 1. It would seem that sorrow does not weaken all activity. Because carefulness is caused by sorrow, as is clear from the passage of the Apostle quoted above (A. 2, *Obj.* 1). But carefulness conduces to good work: wherefore the Apostle says (2 Tim. ii. 15): *Carefully study to present thyself . . . a workman that needeth not to be ashamed.* Therefore sorrow is not a hindrance to work, but helps one to work well.

*Obj.* 2. Further, sorrow causes desire in many cases, as stated in *Ethic.* vii. 14. But desire causes intensity of action. Therefore sorrow does too.

*Obj.* 3. Further, as some actions are proper to the joyful, so are others proper to the sorrowful; for instance, to mourn. Now a thing is improved by that which is suitable to it. Therefore certain actions are not hindered but improved by reason of sorrow.

*On the contrary,* The Philosopher says (*Ethic.* x. 4) that *pleasure perfects action*, whereas on the other hand, *sorrow hinders it* (*ibid.* 5).

*I answer that*, As stated above (A. 2), sorrow at times does not depress or consume the soul, so as to shut out all movement, internal or external; but certain movements are sometimes caused by sorrow itself. Accordingly action stands in a twofold relation to sorrow. First, as being the object of sorrow: and thus sorrow hinders any action: for we never do that which we do with sorrow, so well as that which we do with pleasure, or without sorrow. The reason for this is that the will is the cause of human actions: and consequently when we do something that gives pain, the action must of necessity be weakened in consequence.—Secondly, action stands in relation to sorrow, as to its principle and cause: and such action must needs be improved by sorrow: thus the more one sorrows on account of a certain thing, the more one strives to shake off sorrow, provided there is a hope of shaking it off: otherwise no movement or action would result from that sorrow.

From what has been said the replies to the objections are evident.

## FOURTH ARTICLE.

### WHETHER SORROW IS MORE HARMFUL TO THE BODY THAN THE OTHER PASSIONS OF THE SOUL ?

*We proceed thus to the Fourth Article :—*

*Objection* 1. It would seem that sorrow is not most harmful to the body. For sorrow has a spiritual existence in the soul. But those things which have only a spiritual existence do not cause a transmutation in the body: as is evident with regard to the images of colours, which images are in the air and do not give colour to bodies. Therefore sorrow is not harmful to the body.

*Obj.* 2. Further if it be harmful to the body, this can only be due to its having a bodily transmutation in conjunction with it. But bodily transmutation takes place in all the passions of the soul, as stated above (Q. XXII., AA. 1, 3).

Therefore sorrow is not more harmful to the body than the other passions of the soul.

*Obj.* 3. Further, the Philosopher says (*Ethic.* vii. 3) that *anger and desire drive some to madness*: which seems to be a very great harm, since reason is the most excellent thing in man.   Moreover, despair seems to be more harmful than sorrow; for it is the cause of sorrow.   Therefore sorrow is not more harmful to the body than the other passions of the soul.

*On the contrary,* It is written (Prov. xvii. 22): *A joyful mind maketh age flourishing: a sorrowful spirit drieth up the bones :* and (*ibid.* xxv. 20): *As a moth doth by a garment, and a worm by the wood : so the sadness of a man consumeth the heart :* and (Ecclus. xxxviii. 19): *Of sadness cometh death.*

*I answer that,* Of all the soul's passions, sorrow is most harmful to the body.   The reason of this is because sorrow is repugnant to man's life in respect of the species of its movement, and not merely in respect of its measure or quantity, as is the case with the other passions of the soul. For man's life consists in a certain movement, which flows from the heart to the other parts of the body: and this movement is befitting to human nature according to a certain fixed measure.   Consequently if this movement goes beyond the right measure, it will be repugnant to man's life in respect of the measure of quantity; but not in respect of its specific character: whereas if this movement be hindered in its progress, it will be repugnant to life in respect of its species.

Now it must be noted that, in all the passions of the soul, the bodily transmutation which is their material element, is in conformity with and in proportion to the appetitive movement, which is the formal element: just as in everything matter is proportionate to form.   Consequently those passions that imply a movement of the appetite in pursuit of something, are not repugnant to the vital movement as regards its species, but they may be repugnant thereto as regards its measure: such are love, joy, desire and the like; wherefore these passions conduce to the well-being of the body; though, if they be excessive, they may be harmful to it.—On the other hand, those passions which denote in the appetite a movement of flight or contraction, are repugnant to the vital movement, not only as regards its measure, but also as regards its species; wherefore they are simply harmful: such are fear and despair, and above all sorrow which depresses the soul by reason of a present evil, which makes a stronger impression than future evil.

*Reply Obj.* 1. Since the soul naturally moves the body, the spiritual movement of the soul is naturally the cause of bodily transmutation. Nor is there any parallel with spiritual images, because they are not naturally ordained to move such other bodies as are not naturally moved by the soul.

*Reply Obj.* 2. Other passions imply a bodily transmutation which is specifically in conformity with the vital move_ment: whereas sorrow implies a transmutation that is repugnant thereto, as stated above.

*Reply Obj.* 3. A lesser cause suffices to hinder the use of reason, than to destroy life: since we observe that many ailments deprive one of the use of reason, before depriving one of life. Nevertheless fear and anger cause very great harm to the body, by reason of the sorrow which they imply, and which arises from the absence of the thing desired. Moreover sorrow too sometimes deprives man of the use of reason: as may be seen in those who through sorrow become a prey to melancholy or madness.

# QUESTION XXXVIII.

## OF THE REMEDIES OF SORROW OR PAIN.

### (*In Five Articles*.)

WE must now consider the remedies of pain or sorrow: under which head there are five points of inquiry: (1) Whether pain or sorrow is assuaged by every pleasure? (2) Whether it is assuaged by weeping? (3) Whether it is assuaged by the sympathy of friends? (4) Whether it is assuaged by contemplating the truth? (5) Whether it is assuaged by sleep and baths?

### FIRST ARTICLE.

#### WHETHER PAIN OR SORROW IS ASSUAGED BY EVERY PLEASURE?

*We proceed thus to the First Article :—*

*Objection* 1. It would seem that not every pleasure assuages every pain or sorrow. For pleasure does not assuage sorrow, save in so far as it is contrary to it: for *remedies work by contraries* (*Ethic*. ii. 3). But not every pleasure is contrary to every sorrow; as stated above (Q. XXXV., A. 4). Therefore not every pleasure assuages every sorrow.

*Obj*. 2. Further, that which causes sorrow does not assuage it. But some pleasures cause sorrow; since, as stated in *Ethic*. ix. 4, *the wicked man feels pain at having been pleased*. Therefore not every pleasure assuages sorrow.

*Obj*. 3. Further, Augustine says (*Conf*. iv. 7) that he fled from his country, where he had been wont to associate with his friend, now dead: *for so should his eyes look for him less, where they were not wont to see him*. Hence we may gather that those things which united us to our dead or absent friends, become burdensome to us when we mourn their death or absence. But nothing united us more than the pleasures we enjoyed in common. Therefore these very pleasures become burdensome to us when we mourn. Therefore not every pleasure assuages every sorrow.

*On the contrary,* The Philosopher says (*Ethic.* vii. 14) that *sorrow is driven forth by pleasure, both by a contrary pleasure and by any other, provided it be intense.*

*I answer that,* As is evident from what has been said above (Q. XXIII., A. 4), pleasure is a kind of repose of the appetite in a suitable good; while sorrow arises from something unsuited to the appetite. Consequently in movements of the appetite pleasure is to sorrow, what, in bodies, repose is to weariness, which is due to a non-natural transmutation; for sorrow itself implies a certain weariness or ailing of the appetitive faculty. Therefore just as all repose of the body brings relief to any kind of weariness, ensuing from any non-natural cause; so every pleasure brings relief by assuaging any kind of sorrow, due to any cause whatever.

*Reply Obj.* 1. Although not every pleasure is specifically contrary to every sorrow, yet it is generically, as stated above (Q. XXXV., A. 4). And consequently, on the part of the disposition of the subject, any sorrow can be assuaged by any pleasure.

*Reply Obj.* 2. The pleasures of wicked men are not a cause of sorrow while they are enjoyed, but afterwards: that is to say, in so far as wicked men repent of those things in which they took pleasure. This sorrow is healed by contrary pleasures.

*Reply Obj.* 3. When there are two causes inclining to contrary movements, each hinders the other; yet the one which is stronger and more persistent, prevails in the end. Now when a man is made sorrowful by those things in which he took pleasure in common with a deceased or absent friend, there are two causes producing contrary movements. For the thought of the friend's death or absence, inclines him to sorrow: whereas the present good inclines him to pleasure. Consequently each is modified by the other. And yet, since the perception of the present moves more strongly than the memory of the past, and since love of self is more persistent than love of another; hence it is that, in the end, the pleasure drives out the sorrow. Wherefore a little further on (*loc. cit.*, 8) Augustine says that his *sorrow gave way to his former pleasures.*

## SECOND ARTICLE.

### WHETHER PAIN OR SORROW IS ASSUAGED BY TEARS?

*We proceed thus to the Second Article :—*

*Objection* 1. It would seem that tears do not assuage sorrow. Because no effect diminishes its cause. But tears or groans are an effect of sorrow. Therefore they do not diminish sorrow.

*Obj.* 2. Further, just as tears or groans are an effect of sorrow, so laughter is an effect of joy. But laughter does not lessen joy. Therefore tears do not lessen sorrow.

*Obj.* 3. Further, when we weep, the evil that saddens us is present to the imagination. But the image of that which saddens us increases sorrow, just as the image of a pleasant thing adds to joy. Therefore it seems that tears do not assuage sorrow.

*On the contrary,* Augustine says (*Conf.* iv. 7) that when he mourned the death of his friend, *in groans and in tears alone did he find some little refreshment.*

*I answer that,* Tears and groans naturally assuage sorrow: and this for two reasons. First, because a hurtful thing hurts yet more if we keep it shut up, because the soul is more intent on it: whereas if it be allowed to escape, the soul's intention is dispersed as it were on outward things, so that the inward sorrow is lessened. This is why when men, burdened with sorrow, make outward show of their sorrow, by tears or groans or even by words, their sorrow is assuaged.—Secondly, because an action, that befits a man according to his actual disposition, is always pleasant to him. Now tears and groans are actions befitting a man who is in sorrow or pain; and consequently they become pleasant to him. Since then, as stated above (A. 1), every pleasure assuages sorrow or pain somewhat, it follows that sorrow is assuaged by weeping and groans.

*Reply Obj.* 1. This relation of the cause to the effect is opposed to the relation existing between the cause of sorrow and the sorrowing man. For every effect is suited to its cause, and consequently is pleasant to it; but the cause of sorrow is disagreeable to him that sorrows. Hence the effect of sorrow is not related to him that sorrows in the same way as the cause of sorrow is. For this reason sorrow is assuaged by its effect, on account of the aforesaid contrariety.

*Reply Obj.* 2. The relation of effect to cause is like the relation of the object of pleasure to him that takes pleasure in it: because in each case the one agrees with the other. Now every like thing increases its like. Therefore joy is increased by laughter and the other effects of joy: except they be excessive, in which case, accidentally, they lessen it.

*Reply Obj.* 3. The image of that which saddens us, considered in itself, has a natural tendency to increase sorrow: yet from the very fact that a man imagines himself to be doing that which is fitting according to his actual state, he feels a certain amount of pleasure. For the same reason if laughter escapes a man when he is so disposed that he thinks he ought to weep, he is sorry for it, as having done something unbecoming to him, as Cicero says (*De Tusc. Quaest.* iii. 27).

### THIRD ARTICLE.

#### WHETHER PAIN AND SORROW ARE ASSUAGED BY THE SYMPATHY OF FRIENDS?

*We proceed thus to the Third Article :—*

*Objection* 1. It would seem that the sorrow of sympathizing friends does not assuage our own sorrow. For contraries have contrary effects. Now as Augustine says (*Conf.* viii. 4), *when many rejoice together, each one has more exuberant joy, for they are kindled and inflamed one by the other.* Therefore,

in like manner, when many are sorrowful, it seems that
their sorrow is greater.

*Obj.* 2. Further, friendship demands mutual love, as
Augustine declares (*Conf.* iv. 9). But a sympathizing friend
is pained at the sorrow of his friend with whom he sympathizes. Consequently the pain of a sympathizing friend
becomes, to the friend in sorrow, a further cause of sorrow:
so that his pain being doubled his sorrow seems to increase.

*Obj.* 3. Further, sorrow arises from every evil affecting a
friend, as though it affected oneself: since *a friend is one's
other self* (*Ethic.* ix. 4, 9). But sorrow is an evil. Therefore
the sorrow of the sympathizing friend increases the sorrow
of the friend with whom he sympathizes.

*On the contrary,* The Philosopher says (*Ethic.* ix. 11) that
those who are in pain are consoled when their friends sym-
pathize with them.

*I answer that,* When one is in pain, it is natural that the
sympathy of a friend should afford consolation: whereof
the Philosopher indicates a twofold reason (*Ethic.* ix. *ibid.*).
The first is because, since sorrow has a depressing effect, it
is like a weight whereof we strive to unburden ourselves: so
that when a man sees others saddened by his own sorrow,
it seems as though others were bearing the burden with
him, striving, as it were, to lessen its weight; wherefore the
load of sorrow becomes lighter for him: something like what
occurs in the carrying of bodily burdens.—The second and
better reason is because when a man's friends condole with
him, he sees that he is loved by them, and this affords him
pleasure, as stated above (Q. XXXII., A. 5). Consequently,
since every pleasure assuages sorrow, as stated above
(A. 1), it follows that sorrow is mitigated by a sympathizing
friend.

*Reply Obj.* 1. In either case there is a proof of friendship,
viz., when a man rejoices with the joyful, and when he
sorrows with the sorrowful. Consequently each becomes an
object of pleasure by reason of its cause.

*Reply Obj.* 2. The friend's sorrow itself would be a cause

of sorrow: but consideration of its cause, viz., his love, gives rise rather to pleasure.

And this suffices for the reply to the Third Objection.

## Fourth Article.

### WHETHER PAIN AND SORROW ARE ASSUAGED BY THE CONTEMPLATION OF TRUTH ?

*We proceed thus to the Fourth Article :—*

*Objection* 1. It would seem that the contemplation of truth does not assuage sorrow. For it is written (Eccles i. 18): *He that addeth knowledge addeth also sorrow* (Vulg.,—*labour*). But knowledge pertains to the contemplation of truth. Therefore the contemplation of truth does not assuage sorrow.

*Obj.* 2. Further, the contemplation of truth belongs to the speculative intellect. But *the speculative intellect is not a principle of movement ;* as stated in *De Anima* iii. 11. Therefore, since joy and sorrow are movements of the soul, it seems that the contemplation of truth does not help to assuage sorrow.

*Obj.* 3. Further, the remedy for an ailment should be applied to the part which ails. But contemplation of truth is in the intellect. Therefore it does not assuage bodily pain, which is in the senses.

*On the contrary,* Augustine says (*Soliloq.* i. 12): *It seemed to me that if the light of that truth were to dawn on our minds, either I should not feel that pain, or at least that the pain would seem nothing to me.*

*I answer that,* As stated above (Q. III., A. 5), the greatest of all pleasures consists in the contemplation of truth. Now every pleasure assuages pain as stated above (A. 1): hence the contemplation of truth assuages pain or sorrow, and the more so, the more perfectly one is a lover of wisdom. And therefore in the midst of tribulations men rejoice in the contemplation of Divine things and of future Happiness, according to James i. 2: *My brethren, count it all joy, when you shall fall into divers temptations*: and, what is more, even in the midst of bodily tortures this joy is found; as the *martyr*

*Tiburtius, when he was walking barefoot on the burning coals, said : Methinks, I walk on roses, in the name of Jesus Christ.*\*

*Reply Obj. 1. He that addeth knowledge, addeth sorrow,* either on account of the difficulty and disappointment in the search of truth; or because knowledge makes man acquainted with many things that are contrary to his will. Accordingly, on the part of the things known, knowledge causes sorrow: but on the part of the contemplation of truth, it causes pleasure.

*Reply Obj. 2.* The speculative intellect does not move the mind on the part of the thing contemplated: but on the part of contemplation itself, which is man's good and naturally pleasant to him.

*Reply Obj. 3.* In the powers of the soul there is an overflow from the higher to the lower powers: and accordingly, the pleasure of contemplation, which is in the higher part, overflows so as to mitigate even that pain which is in the senses.

### FIFTH ARTICLE.

#### WHETHER PAIN AND SORROW ARE ASSUAGED BY SLEEP AND BATHS ?

*We proceed thus to the Fifth Article :—*

*Objection 1.* It would seem that sleep and baths do not assuage sorrow.   For sorrow is in the soul: whereas sleep and baths regard the body.   Therefore they do not conduce to the assuaging of sorrow.

*Obj. 2.* Further, the same effect does not seem to ensue from contrary causes.   But these, being bodily things, are incompatible with the contemplation of truth which is a cause of the assuaging of sorrow, as stated above (A. 4). Therefore sorrow is not mitigated by the like.

*Obj. 3.* Further, sorrow and pain, in so far as they affect the body, denote a certain transmutation of the heart. But such remedies as these seem to pertain to the outward

\* *Cf.* Dominican Breviary, August 11th, commemoration of S. Tiburtius.

senses and limbs, rather than to the interior disposition of the heart. Therefore they do not assuage sorrow.

*On the contrary*, Augustine says (*Conf.* ix. 12): *I had heard that the bath had its name** . . . *from the fact of its driving sadness from the mind.* And further on, he says: *I slept, and woke up again, and found my grief not a little assuaged:* and quotes the words from the hymn of Ambrose,† in which it is said that *Sleep restores the tired limbs to labour, refreshes the weary mind, and banishes sorrow.*

*I answer that*, As stated above (Q. XXXVII., A. 4), sorrow, by reason of its specific nature, is repugnant to the vital movement of the body; and consequently whatever restores the bodily nature to its due state of vital movement, is opposed to sorrow and assuages it.—Moreover such remedies, from the very fact that they bring nature back to its normal state, are causes of pleasure; for this is precisely in what pleasure consists, as stated above (Q. XXXI., A. 1). Therefore, since every pleasure assuages sorrow, sorrow is assuaged by suchlike bodily remedies.

*Reply Obj.* 1. The normal disposition of the body, so far as it is felt, is itself a cause of pleasure, and consequently assuages sorrow.

*Reply Obj.* 2. As stated above (Q. XXXI., A. 8), one pleasure hinders another; and yet every pleasure assuages sorrow. Consequently it is not unreasonable that sorrow should be assuaged by causes which hinder one another.

*Reply Obj.* 3. Every good disposition of the body reacts somewhat on the heart, which is the beginning and end of bodily movements, as stated in *De Causa Mot. Animal.* xi.

* *Balneum*, from the Greek βαλανεῖον.
† *Cf.* Sarum Breviary: First Sunday after the octave of the Epiphany, Hymn for first Vespers.

# QUESTION XXXIX.

## OF THE GOODNESS AND MALICE OF SORROW OR PAIN

### (*In Four Articles.*)

WE must now consider the goodness and malice of pain or sorrow: under which head there are four points of inquiry: (1) Whether all sorrow is evil? (2) Whether sorrow can be a virtuous good? (3) Whether it can be a useful good? (4) Whether bodily pain is the greatest evil?

## FIRST ARTICLE.

### WHETHER ALL SORROW IS EVIL?

*We proceed thus to the First Article:—*

*Objection* 1. It would seem that all sorrow is evil. For Gregory of Nyssa* says: *All sorrow is evil, from its very nature.* Now what is naturally evil, is evil always and everywhere. Therefore all sorrow is evil.

*Obj.* 2. Further, that which all, even the virtuous, avoid, is evil. But all avoid sorrow, even the virtuous, since as stated in *Ethic.* vii. 11, *though the prudent man does not aim at pleasure, yet he aims at avoiding sorrow.* Therefore sorrow is evil.

*Obj.* 3. Further, just as bodily evil is the object and cause of bodily pain, so spiritual evil is the object and cause of sorrow in the soul. But every bodily pain is a bodily evil. Therefore every spiritual sorrow is an evil of the soul.

*On the contrary,* Sorrow for evil is contrary to pleasure in evil. But pleasure in evil is evil: wherefore in condemnation of certain men, it is written (Prov. ii. 14), that *they are glad when they have done evil.* Therefore sorrow for evil is good.

* Nemesius, *De Nat. Hom.* xix.

*I answer that,* A thing may be good or evil in two ways: first considered simply and in itself; and thus all sorrow is an evil, because the mere fact of a man's appetite being uneasy about a present evil, is itself an evil, because it hinders the repose of the appetite in good.—Secondly, a thing is said to be good or evil, on the supposition of something else: thus shame is said to be good, on the supposition of a shameful deed done, as stated in *Ethic.* iv. 9. Accordingly, supposing the presence of something saddening or painful, it is a sign of goodness if a man is in sorrow or pain on account of this present evil. For if he were not to be in sorrow or pain, this could only be either because he feels it not, or because he does not reckon it as something unbecoming, both of which are manifest evils. Consequently it is a condition of goodness, that, supposing an evil to be present, sorrow or pain should ensue. Wherefore Augustine says (*Gen. ad lit.* viii. 14): *It is also a good thing that he sorrows for the good he has lost: for had not some good remained in his nature, he could not be punished by the loss of good.*—Because, however, in the science of Morals, we consider things individually,—for actions are concerned about individuals,—that which is good on some supposition, should be considered as good: just as that which is voluntary on some supposition, is judged to be voluntary, as stated in *Ethic.* iii. 1, and likewise above (Q. VI., A. 6).

*Reply Obj.* 1. Gregory of Nyssa* is speaking of sorrow on the part of the evil that causes it, but not on the part of the subject that feels and rejects the evil.—And from this point of view all shun sorrow, inasmuch as they shun evil: but they do not shun the perception and rejection of evil.—The same also applies to bodily pain: because the perception and rejection of bodily evil is the proof of the goodness of nature.

This suffices for the Replies to the Second and Third Objections.

* Nemesius.

## SECOND ARTICLE.

### WHETHER SORROW CAN BE A VIRTUOUS GOOD?

*We proceed thus to the Second Article :—*

*Objection* 1. It would seem that sorrow is not a virtuous good. For that which leads to hell is not a virtuous good. But, as Augustine says (*Gen. ad lit.* xii. 33), *Jacob seems to have feared lest he should be troubled overmuch by sorrow, and so, instead of entering into the rest of the blessed, be consigned to the hell of sinners.* Therefore sorrow is not a virtuous good.

*Obj.* 2. Further, the virtuous good is praiseworthy and meritorious. But sorrow lessens praise or merit: for the Apostle says (2 Cor. ix. 7): *Everyone, as he hath determined in his heart, not with sadness, or of necessity.* Therefore sorrow is not a virtuous good.

*Obj.* 3. Further, as Augustine says (*De Civ. Dei* xiv. 15), *sorrow is concerned about those things which happen against our will.* But not to will those things which are actually taking place, is to have a will opposed to the decree of God, to Whose providence whatever is done is subject. Since, then, conformity of the human to the Divine will is a condition of the rectitude of the will, as stated above (Q. XIX., A. 9), it seems that sorrow is incompatible with rectitude of the will, and that consequently it is not virtuous.

*On the contrary*, Whatever merits the reward of eternal life is virtuous. But such is sorrow; as is evident from Matth. v. 5: *Blessed are they that mourn, for they shall be comforted.* Therefore sorrow is a virtuous good.

*I answer that*, In so far as sorrow is good, it can be a virtuous good. For it has been said above (A. 1) that sorrow is a good inasmuch as it denotes perception and rejection of evil. These two things, as regards bodily pain, are a proof of the goodness of nature, to which it is due that the senses perceive, and that nature shuns, the harmful thing that causes pain. As regards interior sorrow, perception of the evil is sometimes due to a right judgment of reason; while the rejection of the evil is the act of the will, well disposed and detesting that evil. Now every virtuous good results from these two things, the rectitude of the reason and of the will. Wherefore it is evident that sorrow may be a virtuous good.

*Reply Obj.* 1. All the passions of the soul should be regulated according to the rule of reason, which is the root of the virtuous good: but excessive sorrow, of which Augustine is speaking, oversteps this rule, and therefore it fails to be a virtuous good.

*Reply Obj.* 2. Just as sorrow for an evil arises from a right will and reason, which detest the evil, so sorrow for a good is due to a perverse reason and will, which detest the good. Consequently such sorrow is an obstacle to the praise and merit of the virtuous good; for instance, when a man gives an alms sorrowfully.

*Reply Obj.* 3. Some things do actually happen, not because God wills, but because He permits them to happen—such as sins. Consequently a will that is opposed to sin, whether in oneself or in another, is not discordant from the Divine will.—Penal evils happen actually, even by God's will. But it is not necessary for the rectitude of his will, that man should will them in themselves: but only that he should not revolt against the order of Divine justice, as stated above (Q. XIX., A. 10).

## Third Article.

### WHETHER SORROW CAN BE A USEFUL GOOD?

*We proceed thus to the Third Article :—*

*Objection* 1. It would seem that sorrow cannot be a useful good. For it is written (*Ecclus.* xxx. 25): *Sadness hath killed many, and there is no profit in it.*

*Obj.* 2. Further, choice is of that which is useful to an end. But sorrow is not an object of choice; in fact, *a thing without sorrow is to be chosen rather than the same thing with sorrow* (*Topic.* iii. 2). Therefore sorrow is not a useful good.

*Obj.* 3. Further, *Everything is for the sake of its own operation*, as stated in *De Cœlo* ii. 3. But *sorrow hinders operation,* as stated in *Ethic.* x. 5.   Therefore sorrow is not a useful good.

*On the contrary*, The wise man seeks only that which is useful.   But according to Eccles. vii. 5, *the heart of the wise is where there is mourning, and the heart of fools where there is mirth*.   Therefore sorrow is useful.

*I answer that*, A twofold movement of the appetite ensues from a present evil.   One is that whereby the appetite is opposed to the present evil; and, in this respect, sorrow is of no use; because that which is present, cannot be not present.—The other movement arises in the appetite to the effect of avoiding or expelling the saddening evil: and, in this respect, sorrow is of use, if it be for something which ought to be avoided.   Because there are two reasons for which it may be right to avoid a thing.   First, because it should be avoided in itself, on account of its being contrary to good; for instance, sin.   Wherefore sorrow for sin is useful as inducing man to avoid sin: hence the Apostle says (2 Cor. vii. 9): *I am glad : not because you were made sorrowful, but because you were made sorrowful unto penance.* —Secondly, a thing is to be avoided, not as though it were evil in itself, but because it is an occasion of evil; either through one's being attached to it, and loving it too much, or through one's being thrown headlong thereby into an evil, as is evident in the case of temporal goods.   And, in this respect, sorrow for temporal goods may be useful; according to Eccles. vii. 3: *It is better to go to the house of mourning, than to the house of feasting : for in that we are put in mind of the end of all.*

Moreover, sorrow for that which ought to be avoided is always useful, since it adds another motive for avoiding it. Because the very evil is in itself a thing to be avoided: while everyone avoids sorrow for its own sake, just as everyone seeks the good, and pleasure in the good.   Therefore just as pleasure in the good makes one seek the good more earnestly so sorrow for evil makes one avoid evil more eagerly.

*Reply Obj.* 1. This passage is to be taken as referring to excessive sorrow, which consumes the soul: for such sorrow paralyzes the soul, and hinders it from shunning evil, as stated above (Q. XXXVII., A. 2).

*Reply Obj.* 2. Just as any object of choice becomes less eligible by reason of sorrow, so that which ought to be shunned is still more to be shunned by reason of sorrow: and, in this respect, sorrow is useful.

*Reply Obj.* 3. Sorrow caused by an action hinders that action: but sorrow for the cessation of an action, makes one do it more earnestly.

## Fourth Article.

### WHETHER BODILY PAIN IS THE GREATEST EVIL ?

*We proceed thus to the Fourth Article :—*

*Objection* 1. It would seem that pain is the greatest evil. Because *the worst is contrary to the best* (*Ethic.* viii. 10). But a certain pleasure is the greatest good, viz., the pleasure of bliss. Therefore a certain pain is the greatest evil.

*Obj.* 2. Further, happiness is man's greatest good, because it is his last end. But man's Happiness consists in his *having whatever he will, and in willing naught amiss*, as stated above (Q. III., A. 4, *Obj.* 5; Q. V., A. 8, *Obj.* 3). Therefore man's greatest good consists in the fulfilment of his will. Now pain consists in something happening contrary to the will, as Augustine declares (*De Civ. Dei* xiv. 6, 15). Therefore pain is man's greatest evil.

*Obj.* 3. Further, Augustine argues thus (*Soliloq.* i. 12): *We are composed of two parts, i.e. of a soul and a body, whereof the body is the inferior. Now the sovereign good is the greatest good of the better part : while the supreme evil is the greatest evil of the inferior part. But wisdom is the greatest good of the soul ; while the worst thing in the body is pain. Therefore man's greatest good is to be wise : while his greatest evil is to suffer pain.*

*On the contrary*, Guilt is a greater evil than punishment as was stated in the First Part (Q. XLVIII., A. 6). But sorrow or pain belongs to the punishment of sin, just as the enjoyment of changeable things is an evil of guilt. For

Augustine says (*De Vera Relig.* xii.): *What is pain of the soul, except for the soul to be deprived of that which it was wont to enjoy, or had hoped to enjoy? And this is all that is called evil, i.e. sin, and the punishment of sin.* Therefore sorrow or pain is not man's greatest evil.

*I answer that,* It is impossible for any sorrow or pain to be man's greatest evil. For all sorrow or pain is either for something that is truly evil, or for something that is apparently evil, but good in reality. Now pain or sorrow for that which is truly evil cannot be the greatest evil: for there is something worse, namely, either not to reckon as evil that which is really evil, or not to reject it. Again, sorrow or pain, for that which is apparently evil, but really good, cannot be the greatest evil, for it would be worse to be altogether separated from that which is truly good. Hence it is impossible for any sorrow or pain to be man's greatest evil.

*Reply Obj.* 1. Pleasure and sorrow have two good points in common: namely, a true judgment concerning good and evil; and the right order of the will in approving of good and rejecting evil. Thus it is clear that in pain or sorrow there is a good, by the removal of which they become worse: and yet there is not an evil in every pleasure, by the removal of which the pleasure is better. Consequently, a pleasure can be man's highest good, in the way above stated (Q. XXXIV., A. 3): whereas sorrow cannot be man's greatest evil.

*Reply Obj.* 2. The very fact of the will being opposed to evil is a good. And for this reason, sorrow or pain cannot be the greatest evil; because it has an admixture of good.

*Reply Obj.* 3. That which harms the better thing is worse than that which harms the worse. Now a thing is called evil *because it harms*, as Augustine says (*Enchirid.* xii.). Therefore that which is an evil to the soul is a greater evil than that which is an evil to the body. Therefore this argument does not prove: nor does Augustine give it as his own, but as taken from another.*

* Cornelius Celsus.

# QUESTION XL.

## OF THE IRASCIBLE PASSIONS, AND FIRST, OF HOPE AND DESPAIR.

### (*In Eight Articles*.)

WE must now consider the irascible passions: (1) Hope and despair; (2) Fear and daring; (3) Anger. Under the first head there are eight points of inquiry: (1) Whether hope is the same as desire or cupidity? (2) Whether hope is in the apprehensive, or in the appetitive faculty? (3) Whether hope is in dumb animals? (4) Whether despair is contrary to hope? (5) Whether experience is a cause of hope? (6) Whether hope abounds in young men and drunkards? (7) Concerning the order of hope to love? (8) Whether hope conduces to action?

### FIRST ARTICLE.

#### WHETHER HOPE IS THE SAME AS DESIRE OR CUPIDITY?

*We proceed thus to the First Article :—*

*Objection* 1. It would seem that hope is the same as desire or cupidity. Because hope is reckoned as one of the four principal passions. But Augustine in setting down the four principal passions puts cupidity in the place of hope (*De Civ. Dei* xiv. 3, 7). Therefore hope is the same as cupidity or desire.

*Obj.* 2. Further, passions differ according to their objects. But the object of hope is the same as the object of cupidity or desire, viz., the future good. Therefore hope is the same as cupidity or desire.

*Obj.* 3. If it be said that hope, in addition to desire, denotes

455

the possibility of obtaining the future good; on the contrary, whatever is accidental to the object does not make a different species of passion. But possibility of acquisition is accidental to a future good, which is the object of cupidity or desire, and of hope. Therefore hope does not differ specifically from desire or cupidity.

*On the contrary*, To different powers belong different species of passions. But hope is in the irascible power; whereas desire or cupidity is in the concupiscible. Therefore hope differs specifically from desire or cupidity.

*I answer that*, The species of a passion is taken from the object. Now, in the object of hope, we may note four conditions. First, that it is something good; since, properly speaking, hope regards only the good; in this respect, hope differs from fear, which regards evil.—Secondly, that it is future; for hope does not regard that which is present and already possessed: in this respect, hope differs from joy which regards a present good.—Thirdly, that it must be something arduous and difficult to obtain, for we do not speak of any one hoping for trifles, which are in one's power to have at any time: in this respect, hope differs from desire or cupidity, which regards the future good absolutely: wherefore it belongs to the concupiscible, while hope belongs to the irascible faculty.—Fourthly, that this difficult thing is something possible to obtain: for one does not hope for that which one cannot get at all: and, in this respect, hope differs from despair. It is therefore evident that hope differs from desire, as the irascible passions differ from the concupiscible. For this reason, moreover, hope presupposes desire: just as all the irascible passions presuppose the passions of the concupiscible faculty, as stated above (Q. XXV., A. 1).

*Reply Obj*. 1. Augustine mentions desire instead of hope, because each regards future good; and because the good which is not arduous is reckoned as nothing: thus implying that desire seems to tend chiefly to the arduous good, to which hope tends likewise.

*Reply Obj*. 2. The object of hope is the future good considered, not absolutely, but as arduous and difficult of attainment, as stated above.

*Reply Obj.* 3. The object of hope adds not only possibility to the object of desire, but also difficulty: and this makes hope belong to another power, viz. the irascible, which regards something difficult, as stated in the First Part (Q. LXXXI., A. 2). Moreover, possibility and impossibility are not altogether accidental to the object of the appetitive power: because the appetite is a principle of movement; and nothing is moved to anything except under the aspect of being possible; for no one is moved to that which he reckons impossible to get. Consequently hope differs from despair according to the difference of possible and impossible.

## SECOND ARTICLE.

### WHETHER HOPE IS IN THE APPREHENSIVE OR IN THE APPETITIVE POWER ?

*We proceed thus to the Second Article :—*

*Objection* 1. It would seem that hope belongs to the cognitive power. Because hope, seemingly, is a kind of awaiting; for the Apostle says (Rom. viii. 25): *If we hope for that which we see not ; we wait for it with patience.* But awaiting seems to belong to the cognitive power, which we exercise by *looking out.* Therefore hope belongs to the cognitive power.

*Obj.* 2. Further, apparently hope is the same as confidence; hence when a man hopes he is said to be confident, as though to hope and to be confident were the same thing. But confidence, like faith, seems to belong to the cognitive power. Therefore hope does too.

*Obj.* 3. Further, certainty is a property of the cognitive power. But certainty is ascribed to hope. Therefore hope belongs to the cognitive power.

*On the contrary,* Hope regards good, as stated above (A. 1). Now good, as such, is not the object of the cognitive, but of the appetitive power. Therefore hope belongs, not to the cognitive, but to the appetitive power.

*I answer that,* Since hope denotes a certain stretching out of the appetite towards good, it evidently belongs to the appetitive power; since movement towards things belongs properly to the appetite: whereas the action of the cognitive power is accomplished not by the movement of the knower towards things, but rather according as the things known are in the knower. But since the cognitive power moves the appetite, by presenting its object to it; there arise in the appetite various movements according to various aspects of the apprehended object. For the apprehension of good gives rise to one kind of movement in the appetite, while the apprehension of evil gives rise to another: in like manner various movements arise from the apprehension of something present and of something future; of something considered absolutely, and of something considered as arduous; of something possible, and of something impossible. And accordingly hope is a movement of the appetitive power ensuing from the apprehension of a future good, difficult but possible to obtain; namely, a stretching forth of the appetite to such a good.

*Reply Obj.* 1. Since hope regards a possible good, there arises in man a twofold movement of hope; for a thing may be possible to him in two ways, viz. by his own power, or by another's. Accordingly when a man hopes to obtain something by his own power, he is not said to wait for it, but simply to hope for it. But, properly speaking, he is said to await that which he hopes to get by another's help as though to await (*exspectare*) implied keeping one's eyes on another (*ex alio spectare*), in so far as the apprehensive power, by going ahead, not only keeps its eye on the good which man intends to get, but also on the thing by whose power he hopes to get it; according to Ecclus. li. 10: *I looked for the succour of men.* Wherefore the movement of hope is sometimes called expectation, on account of the preceding inspection of the cognitive power.

*Reply Obj.* 2. When a man desires a thing and reckons that he can get it, he believes that he will get it; and from this belief which precedes in the cognitive power, the ensuing movement in the appetite is called confidence. Because the movement of the appetite takes its name from the knowledge that precedes it, as an effect from a cause which is better known; for the apprehensive power knows its own act better than that of the appetite.

*Reply Obj.* 3. Certainty is ascribed to the movement, not only of the sensitive, but also of the natural appetite; thus we say that a stone is certain to tend downwards. This is owing to the inerrancy which the movement of the sensitive or even natural appetite derives from the certainty of the knowledge that precedes it.

### THIRD ARTICLE.

#### WHETHER HOPE IS IN DUMB ANIMALS?

*We proceed thus to the Third Article :—*

*Objection* 1. It would seem that there is no hope in dumb animals. Because hope is for some future good, as Damascene says (*De Fide Orthod.* ii. 12). But knowledge of the future is not in the competency of dumb animals, whose knowledge is confined to the senses and does not extend to the future. Therefore there is no hope in dumb animals.

*Obj.* 2. Further, the object of hope is a future good, possible of attainment. But possible and impossible are differences of the true and the false, which are only in the mind, as the Philosopher states (*Metaph.* vi. 4). Therefore there is no hope in dumb animals, since they have no mind.

*Obj.* 3. Further, Augustine says (*Gen. ad lit.* ix. 14) that *animals are moved by the things that they see.* But hope is of things unseen: *for what a man seeth, why doth he hope for?* (Rom. viii. 24). Therefore there is no hope in dumb animals.

*On the contrary*, Hope is an irascible passion. But the irascible faculty is in dumb animals. Therefore hope is also.

*I answer that*, The internal passions of animals can be gathered from their outward movements: from which it is clear that hope is in dumb animals. For if a dog see a hare, or a hawk see a bird, too far off, it makes no movement towards it, as having no hope to catch it: whereas, if it be near, it makes a movement towards it, as being in hopes of catching it. Because, as stated above (Q. I., A. 2; Q. XXVI., A. 1; Q. XXXV., A. 1), the sensitive appetite of dumb animals, and likewise the natural appetite of insensible things, result from the apprehension of an intellect, just as the appetite of the intellectual nature, which is called the will. But there is a difference, in that the will is moved by an apprehension of the intellect in the same subject; whereas the movement of the natural appetite results from the apprehension of the separate Intellect, Who is the Author of nature; as does also the sensitive appetite of dumb animals, who act from a certain natural instinct. Consequently, in the actions of irrational animals and of other natural things, we observe a procedure which is similar to that which we observe in the actions of art: and in this way hope and despair are in dumb animals.

*Reply Obj.* 1. Although dumb animals do not know the future, yet an animal is moved by its natural instinct to something future, as though it foresaw the future. Because this instinct is planted in them by the Divine Intellect that foresees the future.

*Reply Obj.* 2. The object of hope is not the possible as differentiating the true, for thus the possible ensues from the relation of a predicate to a subject. The object of hope is the possible as compared to a power. For such is the division of the possible given in *Metaph.* v. 12, i.e., into the two kinds we have just mentioned.

*Reply Obj.* 3. Although the thing which is future does not come under the object of sight; nevertheless through seeing something present, an animal's appetite is moved to seek or avoid something future.

## Fourth Article.

### WHETHER DESPAIR IS CONTRARY TO HOPE?

*We proceed thus to the Fourth Article :—*

*Objection* 1. It would seem that despair is not contrary to hope. Because *to one thing there is one contrary* (*Metaph.* x.

5). But fear is contrary to hope. Therefore despair is not contrary to hope.

*Obj.* 2. Further, contraries seem to bear on the same thing. But hope and despair do not bear on the same thing: since hope regards the good, whereas despair arises from some evil that is in the way of obtaining good. Therefore hope is not contrary to despair.

*Obj.* 3. Further, movement is contrary to movement; while repose is in opposition to movement as a privation thereof. But despair seems to imply immobility rather than movement. Therefore it is not contrary to hope, which implies movement of stretching out towards the hoped-for good.

*On the contrary,* The very name of despair (*desperatio*) implies that it is contrary to hope (*spes*).

*I answer that,* As stated above (Q. XXIII., A. 2), there is a twofold contrariety of movements. One is in respect of approach to contrary terms: and this contrariety alone is to be found in the concupiscible passions, for instance between love and hatred. The other is according to approach and withdrawal with regard to the same term; and is to be found in the irascible passions, as stated above (*loc. cit.*). Now the object of hope, which is the arduous good, has the character of a principle of attraction, if it be considered in the light of something attainable; and thus hope tends thereto, for it denotes a kind of approach. But in so far as it is considered as unobtainable, it has the character of a principle of repulsion, because, as stated in *Ethic.* iii. 3, *when men come to an impossibility they disperse.* And this is how despair stands in regard to this object, wherefore it implies a movement of withdrawal: and consequently it is contrary to hope, as withdrawal is to approach.

*Reply Obj.* 1. Fear is contrary to hope, because their objects, *i.e.* good and evil, are contrary: for this contrariety is found in the irascible passions, according as they ensue from the passions of the concupiscible. But despair is contrary to hope, only by contrariety of approach and withdrawal.

*Reply Obj.* 2. Despair does not regard evil as such; sometimes, however, it regards evil accidentally, as making the difficult good impossible to obtain.  But it can arise from the mere excess of good.

*Reply Obj.* 3. Despair implies not only privation of hope, but also a recoil from the thing desired, by reason of its being esteemed impossible to get.  Hence despair, like hope, presupposes desire; because we neither hope for nor despair of that which we do not desire to have.  For this reason, too, each of them regards the good, which is the object of desire.

## Fifth Article.

### WHETHER EXPERIENCE IS A CAUSE OF HOPE ?

*We proceed thus to the Fifth Article :—*

*Objection* 1. It would seem that experience is not a cause of hope.  Because experience belongs to the cognitive power; wherefore the Philosopher says (*Ethic.* ii. 1) that *intellectual virtue needs experience and time.*  But hope is not in the cognitive power, but in the appetite, as stated above (A. 2). Therefore experience is not a cause of hope.

*Obj.* 2. Further, the Philosopher says (*Rhet.* ii. 13) that *the old are slow to hope, on account of their experience;* whence it seems to follow that experience causes want of hope.  But the same cause is not productive of opposites.  Therefore experience is not a cause of hope.

*Obj.* 3. Further, the Philosopher says (*De Cœlo* ii. 5) that *to have something to say about everything, without leaving anything out, is sometimes a proof of folly.*  But to attempt everything seems to point to great hopes; while folly arises from inexperience.  Therefore inexperience, rather than experience, seems to be a cause of hope.

*On the contrary,* The Philosopher says (*Ethic.* iii. 8) *some are hopeful, through having been victorious often and over many opponents*: which seems to pertain to experience.  Therefore experience is a cause of hope.

*I answer that,* As stated above (A. 1), the object of hope is a future good, difficult but possible to obtain.  Consequently a thing may be a cause of hope, either because it makes something possible to a man: or because it makes him think something possible. In the first way hope is caused by everything that increases a man's power; *e.g.* riches, strength, and, among others, experience: since by experience man acquires the faculty of doing something easily, and the result of this is hope. Wherefore Vegetius says (*De Re Milit.* i.): *No one fears to do that which he is sure of having learnt well.*

In the second way, hope is caused by everything that makes man think that he can obtain something: and thus both teaching and persuasion may be a cause of hope. And then again experience is a cause of hope, in so far as it makes him reckon something possible, which before his experience he looked upon as impossible.—However, in this way, experience can cause a lack of hope: because just as it makes a man think possible what he had previously thought impossible; so, conversely, experience makes a man consider as impossible that which hitherto he had thought possible. Accordingly experience causes hope in two ways, despair in one way: and for this reason we may say rather that it causes hope.

*Reply Obj.* 1. Experience in matters pertaining to action not only produces knowledge; it also causes a certain habit, by reason of custom, which renders the action easier. Moreover, the intellectual virtue itself adds to the power of acting with ease: because it shows something to be possible; and thus is a cause of hope.

*Reply Obj.* 2. The old are wanting in hope because of their experience, in so far as experience makes them think something impossible. Hence he adds (*ibid.*) that *many evils have befallen them.*

*Reply Obj.* 3. Folly and inexperience can be a cause of hope accidentally as it were, by removing the knowledge which would help one to judge truly a thing to be impossible. Wherefore inexperience is a cause of hope, for the same reason as experience causes lack of hope.

### SIXTH ARTICLE.

#### WHETHER HOPE ABOUNDS IN YOUNG MEN AND DRUNKARDS ?

*We proceed thus to the Sixth Article :—*

*Objection* 1. It would seem that youth and drunkenness are not causes of hope. Because hope implies certainty and steadiness; so much so that it is compared to an anchor (Heb. vi. 19). But young men and drunkards are wanting in steadiness; since their minds are easily changed. Therefore youth and drunkenness are not causes of hope.

*Obj.* 2. Further, as stated above (A. 5), the cause of hope is chiefly whatever increases one's power. But youth and drunkenness are united to weakness. Therefore they are not causes of hope.

*Obj.* 3. Further, experience is a cause of hope, as stated above (A. 5). But youth lacks experience. Therefore it is not a cause of hope.

*On the contrary*, The Philosopher says (*Ethic*. iii. 8) that *drunken men are hopeful*: and (*Rhet*. ii. 12) that *the young are full of hope*.

*I answer that*, Youth is a cause of hope for three reasons, as the Philosopher states in *Rhet*. ii. *ibid.*: and these three reasons may be gathered from the three conditions of the good which is the object of hope—namely, that it is future, arduous and possible, as stated above (A. 1). For youth has much of the future before it, and little of the past: and therefore since memory is of the past, and hope of the future, it has little to remember and lives very much in hope.— Again, youths, on account of the heat of their nature, are full of spirit; so that their heart expands: and it is owing to the heart being expanded that one tends to that which is arduous; wherefore youths are spirited and hopeful.—Likewise they who have not suffered defeat, nor had experience of obstacles to their efforts, are prone to count a thing possible to them. Wherefore youths, through inexperience of obstacles and of their own shortcomings, easily count a thing possible; and consequently are of good hope. Two of these causes are also in those who are in drink—viz., heat and high spirits, on account of wine, and heedlessness of dangers and shortcomings.—For the same reason all foolish and thoughtless persons attempt everything and are full of hope.

*Reply Obj.* 1. Although youths and men in drink lack steadiness in reality, yet they are steady in their own estimation, for they think that they will steadily obtain that which they hope for.

In like manner, in reply to the Second Objection, we must observe that young people and men in drink are indeed unsteady in reality: but, in their own estimation, they are capable, for they know not their shortcomings.

*Reply Obj.* 3. Not only experience, but also lack of experience, is, in some way, a cause of hope, as explained above, (A. 5 *ad* 3).

## Seventh Article.

### WHETHER HOPE IS A CAUSE OF LOVE ?

*We proceed thus to the Seventh Article :—*

*Objection* 1. It would seem that hope is not a cause of love. Because, according to Augustine (*De Civ. Dei* xiv. 7, 9), love is the first of the soul's emotions. But hope is an emotion of the soul. Therefore love precedes hope, and consequently hope does not cause love.

*Obj.* 2. Further, desire precedes hope. But desire is caused by love, as stated above (Q. XXV., A. 2). Therefore hope, too, follows love, and consequently is not its cause.

*Obj.* 3. Further, hope causes pleasure, as stated above (Q. XXXII., A. 3). But pleasure is only of the good that is loved. Therefore love precedes hope.

*On the contrary*, The gloss commenting on Matth. i. 2, *Abraham begot Isaac, and Isaac begot Jacob*, says, *i.e., faith begets hope, and hope begets charity*. But charity is love. Therefore love is caused by hope.

*I answer that,* Hope can regard two things. For it regards as its object, the good which one hopes for. But since the good we hope for is something difficult but possible to obtain; and since it happens sometimes that what is difficult becomes possible to us, not through ourselves but through others; hence it is that hope regards also that by which something becomes possible to us.

In so far, then, as hope regards the good we hope to get, it is caused by love: since we do not hope save for that which we desire and love.—But in so far as hope regards one through whom something becomes possible to us, love is caused by hope, and not vice versa. Because by the very fact that we hope that good will accrue to us through someone, we are moved towards him as to our own good; and thus we begin to love him. Whereas from the fact that we love someone we do not hope in him, except accidentally, that is, in so far as we think that he returns our love. Wherefore the fact of being loved by another makes us hope in him; but our love for him is caused by the hope we have in him.

Wherefore the Replies to the Objections are evident.

### Eighth Article.

#### WHETHER HOPE IS A HELP OR A HINDRANCE TO ACTION ?

*We proceed thus to the Eighth Article :*

*Objection* 1. It would seem that hope is not a help but a hindrance to action. Because hope implies security. But security begets negligence which hinders action. Therefore hope is a hindrance to action.

*Obj.* 2. Further, sorrow hinders action, as stated above (Q. XXXVII., A. 3). But hope sometimes causes sorrow: for it is written (Prov. xiii. 12): *Hope that is deferred afflicteth the soul.* Therefore hope hinders action.

*Obj.* 3. Further, despair is contrary to hope, as stated above (A. 4). But despair, especially in matters of war, conduces to action; for it is written (2 Kings ii. 26), that *it is dangerous to drive people to despair.* Therefore hope has a contrary effect, namely, by hindering action.

*On the contrary,* It is written (1 Cor. ix. 10) that *he that plougheth should plough in hope . . . to receive fruit*: and the same applies to all other actions.

*I answer that*, Hope of its very nature is a help to action by making it more intense: and this for two reasons. First, by reason of its object, which is a good, difficult but possible. For the thought of its being difficult arouses our attention; while the thought that it is possible is no drag on our effort. Hence it follows that by reason of hope man is intent on his action. Secondly, on account of its effect. Because hope, as stated above (Q. XXXII., A. 3), causes pleasure; which is a help to action, as stated above (Q. XXXIII., A. 4). Therefore hope is conducive to action.

*Reply Obj.* 1. Hope regards a good to be obtained; security regards an evil to be avoided. Wherefore security seems to be contrary to fear rather than to belong to hope. Yet security does not beget negligence, save in so far as it lessens the idea of difficulty: whereby it also lessens the character of hope: for the things in which a man fears no hindrance, are no longer looked upon as difficult.

*Reply Obj.* 2. Hope of itself causes pleasure; it is by accident that it causes sorrow, as stated above (Q. XXXII., A. 3 *ad* 2).

*Reply Obj.* 3. Despair threatens danger in war, on account of a certain hope that attaches to it. For they who despair of flight, strive less to fly, but hope to avenge their death: and therefore in this hope they fight the more bravely, and consequently prove dangerous to the foe.

# QUESTION XLI.

## OF FEAR, IN ITSELF.

### (*In Four Articles.*)

WE must now consider, in the first place, fear; and, secondly, daring.   With regard to fear, four things must be considered: (1) Fear, in itself; (2) Its object; (3) Its cause; (4) Its effect. Under the first head there are four points of inquiry: (1) Whether fear is a passion of the soul?   (2) Whether fear is a special passion?   (3) Whether there is a natural fear? (4) Of the species of fear.

## FIRST ARTICLE.

### WHETHER FEAR IS A PASSION OF THE SOUL?

*We proceed thus to the First Article :—*

*Objection* 1. It would seem that fear is not a passion of the soul.   For Damascene says (*De Fide Orthod.* iii. 23) that *fear is a power, by way of* συστολή—i.e., of contraction—*desirous of vindicating nature.*   But no virtue is a passion, as is proved in *Ethic.* ii. 5.   Therefore fear is not a passion.

*Obj.* 2. Further, every passion is an effect due to the presence of an agent.   But fear is not of something present, but of something future, as Damascene declares (*De Fide Orthod.* ii. 12).   Therefore fear is not a passion.

*Obj.* 3. Further, every passion of the soul is a movement of the sensitive appetite, in consequence of an apprehension of the senses.   But sense apprehends, not the future but the present.   Since, then, fear is of future evil, it seems that it is not a passion of the soul.

*On the contrary*, Augustine (*De Civ. Dei* xiv. 5 *sqq.*) reckons fear among the other passions of the soul.

*I answer that,* Among the other passions of the soul, after sorrow, fear chiefly has the character of passion. For as we have stated above (Q. XXII.), the notion of passion implies first of all a movement of a passive power—*i.e.*, of a power whose object is compared to it as its active principle: since passion is the effect of an agent. In this way, both *to feel* and *to understand* are passions. Secondly, more properly speaking, passion is a movement of the appetitive power; and more properly still, it is a movement of an appetitive power that has a bodily organ, such movement being accompanied by a bodily transmutation. And, again, most properly those movements are called passions, which imply some deterioration. Now it is evident that fear, since it regards evil, belongs to the appetitive power, which of itself regards good and evil. Moreover, it belongs to the sensitive appetite: for it is accompanied by a certain transmutation—*i.e.*, contraction—as Damascene says (*cf. Obj.* 1). Again, it implies relation to evil as overcoming, so to speak, some particular good. Wherefore it has most properly the character of passion; less, however, than sorrow, which regards the present evil: because fear regards future evil, which is not so strong a motive as present evil.

*Reply Obj.* 1. Virtue denotes a principle of action: wherefore, in so far as the interior movements of the appetitive faculty are principles of external action, they are called virtues. But the Philosopher denies that passion is a virtue by way of habit.

*Reply Obj.* 2. Just as the passion of a natural body is due to the bodily presence of an agent, so is the passion of the soul due to the agent being present to the soul, although neither corporally nor really present: that is to say, in so far as the evil which is really future, is present in the apprehension of the soul.

*Reply Obj.* 3. The senses do not apprehend the future: but from apprehending the present, an animal is moved by natural instinct to hope for a future good, or to fear a future evil.

## SECOND ARTICLE.

### WHETHER FEAR IS A SPECIAL PASSION?

*We proceed thus to the Second Article :—*

*Objection* 1. It would seem that fear is not a special passion. For Augustine says (QQ. LXXXIII., qu. 33) that *the man who is not distraught by fear, is neither harassed by desire, nor wounded by sickness*—i.e., sorrow—*nor tossed about in transports of empty joys.* Wherefore it seems that, if fear be set aside, all the other passions are removed. Therefore fear is not a special but a general passion.

*Obj.* 2. Further, the Philosopher says (*Ethic.* vi. 2) that *pursuit and avoidance in the appetite are what affirmation and denial are in the intellect.* But denial is nothing special in the intellect, as neither is affirmation, but something common to many. Therefore neither is avoidance anything special in the appetite. But fear is nothing but a kind of avoidance of evil. Therefore it is not a special passion.

*Obj.* 3. Further, if fear were a special passion, it would be chiefly in the irascible part. But fear is also in the concupiscible: since the Philosopher says (*Rhet.* ii. 5) that *fear is a kind of sorrow*; and Damascene says (*De Fide Orthod.* iii. 23) that fear is *a power of desire*: and both sorrow and desire are in the concupiscible faculty, as stated above (Q. XXIII., A. 4). Therefore fear is not a special passion, since it belongs to different powers.

*On the contrary,* Fear is condivided with the other passions of the soul, as is clear from Damascene (*De Fide Orthod.* ii. 12, 15).

*I answer that,* The passions of the soul derive their species from their objects: hence that is a special passion, which has a special object. Now fear has a special object, as hope has. For just as the object of hope is a future good, difficult but possible to obtain; so the object of fear is a future evil, difficult and irresistible. Consequently fear is a special passion of the soul.

*Reply Obj.* 1. All the passions of the soul arise from one

source, viz., love, wherein they are connected with one another. By reason of this connection, when fear is put aside, the other passions of the soul are dispersed; not, however, as though it were a general passion.

*Reply Obj.* 2. Not every avoidance in the appetite is fear, but avoidance of a special object, as stated. Wherefore, though avoidance be something common, yet fear is a special passion.

*Reply Obj.* 3. Fear is nowise in the concupiscible: for it regards evil, not absolutely, but as difficult or arduous, so as to be almost unavoidable. But since the irascible passions arise from the passions of the concupiscible faculty, and terminate therein, as stated above (Q. XXV., A. 1); hence it is that what belongs to the concupiscible is ascribed to fear. For fear is called sorrow, in so far as the object of fear causes sorrow when present: wherefore the Philosopher says (*loc. cit.*) that fear arises *from the representation of a future evil which is either corruptive or painful.* In like manner desire is ascribed by Damascene to fear, because just as hope arises from the desire of good, so fear arises from avoidance of evil; while avoidance of evil arises from the desire of good, as is evident from what has been said above (Q. XXV., A. 2; Q. XXIX., A. 2; Q. XXXVI., A. 2).

## THIRD ARTICLE.

### WHETHER THERE IS A NATURAL FEAR?

*We proceed thus to the Third Article :—*

*Objection* 1. It would seem that there is a natural fear. For Damascene says (*De Fide Orthod.* iii. 23) that *there is a natural fear, through the soul refusing to be severed from the body.*

*Obj.* 2. Further, fear arises from love, as stated above (A. 2 *ad* 1). But there is a natural love, as Dionysius states (*Div. Nom.* iv.). Therefore there is also a natural fear.

*Obj.* 3. Further, fear is opposed to hope, as stated above (Q. XL., A. 4 *ad* 1). But there is a hope of nature, as is evident from Rom. iv. 18, where it is said of Abraham that *against hope* of nature, *he believed in hope* of grace.   Therefore there is also a fear of nature.

*On the contrary*, That which is natural is common to things animate and inanimate.   But fear is not in things inanimate. Therefore there is no natural fear.

*I answer that*, A movement is said to be natural, because nature inclines thereto.   Now this happens in two ways. First, so that it is entirely accomplished by nature, without any operation of the apprehensive faculty: thus to have an upward movement is natural to fire, and to grow is the natural movement of animals and plants.—Secondly, a movement is said to be natural, if nature inclines thereto, though it be accomplished by the apprehensive faculty alone: since, as stated above (Q. X., A. 1), the movements of the cognitive and appetitive faculties are reducible to nature as to their first principle.   In this way, even the acts of the apprehensive power, such as understanding, feeling, and remembering, as well as the movements of the animal appetite, are sometimes said to be natural.

And in this sense we may say that there is a natural fear; and it is distinguished from non-natural fear, by reason of the diversity of its object.   For, as the Philosopher says (*Rhet*. ii. 5), there is a fear of *corruptive evil*, which nature shrinks from on account of its natural desire to exist; and such fear is said to be natural.   Again, there is a fear of *painful evil*, which is repugnant not to nature, but to the desire of the appetite; and such fear is not natural.   In this sense we have stated above (Q. XXVI., A. 1; Q. XXX. A. 3; Q. XXXI., A. 7) that love, desire, and pleasure are divisible into natural and non-natural.

But in the first sense of the word *natural*, we must observe that certain passions of the soul are sometimes said to be natural, as love, desire, and hope; whereas the others cannot be called natural.   The reason of this is because love and hatred, desire and avoidance, imply a certain inclination to pursue what is good or to avoid what is evil; which inclination is to be found in the natural appetite also.   Consequently there is a natural love; while we may also speak of desire and

hope as being even in natural things devoid of knowledge.—
On the other hand the other passions of the soul denote
certain movements, whereto the natural inclination is nowise
sufficient. This is due either to the fact that perception or
knowledge is essential to these passions (thus we have said,
Q. XXXI., AA. 1, 3; Q. XXXV., A. 1, that apprehension
is a necessary condition of pleasure and sorrow), wherefore
things devoid of knowledge cannot be said to take pleasure
or to be sorrowful: or else it is because suchlike movements
are contrary to the very nature of natural inclination: for
instance, despair flies from good on account of some difficulty;
and fear shrinks from repelling a contrary evil; both of
which are contrary to the inclination of nature. Wherefore
suchlike passions are in no way ascribed to inanimate
beings.

Thus the Replies to the Objections are evident.

## FOURTH ARTICLE.

### WHETHER THE SPECIES OF FEAR ARE SUITABLY ASSIGNED ?

*We proceed thus to the Fourth Article :—*

*Objection* 1. It would seem that six species of fear are unsuitably assigned by Damascene (*De Fide Orthod.* ii. 15);
namely, *laziness, shamefacedness, shame, amazement, stupor,
and anxiety.* Because, as the Philosopher says (*Rhet.* ii. 5),
*fear regards a saddening evil.* Therefore the species of fear
should correspond to the species of sorrow. Now there are
four species of sorrow, as stated above (Q. XXXV., A. 8).
Therefore there should only be four species of fear corresponding to them.

*Obj.* 2. Further, that which consists in an action of our
own is in our power. But fear regards an evil that surpasses
our power, as stated above (A. 2). Therefore laziness,
shamefacedness, and shame, which regard our own actions,
should not be reckoned as species of fear.

*Obj.* 3. Further, fear is of the future, as stated above
(AA. 1, 2). But *shame regards a disgraceful deed already*

*done*, as Gregory of Nyssa* says.  Therefore shame is not a species of fear.

*Obj.* 4.  Further, fear is only of evil.  But amazement and stupor regard great and unwonted things, whether good or evil.  Therefore amazement and stupor are not species of fear.

*Obj.* 5.  Further, Philosophers have been led by amazement to seek the truth, as stated at the beginning of *Metaph*. But fear leads to flight rather than to search.  Therefore amazement is not a species of fear.

*On the contrary* suffices the authority of Damascene and Gregory of Nyssa† (*cf. Obj.* 1, 3).

*I answer that*, As stated above (A. 2), fear regards a future evil which surpasses the power of him that fears, so that it is irresistible.  Now man's evil, like his good, may be considered either in his action or in external things.  In his action he has a twofold evil to fear.  First, there is the toil that burdens his nature: and hence arises *laziness*, as when a man shrinks from work for fear of too much toil.—Secondly, there is the disgrace which damages him in the opinion of others.  And thus, if disgrace is feared in a deed that is yet to be done, there is *shamefacedness*; if, however, it be in a deed already done, there is *shame*.

On the other hand, the evil that consists in external things may surpass man's faculty of resistance in three ways. First by reason of its magnitude; when, that is to say, a man considers some great evil the outcome of which he is unable to gauge: and then there is *amazement*.—Secondly, by reason of its being unwonted; because, to wit, some unwonted evil arises before us, and on that account is great in our estimation: and then there is *stupor*, which is caused by the representation of something unwonted.—Thirdly, by reason of its being unforeseen; because, to wit, it cannot be foreseen: thus future misfortunes are feared, and fear of this kind is called *anxiety*.

*Reply Obj.* 1.  Those species of sorrow given above are not derived from the diversity of objects, but from the

* Nemesius, *De Nat. Hom.* xx.                    † Nemesius.

diversity of effects, and for certain special reasons. Consequently there is no need for those species of sorrow to correspond with these species of fear, which are derived from the proper division of the object of fear itself.

*Reply Obj.* 2. A deed considered as being actually done, is in the power of the doer. But it is possible to take into consideration something connected with the deed, and surpassing the faculty of the doer, for which reason he shrinks from the deed. It is in this sense that laziness, shamefacedness, and shame are reckoned as species of fear.

*Reply Obj.* 3. The past deed may be the occasion of fear of future reproach or disgrace: and in this sense shame is a species of fear.

*Reply Obj.* 4. Not every amazement and stupor are species of fear, but that amazement which is caused by a great evil, and that stupor which arises from an unwonted evil.—Or else we may say that, just as laziness shrinks from the toil of external work, so amazement and stupor shrink from the difficulty of considering a great and unwonted thing, whether good or evil: so that amazement and stupor stand in relation to the act of the intellect, as laziness does to external work.

*Reply Obj.* 5. He who is amazed shrinks at present from forming a judgment of that which amazes him, fearing to fall short of the truth, but inquires afterwards: whereas he who is overcome by stupor fears both to judge at present, and to inquire afterwards. Wherefore amazement is a beginning of philosophical research: whereas stupor is a hindrance thereto.

# QUESTION XLII.

## OF THE OBJECT OF FEAR.

### (*In Six Articles.*)

WE must now consider the object of fear: under which head there are six points of inquiry: (1) Whether good or evil is the object of fear? (2) Whether evil of nature is the object of fear? (3) Whether the evil of sin is an object of fear? (4) Whether fear itself can be feared? (5) Whether sudden things are especially feared? (6) Whether those things are more feared against which there is no remedy?

## FIRST ARTICLE.

### WHETHER THE OBJECT OF FEAR IS GOOD OR EVIL?

*We proceed thus to the First Article :—*

*Objection* 1. It would seem that good is the object of fear. For Augustine says (QQ. LXXXIII., qu. 33) that *we fear nothing save to lose what we love and possess, or not to obtain that which we hope for.* But that which we love is good. Therefore fear regards good as its proper object.

*Obj.* 2. Further, the Philosopher says (*Rhet.* ii. 5) that *power and to be above another is a thing to be feared.* But this is a good thing. Therefore good is the object of fear.

*Obj.* 3. Further, there can be no evil in God. But we are commanded to fear God, according to Ps. xxxiii. 10: *Fear the Lord, all ye saints.* Therefore even the good is an object of fear.

*On the contrary,* Damascene says (*De Fide Orthod.* ii. 12) that fear is of future evil.

*I answer that,* Fear is a movement of the appetitive power.

Now it belongs to the appetitive power to pursue and to avoid, as stated in *Ethic.* vi. 2: and pursuit is of good, while avoidance is of evil. Consequently whatever movement of the appetitive power implies pursuit, has some good for its object: and whatever movement implies avoidance, has an evil for its object. Wherefore, since fear implies an avoidance, in the first place and of its very nature it regards evil as its proper object.

It can, however, regard good also, in so far as referable to evil. This can be in two ways. In one way, inasmuch as an evil causes privation of good. Now a thing is evil from the very fact that it is a privation of some good. Wherefore, since evil is shunned because it is evil, it follows that it is shunned because it deprives one of the good that one pursues through love thereof. And in this sense Augustine says that there is no cause for fear, save loss of the good we love.

In another way, good stands related to evil as its cause: in so far as some good can by its power bring harm to the good we love: and so, just as hope, as stated above (Q. XL., A. 7), regards two things, namely, the good to which it tends, and the thing through which there is a hope of obtaining the desired good; so also does fear regard two things, namely, the evil from which it shrinks, and that good which, by its power, can inflict that evil. In this way God is feared by man, inasmuch as He can inflict punishment, spiritual or corporal. In this way, too, we fear the power of man; especially when it has been thwarted, or when it is unjust, because then it is more likely to do us a harm.

In like manner one fears *to be over another*, i.e., to lean on another, so that it is in his power to do us a harm: thus a man fears another, who knows him to be guilty of a crime, lest he reveal it to others.

This suffices for the Replies to the Objections.

## SECOND ARTICLE.

### WHETHER EVIL OF NATURE IS AN OBJECT OF FEAR ?

*We proceed thus to the Second Article :—*

*Objection* 1. It would seem that evil of nature is not an object of fear.  For the Philosopher says (*Rhet.* ii. 5) that *fear makes us take counsel.*   But we do not take counsel about things which happen naturally, as stated in *Ethic.* iii. 3. Therefore evil of nature is not an object of fear.

*Obj.* 2. Further, natural defects such as death and the like are always threatening man.  If therefore suchlike evils were an object of fear, man would needs be always in fear.

*Obj.* 3. Further, nature does not move to contraries. But evil of nature is an effect of nature.   Therefore if a man shrinks from suchlike evils through fear thereof, this is not an effect of nature.   Therefore natural fear is not of the evil of nature; and yet it seems that it should be.

*On the contrary*, The Philosopher says (*Ethic.* iii. 6) that *the most terrible of all things is death,* which is an evil of nature.

*I answer that*, As the Philosopher says (*Rhet.* ii. 5), fear is caused by the *imagination of a future evil which is either corruptive or painful.*  Now just as a painful evil is that which is contrary to the will, so a corruptive evil is that which is contrary to nature: and this is the evil of nature. Consequently evil of nature can be the object of fear.

But it must be observed that evil of nature sometimes arises from a natural cause; and then it is called evil of nature, not merely from being a privation of the good of nature, but also from being an effect of nature; such are natural death and other like defects.  But sometimes evil of nature arises from a non-natural cause; such as violent death inflicted by an assailant.   In either case evil of nature is feared to a certain extent, and to a certain extent not. For since fear arises *from the imagination of future evil,* as the Philosopher says (*loc. cit.*), whatever removes the imagination of the future evil, removes fear also.   Now it may happen in two ways that an evil may not appear as about to be. First, through being remote and far off: for, on account of the distance, such a thing is considered as though it were not to be. Hence we either do not fear it, or fear it but little; for, as the Philosopher says (*Rhet*. ii. 5), *we do not fear things that are very far off ; since all know that they shall die, but as death is not near, they heed it not.*—Secondly, a future evil is considered as though it were not to be, on account of its being inevitable, wherefore we look upon it as already present. Hence the Philosopher says (*Rhet*. ii. 5) that *those who are already on the scaffold, are not afraid,* seeing that they are on the very point of a death from which there is no escape; *but in order that a man be afraid, there must be some hope of escape for him.*

Consequently evil of nature is not feared if it be not apprehended as future: but if evil of nature, that is corruptive, be apprehended as near at hand, and yet with some hope of escape, then it will be feared.

*Reply Obj.* 1. The evil of nature sometimes is not an effect of nature, as stated above. But in so far as it is an effect of nature, although it may be impossible to avoid it entirely, yet it may be possible to delay it. And with this hope one may take counsel about avoiding it.

*Reply Obj.* 2. Although evil of nature ever threatens, yet it does not always threaten from near at hand: and consequently it is not always feared.

*Reply Obj.* 3. Death and other defects of nature are the effects of the common nature; and yet the individual nature rebels against them as far as it can. Accordingly, from the inclination of the individual nature arise pain and sorrow for suchlike evils, when present; fear when threatening in the future.

### Third Article.

#### WHETHER THE EVIL OF SIN IS AN OBJECT OF FEAR ?

*We proceed thus to the Third Article :—*

*Objection* 1. It would seem that the evil of sin can be an object of fear. For Augustine says on the canonical Epistle of John (*Tract*. ix.), that *by chaste fear man fears to be severed from God*.   Now nothing but sin severs us from God; according to Isa. lix. 2: *Your iniquities have divided between you and your God*.   Therefore the evil of sin can be an object of fear.

*Obj*. 2.   Further, Cicero says (*Quæst. Tusc*. iv. 4, 6) that *we fear when they are yet to come, those things which give us pain when they are present*.   But it is possible for one to be pained or sorrowful on account of the evil of sin.   Therefore one can also fear the evil of sin.

*Obj*. 3.   Further, hope is contrary to fear.   But the good of virtue can be the object of hope, as the Philosopher declares (*Ethic*. ix. 4): and the Apostle says (Gal. v. 10): *I have confidence in you in the Lord, that you will not be of another mind*.   Therefore fear can regard evil of sin.

*Obj*. 4.   Further, shame is a kind of fear, as stated above (Q. XLI., A. 4).   But shame regards a disgraceful deed, which is an evil of sin.   Therefore fear does so likewise.

*On the contrary*, The Philosopher says (*Rhet*. ii. 5) that *not all evils are feared, for instance that someone be unjust or slow*.

*I answer that*, As stated above (Q. XL., A. 1; Q. XLI., A. 2), as the object of hope is a future good difficult but possible to obtain, so the object of fear is a future evil, arduous and not to be easily avoided.   From this we may gather that whatever is entirely subject to our power and will, is not an object of fear; and that nothing gives rise to fear save what is due to an external cause.   Now human will is the proper cause of the evil of sin: and consequently evil of sin, properly speaking, is not an object of fear.

But since the human will may be inclined to sin by an extrinsic cause; if this cause have a strong power of inclination, in that respect a man may fear the evil of sin, in so far as it arises from that extrinsic cause: as when he fears to dwell in the company of wicked men, lest he be led by them to sin.   But, properly speaking, a man thus disposed, fears the being led astray rather than the sin considered in its proper nature, *i.e.*, as a voluntary act; for considered in this light it is not an object of fear to him.

*Reply Obj.* 1. Separation from God is a punishment resulting from sin: and every punishment is, in some way, due to an extrinsic cause.

*Reply Obj.* 2. Sorrow and fear agree in one point, since each regards evil: they differ, however, in two points. First, because sorrow is about present evil, whereas fear is future evil. Secondly, because sorrow, being in the concupiscible faculty, regards evil absolutely; wherefore it can be about any evil, great or small; whereas fear, being in the irascible part, regards evil with the addition of a certain arduousness or difficulty; which difficulty ceases in so far as a thing is subject to the will. Consequently not all things that give us pain when they are present, make us fear when they are yet to come, but only some things, namely, those that are difficult.

*Reply Obj.* 3. Hope is of good that is obtainable. Now one may obtain a good either of oneself, or through another: and so, hope may be of an act of virtue, which lies within our own power. On the other hand, fear is of an evil that does not lie in our own power: and consequently the evil which is feared is always from an extrinsic cause; while the good that is hoped for may be both from an intrinsic and from an extrinsic cause.

*Reply Obj.* 4. As stated above (Q. XLI., A. 4 *ad* 2, 3), shame is not fear of the very act of sin, but of the disgrace or ignominy which arises therefrom, and which is due to an extrinsic cause.

## Fourth Article.

### whether fear itself can be feared ?

*We proceed thus to the Fourth Article :—*

*Objection* 1. It would seem that fear cannot be feared. For whatever is feared, is prevented from being lost, through fear thereof: thus a man who fears to lose his health, keeps it, through fearing its loss. If therefore a man be afraid of fear, he will keep himself from fear by being afraid: which seems absurd.

*Obj.* 2. Further, fear is a kind of flight. But nothing

flies from itself. Therefore fear cannot be the object of fear.

*Obj.* 3. Further, fear is about the future. But fear is present to him that fears. Therefore it cannot be the object of his fear.

*On the contrary*, A man can love his own love, and can grieve at his own sorrow. Therefore, in like manner, he can fear his own fear.

*I answer that*, As stated above (A. 3), nothing can be an object of fear, save what is due to an extrinsic cause; but not that which ensues from our own will. Now fear partly arises from an extrinsic cause, and is partly subject to the will. It is due to an extrinsic cause, in so far as it is a passion resulting from the imagination of an imminent evil. In this sense it is possible for fear to be the object of fear, *i.e.*, a man may fear lest he should be threatened by the necessity of fearing, through being assailed by some great evil.—It is subject to the will, in so far as the lower appetite obeys reason; wherefore man is able to drive fear away. In this sense fear cannot be the object of fear, as Augustine says (QQ. LXXXIII., qu. 33). Lest, however, anyone make use of his arguments, in order to prove that fear cannot at all be the object of fear, we must add a solution to the same.

*Reply Obj.* 1. Not every fear is identically the same; there are various fears according to the various objects of fear. Nothing, then, prevents a man from keeping himself from fearing one thing, by fearing another, so that the fear which he has preserves him from the fear which he has not.

*Reply Obj.* 2. Since fear of an imminent evil is not identical with the fear of the fear of an imminent evil; it does not follow that a thing flies from itself, or that it is the same flight in both cases.

*Reply Obj.* 3. On account of the various kinds of fear already alluded to (*ad* 2) a man's present fear may have a future fear for its object.

## FIFTH ARTICLE.

### WHETHER SUDDEN THINGS ARE ESPECIALLY FEARED ?

*We proceed thus to the Fifth Article :—*

*Objection* 1. It would seem that unwonted and sudden things are not especially feared. Because, as hope is about good things, so fear is about evil things. But experience conduces to the increase of hope in good things. Therefore it also adds to fear in evil things.

*Obj.* 2. Further, the Philosopher says (*Rhet.* ii. 5) that *those are feared most, not who are quick-tempered, but who are gentle and cunning.* Now it is clear that those who are quick-tempered are more subject to sudden emotions. Therefore sudden things are less to be feared.

*Obj.* 3. Further, we think less about things that happen suddenly. But the more we think about a thing, the more we fear it; hence the Philosopher says (*Ethic.* iii. 8) that *some appear to be courageous through ignorance, but as soon as they discover that the case is different from what they expected, they run away.* Therefore sudden things are feared less.

*On the contrary*, Augustine says (*Conf.* ii. 6): *Fear is startled at things unwonted and sudden, which endanger things beloved, and takes forethought for their safety.*

*I answer that*, As stated above (A. 3; Q. XLI., A. 2), the object of fear is an imminent evil, which can be repelled, but with difficulty. Now this is due to one of two causes: to the greatness of the evil, or to the weakness of him that fears; while unwontedness and suddenness conduce to both of these causes. First, it helps an imminent evil to seem greater. Because all material things, whether good or evil, the more we consider them, the smaller they seem. Consequently, just as sorrow for a present evil is mitigated in course of time, as Cicero states (*De Quæst. Tusc.* iii. 30); so, too, fear of a future evil is diminished by thinking about it beforehand.—Secondly, unwontedness and suddenness increase the weakness of him that fears, in so far as they deprive him of the remedies with which he might otherwise provide himself to forestall the coming evil, were it not for the evil taking him by surprise.

*Reply Obj*. 1. The object of hope is a good that it is possible to obtain. Consequently whatever increases a man's power, is of a nature to increase hope, and, for the same reason, to diminish fear, since fear is about an evil which cannot be easily repelled. Since, therefore, experience increases a man's power of action, therefore, as it increases hope, so does it diminish fear.

*Reply Obj*. 2. Those who are quick-tempered do not hide their anger; wherefore the harm they do others is not so sudden, as not to be foreseen. On the other hand, those who are gentle or cunning hide their anger; wherefore the harm which may be impending from them, cannot be foreseen, but takes one by surprise. For this reason the Philosopher says that such men are feared more than others.

*Reply Obj*. 3. Bodily good or evil, considered in itself, seems greater at first. The reason for this is that a thing is more obvious when seen in juxtaposition with its contrary. Hence when a man passes unexpectedly from penury to wealth, he thinks more of his wealth on account of his previous poverty: while, on the other hand, the rich man who suddenly becomes poor, finds poverty all the more disagreeable. For this reason sudden evil is feared more, because it seems more to be evil.—However, it may happen through some accident that the greatness of some evil is hidden; for instance if the foe hides himself in ambush: and then it is true that evil inspires greater fear through being much thought about.

## SIXTH ARTICLE.

### WHETHER THOSE THINGS ARE MORE FEARED, FOR WHICH THERE IS NO REMEDY?

*We proceed thus to the Sixth Article :—*

*Objection* 1. It would seem that those things are not more to be feared, for which there is no remedy. Because it is a condition of fear, that there be some hope of safety, as stated above (A. 2).    But an evil that cannot be remedied leaves no hope of escape.    Therefore such things are not feared at all.

*Obj.* 2. Further, there is no remedy for the evil of death: since, in the natural course of things, there is no return from death to life.    And yet death is not the most feared of all things, as the Philosopher says (*Rhet.* ii. 5).    Therefore those things are not feared most, for which there is no remedy.

*Obj.* 3. Further, the Philosopher says (*Ethic.* i. 6) that *a thing which lasts long is no better than that which lasts but one day : nor is that which lasts for ever any better than that which is not everlasting :* and the same applies to evil.    But things that cannot be remedied seem to differ from other things, merely in the point of their lasting long or for ever.    Consequently they are not therefore any worse or more to be feared.

*On the contrary*, the Philosopher says (*Rhet.* ii. 5) that *those things are most to be feared which when done wrong cannot be put right, . . . or for which there is no help, or which are not easy.*

*I answer that*, The object of fear is evil: consequently whatever tends to increase evil, conduces to the increase of fear.    Now evil is increased not only in its species of evil, but also in respect of circumstances, as stated above (Q. XVIII., A. 3).    And of all the circumstances, long-lastingness, or even everlastingness, seems to have the greatest bearing on the increase of evil.    Because things that exist in time are measured, in a way, according to the duration of time: wherefore if it be an evil to suffer something for a certain length of time, we should reckon the evil doubled, if it be suffered for twice that length of time. And, accordingly, to suffer the same thing for an infinite length of time, *i.e.*, for ever, implies, so to speak, an infinite increase.    Now those evils which, after they have come, cannot be remedied at all, or at least not easily, are considered as lasting for ever or for a long time: for which reason they inspire the greatest fear.

*Reply Obj.* 1. Remedy for an evil is twofold.    One, by which a future evil is warded off from coming.    If such a

remedy be removed, there is an end to hope and consequently to fear; wherefore we do not speak now of remedies
of that kind.   The other remedy is one by which an already
present evil is removed: and of such a remedy we speak now.

*Reply Obj.* 2. Although death be an evil without remedy,
yet, since it threatens not from near, it is not feared, as
stated above (A. 2).

*Reply Obj.* 3. The Philosopher is speaking there of things
that are good in themselves, *i.e.*, good specifically. And
such like good is no better for lasting long or for ever: its
goodness depends on its very nature.

# QUESTION XLIII.

## OF THE CAUSE OF FEAR.

### (*In Two Articles.*)

WE must now consider the cause of fear: under which head there are two points of inquiry: (1) Whether love is the cause of fear? (2) Whether defect is the cause of fear?

### FIRST ARTICLE.

#### WHETHER LOVE IS THE CAUSE OF FEAR?

*We proceed thus to the First Article :—*

*Objection* 1. It would seem that love is not the cause of fear. For that which leads to a thing is its cause. But *fear leads to the love of charity* as Augustine says on the canonical epistle of John (*Tract.* ix.). Therefore fear is the cause of love, and not conversely.

*Obj.* 2. Further, the Philosopher says (*Rhet.* ii. 5) that *those are feared most from whom we dread the advent of some evil.* But the dread of evil being caused by someone, makes us hate rather than love him. Therefore fear is caused by hate rather than by love.

*Obj.* 3. Further, it has been stated above (Q. XLII., A. 3) that those things which occur by our own doing are not fearful. But that which we do from love, is done from our inmost heart. Therefore fear is not caused by love.

*On the contrary*, Augustine says (QQ. LXXXIII., qu. 33): *There can be no doubt that there is no cause for fear save the loss of what we love, when we possess it, or the failure to obtain what we hope for.* Therefore all fear is caused by our loving something: and consequently love is the cause of fear.

487

*I answer that,* The objects of the soul's passions stand in relation thereto as the forms to things natural or artificial: because the passions of the soul take their species from their objects, as the aforesaid things do from their forms. Therefore, just as whatever is a cause of the form, is a cause of the thing constituted by that form, so whatever is a cause, in any way whatever, of the object, is a cause of the passion. Now a thing may be a cause of the object, either by way of efficient cause, or by way of material disposition. Thus the object of pleasure is good apprehended as suitable and conjoined: and its efficient cause is that which causes the conjunction, or the suitableness, or goodness, or apprehension of that good thing; while its cause by way of material disposition, is a habit or any sort of disposition by reason of which this conjoined good becomes suitable or is apprehended as such.

Accordingly, as to the matter in question, the object of fear is something reckoned as an evil to come, near at hand and difficult to avoid. Therefore that which can inflict such an evil, is the efficient cause of the object of fear, and, consequently, of fear itself. While that which renders a man so disposed that a thing is such an evil to him, is a cause of fear and of its object, by way of material disposition. And thus it is that love causes fear: since it is through his loving a certain good, that whatever deprives a man of that good is an evil to him, and that consequently he fears it as an evil.

*Reply Obj.* 1. As stated above (Q. XLII., A. 1), fear, of itself and in the first place, regards the evil from which it recoils as being contrary to some loved good: and thus fear, of itself, is born of love.—But, in the second place, it regards the cause from which that evil ensues: so that sometimes, accidentally, fear gives rise to love; in so far as, for instance, through fear of God's punishments, man keeps His commandments, and thus begins to hope, while hope leads to love, as stated above (Q. XL., A. 7).

*Reply Obj.* 2. He, from whom evil is expected, is indeed hated at first; but afterwards, when once we begin to hope for good from him, we begin to love him. But the good, the contrary evil of which is feared, was loved from the beginning.

*Reply Obj*. 3. This argument is true of that which is the efficient cause of the evil to be feared: whereas love causes fear by way of material disposition, as stated above.

SECOND ARTICLE.

WHETHER DEFECT IS THE CAUSE OF FEAR ?

*We proceed thus to the Second Article :—*

*Objection* 1. It would seem that defect is not a cause of fear. Because those who are in power are very much feared. But defect is contrary to power. Therefore defect is not a cause of fear.

*Obj*. 2. Further, the defect of those who are already being executed is extreme. But suchlike do not fear as stated in *Rhet*. ii. 5. Therefore defect is not a cause of fear.

*Obj*. 3. Further, contests arise from strength not from defect. But *those who contend fear those who contend with them* (*Rhet*. ii. 5). Therefore defect is not a cause of fear.

*On the contrary*, Contraries ensue from contrary causes. But *wealth, strength, a multitude of friends, and power drive fear away* (*Rhet*. ii. *ibid*.). Therefore fear is caused by lack of these.

*I answer that*, As stated above (A. 1), fear may be set down to a twofold cause: one is by way of a material disposition, on the part of him that fears; the other is by way of efficient cause, on the part of the person feared. As to the first then, some defect is, of itself, the cause of fear: for it is owing to some lack of power that one is unable easily to repulse a threatening evil. And yet, in order to cause fear, this defect must be according to a measure. For the defect which causes fear of a future evil, is less than the defect caused by evil present, which is the object of sorrow. And still greater would be the defect, if perception of the evil, or love of the good whose contrary is feared, were entirely absent.

But as to the second, power and strength are, of themselves, the cause of fear: because it is owing to the fact that the cause apprehended as harmful is powerful, that its effect cannot be repulsed. It may happen, however, in this respect, that some defect causes fear accidentally, in so far as owing to some defect someone wishes to hurt another; for instance, by reason of injustice, either because that other has already done him a harm, or because he fears to be harmed by him.

*Reply Obj.* 1. This argument is true of the cause of fear, on the part of the efficient cause.

*Reply Obj.* 2. Those who are already being executed, are actually suffering from a present evil; wherefore their defect exceeds the measure of fear.

*Reply Obj.* 3. Those who contend with one another are afraid, not on account of the power which enables them to contend: but on account of the lack of power, owing to which they are not confident of victory.

# QUESTION XLIV.

## OF THE EFFECTS OF FEAR

### (*In Four Articles.*)

WE must now consider the effects of fear: under which head there are four points of inquiry: (1) Whether fear causes contraction ? (2) Whether it makes men suitable for counsel ? (3) Whether it makes one tremble ? (4) Whether it hinders action ?

### FIRST ARTICLE.

#### WHETHER FEAR CAUSES CONTRACTION ?

*We proceed thus to the First Article :—*

*Objection* 1. It would seem that fear does not cause contraction. For when contraction takes place, the heat and vital spirits are withdrawn inwardly. But accumulation of heat and vital spirits in the interior parts of the body, dilates the heart unto endeavours of daring, as may be seen in those who are angered: while the contrary happens in those who are afraid. Therefore fear does not cause contraction.

*Obj.* 2. Further, when, as a result of contraction, the vital spirits and heat are accumulated in the interior parts, man cries out, as may be seen in those who are in pain. But those who fear utter nothing: on the contrary they lose their speech. Therefore fear does not cause contraction.

*Obj.* 3. Further, shame is a kind of fear, as stated above (Q. XLI., A. 4). But *those who are ashamed blush*, as Cicero (*De Quaest. Tusc.* iv. 8), and the Philosopher (*Ethic.* iv. 9) observe. But blushing is an indication, not of contraction, but of the reverse.   Therefore contraction is not an effect of fear.

*On the contrary*, Damascene says (*De Fide Orthod*. iii. 23) that *fear is a power according to* συστολή, i.e., contraction.

*I answer that*, As stated above (Q. XXVIII., A. 5), in the passions of the soul, the formal element is the movement of the appetitive power, while the bodily transmutation is the material element.   Both of these are mutually proportionate; and consequently the bodily transmutation assumes a resemblance to and the very nature of the appetitive movement. Now, as to the appetitive movement of the soul, fear implies a certain contraction: the reason of which is that fear arises from the imagination of some threatening evil which is difficult to repel, as stated above (Q. XLI., A. 2).   But that a thing be difficult to repel is due to lack of power, as stated above (Q. XLIII., A. 2): and the weaker a power is, the fewer the things to which it extends.   Wherefore from the very imagination that causes fear there ensues a certain contraction in the appetite.   Thus we observe in one who is dying that nature withdraws inwardly, on account of the lack of power: and again we see the inhabitants of a city, when seized with fear, leave the outskirts, and, as far as possible, make for the inner quarters.   It is in resemblance to this contraction, which pertains to the appetite of the soul, that in fear a similar contraction of heat and vital spirits towards the inner parts takes place in regard to the body.

*Reply Obj*. 1. As the Philosopher says (*De Problem*. xxvii. 3), although in those who fear, the vital spirits recede from the outer to the inner parts of the body, yet the movement of vital spirits is not the same in those who are angry and those who are afraid.   For in those who are angry, by reason of the heat and subtlety of the vital spirits, which result from the craving for vengeance, the inward movement has an upward direction: wherefore the vital spirits and heat concentrate around the heart: the result being that an angry man is quick and brave in attacking.—But in those who are afraid, on account of the condensation caused by the cold, the vital spirits have a downward movement; the said cold being due to the imagined lack of power. Consequently the heat and vital spirits abandon the heart instead of concentrating around it: the result being that a man who is afraid is not quick to attack, but is more inclined to run away.

*Reply Obj.* 2. To everyone that is in pain, whether man or animal, it is natural to use all possible means of repelling the harmful thing that causes pain by its presence: thus we observe that animals, when in pain, attack with their jaws or with their horns. Now the greatest help for all purposes, in animals, is heat and vital spirits: wherefore when they are in pain, their nature stores up the heat and vital spirits within them, in order to make use thereof in repelling the harmful object. Hence the Philosopher says (*De Problem.* xxvii. 9) when the vital spirits and heat are concentrated together within, they require to find a vent in the voice: for which reason those who are in pain can scarcely refrain from crying aloud.—On the other hand, in those who are afraid, the internal heat and vital spirits move from the heart downwards, as stated above (*ad* 1): wherefore fear hinders speech which ensues from the emission of the vital spirits in an upward direction through the mouth: the result being that fear makes its subject speechless. For this reason, too, fear *makes its subject tremble*, as the Philosopher says (*De Problem.* xxvii. 1, 6, 7).

*Reply Obj.* 3. Mortal perils are contrary not only to the appetite of the soul, but also to nature. Consequently in suchlike fear, there is contraction not only in the appetite, but also in the corporeal nature: for when an animal is moved by the imagination of death, it experiences a contraction of heat towards the inner parts of the body, as though it were threatened by a natural death. Hence it is that *those who are in fear of death turn pale* (*Ethic.* iv. 9).—But the evil that shame fears, is contrary, not to nature, but only to the appetite of the soul. Consequently there results a contraction in this appetite, but not in the corporeal nature; in

fact, the soul, as though contracted in itself, is free to set
the vital spirits and heat in movement, so that they spread
to the outward parts of the body: the result being that those
who are ashamed blush.

## SECOND ARTICLE.

#### WHETHER FEAR MAKES ONE SUITABLE FOR COUNSEL ?

*We proceed thus to the Second Article :—*

*Objection* 1. It would seem that fear does not make one
suitable for counsel.   For the same thing cannot be conducive to counsel, and a hindrance thereto.   But fear hinders
counsel: because every passion disturbs repose, which is
requisite for the good use of reason.   Therefore fear does
not make a man suitable for counsel.

*Obj.* 2. Further, counsel is an act of reason, in thinking
and deliberating about the future.   But a certain fear
*drives away all thought, and dislocates the mind*, as Cicero
observes (*De Quaest. Tusc.* iv. 8).   Therefore fear does not
conduce to counsel, but hinders it.

*Obj.* 3. Further, just as we have recourse to counsel in
order to avoid evil, so do we, in order to attain good things.
But whereas fear is of evil to be avoided, so is hope of good
things to be obtained.   Therefore fear is not more conducive
to counsel, than hope is.

*On the contrary,* The Philosopher says (*Rhet.* ii. 5) that *fear
makes men of counsel.*

*I answer that,* A man of counsel may be taken in two
ways.   First, from his being willing or anxious to take
counsel.   And thus fear makes men of counsel.   Because,
as the Philosopher says (*Ethic.* iii. 3), *we take counsel on
great matters, because therein we distrust ourselves*.   Now
things which make us afraid, are not simply evil, but have
a certain magnitude, both because they seem difficult to
repel, and because they are apprehended as near to us, as
stated above (Q. XLII., A. 2).   Wherefore men seek for
counsel especially when they are afraid.

Secondly, a man of counsel means one who is apt for

giving good counsel: and in this sense, neither fear nor any passion makes men of counsel. Because when a man is affected by a passion, things seem to him greater or smaller than they really are: thus to a lover, what he loves seems better; to him that fears, what he fears seems more dreadful. Consequently owing to the want of right judgment, every passion, considered in itself, hinders the faculty of giving good counsel.

This suffices for the Reply to the First Objection.

*Reply Obj.* 2. The stronger a passion is, the greater hindrance is it to the man who is swayed by it. Consequently, when fear is intense, man does indeed wish to take counsel, but his thoughts are so disturbed, that he can find no counsel. If, however, the fear be slight, so as to make a man wish to take counsel, without gravely disturbing the reason; it may even make it easier for him to take good counsel, by reason of his ensuing carefulness.

*Reply Obj.* 3. Hope also makes man a good counsellor: because, as the Philosopher says (*Rhet.* ii. 5), *no man takes counsel in matters he despairs of*, nor about impossible things, as he says in *Ethic.* iii. 3. But fear incites to counsel more than hope does. Because hope is of good things, as being possible of attainment; whereas fear is of evil things, as being difficult to repel, so that fear regards the aspect of difficulty more than hope does. And it is in matters of difficulty, especially when we distrust ourselves, that we take counsel, as stated above.

## THIRD ARTICLE.

### WHETHER FEAR MAKES ONE TREMBLE ?

*We proceed thus to the Third Article :—*

*Objection* 1. It would seem that trembling is not an effect of fear. Because trembling is occasioned by cold; thus we observe that a cold person trembles. Now fear does not seem to make one cold, but rather to cause a parching heat: a sign whereof is that those who fear are thirsty, especially if their fear be very great, as in the case of those who are

being led to execution. Therefore fear does not cause
trembling.

*Obj.* 2. Further, fæcal evacuation is occasioned by heat;
hence laxative medicines are generally warm. But these
evacuations are often caused by fear. Therefore fear
apparently causes heat; and consequently does not cause
trembling.

*Obj.* 3. Further, in fear, the heat is withdrawn from the
outer to the inner parts of the body. If, therefore, man
trembles in his outward parts, through the heat being withdrawn thus; it seems that fear should cause this trembling
in all the external members. But such is not the case.
Therefore trembling of the body is not caused by fear.

*On the contrary,* Cicero says (*De Quaest. Tusc.* iv. 8) that
*fear is followed by trembling, pallor and chattering of the teeth.*

*I answer that,* As stated above (A. 1), in fear there takes
place a certain contraction from the outward to the inner
parts of the body, the result being that the outer parts become
cold; and for this reason trembling is occasioned in these
parts, being caused by a lack of power in controlling the
members: which lack of power is due to the want of heat,
which is the instrument whereby the soul moves those
members, as stated in *De Anima* ii. 4.

*Reply Obj.* 1. When the heat withdraws from the outer
to the inner parts, the inward heat increases, especially in
the inferior or nutritive parts. Consequently the humid
element being spent, thirst ensues; sometimes indeed the
result is a loosening of the bowels, and urinary or even
seminal evacuation.—Or else suchlike evacuations are due
to contraction of the abdomen and testicles, as the Philosopher says (*De Problem.* xxii. 11).

This suffices for the Reply to the Second Objection.

*Reply Obj.* 3. In fear, heat abandons the heart, with a
downward movement: hence in those who are afraid the
heart especially trembles, as also those members which are
connected with the breast where the heart resides. Hence
those who fear tremble especially in their speech, on account
of the tracheal artery being near the heart. The lower lip,

too, and the lower jaw tremble, through their connection with the heart; which explains the chattering of the teeth. For the same reason the arms and hands tremble.—Or else because the aforesaid members are more mobile. For which reason the knees tremble in those who are afraid, according to Isa. xxxv. 3: *Strengthen ye the feeble hands, and confirm the trembling* (Vulg., *weak*) *knees*.

## FOURTH ARTICLE.

### WHETHER FEAR HINDERS ACTION ?

*We proceed thus to the Fourth Article :—*

*Objection* 1. It would seem that fear hinders action. For action is hindered chiefly by a disturbance in the reason, which directs action. But fear disturbs reason, as stated above (A. 2). Therefore fear hinders action.

*Obj.* 2. Further, those who fear while doing anything, are more apt to fail: thus a man who walks on a plank placed aloft, easily falls through fear; whereas, if he were to walk on the same plank down below, he would not fall, through not being afraid. Therefore fear hinders action.

*Obj.* 3. Further, laziness or sloth is a kind of fear. But laziness hinders action. Therefore fear does too.

*On the contrary,* The Apostle says (Phil. ii. 12): *With fear and trembling work out your salvation*: and he would not say this if fear were a hindrance to a good work. Therefore fear does not hinder a good action.

*I answer that,* Man's exterior actions are caused by the soul as first mover, but by the bodily members as instruments. Now action may be hindered both by defect of the instrument, and by defect of the principal mover. On the part of the bodily instruments, fear, considered in itself, is always apt to hinder exterior action, on account of the outward members being deprived, through fear, of their heat. But on the part of the soul, if the fear be moderate, without much disturbance of the reason, it conduces to working well, in so far as it causes a certain solicitude, and makes a man take counsel and work with greater attention.

II. i.                                                                   32

—If, however, fear increases so much as to disturb the reason, it hinders action even on the part of the soul. But of such a fear the Apostle does not speak.

This suffices for the Reply to the First Objection.

*Reply Obj.* 2. He that falls from a plank placed aloft, suffers a disturbance of his imagination, through fear of the fall that is pictured to his imagination.

*Reply Obj.* 3. Everyone in fear shuns that which he fears: and therefore, since laziness is a fear of work itself as being toilsome, it hinders work by withdrawing the will from it. But fear of other things conduces to action, in so far as it inclines the will to do that whereby a man escapes from what he fears.

# QUESTION XLV.

## OF DARING.

### (*In Four Articles.*)

WE must now consider daring: under which head there are four points of inquiry: (1) Whether daring is contrary to fear? (2) How is daring related to hope? (3) Of the cause of daring: (4) Of its effect.

## FIRST ARTICLE.

### WHETHER DARING IS CONTRARY TO FEAR?

*We proceed thus to the First Article :—*

*Objection* 1. It would seem that daring is not contrary to fear. For Augustine says (QQ. LXXXIII., qu. 31) that *daring is a vice*. Now vice is contrary to virtue. Since, therefore, fear is not a virtue but a passion, it seems that daring is not contrary to fear.

*Obj.* 2. Further, to one thing there is one contrary. But hope is contrary to fear. Therefore daring is not contrary to fear.

*Obj.* 3. Further, every passion excludes its opposite. But fear excludes safety; for Augustine says (*Conf.* ii. 6) that *fear takes forethought for safety*. Therefore safety is contrary to fear. Therefore daring is not contrary to fear.

*On the contrary*, The Philosopher says (*Rhet.* ii. 5) that *daring is contrary to fear*.

*I answer that*, It is of the essence of contraries to be *farthest removed from one another*, as stated in *Metaph.* x. 4. Now that which is farthest removed from fear, is daring: since fear turns away from the future hurt, on account of its victory over him that fears it; whereas daring turns on threatened danger, because of its own victory over that same danger. Consequently it is evident that daring is contrary to fear.

*Reply Obj.* 1. Anger, daring and all the names of the passions can be taken in two ways. First, as denoting absolutely movements of the sensitive appetite in respect of some object, good or bad: and thus they are names of passions.—Secondly, as denoting besides this movement, a straying from the order of reason: and thus they are names of vices. It is in this sense that Augustine speaks of daring: but we are speaking of it in the first sense.

*Reply Obj.* 2. To one thing, in the same respect, there are not several contraries; but in different respects nothing prevents one thing having several contraries. Accordingly it has been said above (Q. XXIII., A. 2; Q. XL., A. 4) that the irascible passions admit of a twofold contrariety: one, according to the opposition of good and evil, and thus fear is contrary to hope: the other, according to the opposition of approach and withdrawal, and thus daring is contrary to fear, and despair contrary to hope.

*Reply Obj.* 3. Safety does not denote something contrary to fear, but merely the exclusion of fear: for he is said to be safe, who fears not. Wherefore safety is opposed to fear, as a privation: while daring is opposed thereto as a contrary. And as contrariety implies privation, so daring implies safety.

## SECOND ARTICLE.

### WHETHER DARING ENSUES FROM HOPE?

*We proceed thus to the Second Article :—*

*Objection* 1. It would seem that daring does not ensue from hope. Because daring regards evil and fearful things, as stated in *Ethic.* iii. 7. But hope regards good things, as stated above (Q. XL., A. 1). Therefore they have different objects and are not in the same order. Therefore daring does not ensue from hope.

*Obj.* 2. Further, just as daring is contrary to fear, so is despair contrary to hope. But fear does not ensue from despair: in fact despair excludes fear, as the Philosopher says (*Rhet.* ii. 5). Therefore daring does not result from hope.

*Obj.* 3. Further, daring is intent on something good, viz., victory. But it belongs to hope to tend to that which is good and difficult. Therefore daring is the same as hope; and consequently does not result from it.

*On the contrary,* The Philosopher says (*Ethic.* iii. 8) that *those who are hopeful are full of daring.* Therefore it seems that daring ensues from hope.

*I answer that,* As we have often stated (Q. XXII., A. 2; Q. XXXV., A. 1; Q. XLI., A. 1), all these passions belong to the appetitive power. Now every movement of the appetitive power is reducible to one either of pursuit or of avoidance. Again, pursuit or avoidance is of something either by reason of itself or by reason of something else. By reason of itself, good is the object of pursuit, and evil, the object of avoidance: but by reason of something else, evil can be the object of pursuit, through some good attaching to it; and good can be the object of avoidance, through some evil attaching to it. Now that which is by reason of something else, follows that which is by reason of itself. Consequently pursuit of evil follows pursuit of good; and avoidance of good follows avoidance of evil. Now these four things belong to four passions, since pursuit of good belongs to hope, avoidance of evil to fear, the pursuit of the fearful evil belongs to daring, and the avoidance of good to despair. It follows, therefore, that daring results from hope; since it is in the hope of overcoming the threatening object of fear, that one attacks it boldly. But despair results from fear: since the reason why a man despairs is because he fears the difficulty attaching to the good he should hope for.

*Reply Obj.* 1. This argument would hold, if good and evil were not co-ordinate objects. But because evil has a certain relation to good, since it comes after good, as privation comes after habit; consequently daring which pursues evil, comes after hope which pursues good.

*Reply Obj.* 2. Although good, absolutely speaking, is prior to evil, yet avoidance of evil precedes avoidance of good; just as the pursuit of good precedes the pursuit of evil. Consequently just as hope precedes daring, so fear precedes despair.   And just as fear does not always lead to despair, but only when it is intense; so hope does not always lead to daring, save only when it is strong.

*Reply Obj.* 3. Although the object of daring is an evil to which, in the estimation of the daring man, the good of victory is conjoined; yet daring regards the evil, and hope regards the conjoined good.   In like manner despair regards directly the good which it turns away from, while fear regards the conjoined evil.   Hence, properly speaking, daring is not a part of hope, but its effect: just as despair is an effect, not a part, of fear.   For this reason, too, daring cannot be a principal passion.

### Third Article.
#### WHETHER SOME DEFECT IS A CAUSE OF DARING?

*We proceed thus to the Third Article :—*

*Objection* 1. It would seem that some defect is a cause of daring.   For the Philosopher says (*De Problem.* xxvii. 4) that *lovers of wine are strong and daring*.   But from wine ensues the defect of drunkenness.   Therefore daring is caused by a defect.

*Obj.* 2. Further, the Philosopher says (*Rhet.* ii. 5) that *those who have no experience of danger are bold*.   But want of experience is a defect.   Therefore daring is caused by a defect.

*Obj.* 3. Further, those who have suffered wrongs are wont to be daring; *like the beasts when beaten*, as stated in *Ethic.* iii. 5.   But the suffering of wrongs pertains to defect.   Therefore daring is caused by a defect.

*On the contrary*, The Philosopher says (*Rhet.* ii. 5) that the cause of daring *is the presence in the imagination of the hope that the means of safety are nigh, and that the things to be feared are either non-existent or far off.* But anything pertaining to defect implies either the removal of the means of safety, or the proximity of something to be feared. Therefore nothing pertaining to defect is a cause of daring.

*I answer that,* As stated above (AA. 1, 2) daring results from hope and is contrary to fear: wherefore whatever is naturally apt to cause hope or banish fear, is a cause of daring. Since, however, fear and hope, and also daring, being passions, consist in a movement of the appetite, and in a certain bodily transmutation; a thing may be considered as the cause of daring in two ways, whether by raising hope, or by banishing of fear; in one way, on the part of the appetitive movement; in another way, on the part of the bodily transmutation.

On the part of the appetitive movement which follows apprehension, hope that leads to daring is roused by those things that make us reckon victory as possible. Such things regard either our own power, as bodily strength, experience of dangers, abundance of wealth, and the like; or they regard the power of others, such as having a great number of friends or any other means of help, especially if a man trust in the Divine assistance; wherefore *those are more daring, with whom it is well in regard to godlike things,* as the Philosopher says (*Rhet.* ii. 5). Fear is banished, in this way, by the removal of threatening causes of fear; for instance, by the fact that a man has no enemies, through having harmed nobody, so that he is not aware of any imminent danger; since those especially appear to be threatened by danger, who have harmed others.

On the part of the bodily transmutation, daring is caused through the incitement of hope and the banishment of fear, by those things which raise the temperature about the heart. Wherefore the Philosopher says (*De Part. Animal.* iii. 4) that *those whose heart is small in size, are more daring; while animals whose heart is large are timid; because the natural heat is unable to give the same degree of temperature to a large as to a small heart; just as a fire does not heat a large house*

*as well as it does a small house.*   He says also (*De Problem.*
xxvii. 4) that *those whose lungs contain much blood, are more
daring, through the heat in the heart that results therefrom.*   He
says also in the same passage that *lovers of wine are more
daring, on account of the heat of the wine*: hence it has been
said above (Q. XL., A. 6) that drunkenness conduces to
hope, since the heat in the heart banishes fear and raises
hope, by reason of the dilatation and enlargement of the
heart.

*Reply Obj.* 1. Drunkenness causes daring, not through
being a defect, but through dilating the heart: and again
through making a man think greatly of himself.

*Reply Obj.* 2. Those who have no experience of dangers
are more daring, not on account of a defect, but accidentally,
*i.e.*, in so far as through being inexperienced they do not
know their own failings, nor the dangers that threaten.
Hence it is that the removal of the cause of fear gives rise
to daring.

*Reply Obj.* 3. As the Philosopher says (*Rhet.* ii. 5) *those who
have been wronged are courageous, because they think that God
comes to the assistance of those who suffer unjustly.*

Hence it is evident that no defect causes daring except
accidentally, *i.e.*, in so far as some excellence attaches thereto,
real or imaginary, either in oneself or in another.

## Fourth Article.

### WHETHER THE BRAVE ARE MORE EAGER AT FIRST THAN IN THE MIDST OF DANGER ?

*We proceed thus to the Fourth Article :—*

*Objection* 1. It would seem that the daring are not more
eager at first than in the midst of danger.   Because trembling is caused by fear, which is contrary to daring, as
stated above (A. 1; Q. XLIV., A. 3).   But the daring sometimes tremble at first, as the Philosopher says (*De Problem.*
xxvii. 3).   Therefore they are not more eager at first than
in the midst of danger.

*Obj.* 2. Further, passion is intensified by an increase in

its object: thus since a good is lovable, what is better is yet more lovable. But the object of daring is something difficult. Therefore the greater the difficulty, the greater the daring. But danger is more arduous and difficult when present. It is then therefore that daring is greatest.

*Obj.* 3. Further, anger is provoked by the infliction of wounds. But anger causes daring; for the Philosopher says (*Rhet.* ii. 5) that *anger makes man bold.* Therefore when man is in the midst of danger and when he is being beaten, then is he most daring.

*On the contrary,* It is said in *Ethic.* iii. 7 that *the daring are precipitate and full of eagerness before the danger, yet in the midst of dangers they stand aloof.*

*I answer that,* Daring, being a movement of the sensitive appetite, follows an apprehension of the sensitive faculty. But the sensitive faculty cannot make comparisons, nor can it inquire into circumstances; its judgment is instantaneous. Now it happens sometimes that it is impossible for a man to take note in an instant of all the difficulties of a certain situation: hence there arises the movement of daring to face the danger; so that when he comes to experience the danger, he feels the difficulty to be greater than he expected, and so gives way.

On the other hand, reason discusses all the difficulties of a situation. Consequently men of fortitude who face danger according to the judgment of reason, at first seem slack, because they face the danger not from passion but with due deliberation. Yet when they are in the midst of danger, they experience nothing unforeseen, but sometimes the difficulty turns out to be less than they anticipated; wherefore they are more persevering.—Moreover, it may be because they face the danger on account of the good of virtue which is the abiding object of their will, however great the danger may prove: whereas men of daring face the danger on account of a mere thought giving rise to hope and banishing fear, as stated above (A. 3).

*Reply Obj.* 1. Trembling does occur in men of daring, on account of the heat being withdrawn from the outer to the inner parts of the body, as occurs also in those who are afraid. But in men of daring the heat withdraws to the heart; whereas in those who are afraid, it withdraws to the inferior parts.

*Reply Obj.* 2. The object of love is good simply, wherefore if it be increased, love is increased simply. But the object of daring is a compound of good and evil; and the movement of daring towards evil presupposes the movement of hope towards good. If, therefore, so much difficulty be added to the danger that it overcomes hope, the movement of daring does not ensue, but fails.—But if the movement of daring does ensue, the greater the danger, the greater is the daring considered to be.

*Reply Obj.* 3. Hurt does not give rise to anger unless there be some kind of hope, as we shall see later on (Q. XLVI., A. 1). Consequently if the danger be so great as to banish all hope of victory, anger does not ensue.—It is true, however, that if anger does ensue, there will be greater daring.

# QUESTION XLVI.

## OF ANGER, IN ITSELF.

### (*In Eight Articles.*)

WE must now consider anger: and (1) anger in itself: (2) the cause of anger and its remedy: (3) the effect of anger.

Under the first head there are eight points of inquiry: (1) Whether anger is a special passion ?  (2) Whether the object of anger is good or evil ?  (3) Whether anger is in the concupiscible faculty ?  (4) Whether anger is accompanied by an act of reason ?  (5) Whether anger is more natural than desire ?  (6) Whether anger is more grievous than hatred ?  (7) Whether anger is only towards those with whom we have a relation of justice ?  (8) Of the species of anger.

## FIRST ARTICLE.

### WHETHER ANGER IS A SPECIAL PASSION ?

*We proceed thus to the First Article :—*

*Objection* 1. It would seem that anger is not a special passion.   For the irascible power takes its name from anger (*ira*).   But there are several passions in this power, not only one.   Therefore anger is not one special passion.

*Obj.* 2. Further, to every special passion there is a contrary passion; as is evident by going through them one by one.   But no passion is contrary to anger, as stated above (Q. XXIII., A. 3).   Therefore anger is not a special passion.

*Obj.* 3. Further, one special passion does not include another.   But anger includes several passions: since it accompanies sorrow, pleasure, and hope, as the Philosopher states (*Rhet.* ii. 2).   Therefore anger is not a special passion.

*On the contrary*, Damascene (*De Fide Orthod.* ii. 16) calls anger a special passion: and so does Cicero (*De Quæst. Tusc.* iv. 7).

*I answer that*, A thing is said to be general in two ways. First, by predication; thus *animal* is general in respect of all animals.—Secondly, by causality; thus the sun is the general cause of all things generated here below, according to Dionysius (*Div. Nom.* iv.). Because just as a genus contains potentially many differences, according to a likeness of matter; so an efficient cause contains many effects according to its active power.—Now it happens that an effect is produced by the concurrence of various causes; and since every cause remains somewhat in its effect, we may say that, in yet a third way, an effect which is due to the concurrence of several causes, has a certain generality, inasmuch as several causes are, in a fashion, actually existing therein.

Accordingly in the first way, anger is not a general passion, but is condivided with the other passions, as stated above (Q. XXIII., A. 4).—In like manner, neither is it in the second way: since it is not a cause of the other passions. But in this way love may be called a general passion, as Augustine declares (*De Civ. Dei* xiv. 7, 9), because love is the primary root of all the other passions, as stated above (Q. XXVII., A. 4). But, in the third way, anger may be called a general passion, inasmuch as it is caused by a concurrence of several passions. Because the movement of anger does not arise save on account of some pain inflicted, and unless there be desire and hope of revenge: for, as the Philosopher says (*Rhet.* ii. 2), *the angry man hopes to punish ; since he craves for revenge as being possible*. Consequently if the person, who inflicted the injury, excel very much, anger does not ensue, but only sorrow, as Avicenna states (*De Anima* iv. 6).

*Reply Obj.* 1. The irascible power takes its name from *ira* (anger), not because every movement of that power is one of anger; but because all its movements terminate in anger; and because, of all these movements, anger is the most patent.

*Reply Obj.* 2. From the very fact that anger is caused by

contrary passions, *i.e.*, by hope, which is of good, and by sorrow, which is of evil, it includes in itself contrariety: and consequently it has no contrary outside itself. Thus also in mixed colours there is no contrariety, except that of the simple colours from which they are made.

*Reply Obj.* 3. Anger includes several passions, not indeed as a genus includes several species; but rather according to the inclusion of cause and effect.

### SECOND ARTICLE.

#### WHETHER THE OBJECT OF ANGER IS GOOD OR EVIL?

*We proceed thus to the Second Article :—*

*Objection* 1. It would seem that the object of anger is evil. For Gregory of Nyssa* says that anger is *the sword-bearer of desire*, inasmuch, to wit, as it assails whatever obstacle stands in the way of desire. But an obstacle has the character of evil. Therefore anger regards evil as its object.

*Obj.* 2. Further, anger and hatred agree in their effect, since each seeks to inflict harm on another. But hatred regards evil as its object, as stated above (Q. XXIX., A. 1). Therefore anger does also.

*Obj.* 3. Further, anger arises from sorrow; wherefore the Philosopher says (*Ethic.* vii. 6) that *anger acts with sorrow*. But evil is the object of sorrow. Therefore it is also the object of anger.

*On the contrary*, Augustine says (*Conf.* ii. 6) that *anger craves for revenge*. But the desire for revenge is a desire for something good: since revenge belongs to justice. Therefore the object of anger is good.

2. Moreover, anger is always accompanied by hope, wherefore it causes pleasure, as the Philosopher says (*Rhet.* ii. 2). But the object of hope and of pleasure is good. Therefore good is also the object of anger.

*I answer that*, The movement of the appetitive power follows an act of the apprehensive power. Now the apprehensive power apprehends a thing in two ways. First, by

---

* Nemesius, *De Nat. Hom.* xxi.

way of an incomplex object, as when we understand what a man is; secondly, by way of a complex object, as when we understand that whiteness is in a man. Consequently in each of these ways the appetitive power can tend to both good and evil:—by way of a simple and incomplex object, when the appetite simply follows and adheres to good, or recoils from evil: and such movements are desire, hope, pleasure, sorrow, and so forth:—by way of a complex object, as when the appetite is concerned with some good or evil being in, or being done to, another, either seeking this or recoiling from it. This is evident in the case of love and hatred: for we love someone, in so far as we wish some good to be in him; and we hate someone, in so far as we wish some evil to be in him. It is the same with anger; for when a man is angry, he wishes to be avenged on someone. Hence the movement of anger has a twofold tendency: viz., to vengeance itself, which it desires and hopes for as being a good, wherefore it takes pleasure in it; and to the person on whom it seeks vengeance, as to something contrary and hurtful, which bears the character of evil.

We must, however, observe a twofold difference in this respect, between anger on the one side, and hatred and love on the other. The first difference is that anger always regards two objects: whereas love and hatred sometimes regard but one object, as when a man is said to love wine or something of the kind, or to hate it.—The second difference is, that both the objects of love are good: since the lover wishes good to someone, as to something agreeable to himself: while both the objects of hatred bear the character of evil: for the man who hates, wishes evil to someone, as to something disagreeable to him. Whereas anger regards one object under the aspect of good, viz., vengeance, which it desires to have; and the other object under the aspect of evil, viz., the noxious person, on whom it seeks to be avenged. Consequently it is a passion somewhat made up of contrary passions.

This suffices for the Replies to the Objections.

### THIRD ARTICLE.

#### WHETHER ANGER IS IN THE CONCUPISCIBLE FACULTY?

*We proceed thus to the Third Article :—*

*Objection* 1. It would seem that anger is in the concupis-cible faculty. For Cicero says (*De Quæst. Tusc.* iv. 9) that anger is a kind of *desire*. But desire is in the concupiscible faculty. Therefore anger is too.

*Obj.* 2. Further, Augustine says in his Rule, that *anger grows into hatred:* and Cicero says (*loc. cit.*) that *hatred is inveterate anger*. But hatred, like love, is a concupiscible passion. Therefore anger is in the concupiscible faculty.

*Obj.* 3. Further, Damascene (*De Fide Orthod.* ii. 16) and Gregory of Nyssa* say that *anger is made up of sorrow and desire*. Both of these are in the concupiscible faculty. Therefore anger is a concupiscible passion.

*On the contrary*, The concupiscible is distinct from the irascible faculty. If, therefore, anger were in the con-cupiscible power, the irascible would not take its name from it.

*I answer that*, As stated above (Q. XXIII., A. 1), the passions of the irascible part differ from the passions of the concupiscible faculty, in that the objects of the concupiscible passions are good and evil absolutely considered, whereas the objects of the irascible passions are good and evil of a certain elevation or arduousness. Now it has been stated (A. 2) that anger regards two objects: viz., the vengeance that it seeks; and the person on whom it seeks vengeance; and in respect of both, anger requires a certain arduousness: for the movement of anger does not arise, unless there be some magnitude about both these objects; since *we make no ado about things that are naught or very minute*, as the Philosopher observes (*Rhet.* ii. 2). It is therefore evident that anger is not in the concupiscible, but in the irascible faculty.

*Reply Obj.* 1. Cicero gives the name of desire to any kind of craving for a future good, without discriminating between

* Nemesius, *De Nat. Hom.* xxi.

that which is arduous and that which is not. Accordingly he reckons anger as a kind of desire, inasmuch as it is a desire of vengeance. In this sense, however, desire is common to the irascible and concupiscible faculties.

*Reply Obj.* 2. Anger is said to grow into hatred, not as though the same passion which at first was anger, afterwards becomes hatred by becoming inveterate; but by a process of causality. For anger when it lasts a long time engenders hatred.

*Reply Obj.* 3. Anger is said to be composed of sorrow and desire, not as though they were its parts, but because they are its causes: and it has been said above (Q. XXV., A. 2) that the concupiscible passions are the causes of the irascible passions.

## FOURTH ARTICLE.

### WHETHER ANGER REQUIRES AN ACT OF REASON?

*We proceed thus to the Fourth Article :—*

*Objection* 1. It would seem that anger does not require an act of reason. For, since anger is a passion, it is in the sensitive appetite. But the sensitive appetite follows an apprehension, not of reason, but of the sensitive faculty. Therefore anger does not require an act of reason.

*Obj.* 2. Further, dumb animals are devoid of reason: and yet they are seen to be angry. Therefore anger does not require an act of reason.

*Obj.* 3. Further, drunkenness fetters the reason; whereas it is conducive to anger. Therefore anger does not require an act of reason.

*On the contrary*, The Philosopher says (*Ethic.* vii. 6) that *anger listens to reason somewhat.*

*I answer that*, As stated above (A. 2), anger is a desire for vengeance. Now vengeance implies a comparison between the punishment to be inflicted and the hurt done; wherefore the Philosopher says (*Ethic.* vii. *loc. cit.*) that *anger, as if it had drawn the inference that it ought to quarrel with such a person, is therefore immediately exasperated.* Now to compare and to draw an inference is an act of reason. Therefore anger, in a fashion, requires an act of reason.

*Reply Obj.* 1. The movement of the appetitive power may follow an act of reason in two ways. In the first way, it follows the reason in so far as the reason commands: and thus the will follows reason, wherefore it is called the rational appetite. In another way, it follows reason in so far as the reason denounces, and thus anger follows reason. For the Philosopher says (*De Problem.* xxviii. 3) that *anger follows reason, not in obedience to reason's command, but as a result of reason's denouncing the injury*. Because the sensitive appetite is subject to the reason, not immediately but through the will.

*Reply Obj.* 2. Dumb animals have a natural instinct imparted to them by the Divine Reason, in virtue of which they are gifted with movements, both internal and external, like unto rational movements, as stated above (Q. XL., A. 3).

*Reply Obj.* 3. As stated in *Ethic.* vii. 6, *anger listens somewhat to reason* in so far as reason denounces the injury inflicted, *but listens not perfectly*, because it does not observe the rule of reason as to the measure of vengeance. Anger, therefore, requires an act of reason; and yet proves a hindrance to reason. Wherefore the Philosopher says (*De Problem.* iii. 2, 27) that those who are very drunk, so as to be incapable of the use of reason, do not get angry: but those who are slightly drunk, do get angry, through being still able, though hampered, to form a judgment of reason.

## FIFTH ARTICLE.

### WHETHER ANGER IS MORE NATURAL THAN DESIRE ?

*We proceed thus to the Fifth Article :—*

*Objection* 1. It would seem that anger is not more natural than desire. Because it is proper to man to be by nature a gentle animal. But *gentleness is contrary to anger*, as the Philosopher states (*Rhet.* ii. 3). Therefore anger is not more natural than desire, in fact it seems to be altogether unnatural to man.

II. i.

*Obj.* 2. Further, reason is contrasted with nature: since those things that act according to reason, are not said to act according to nature. Now *anger requires an act of reason, but desire does not*, as stated in *Ethic*. vii. 6.   Therefore desire is more natural than anger.

*Obj.* 3. Further, anger is a craving for vengeance: while desire is a craving for those things especially which are pleasant to the touch, viz., for pleasures of the table and for sexual pleasures.   But these things are more natural to man than vengeance.   Therefore desire is more natural than anger.

*On the contrary*, The Philosopher says (*Ethic*. vii. *loc. cit.*) that *anger is more natural than desire*.

*I answer that*, By *natural* we mean that which is caused by nature, as stated in *Phys*. ii. 1.   Consequently the question as to whether a particular passion is more or less natural cannot be decided without reference to the cause of that passion.   Now the cause of a passion, as stated above (Q. XXXVI., A. 2), may be considered in two ways: first, on the part of the object; secondly, on the part of the subject.   If then we consider the cause of anger and of desire, on the part of the object, thus desire, especially of pleasures of the table, and of sexual pleasures, is more natural than anger; in so far as these pleasures are more natural to man than vengeance.

If, however, we consider the cause of anger on the part of the subject, thus anger, in a manner, is more natural; and, in a manner, desire is more natural.   Because the nature of an individual man may be considered either as to the generic, or as to the specific nature, or again as to the particular temperament of the individual.   If then we consider the generic nature, *i.e.*, the nature of this man considered as an animal; thus desire is more natural than anger; because it is from this very generic nature that man is inclined to desire those things which tend to preserve in him the life both of the species and of the individual.—If, however, we consider the specific nature, *i.e.*, the nature of this man as a rational being; then anger is more natural to man than desire, in so far as anger follows reason more than desire does. Wherefore the Philosopher says (*Ethic*. iv. 5) that *revenge* which pertains to anger *is more natural to man than meekness*: for it is natural to everything to rise up against things contrary and hurtful.—And if we consider the nature of the individual, in respect of his particular temperament, thus anger is more natural than desire; for the reason that anger is prone to ensue from the natural tendency to anger, more than desire, or any other passion, is to ensue from a natural tendency to desire, which tendencies result from a man's individual temperament. Because disposition to anger is due to a bilious temperament; and of all the humours, the bile moves quickest; for it is like fire. Consequently he that is temperamentally disposed to anger is sooner incensed with anger, than he that is temperamentally disposed to desire, is inflamed with desire: and for this reason the Philosopher says (*Ethic*. vii. 6) that a disposition to anger is more liable to be transmitted from parent to child, than a disposition to desire.

*Reply Obj.* 1. We may consider in man both the natural temperament on the part of the body, and the reason. On the part of the bodily temperament, a man, considered specifically, does not naturally excel others either in anger or in any other passion, on account of the moderation of his temperament. But other animals, for as much as their temperament recedes from this moderation and approaches to an extreme disposition, are naturally disposed to some excess of passion, such as the lion in daring, the hound in anger, the hare in fear, and so forth.—On the part of reason, however, it is natural to man, both to be angry and to be gentle: in so far as reason somewhat causes anger, by denouncing the injury which causes anger; and somewhat appeases anger, in so far as the angry man *does not listen perfectly to the command of reason*, as stated above (A. 4 *ad* 3).

*Reply Obj.* 2. Reason itself belongs to the nature of man: wherefore from the very fact that anger requires an act of reason, it follows that it is, in a manner, natural to man.

*Reply Obj.* 3. This argument regards anger and desire on the part of the object.

## Sixth Article.

### WHETHER ANGER IS MORE GRIEVOUS THAN HATRED ?

*We proceed thus to the Sixth Article :—*

*Objection* 1. It would seem that anger is more grievous than hatred.  For it is written (Prov. xxvii. 4) that *anger hath no mercy, nor fury when it breaketh forth*.  But hatred sometimes has mercy.   Therefore anger is more grievous than hatred.

*Obj.* 2. Further, it is worse to suffer evil and to grieve for it, than merely to suffer it.  But when a man hates, he is contented if the object of his hatred suffer evil: whereas the angry man is not satisfied unless the object of his anger know it and be aggrieved thereby, as the Philosopher says (*Rhet.* ii. 4).   Therefore, anger is more grievous than hatred.

*Obj.* 3. Further, a thing seems to be so much the more firm according as more things concur to set it up: thus a habit is all the more settled through being caused by several acts.  But anger is caused by the concurrence of several passions, as stated above (A. 1): whereas hatred is not.   Therefore anger is more settled and more grievous than hatred.

*On the contrary*, Augustine, in his Rule, compares hatred to *a beam*, but anger to *a mote*.

*I answer that*, The species and nature of a passion are taken from its object.  Now the object of anger is the same in substance as the object of hatred; since, just as the hater wishes evil to him whom he hates, so does the angry man wish evil to him with whom he is angry.  But there is a difference of aspect: for the hater wishes evil to his enemy, as evil, whereas the angry man wishes evil to him with whom he is angry, not as evil but in so far as it has an aspect of good, that is, in so far as he reckons it as just, since it is a means of vengeance.   Wherefore also it has been said above (A. 2) that hatred implies application of evil to evil, whereas anger denotes application of good to evil.—Now it is evident that to seek evil under the aspect of justice, is a lesser evil, than simply to seek evil to someone. Because to wish evil to someone under the aspect of justice, may be according to the virtue of justice, if it be in conformity with the order of reason; and anger fails only in this, that it does not obey the precept of reason in taking vengeance. Consequently it is evident that hatred is far worse and graver than anger.

*Reply Obj.* 1. In anger and hatred two points may be considered: namely, the thing desired, and the intensity of the desire. As to the thing desired, anger has more mercy than hatred has. For since hatred desires another's evil for evil's sake, it is satisfied with no particular measure of evil: because those things that are desired for their own sake, are desired without measure, as the Philosopher states (*Polit.* i. 3), instancing a miser with regard to riches. Hence it is written (Ecclus. xii. 16): *An enemy . . . if he find an opportunity, will not be satisfied with blood.*—Anger, on the other hand, seeks evil only under the aspect of a just means of vengeance. Consequently when the evil inflicted goes beyond the measure of justice according to the estimate of the angry man, then he has mercy. Wherefore the Philosopher says (*Rhet.* ii. 4) that *the angry man is appeased if many evils befall, whereas the hater is never appeased.*

As to the intensity of the desire, anger excludes mercy more than hatred does; because the movement of anger is more impetuous, through the heating of the bile. Hence the passage quoted continues: *Who can bear the violence of one provoked?*

*Reply Obj.* 2. As stated above, an angry man wishes evil to someone, in so far as this evil is a means of just vengeance. Now vengeance is wrought by the infliction of a punishment: and the nature of punishment consists in being contrary to the will, painful, and inflicted for some fault. Consequently an angry man desires this, that the person whom he is hurting, may feel it and be in pain, and know that this has befallen him on account of the harm he has done the other. The hater, on the other hand, cares not for all this, since he desires another's evil as such.—It is not true, however, that an evil is worse through giving pain: because *injustice and imprudence, although evil,* yet, being voluntary, *do not grieve those in whom they are,* as the Philosopher observes (*Rhet.* ii. 4).

*Reply Obj.* 3. That which proceeds from several causes, is more settled when these causes are of one kind: but it may be that one cause prevails over many others. Now hatred ensues from a more lasting cause than anger does. Because anger arises from an emotion of the soul due to the wrong inflicted; whereas hatred ensues from a disposition in a man, by reason of which he considers that which he hates to be contrary and hurtful to him. Consequently, as passion is more transitory than disposition or habit, so anger is less lasting than hatred; although hatred itself is a passion ensuing from this disposition. Hence the Philosopher says (*Rhet.* ii. 4) that *hatred is more incurable than anger.*

## SEVENTH ARTICLE.

### WHETHER ANGER IS ONLY TOWARDS THOSE TO WHOM ONE HAS AN OBLIGATION OF JUSTICE ?

*We proceed thus to the Seventh Article :—*

*Objection* 1. It would seem that anger is not only towards those to whom one has an obligation of justice. For there is no justice between man and irrational beings. And yet sometimes one is angry with irrational beings; thus, out of anger, a writer throws away his pen, or a rider strikes his horse. Therefore anger is not only towards those to whom one has an obligation of justice.

*Obj.* 2. Further, *there is no justice towards oneself . . . nor is there justice towards one's own* (*Ethic.* v. 6). But sometimes a man is angry with himself; for instance, a penitent, on account of his sin; hence it is written (Ps. iv. 5): *Be ye angry and sin not.* Therefore anger is not only towards those with whom one has a relation of justice.

*Obj.* 3. Further, justice and injustice can be of one man towards an entire class, or a whole community: for instance, when the state injures an individual. But anger is not towards a class but only towards an individual, as the

Philosopher states (*Rhet.* ii. 4). Therefore properly speaking, anger is not towards those with whom one is in relation of justice or injustice.

*The contrary*, however, may be gathered from the Philosopher (*Rhet.* ii. 2, 3).

*I answer that*, As stated above (A. 6), anger desires evil as being a means of just vengeance. Consequently, anger is towards those to whom we are just or unjust: since vengeance is an act of justice, and wrong-doing is an act of injustice. Therefore both on the part of the cause, viz., the harm done by another, and on the part of the vengeance sought by the angry man, it is evident that anger concerns those to whom one is just or unjust.

*Reply Obj.* 1. As stated above (A. 4 *ad* 2), anger, though it follows an act of reason, can nevertheless be in dumb animals that are devoid of reason, in so far as through their natural instinct they are moved by their imagination to something like rational action. Since then in man there is both reason and imagination, the movement of anger can be aroused in man in two ways. First, when only his imagination denounces the injury: and, in this way, man is aroused to a movement of anger even against irrational and inanimate beings, which movement is like that which occurs in animals against anything that injures them.—Secondly, by the reason denouncing the injury: and thus, according to the Philosopher (*Rhet.* ii. 3), *it is impossible to be angry with insensible things, or with the dead*: both because they feel no pain, which is, above all, what the angry man seeks in those with whom he is angry: and because there is no question of vengeance on them, since they can do us no harm.

*Reply Obj.* 2. As the Philosopher says (*Ethic.* v. 11), *metaphorically speaking there is a certain justice and injustice between a man and himself*, in so far as the reason rules the irascible and concupiscible parts of the soul. And in this sense a man is said to be avenged on himself, and consequently, to be angry with himself. But properly, and in accordance with the nature of things, a man is never angry with himself.

*Reply Obj.* 3. The Philosopher (*Rhet.* ii. 4) assigns as one difference between hatred and anger, that *hatred may be felt towards a class, as we hate the entire class of thieves; whereas anger is directed only towards an individual.* The reason is that hatred arises from our considering a quality as disagreeing with our disposition; and this may refer to a thing in general or in particular. Anger, on the other hand, ensues from someone having injured us by his action. Now all actions are the deeds of individuals: and consequently anger is always pointed at an individual.—When the whole state hurts us, the whole state is reckoned as one individual.*

## Eighth Article.

### WHETHER THE SPECIES OF ANGER ARE SUITABLY ASSIGNED?

*We proceed thus to the Eighth Article :—*

*Objection* 1. It would seem that Damascene (*De Fide Orthod.* ii. 16) unsuitably assigns three species of anger,—*wrath, ill-will* and *rancour.* For no genus derives its specific differences from accidents. But these three are diversified in respect of an accident: because *the beginning of the movement of anger is called wrath* (χόλος), *if anger continue it is called ill-will* (μῆνις); *while rancour* (κότος) *is anger waiting for an opportunity of vengeance.* Therefore these are not different species of anger.

*Obj.* 2. Further, Cicero says (*De Quaest. Tusc.* iv. 9) that *excandescentia* (*irascibility*) *is what the Greeks call* θυμῶσις, *and is a kind of anger that arises and subsides intermittently*; while according to Damascene θυμῶσις is the same as κότος (*rancour*). Therefore κότος does not bide its time for taking vengeance, but in course of time spends itself.

*Obj.* 3. Further, Gregory (*Moral.* xxi. 4) gives three degrees of anger, namely, *anger without utterance, anger with utterance, and anger with perfection of speech,* corresponding to

* *Cf.* Q. XXIX. 6.

# QUESTION XLVII.

## OF THE CAUSE THAT PROVOKES ANGER, AND OF THE REMEDIES OF ANGER.*

### (*In Four Articles.*)

WE must now consider the cause that provokes anger, and its remedies. Under this head there are four points of inquiry: (1) Whether the motive of anger is always something done against the one who is angry? (2) Whether slight or contempt is the sole motive of anger? (3) Of the cause of anger on the part of the angry person. (4) Of the cause of anger on the part of the person with whom one is angry.

### FIRST ARTICLE.

#### WHETHER THE MOTIVE OF ANGER IS ALWAYS SOMETHING DONE AGAINST THE ONE WHO IS ANGRY?

*We proceed thus to the First Article :—*

*Objection* 1. It would seem that the motive of anger is not always something done against the one who is angry. Because man, by sinning, can do nothing against God; since it is written (Job xxxv. 6): *If thy iniquities be multiplied, what shalt thou do against Him?* And yet God is spoken of as being angry with man on account of sin, according to Ps. cv. 40: *The Lord was exceedingly angry with His people.* Therefore it is not always on account of something done against him, that a man is angry.

*Obj.* 2. Further, anger is a desire for vengeance. But one may desire vengeance for things done against others.

---

\* There is no further mention of these remedies in the text, except in Art. 4.

Therefore we are not always angry on account of something done against us.

*Obj*. 3. Further, as the Philosopher says (*Rhet*. ii. 2) man is angry especially with those *who despise what he takes a great interest in ; thus men who study philosophy are angry with those who despise philosophy*, and so forth.   But contempt of philosophy does not harm the philosopher.   Therefore it is not always a harm done to us that makes us angry.

*Obj*. 4. Further, he that holds his tongue when another insults him, provokes him to greater anger, as Chrysostom observes (*Hom*. xxii. *in Ep. ad Rom.*).   But by holding his tongue he does the other no harm.   Therefore a man is not always provoked to anger by something done against him.

*On the contrary*, The Philosopher says (*Rhet*. ii. 4) that *anger is always due to something done to oneself : whereas hatred may arise without anything being done to us, for we hate a man simply because we think him such.*

*I answer that*, As stated above (Q. XLVI., A. 6), anger is the desire to hurt another for the purpose of just vengeance. Now unless some injury has been done, there is no question of vengeance: nor does any injury provoke one to vengeance, but only that which is done to the person who seeks vengeance: for just as everything naturally seeks its own good, so does it naturally repel its own evil.   But injury done by anyone does not affect a man unless in some way it be something done against him.   Consequently the motive of a man's anger is always something done against him.

*Reply Obj*. 1. We speak of anger in God, not as of a passion of the soul but as of a judgment of justice, inasmuch as He wills to take vengeance on sin.   Because the sinner, by sinning, cannot do God any actual harm: but so far as he himself is concerned, he acts against God in two ways. First, in so far as he despises God in His commandments. Secondly, in so far as he harms himself or another; which injury redounds to God, inasmuch as the person injured is an object of God's providence and protection.

*Reply Obj*. 2. If we are angry with those who harm others,

and seek to be avenged on them, it is because those who are injured belong in some way to us: either by some kinship or by friendship, or at least because of the nature we have in common.

*Reply Obj.* 3. When we take a very great interest in a thing, we look upon it as our own good; so that if anyone despise it, it seems as though we ourselves were despised and injured.

*Reply Obj.* 4. Silence provokes the insulter to anger when he thinks it is due to contempt, as though his anger were slighted: and a slight is an action.

## Second Article.

### Whether the sole motive of anger is slight or contempt ?

*We proceed thus to the Second Article :—*

*Objection* 1. It would seem that slight or contempt is not the sole motive of anger. For Damascene says (*De Fide Orthod.* ii. 16) that we are angry *when we suffer, or think that we are suffering, an injury*. But one may suffer an injury without being despised or slighted. Therefore a slight is not the only motive of anger.

*Obj.* 2. Further, desire for honour and grief for a slight belong to the same subject. But dumb animals do not desire honour. Therefore they are not grieved by being slighted. And yet *they are roused to anger, when wounded*, as the Philosopher says (*Ethic.* iii. 8). Therefore a slight is not the sole motive of anger.

*Obj.* 3. Further, the Philosopher (*Rhet.* ii. 2) gives many other causes of anger, for instance, *being forgotten by others ; that others should rejoice in our misfortunes ; that they should make known our evils; being hindered from doing as we like*. Therefore being slighted is not the only motive for being angry.

*On the contrary*, The Philosopher says (*Rhet.* ii. *loc. cit.*) that anger is *a desire, with sorrow, for vengeance, on account of a seeming slight done unbecomingly.*

*I answer that,* All the causes of anger are reduced to slight. For slight is of three kinds, as stated in *Rhet* ii., *ibid.*, viz., *contempt, despiteful treatment, i.e.,* hindering one from doing one's will, and *insolence*: and all motives of anger are reduced to these three. Two reasons may be assigned for this. First, because anger seeks another's hurt as being a means of just vengeance: wherefore it seeks vengeance in so far as it seems just. Now just vengeance is taken only for that which is done unjustly; hence that which provokes anger is always something considered in the light of an injustice. Wherefore the Philosopher says (*Rhet.* ii. 3) that *men are not angry,—if they think they have wronged some one and are suffering justly on that account; because there is no anger at what is just.* Now injury is done to another in three ways: namely, through ignorance, through passion, and through choice. Then, most of all, a man does an injustice, when he does an injury from choice, on purpose, or from deliberate malice, as stated in *Ethic.* v, 8. Wherefore we are most of all angry with those who, in our opinion, have hurt us on purpose. For if we think that some one has done us an injury through ignorance or through passion, either we are not angry with them at all, or very much less: since to do anything through ignorance or through passion takes away from the notion of injury, and to a certain extent calls for mercy and forgiveness. Those, on the other hand, who do an injury on purpose, seem to sin from contempt; wherefore we are angry with them most of all. Hence the Philosopher says (*Rhet.* ii. 3) that *we are either not angry at all, or not very angry with those who have acted through anger, because they do not seem to have acted slightingly.*

The second reason is because a slight is opposed to a man's excellence: because *men think little of things that are not worth much ado (Rhet.* ii. 2). Now we seek for some kind of excellence from all our goods. Consequently whatever injury is inflicted on us, in so far as it is derogatory to our excellence, seems to savour of a slight.

*Reply Obj.* 1. Any other cause, besides contempt, through which a man suffers an injury, takes away from the notion of injury: contempt or slight alone adds to the motive of anger, and consequently is of itself the cause of anger.

*Reply Obj.* 2. Although a dumb animal does not seek honour as such, yet it naturally seeks a certain superiority, and is angry with anything derogatory thereto.

*Reply Obj.* 3. Each of those causes amounts to some kind of slight. Thus forgetfulness is a clear sign of slight esteem, for the more we think of a thing the more is it fixed in our memory. Again if a man does not hesitate by his remarks to give pain to another, this seems to show that he thinks little of him: and those too who show signs of hilarity when another is in misfortune, seem to care little about his good or evil. Again he that hinders another from carrying out his will, without deriving thereby any profit to himself, seems not to care much for his friendship. Consequently all those things, in so far as they are signs of contempt, provoke anger.

### THIRD ARTICLE.

#### WHETHER A MAN'S EXCELLENCE IS THE CAUSE OF HIS BEING ANGRY?

*We proceed thus to the Third Article :—*

*Objection* 1. It would seem that a man's excellence is not the cause of his being more easily angry. For the Philosopher says (*Rhet.* ii. 2) that *some are angry especially when they are grieved, for instance, the sick, the poor, and those who are disappointed.* But these things seem to pertain to defect. Therefore defect rather than excellence makes one prone to anger.

*Obj.* 2. Further, the Philosopher says (*ibid.*) that *some are very much inclined to be angry when they are despised for some failing or weakness of the existence of which there are grounds for suspicion; but if they think they excel in those points, they do not trouble.* But a suspicion of this kind is due to some defect. Therefore defect rather than excellence is a cause of a man being angry.

*Obj.* 3. Further, whatever savours of excellence makes a man agreeable and hopeful. But the Philosopher says

(*Rhet.* ii. 3) that *men are not angry when they play, make jokes, or take part in a feast, nor when they are prosperous or successful, nor in moderate pleasures and well-founded hope.*   Therefore excellence is not a cause of anger.

*On the contrary,* The Philosopher says (*ibid.* 9) that excellence makes men prone to anger.

*I answer that,* The cause of anger, in the man who is angry, may be taken in two ways.   First in respect of the motive of anger: and thus excellence is the cause of a man being easily angered.   Because the motive of anger is an unjust slight, as stated above (A. 2).   Now it is evident that the more excellent a man is, the more unjust is a slight offered him in the matter in which he excels.   Consequently those who excel in any matter, are most of all angry, if they be slighted in that matter; for instance, a wealthy man in his riches, or an orator in his eloquence, and so forth.

Secondly, the cause of anger, in the man who is angry, may be considered on the part of the disposition produced in him by the motive aforesaid.   Now it is evident that nothing moves a man to anger except a hurt that grieves him: while whatever savours of defect is above all a cause of grief; since men who suffer from some defect are more easily hurt.   And this is why men who are weak, or subject to some other defect, are more easily angered, since they are more easily grieved.

This suffices for the Reply to the First Objection.

*Reply Obj.* 2. If a man be despised in a matter in which he evidently excels greatly, he does not consider himself the loser thereby, and therefore is not grieved: and in this respect he is less angered.   But in another respect, in so far as he is more undeservedly despised, he has more reason for being angry: unless perhaps he thinks that he is envied or insulted not through contempt but through ignorance, or some other like cause.

*Reply Obj.* 3. All these things hinder anger in so far as they hinder sorrow.   But in another respect they are naturally apt to provoke anger, because they make it more unseemly to insult anyone.

## Fourth Article.

### WHETHER A PERSON'S DEFECT IS A REASON FOR BEING MORE EASILY ANGRY WITH HIM?

*We proceed thus to the Fourth Article :—*

*Objection* 1. It would seem that a person's defect is not a reason for being more easily angry with him. For the Philosopher says (*Rhet.* ii. 3) that *we are not angry with those who confess and repent and humble themselves ; on the contrary, we are gentle with them. Wherefore dogs bite not those who sit down.* But these things savour of littleness and defect. Therefore littleness of a person is a reason for being less angry with him.

*Obj.* 2. Further, there is no greater defect than death. But anger ceases at the sight of death. Therefore defect of a person does not provoke anger against him.

*Obj.* 3. Further, no one thinks little of a man through his being friendly towards him. But we are more angry with friends, if they offend us or refuse to help us; hence it is written (Ps. liv. 13): *If my enemy had reviled me I would verily have borne with it.* Therefore a person's defect is not a reason for being more easily angry with him.

*On the contrary,* The Philosopher says (*Rhet.* ii. 2) that *the rich man is angry with the poor man, if the latter despise him ; and in like manner the prince is angry with his subject.*

*I answer that,* As stated above (AA. 2, 3), unmerited contempt more than anything else is a provocative of anger. Consequently deficiency or littleness in the person with whom we are angry, tends to increase our anger, in so far as it adds to the unmeritedness of being despised. For just as the higher a man's position is, the more undeservedly he is despised; so the lower it is, the less reason he has for despising. Thus a nobleman is angry if he be insulted by a peasant; a wise man, if by a fool; a master, if by a servant.

If, however, the littleness or deficiency lessens the unmerited contempt, then it does not increase but lessens anger. In this way those who repent of their ill-deeds,

34

and confess that they have done wrong, who humble themselves and ask pardon, mitigate anger, according to Prov. xv. 1: *A mild answer breaketh wrath*: because, to wit, they seem not to despise, but rather to think much of those before whom they humble themselves.

This suffices for the Reply to the First Objection.

*Reply Obj.* 2. There are two reasons why anger ceases at the sight of death. One is because the dead are incapable of sorrow and sensation; and this is chiefly what the angry seek in those with whom they are angered.—Another reason is because the dead seem to have attained to the limit of evils. Hence anger ceases in regard to all who are grievously hurt, in so far as this hurt surpasses the measure of just retaliation.

*Reply Obj.* 3. To be despised by one's friends seems also a greater indignity. Consequently if they despise us by hurting or by failing to help, we are angry with them for the same reason for which we are angry with those who are beneath us.

# QUESTION XLVIII.

## OF THE EFFECTS OF ANGER.

### (*In Four Articles.*)

WE must now consider the effects of anger: under which head there are four points of inquiry: (1) Whether anger causes pleasure? (2) Whether above all it causes heat in the heart? (3) Whether above all it hinders the use of reason? (4) Whether it causes taciturnity?

### FIRST ARTICLE.

#### WHETHER ANGER CAUSES PLEASURE?

*We proceed thus to the First Article:—*

*Objection* 1. It would seem that anger does not cause pleasure. Because sorrow excludes pleasure. But anger is never without sorrow, since, as stated in *Ethic.* vii. 6, *everyone that acts from anger, acts with pain.* Therefore anger does not cause pleasure.

*Obj.* 2. Further, the Philosopher says (*Ethic.* iv. 5) that *vengeance makes anger to cease, because it substitutes pleasure for pain*: whence we may gather that the angry man derives pleasure from vengeance, and that vengeance quells his anger. Therefore on the advent of pleasure, anger departs: and consequently anger is not an effect united with pleasure.

*Obj.* 3. Further, no effect hinders its cause, since it is conformed to its cause. But pleasure hinders anger, as stated in *Rhet.* ii. 3. Therefore pleasure is not an effect of anger.

*On the contrary,* The Philosopher (*ibid.*) quotes the saying that anger is

"Sweet to the soul as honey to the taste."
—*Iliad*, xviii. 109, 110 (trl. POPE).

*I answer that*, As the Philosopher says (*Ethic*. vii. 14), pleasures, chiefly sensible and bodily pleasures, are remedies against sorrow: and therefore the greater the sorrow or anxiety, the more sensible are we to the pleasure which heals it, as is evident in the case of thirst which increases the pleasure of drink. Now it is clear from what has been said (Q. XLVII., AA. 1, 3), that the movement of anger arises from a wrong done that causes sorrow, for which sorrow vengeance is sought as a remedy. Consequently as soon as vengeance is present, pleasure ensues, and so much the greater according as the sorrow was greater.—Therefore if vengeance be really present, perfect pleasure ensues, entirely excluding sorrow, so that the movement of anger ceases. | But before vengeance is really present, it becomes present to the angry man in two ways:—in one way, by hope; because none is angry except he hopes for vengeance, as stated above (Q. XLVI., A. 1);—in another way, by thinking of it continually, for to everyone that desires a thing it is pleasant to dwell on the thought of what he desires; wherefore the imaginings of dreams are pleasant. Accordingly an angry man takes pleasure in thinking much about vengeance. This pleasure, however, is not perfect, so as to banish sorrow and consequently anger.

*Reply Obj.* 1. The angry man does not grieve and rejoice at the same thing; he grieves for the wrong done, while he takes pleasure in the thought and hope of vengeance. Consequently sorrow is to anger as its beginning; while pleasure is the effect or terminus of anger.

*Reply Obj.* 2. This argument holds in regard to pleasure caused by the real presence of vengeance, which banishes anger altogether.

*Reply Obj.* 3. Pleasure that precedes hinders sorrow from ensuing, and consequently is a hindrance to anger. But pleasure felt in taking vengeance follows from anger.

## Second Article.

### WHETHER ANGER ABOVE ALL CAUSES FERVOUR IN THE HEART?

*We proceed thus to the Second Article :—*

*Objection* 1. It would seem that heat is not above all the effect of anger. For fervour, as stated above (Q. XXVIII., A. 5; Q. XXXVII., A. 2), belongs to love. But love, as above stated, is the beginning and cause of all the passions. Since then the cause is more powerful than its effect, it seems that anger is not the chief cause of fervour.

*Obj.* 2. Further, those things which, of themselves, arouse fervour, increase as time goes on; thus love grows stronger the longer it lasts. But in course of time anger grows weaker; for the Philosopher says (*Rhet.* ii. 3) that *time puts an end to anger.* Therefore fervour is not the proper effect of anger.

*Obj.* 3. Further, fervour added to fervour produces greater fervour. But *the addition of a greater anger banishes already existing anger,* as the Philosopher says (*ibid.*). Therefore anger does not cause fervour.

*On the contrary,* Damascene says (*De Fide Orth.* ii. 16) that *anger is fervour of the blood around the heart, resulting from an exhalation of the bile.*

*I answer that,* As stated above (Q. XLIV., A. 1), the bodily transmutation that occurs in the passions of the soul is proportionate to the movement of the appetite. Now it is evident that every appetite, even the natural appetite, tends with greater force to repel that which is contrary to it, if it be present: hence we see that hot water freezes harder, as though the cold acted with greater force on the hot object. Since then the appetitive movement of anger is caused by some injury inflicted, as by a contrary that is present; it follows that the appetite tends with great force to repel the injury by the desire of vengeance; and hence ensues great vehemence and impetuosity in the movement of anger. And because the movement of anger is not one of recoil, which corresponds to the action of cold, but one of prosecution, which corresponds to the action of heat, the result is that the movement of anger produces fervour of the blood and vital spirits around the heart, which is the instrument of the soul's passions. And hence it is that, on account of the heart being so disturbed by anger, those chiefly who are angry betray signs thereof in their outer members. For, as Gregory says (*Moral.* v. 30) *the heart that is inflamed with the stings of its own anger beats quick, the body trembles, the tongue stammers, the countenance takes fire, the eyes grow fierce, they that are well known are not recognized. With the mouth indeed he shapes a sound, but the understanding knows not what it says.*

*Reply Obj.* 1. *Love itself is not felt so keenly as in the absence of the beloved,* as Augustine observes (*De Trin.* x. 12). Consequently when a man suffers from a hurt done to the excellence that he loves, he feels his love thereof the more: the result being that his heart is moved with greater heat to remove the hindrance to the object of his love; so that anger increases the fervour of love and makes it to be felt more.

Nevertheless, the fervour arising from heat differs according as it is to be referred to love or to anger. Because the fervour of love has a certain sweetness and gentleness; for it tends to the good that one loves: whence it is likened to the warmth of the air and of the blood. For this reason sanguine temperaments are more inclined to love; and hence the saying that *love springs from the liver,* because of the blood being formed there.—On the other hand, the fervour of anger has a certain bitterness with a tendency to destroy, for it seeks to be avenged on the contrary evil: whence it is likened to the heat of fire and of the bile, and for this reason Damascene says (*loc. cit.*) that it *results from an exhalation of the bile whence it takes its name* χολή.

*Reply Obj.* 2. Time, of necessity, weakens all those things, the causes of which are impaired by time. Now it is evident that memory is weakened by time; for things which happened long ago easily slip from our memory. But anger is caused by the memory of a wrong done. Consequently the cause of anger is impaired little by little as time goes on, until at length it vanishes altogether.—Moreover a wrong seems greater when it is first felt; and our estimate thereof is gradually lessened the further the sense of present wrong recedes into the past.—The same applies to love, so long as the cause of love is in the memory alone: wherefore the Philosopher says (*Ethic.* viii. 5) that *if a friend's absence lasts long, it seems to make men forget their friendship*. But in the presence of a friend, the cause of friendship is continually being multiplied by time: wherefore the friendship increases: and the same would apply to anger, were its cause continually multiplied.

Nevertheless the very fact that anger soon spends itself proves the strength of its fervour: for as a great fire is soon spent having burnt up all the fuel; so too anger, by reason of its vehemence, soon dies away.

*Reply Obj.* 3. Every power that is divided in itself is weakened. Consequently if a man being already angry with one, becomes angry with another, by this very fact his anger with the former is weakened. Especially is this so if his anger in the second case be greater: because the wrong done which aroused his former anger, will, in comparison with the second wrong, which is reckoned greater, seem to be of little or no account.

### THIRD ARTICLE.

#### WHETHER ANGER ABOVE ALL HINDERS THE USE OF REASON ?

*We proceed thus to the Third Article :—*

*Objection* 1. It would seem that anger does not hinder the use of reason. Because that which presupposes an act of reason, does not seem to hinder the use of reason. But *anger listens to reason*, as stated in *Ethic.* vii. 6. Therefore anger does not hinder reason.

*Obj.* 2. Further, the more the reason is hindered, the less does man show his thoughts. But the Philosopher says (*Ethic.* vii. 6) that *an angry man is not cunning but is open*. Therefore anger does not seem to hinder the use of reason, as desire does; for desire is cunning, as he also states (*ibid.*).

*Obj.* 3. Further, the judgment of reason becomes more evident by juxtaposition of the contrary: because contraries stand out more clearly when placed beside one another. But this also increases anger: for the Philosopher says (*Rhet.* ii. 2) that *men are more angry if they receive unwonted treatment; for instance, honourable men, if they be dishonoured*: and so forth. Therefore the same cause increases anger, and facilitates the judgment of reason. Therefore anger does not hinder the judgment of reason.

*On the contrary*, Gregory says (*Moral.* v. 30) that anger *withdraws the light of understanding, while by agitating it troubles the mind*.

*I answer that*, Although the mind or reason makes no use of a bodily organ in its proper act, yet, since it needs certain sensitive powers for the execution of its act, the acts of which powers are hindered when the body is disturbed, it follows of necessity that any disturbance in the body hinders even the judgment of reason; as is clear in the case of drunkenness or sleep. Now it has been stated (A. 2) that anger, above all, causes a bodily disturbance in the region of the heart, so much as to effect even the outward members. Consequently, of all the passions, anger is the most manifest obstacle to the judgment of reason, according to Ps. xxx. 10: *My eye is troubled with wrath.*

*Reply Obj.* 1. The beginning of anger is in the reason, as regards the appetitive movement, which is the formal element of anger. But the passion of anger forestalls the perfect judgment of reason, as though it listened but imperfectly to reason, on account of the commotion of the heat urging to instant action, which commotion is the material element of anger. In this respect it hinders the judgment of reason.

*Reply Obj.* 2. An angry man is said to be open, not because it is clear to him what he ought to do, but because he acts openly, without thought of hiding himself. This is due partly to the reason being hindered, so as not to discern what should be hidden and what done openly, nor to devise the means of hiding; and partly to the dilatation of the heart which pertains to magnanimity which is an effect of anger: wherefore the Philosopher says of the magnanimous man (*Ethic.* iv. 3) that *he is open in his hatreds and his friendships* . . . and *speaks and acts openly.*—Desire, on the other hand, is said to lie low and to be cunning, because, in many cases, the pleasurable things that are desired, savour of shame and voluptuousness, wherein man wishes not to be seen. But in those things that savour of manliness and excellence, such as matters of vengeance, man seeks to be in the open.

*Reply Obj. 3.* As stated above (*ad* 1), the movement of anger begins in the reason, wherefore the juxtaposition of one contrary with another facilitates the judgment of reason, on the same grounds as it increases anger. For when a man who is possessed of honour or wealth, suffers a loss therein, the loss seems all the greater, both on account of the contrast, and because it was unforeseen. Consequently it causes greater grief: just as a great good, through being received unexpectedly, causes greater delight. And in proportion to the increase of the grief that precedes, anger is increased also.

## Fourth Article.

### WHETHER ANGER ABOVE ALL CAUSES TACITURNITY?

*We proceed thus to the Fourth Article :—*

*Objection* 1. It would seem that anger does not cause taciturnity. Because taciturnity is opposed to speech. But increase of anger conduces to speech; as is evident from the degrees of anger laid down by Our Lord (Matth. v. 22): where He says: *Whosoever is angry with his brother;* and . . . *whosoever shall say to his brother, 'Raca';* and . . . *whosoever shall say to his brother, 'Thou fool.'* Therefore anger does not cause taciturnity.

*Obj.* 2. Further, through failing to obey reason, man sometimes breaks out into unbecoming words: hence it is written (Prov. xxv. 28): *As a city that lieth open and is not compassed with walls, so is a man that cannot refrain his own spirit in speaking.* But anger, above all, hinders the judgment of reason, as stated above (A. 3). Consequently above all it makes one break out into unbecoming words. Therefore it does not cause taciturnity.

*Obj.* 3. Further, it is written (Matth. xii. 34): *Out of the abundance of the heart the mouth speaketh.* But anger, above all, causes a disturbance in the heart, as stated above (A. 2). Therefore above all it conduces to speech. Therefore it does not cause taciturnity.

*On the contrary,* Gregory says (*Moral.* v. 30) that *when anger does not vent itself outwardly by the lips, inwardly it burns the more fiercely.*

*I answer that,* As stated above (A. 3; Q. XLVI., A. 4), anger both follows an act of reason, and hinders the reason: and in both respects it may cause taciturnity. On the part of the reason, when the judgment of reason prevails so far, that although it does not curb the appetite in its inordinate desire for vengeance, yet it curbs the tongue from unbridled speech. Wherefore Gregory says (*Moral.* v. *loc. cit.*): *Sometimes when the mind is disturbed, anger, as if in judgment, commands silence.*—On the part of the impediment to reason because, as stated above (A. 2), the disturbance of anger reaches to the outward members, and chiefly to those members which reflect more distinctly the emotions of the heart, such as the eyes, face and tongue; wherefore, as observed above (A. 2), *the tongue stammers, the countenance takes fire, the eyes grow fierce.* Consequently anger may cause such a disturbance, that the tongue is altogether deprived of speech; and taciturnity is the result.

*Reply Obj.* 1. Anger sometimes goes so far as to hinder the reason from curbing the tongue: but sometimes it goes yet farther, so as to paralyze the tongue and other outward members.

And this suffices for the Reply to the Second Objection.

*Reply Obj.* 3. The disturbance of the heart may sometimes superabound to the extent that the movements of the outward members are hindered by the inordinate movement of the heart. Thence ensue taciturnity and immobility of the outward members; and sometimes even death.—If, however, the disturbance be not so great, then *out of the abundance of the heart* thus disturbed, the mouth proceeds to speak.